OLD TRAF[

100 YEARS AT THE THEATRE OF DREAMS

BY IAIN MCCARTNEY

EMPIRE
PUBLICATIONS

EMPIRE PUBLICATIONS
1 Newton Street, Manchester M1 1HW
© Iain McCartney 2010

ISBN 1 901 746 60 7 - 9781901746600

Cover design and layout: Ashley Shaw
Proof read by Lindsey Mallory.

Printed in Great Britain.

Contents

ACKNOWLEDGMENTS

I would like to acknowledge the help of the following in the first publication of this title – Dave Twydell of Yore Publishing, Tim Laycock of Hilstone Laurie and Ole Pederson

As regards to the this version, I would like to acknowledge the help of , Mark Wylie – Manchester United Museum, Brian Koffman, Ken Ramsden – Manchester United FC, Dave Weldon, Tom Clare, Alan Tyler, James Thomas, Peter Edwards, Gary James (author of Manchester – A Football History) Stuart Beesley, Tommy Haddock, Tony Smith, Leslie Millman, Tim Ashmore and Pat Crerand – for writing the foreword.

And last, but certainly not least, John Ireland and Ashley Shaw at Empire. Particularly to Ashley for prompting me to do this updated and re-vamped version and for his help in the layout.

Iain Mccartney
FEBRUARY 2010

FOREWORD

CELEBRATING ANY 100TH anniversary is a time for looking back, recalling memorable occasions and stand out events. The one hundred years since the opening of Old Trafford is no different and within the pages of this book, Iain McCartney brings the home of Manchester United to life, creating a picture of the stadium itself as it grew from the vast open space of the early 1900's to the magnificent arena it is today.

There is certainly something special about Old Trafford, a place where I have many happy memories, beginning as a player, back in 1963, through to the present day, where I still enjoy the match-day experience through my work with MUTV.

When Iain asked me what my favourite memories of Old Trafford were, the one that immediately sprang to mind was that never to be forgotten evening in March 1984, when United defeated Barcelona 3-0. Who could ever forget that night?

Steve Bruce's two goals against Sheffield Wednesday in 1993, which paved the way towards ending that long wait for the Championship is another one of those magical Old Trafford moments, while from my own playing days, the 1-0 European Cup semi-final victory over Real Madrid in 1968 is another which readily springs to mind.

I also remember the early redevelopment of the ground for the 1966 World Cup and Paddy McGrath, an old friend of Sir Matt's buying the first of the new executive boxes, right on the half way line, for the sum of £400.

Iain also rekindles the memories of so many other great games played out at the ground, the players who have graced its hallowed turf, whilst revealing countless other stories and events, creating an interesting and detailed account in words and pictures of one hundred years at one of the best known stadiums in world football – Old Trafford, the Theatre of Dreams.

Pat Crerand
FEBRUARY 2010.

INTRODUCTION

IT WAS STILL some six hours until kick off, but the chill of the bright autumn morning could not deter the fans, pilgrims or whatever definition is best to describe those congregated around the main forecourt of the concrete and metal construction called Old Trafford.

The numbers began to increase, as the hours and minutes to the scheduled kick off time ticked away, but time would pass quickly enough for some who were making their first trip

to the Mecca of English football. They would stand, oblivious to all around them, consuming every detail, as they longed for the red gates at the turnstiles to open and admit them to the arena so that they would be swallowed up by the stands of the stadium. For others, it would be merely a fortnightly ritual - a habit or love affair, that may have begun many years before, when they too were brought to the ground for the first time, to stare at the stadium in awe.

No matter the outcome of the match, your first trip to Old Trafford is always memorable. Maybe for a great game, a piece of individualistic skill, a certain incident, or purely just for being there.

Close your eyes for a moment and imagine the stadium packed to capacity, and from the darkened bowels of the Stretford End, the thespians for today's performance are introduced. It is an all time United X1 which includes the famous names from

Manchester United v Leeds United, FA Cup, January 27th 1951.

the past, who have graced the hallowed turf... Meredith, Carey, Edwards, Best, Robson, Cantona, Keane, Ronaldo, Rooney...

Welcome to Old Trafford, home of Manchester United Football Club, the Theatre Of Dreams.

1 - GRASSROOTS

▲ Match Day action at Bank Street: *Notorious for the proximity of an adjacent chemical works, United's second home was a little rough and ready, although the club's home record was impressive. Here they suffer a rare Clayton defeat going down 2-1 to Portsmouth in the FA Cup on 16th January 1907 before 8,000 spectators.*

To THE THOUSANDS who flock to Old Trafford on match days, it is difficult for them to imagine the spartan surroundings that the club had called home prior to 1910 and their arrival at the present site.

Newton Heath, as the club were called when they began their life in the world of football, in 1878, had their first home at North Road, Monsall, in the north-eastern Manchester suburb of the same name, close to the carriage and wagon works of the Lancashire and Yorkshire Railway. Hence the full original name of the original club - Newton Heath Lancashire and Yorkshire Railway Football Club.

The playing surface of the North Road ground left a lot to be desired, with half the pitch as hard as iron, while the other was soft and muddy. The area surrounding this was little better than a quagmire and spectators entering the ground at one end needed the footwork of a first-class forward to avoid numerous pools of water in the bad weather. During the winter months, conditions deteriorated, and proved a sizeable obstacle for both players and followers.

Those players also endured

the additional hardship of having no changing facilities at the ground. At first, they were to use the Three Crowns public house on Oldham Road, later moving to the Shears Hotel (which also became the club headquarters), around half a mile from the ground. After changing there, they had to walk to the ground with little prospect of a bath at the end of their afternoon's endeavours.

The Heathens began their competitive life playing little more than friendlies, before they joined the Football Alliance for season 1889-90, having turned professional in 1885. By 1892, they had achieved First Division status, but there were dark clouds on the horizon despite stepping up to this higher level of football.

The team had to be strengthened and in order to be able to afford the accompanying higher wage bill, it was decided to drop the ˜Lancashire and Yorkshire" part from the club's name and form a limited company in order to raise some capital. This was all very well, but the ground at North Road, which also contained a cricket pitch, belonged to the Manchester Cathedral authorities, but was leased to the Lancashire and Yorkshire Railway, who in turn

paid a nominal rent to the authorities.

Following the final home fixture of 1891-92 against Notts County, the Heathens moved out and the Railway committee reclaimed the ground, but during the close season the difficulties between the two were ironed out, if only temporarily, and all the equipment and whatever that had been carried away in May was returned in time for the new season.

Returning to their old stomping ground, results showed some improvement, while off the field, the drainage system was improved, with work also being carried out on the embankments on either side of the ground. Baths and dressing rooms were also installed beneath a stand built in 1891 which could accommodate 1,000 spectators. The facilities, were far from ideal, but the improvements were certainly welcomed by players and spectators alike.

On October 13th 1892, a Football League record scoreline of 10-1 was recorded against Wolverhampton Wanderers (they had beaten Lincoln City by a similar score line during a Football Alliance fixture in November 1891) and a correspondent for the *Birmingham Daily Gazette*

▲ **Humble beginnings:** *An aerial shot of Bank Street, Clayton (the former ground is at the top in the centre behind Moston Fever Hospital) - image taken c.1920.*

▶**The Three Crowns Pub:** *the hostelry was used as a clubhouse and changing room.*

▼ **The Shears Hotel** *was also used as a club headquarters in the club's formative years.*

FA Cup fourth round: Manchester United v Arsenal 1906: *FA Cup action at Clayton on March 10th 1906, a game United (who played in blue to avoid a colour clash) lost 3-2 in front of 26,500, some of whom can be seen precariously balanced on the roof of the stand.*

reported that "the pitch was in a terrible state, with pools of water here and there and Wolves found it difficult to even stand on the muddy pitch". There was, however, another incident at the ground which made the newspaper headlines, this time in something of a more spectacular scale.

During a training session, which for some reason or another involved throwing a hammer, Stewart let it slip from his grasp and it struck his team mate Donaldson, who was standing close by, on the side of the head. Surprisingly, although the player was carried home and received medical attention, he turned out in his usual position a couple of days later.

A year after having almost been declared homeless, a new home definitely had to be found when the Manchester Cathedral

authorities decided that with the football club now having moved away from the Lancashire and Yorkshire Railway they would end the agreement with railway company. This was despite the landlords having spent a considerable sum on the improvements of twelve months previously.

Today, North Road has gone, along with the Three Crowns and the Shears Hotel. The whole area has seen wholesale changes since those early days, but for a while there was a link between Manchester United and the area, as one time shirt sponsors Sharp™ had their home a goal kick from the patch of land that the Heathens once called home.

So, in 1893, Newton Heath packed whatever belongings they had and moved to a new site, some three miles south, at Bank Lane, Clayton, where a more

spacious enclosure, the Bradford and Clayton athletic ground, was secured. This was let to the club for eight months per year, for two years, for playing purposes, although pre-season training was allowed to take place on occasional nights.

The new ground was ready for the start of season 1893-94 and had a much better playing surface than that at North Road. There were, however, other distinct disadvantages, as the new ground stood beside a chemical works, with a background of chimney stacks, which would emit foul smelling fumes, that engulfed players and spectators alike. It has been claimed that the home side would pass a a message to the neighbouring factories if they were losing for them to stoke the chimneys in an effort to distract the visiting team.

Numerous reports from those distant days at Clayton often mention the conditions at the ground, sometimes the comments would take up more lines than the actual match report itself. One gentleman, going under the name of "Tam", visiting the ground for the F. A. Cup tie against Chelsea on February 1st 1908 gave his uninitiated readers an insight into the sometimes atrocious conditions.

He wrote of "thirteen belching chimneys confronting the spectator in the grandstand; where steam in great volumes threatens to envelope the whole place at any moment if the wind but swings round to the west". He also described the pitch as "but a bed of grit, though it rolls out as flat as a running track". Another report, for a match against Burnley, mentioned that the goal posts were so tainted with smoke and the dullness of their surroundings, as to be hardly discernable.

Rather ironically, those same conditions, no matter how favoured they were by the home team and its supporters, did not prevent the name of Newton Heath from making an early entry into the record books, when Walsall Town Swifts were defeated 14-0 on March 9th 1895. The Midlands side, however, protested about the terrible ground conditions which clearly favoured the home side and after the inquest which followed, the match was declared void.

On April 3rd, the match was replayed and a 9-0 score line, again in Newton Heath's favour, showed clearly that it was not just the playing conditions that had defeated the visitors.

Nevertheless life at Clayton saw the club finances hit rock bottom and in 1902 bankruptcy threatened. At a shareholders meeting in March, club captain Harry Stafford announced that he knew of four men who were prepared to put up the £2,000 required to keep the club going. The four were Mr Taylor of Sale, Mr Brown of Denton, Mr Jones of Manchester and Mr Davies of Old Trafford. It was also suggested that perhaps a change of name would lead to a change of fortune and on April 28th, the *Manchester Guardian* reported that the name of the club from then on would be ˜Manchester United" and a month later the Lancashire Football Association gave formal permission for the name change. The legend was born, with the red and white jerseys, which have since become famous all over the world, the new club colours.

Mr J. H. Davies became the club chairman and president and although he knew little of the game of football, he made up for this with his business acumen. He was for many years the chairman of the Manchester Brewery and a self made man, living a life of luxury, but never looking down on those less fortunate than himself. Along with his wife, he would travel to watch his club wherever they played and the players were often invited to his 17th century mansion home at Bramall Hall, where they would be lavishly entertained.

Prior to the start of season 1902-03, the *Athletic News* wrote "Financial troubles are at an end, in fact money has been spent most lavishly, but to good purpose, in all directions. Close upon £4,000 has been sunk in getting a competent team together, and in such alterations to the ground as to make the latter one of the finest enclosures in the country.

"The stand on the Bank Street side has been roofed in and extended and improvements having been made to the other stand, it is now possible for 8,000 people to watch a match under cover. The architects entrusted with the renovation of the ground say that some 50,000 spectators can now be accommodated and all have a clear view of play.

"A great effort is to be made to lend an air of sociability to the club. Every consideration and comfort will be extended to lady visitors, whilst guinea members are to have quite an ideal position. The players have not been overlooked. They are to be looked after better than they were in the past and the officials of the club are to be commended upon the wisdom they have shown in making an

The Imperial Hotel: *Situated a short walk from Piccadilly Station, it belonged to J H Davies who was persuaded by Harry Stafford to invest some of his money into the beleaguered Newton Heath. Stafford was then installed as licensee, with the pub becoming the headquarters of the newly formed Manchester United.*

Two views of excavation work being carried out on the site which was to become Old Trafford. *Both photographs look towards Warwick Road and what would become the Scoreboard End. Interestingly both were discovered in a skip outside Maine Road during a 'clear-out' and were originally thought to be of the construction of City's ground. The surrounding buildings would indicate otherwise.*

underground passage from the dressing rooms to the field of play for the players and referee."

The *Cricket and Football Field*, another popular publication of the day was slightly more descriptive of the new-look Bank Street ground, following the attendance of one of their correspondents to a pre-season practise match, "On entering the ground one was struck with the great improvements that have been made, and every credit is due to the new management for the manner in which they have catered for the comforts of

the public. Though not quite complete yet, there is no doubt that when finished it will prove one of the best equipped of grounds.

"On the enclosure side, the three stands have been made into one (covered), and underneath will be found well-fitted dressing rooms, reading and recreative rooms for the players, offices etc. The stand behind the goal at one end has been practically rebuilt and covered and will find accommodation for a goodly number. On the other sides, great bankings have been thrown up and an imposing press box and office erected. In every way, improvements have been made and the spectators who visit this ground need have no fear on the score of suitable positions, for a good view is obtainable everywhere. The playing pitch never looked better and the newly painted boards all round make a splendid border."

The midas touch of John Davies seemed to be rubbing off on the club, as each season saw some improvement with promotion to the First Division eventually being achieved at the end of season 1905-06, as runners-up. It had been twelve years since Newton Heath had last appeared in the First Division, following their relegation at the end of season 1893-94. The success continued and in what was only their second season back in the big time the League Championship was won. At long last the loyal band of supporters were getting something to shout about, as the

club were now challenging for a permanent place amongst the top clubs in the country.

Although Mr Davies had helped get the club back on its feet and his financial backing had enabled those supporters to enjoy First Division football again, enjoying the taste of success as much as anyone, he was very concerned about the conditions at Clayton, as he thought that they were an embarrassment to the club and not ideal for the playing of top class football. Nor were they ideal for a club who wanted to play its football in the top flight, although a representative match between the Football League and their Scottish counterparts was played at Bak Street on April 4th 1904.

Neither was John Davies a man to rush into things and he certainly did not squander his money or invest it in projects where there was little or no return. But he had set his sights on finding a new home for his club and he scoured the city for a site worthy of United, before deciding upon a spot to the south-west of the city centre, in Stretford, alongside the Bridgewater Canal at Old Trafford.

Stretford, or Streetford as it was known in Anglo-Saxon times, was a woollen town, which was indicated by the old Bishop Blaize Inn (sounds familiar?), as the Bishop was the patron saint of woolcombers. The construction of the Bridgewater Canal, from Worsley to Manchester in 1761, began an

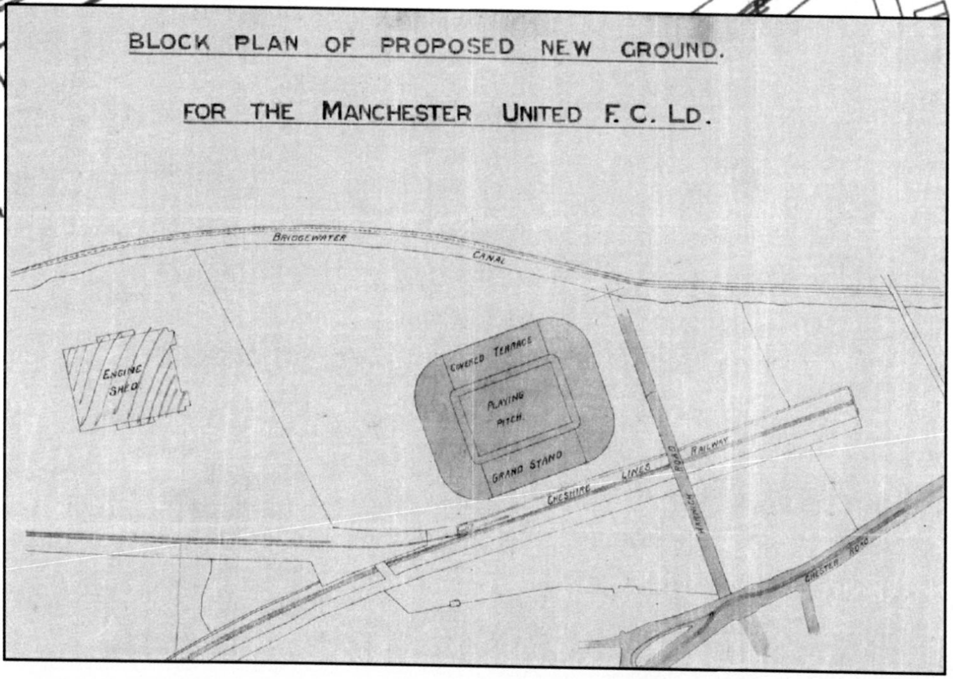

FFORD PARK

CANAL

PROPOSED FOOTBALL GROUND

PARK

CO: DEPOT

Road 25 FT WIDE

600 FT × 30 FT
600 FT × 30 FT
600 FT × 30 FT

Slope 8 FT Wide

DOUBLE SLIPS

FOOTBRIDGE

RAILWAY (MAIN LINE)

WARWICK ROAD

PROPOSED WARWICK ROAD

CHESHIRE LINES

Trafford Park Junc:
Canal Box

▲ **A view of the original plans:** *From June 1908, showing the area outlined for the ground.*

▶ **The original lay-out of the ground:** *Proposed by Leitch and approved by Stretford Urban District Council on February 2nd 1909.*

BLOCK PLAN OF PROPOSED NEW GROUND.

FOR THE MANCHESTER UNITED F.C. LD.

BRIDGEWATER CANAL

ENGINE SHED

COVERED TERRACE

PLAYING PITCH

GRAND STAND

CHESHIRE LINES RAILWAY

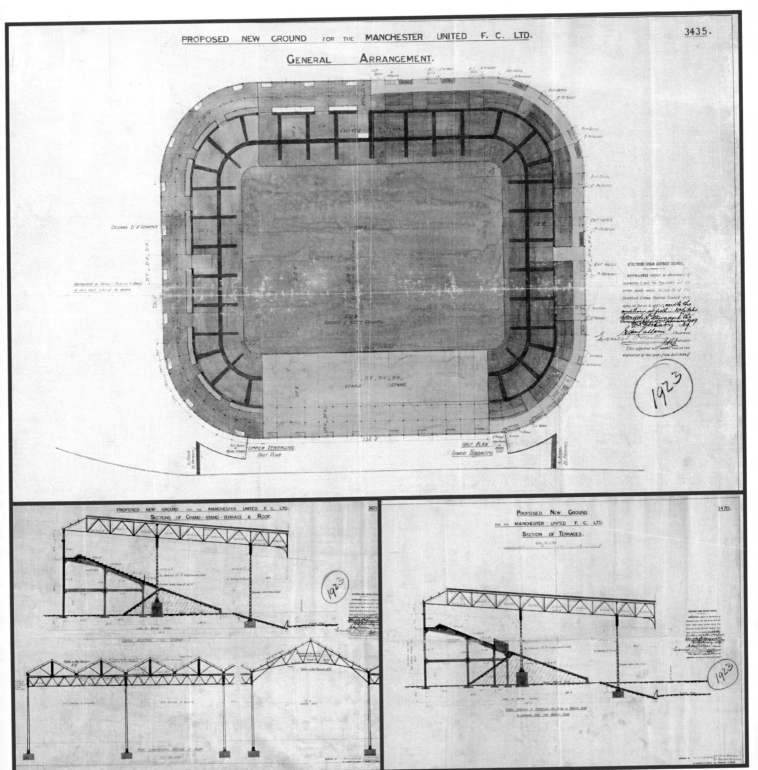

PROPOSED NEW GROUND FOR THE MANCHESTER UNITED F.C. LTD.

GENERAL ARRANGEMENT.

3435.

UPPER TERRACING
HALF PLAN

HALF PLAN
LOWER TERRACING

1923

PROPOSED NEW GROUND FOR THE MANCHESTER UNITED F.C. LTD.
SECTIONS OF GRAND·STAND·TERRACE & ROOF.

3471

1923

PROPOSED NEW GROUND
FOR THE MANCHESTER UNITED F.C. LTD.
SECTION OF TERRACES.

3470.

1923

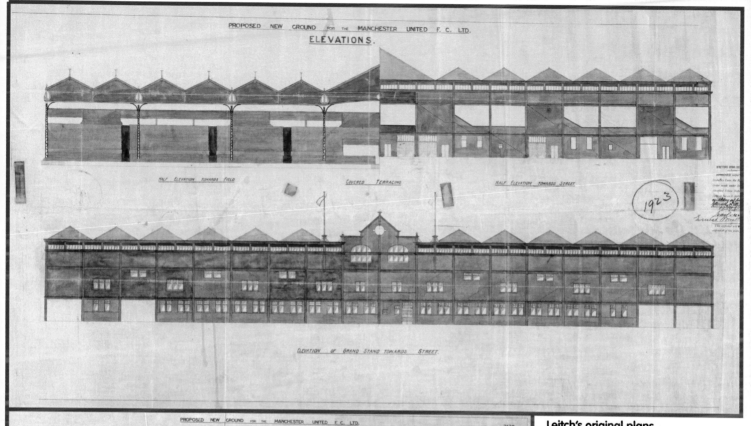

PROPOSED NEW GROUND FOR THE MANCHESTER UNITED F. C. LTD.

ELEVATIONS.

HALF ELEVATION TOWARDS FIELD · COVERED TERRACING · HALF ELEVATION TOWARDS STREET

1923

ELEVATION OF GRAND STAND TOWARDS STREET.

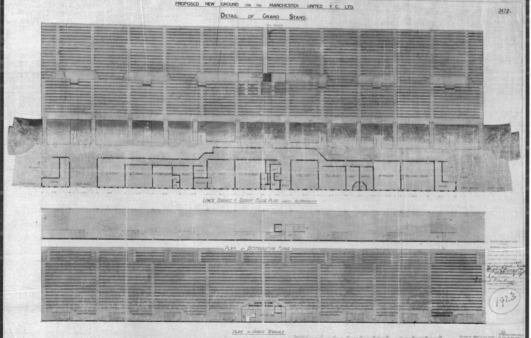

PROPOSED NEW GROUND FOR THE MANCHESTER UNITED F. C. LTD.

DETAIL OF GRAND STAND.

3472.

LOWER TERRACE & GROUND FLOOR PLAN SHOWING ACCOMMODATION

PLAN OF DISTRIBUTING FLOOR

PLAN OF LOWER TERRACE

1923

Leitch's original plans for Old Trafford:

◄◄ **The 'General Arrangement' of the stadium:** *Leitch's stadiums often featured one Main Stand with the rest given over to terracing.*

◄◄▼ **Cross-sections of the Grandstand Terrace, Seating and Roof.**

▲ **Elevations of the Grandstand**

◄ **Details of the Grandstand:** *Including tea-rooms, toilets, dressing rooms and other amenities.*

All plans were approved by Stretford Urban District Council on February 2nd 1909.

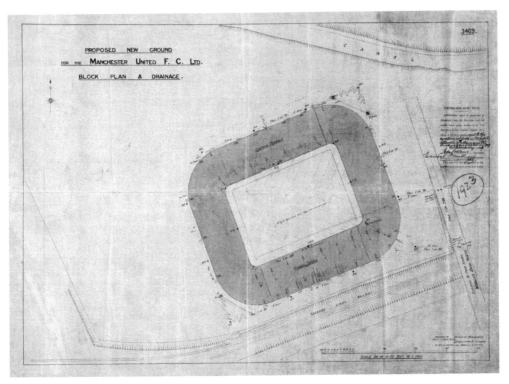

PROPOSED NEW GROUND FOR THE MANCHESTER UNITED F. C. LTD.
BLOCK PLAN & DRAINAGE.

The drainage plan for the new ground

upsurge in development, which continued with the building of the Ship Canal and Trafford Park Industrial Estate.

The sprawl of the area which encompassed Old Trafford, (the name is thought to derived from Old Trafford Hall which was situated where the White City Retail Park on Chester Road is today) and simply abbreviated. This had been owned by the de Trafford family since the 13th century. The family occupied Trafford Hall from around 1017 until the late 1600s before moving to the other end of the

Park, amid the 1,183 acres of land which contained three entrance lodges, Throstles Nest, Barton-upon-Irwell and Old Trafford and three farms, Park Farm, Moss Farm and Waters Meet Farm, making it more than a possibility that the area now occupied by the stadium was once used for sheep and cattle grazing.

With the building of the Ship Canal in 1887 disturbing some, or perhaps much, of the rural peace and quiet, the family decided to put the estate on the market in May 1896, looking for something in the region of £300,000 (over £24m today).

The Manchester

Corporation's Open Spaces Committee showed an early interest, but it was an Ernest Hooley who in the end paid £360,000 (around £30m today) for the bulk of the land in June 1896. Two months later, he had formed Trafford Park Estates Ltd., transferring ownership over to the new company, the world's first industrial park and within two decades the area expanded at an unforeseeable rate.

Perhaps it was this expansion that the businessman in J.H. Davies saw as attractive and certainly important to Manchester United's immediate future, hoping that a large number of those working in and

around Trafford Park would make their way through the gates of the new ground upon finishing work at lunch time on a Saturday.

"Mancunian" of the *Cricket and Football Field* certainly did not share the opinion of John Davies regarding the proposed new home for Manchester United, writing "I consider it too far from the centre of the city. Nor do I think it would be fair to the present supporters, who have stuck to the club through adversity, to take another ground on the opposite side of the city to that from which they have always drawn their patronage, for I don't think they would follow them". How wrong he was to be, not only in the near, but also distant future.

In the *Athletic News* dated March 8th 1909 an article entitled "Pen Picture Of The Undertaking" by a correspondent called "Tityrus" described the proposed move to pastures new in great detail and even today it makes very interesting reading: "The west of Manchester is destined to be the Mecca of sportsmen of that great commercial city. 'To the west, to the west' will be the cry of our football folks when leaves are falling next autumn. Already we have the Lancashire County Cricket ground, the polo ground, the curling pond, the Manchester Gun Club and numerous other organisations of similar character, devoted to pastime and recreation to the west of the city.

"In September, the

Manchester United Football Club will fling open its portals and bid all welcome in the same locality. The contrast between Clayton and the new headquarters of this great football club need not be insisted upon. Clayton is situated in the very heart of the working class community, and dominated on every hand by about forty huge stacks of chimneys belching forth ciminerion smoke and malodorous fumes. No doubt there are those who feel thankful for a football ground in the vicinity, as it does tend to remind the immediate residents that there is some space left where the toiling people can be amused in a healthy and vigorous manner that pleases them. But an ambitious and a vast club like Manchester United appeals to the 800,000 folks of Manchester and Salford, and an area of larger dimensions, with better accommodation for seeing and housing the spectators and situated in a more attractive locality became essential. Hence the decision of the enterprising directors to lay out an enclosure in the west of Manchester. The new ground lies between the Cheshire Lines railway and the Bridgewater Canal, being a little to the left of the Warwick Road North which juts off the Cheshire Road. In other words, walking along the Chester Road towards Stretford, one would turn to the south along Warwick Road for the County cricket ground and exactly opposite to the north for Manchester United football ground.

"The goals in the new arena will be almost west and east, the Streford goal being the west and the Old Trafford goal to the east. This will give the readers an idea of the exact environment in the locality which is expanding. There will not be any difficulty in reaching the new rendezvous. Electric tramcars already run from Clayton to Old Trafford and from the city direct by two routes. It is proposed to lay down a circular tramway siding just off Chester Road so that cars can be turned in there, and the passengers having disembarked, the cars can run round the western end of the circle and return to Manchester for more freight.

"There is here a bridge over the Cheshire Lines railway which is to be widened so as to cope with the traffic, while further north on the other side of the ground it is intended to throw a bridge over the canal. But apart from those approaches we understand that the Cheshire lines committee will open a special station within two or three minutes walk of the western end of this home of sport, so that people can step off the train into the immediate precincts. With such conveniences as these there should never be any difficulty in getting to the place or away from it.

"The Manchester United club have resolved to lay out and equip a huge ground wholly and solely dedicated to football. There will be a running or cycling track around the grass, and for football alone there

Another rare Bank Street action shot: *Note the terraced houses behind the goal at the opposite end of the ground. Bank Street was a far cry from United's new palatial home.*

will be no better enclosure in England. It is to accommodate 100,000 people and if the greatest matches of the day are not in turn brought to Manchester we shall be surprised, especially as the club is not frightened to expend £30,000 on the undertaking.

"When sightseers cross over the railway bridge, they will find themselves in the midst of a clear space which will serve as a gathering ground one hundred and twenty feet broad for spectators and there need not be congestion in gaining access

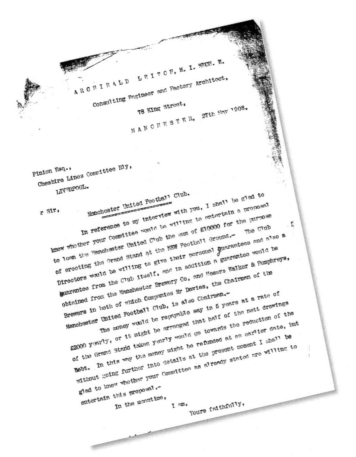

A R C H I B A L D L E I T C H, M. I. MECH. E.

Consulting Engineer and Factory Architect,

78 King Street,

MANCHESTER, 27th May 1908.

Pinion Esq.,
Cheshire Lines Committee Rly,
LIVERPOOL.

Dear Sir, Manchester United Football Club.

In reference to my interview with you, I shall be glad to know whether your Committee would be willing to entertain a proposal to loan the Manchester United Club the sum of £10000 for the purpose of erecting the Grand Stand at the NEW Football Ground.— The Club Directors would be willing to give their personal guarantees and also a guarantee from the Club itself, and in addition a guarantee would be obtained from the Manchester Brewery Co, and Messrs Walker & Pumphreys, Brewers in both of which Companies Mr Davies, the Chairman of the Manchester United Football Club, is also Chairman.—

The money would be repayable say in 5 years at a rate of £2000 yearly, or it might be arranged that half of the nett drawings of the Grand Stand taken yearly would go towards the reduction of the Debt. In this way the money might be refunded at an earlier date, but without going into details at the present moment I shall be glad to know whether your Committee as already stated are willing to entertain this proposal.—

In the meantime,

I am,

Yours faithfully,

Cheshire Lines Committee.

Manager's Office.

Central Station.

Liverpool. May 30th, 190 8.

memorandum.

Manchester United Football Club.
Proposed new Ground in Trafford Park immediately alongside the Cheshire Lines Railway.

The estimated cost of this ground with stands and other accommodation is £60,000.—

The estimated cost of the Station shewn on the plan prepared by Mr Blundell for the accommodation of the traffic to and from is £10,000.—

The ground is to be constructed so as to accommodate 100,000 spectators.— The Football Season extends over a period of 33 weeks and estimating that on twenty Saturdays during the Season matches will be held on the ground and that we obtain the carrying of one-tenth of the number the ground is estimated to accommodate, it would mean the conveyance of 10,000 per match on twenty Saturdays, bringing up an aggregate of 200,000 from Manchester during the Season.—

In addition, on the remaining 20 Saturdays comprising the year it is proposed to hold athletic meetings, cycling meetings, and such like, and that we shall have 1,000 on each such Saturday, making up a total of 20,000 for athletic gatherings or 220,000 passengers

---

▲ **Letter from Archibald Leitch to Mr Pinion of the Cheshire Lines Committee:** *Concerning the building of a railway station at Old Trafford.*
Mr Pinion's reply: *Unfortunately it took another 20 years before the station was finally built.*
▶ **Archibald Leitch**: *Football Ground architect extraordinaire.*

to any portion. With this ground laid out for football alone, the sightseers are brought as near as possible to the playing portion.

"The ground will be rectangle in shape with the corners rounded and it is designed so that everybody will be able to see. The pitch for the game will be excavated to a depth of nine feet from the ground level so that the boundary or containing wall which is to surround the whole place will only be thirty feet high. There are numerous and spacious exits around the ground. Ingress will be easy and

it is estimated that a full ground can be emptied in five minutes.

"Now let us assume that the ordinary spectator has passed through the turnstile. He will find himself in a passage twenty feet broad, which girdles the whole area. From this, access can be obtained from any portion of the popular terracing, which is virtually divided into three sections. There will be one hundred steps of terracing constructed on a special plan and a nicely judged gradient with of course Leitch's patient crush

barriers. The lower portion of this terracing is solid ground, the next higher is formed by the excavated earth and the last and highest is built entirely of ferro-concrete, which is as hard as rock and non-flammable.

"With his practical experience of all the best grounds in these islands, Mr Archibald Leitch M. I. M. E. of Manchester, who has been the only designer, has endeavoured to cope with these problems. There seems every reason to believe that he has solved it.

"Now, from this twenty foot passage, which will of course afford protection from rain until it absolutely necessary to go into the arena, the herds of human beings can melt away at will. Right in front of the visitor, whichever entrance they take, will be a flight of very broad but easy stairs, which end in a wide opening or mouth, sixty feet wide and split into three sections.

"The stream of sightseers mounting these stairs and reaching the opening find themselves rather above the middle of the terracing which they can spread themselves at will. We can picture these great mouths vomiting thousands upon thousands human beings onto this glorious amphitheatre. The advantage of each mouth is its central position. But if the spectator wishes to go right on top of the terracing, any tier above sixteenth, he will take another wide staircase which hugs the inside of the boundary wall and lands him at the top of forty tiers of concrete, resting on foundations of the same material, the space underneath being utilised for refreshment rooms and other conveniences.

"Means are provided for transferring from one portion of the ground to another, but it is expected that in a ground devised on this plan, with so many conveniences for reaching the particular position that the spectator desires, there will be little call for transfers and certainly not to the same extent as on other enclosures.

"The accommodation will, as said, provide for 100,000 people. Of these, 12,000 will be seated in the grandstand and 24,000 standing under steel and slated roofs, so that together there will be room for 36,000 folk under cover and 64,000 in the open, divided between the two arcs of a circle and the mammoth terracing behind each goal. The roofed part for the populace will be on the southern side and will have wide open ends with overhanging eaves so that no portion of this erection will obstruct the view of those who are not fortunate enough to secure its shelter on an inclement day.

"The special feature of the grandstand compared with similar erections is that there will not be a paddock in front of it. The spectators will be seated from the barricade round the pitch direct to the back of the stand, in fifty tiers. These fifty tiers are again divided into three sections, the lower, the middle and the highest. Spectators desiring to be comfortable in the grandstand will enter from the turnstiles facing the mouth of Chester Road. They are especially reserved for grandstand visitors only and there they can only obtain tickets for any part of the stand.

"Entering there, the spectator will find themselves in a corridor along which run tea rooms, referee apartments, the players' facilities, a gym, billiard room and laundry. All of which are to be fitted up in the most modern manner. From this central corridor, there are means of access to three sections of the grandstand. The lowest or front portion will be approached by a number of passages on the ground floor. To the middle or central portion there are stairs which run practically the whole length of the stand. The highest part is to be gained by means of a distributing passage which is as long as the stand and twenty feet broad. Stairs lead from this to the loftiest section. Thus it will be seen that the structure is designed in such a manner that each person will be able to get to his seat with the least discomfort to himself and the minimum inconvenience to his neighbours, because there is a separate means of ingress to each section of the stand.

"The man who wishes to go to the top of the stand has not to disturb those sitting in the lower rungs and this applies to each portion for every detail has been carefully thought out, both by Mr Leitch the mastermind and Messers Bramfield and Smith of Manchester who were responsible for the extensions and improvements at the Clayton ground, the present home of Manchester United F. C.

"Altogether, the entire area of the new home of Manchester United will be sixteen acres. The outward circumference of the ground will be about 2000 feet. The ground will be six hundred and thirty feet long and five hundred and ten feet broad, with the width of the terracing being one hundred and twenty feet. This is a palatial ground which will challenge comparison with any in Great Britain. The executives of the club are to be congratulated on their spirited policy which no doubt be met with reward from the football public."

As a matter of interest, Archibald Leitch, the man behind the construction of Old Trafford was a Glasgwegian consulting engineer and factory architect by profession. His first work on a football stadium was in his native city with Rangers in 1899 and as the years passed by, he was involved in the ground improvements and extensions with the likes of Tottenham, Arsenal, Fulham, Sunderland, Everton and Chelsea, as well as at Hampden Park. His work with United and their Old Trafford project, however, was the first time he was involved in designing a complete stadium.

For those familiar with

FA Cup winners 1909: *The team who moved across Manchester to Old Trafford.*

the ground up until the early sixties, it is not difficult to visualize those vivid plans for the stadium from those bygone days. However, before finalising the plans, Mr J. J. Bentley, the club secretary, suggested several refinements, such as the cycle track, reducing the height of the terracing and omitting the cover on the terracing opposite the main stand. The latter of course meant a reduction in the planned 100,000 capacity, by around 20,000, but the original plans were felt to be a little too ambitious and this reduction did in fact cut the costs of the

project to around £60,000, which was also something of a deciding factor, even though the final figure was twice the sum initially reported.

In an effort to make an indent in the final cost of the new stadium, no matter how small, Archibald Leitch tried to involve the Cheshire Lines Railway in the project. From his Manchester Office, at 78 King Street, he contacted James Pinion, the manager of the Railway Committee and a letter from Leitch on May 27th 1908 set out his proposal.

It read "In reference to my interview with you, I shall be glad to know whether your Committee would be willing to entertain a proposal to loan the Manchester United Club the

sum of £10,000 for the purpose of erecting the Grand Stand at the NEW Football Ground. The Club Directors would be willing to give their personal guarantees and also a guarantee from the Club itself, and in addition a guarantee would be obtained from the Manchester Brewery Co. and Messers Walker and Humphreys, Brewers in both of which Mr Davies, the chairman of the Manchester United Football Club, is also Chairman.

The money would be repayable in five years at a rate of £2,000 yearly, or it might be arranged that half of the net drawings of the grandstand taken yearly would go towards the reduction of the debt. In this way the money might be refunded at an earlier date,

but without going further into details at the present moment I shall be glad to know whether your Committee, as already stated, are willing to entertain this proposal."

Three days after receiving the letter, James Pinion sent a memorandum to all the other Committee members outlining the proposal, whilst also mentioning the construction of a Station, something which was not mentioned in the original letter, but something which must have been brought up by Archibald Leitch at his earlier meeting with James Pinion.

The memorandum, entitled "Manchester United Football Club. Proposed new Ground in Trafford Park immediately alongside the Cheshire Line Railway" read as follows

"The estimated cost of this ground with stands and other accommodation is £60,000. The estimated cost of the Station shewn(sic) on the plan prepared by Mr Blundell for the accommodation of traffic to and from is £10,000. The ground is to be constructed so as to accommodate 100,000 spectators. The football season extends over a period of thirty-three weeks and estimating that on twenty Saturdays during the season, matches will be held on the ground and that we obtain the carrying of one-tenth of the number the ground is estimated to accommodate, it would mean the conveyance of 10,000 per match on twenty Saturdays, bringing up an aggregate of 200,000 from Manchester during

THE NEW HOME OF MANCHESTER UNITED.

A GREAT GROUND FOR THE NORTH.

the season.

"In addition, on the remaining twenty Saturdays comprising the year it is proposed to hold athletic meetings, cycling meetings and such like and that we shall have 1,000 on each such Saturday, making up a total of 20,000 for athletic gatherings or 220,000 passengers altogether in the year.

In addition to this estimate for the Manchester traffic there is to be reckoned traffic from Liverpool, Warrington and other stations on the Cheshire Lines proper and also traffic from such places as Derby, Sheffield, Nottingham etc, on the Parent Companies Lines

and a great many other places on foreign lines, but reckoning the passenger traffic alone from Manchester the proposal appears to be an enticing one from a Cheshire lines point of view.

"I should state that it is the intention of the Football Club to provide elaborate provision for substantial refreshments for large parties coming from a distance so that footballers coming from such remote places as Derby, Sheffield, Nottingham etc, will on arrival on the ground obtain liquid refreshment and refreshments of a more substantial character so that it appears to me the proposal is one to be viewed with

considerable favour.

"I may mention that such a Station as is proposed, with the White City less than half a mile distant and Old Trafford Cricket Ground just half a mile away, would suit admirably for both these places so that the proposal has not alone the football Company's clientele to cater for but also the possibility of a very large traffic for the White City and for the Cricket matches at Old Trafford."

Despite James Pinion obviously being enthusiastic about the proposal, with the idea of the threepenny fare possibly generating around an extra £2,750 per annum

Old Trafford: *An artist's impression of the new stadium - nb. The terrace area opposite the grandstand was not covered until the 1930s.*

particularly appealing and a fair return for the initial £9,800 outlay, a preliminary meeting of the Committee, held on June 1st, thought otherwise. From the minutes of that meeting came the following, "The Committee regret exceedingly their statuary powers do not permit of them lending money for such purposes, otherwise the Manchester United Company's proposal would have every consideration."

2 - A NEW HOME

The United board and staff survey English football's first super stadium: *J.H. Davies (centre with trademark moustache), Louis Rocca (sitting on the hallowed turf with a light coloured overcoat on) and J. J. Bentley to the left of Davies holding a cigar.*

So it was Manchester United Football Club of Old Trafford on top of the letterheads from now on and it was all systems go to have the new stadium ready for the visit of Lancashire neighbours Liverpool, on Saturday February 19th 1910, for the inaugural match. This should really have been the second fixture at the new ground, with the visit of Tottenham Hotspur on January 22nd pencilled in for the opening match. However, with work on various sections of the stadium still incomplete, the supporters had to wait just a little longer to meander through the cobbled streets to their new home ground.

On February 16th, an official inspection of the ground was made by Mr J.H.Davies and his directors, accompanied by a large number of eager, inquisitive journalists. One of whom represented the *Manchester Evening News* and in his report in that day's newspaper, he wrote: "There is accommodation for over 40,000 people on the sixpenny side and the covered stand will hold nearly 13,000. The entire portion (of the stand) is filled with tip up chairs, covered with plush and these have been so arranged that at the close of a match, the coverings can be removed and stocked in a room adjoining, until required again. Behind these are arranged the seats for directors and visiting officials.

"Underneath the stands there is the boardroom, secretary's office, player's recreation rooms, gymnasium, dressing rooms and an elaborate series of baths. The Manchester and Salford Corporation are completing arrangements for carrying the spectators to the ground for the opening match and cars will also run on many Manchester routes. In addition, the cricket ground station will be opened. The task is so far advanced."

The task may well have been far advanced, thanks to Humphrey's the Knightsbridge builders, but their efforts were certainly not appreciated by those with the combination to the safe in the club's office, or the authority to sign the club chequebook, as they had to continually pester the directors over a period of time in order to extract payment for the work that they had done. It actually got to the stage that Humphrey's became so disappointed with the club that a solicitor was employed and for a number of years the club were paying around one third of their gate receipts to the builder.

Humphrey's were certainly not the only ones who had to wait on money owed coming their way, as the more local Ellison's, the Salford turnstile manufacturers, whose work could be found at countless venues, had to wait seven months before a cheque popped through their letter-box.

So, had John Davies and his fellow directors taken on more than they could chew?

The conveying of the expected large numbers of spectators was not as straight forward as had been expected, as two days prior to the inaugural fixture, the *Manchester Evening Chronicle* reported on the "Tramway Difficulty", with their correspondent writing about the "Question of Special Cars to Football Ground" and the "Difficulty that the Stretford Council do not have sufficient plant at their power station to propel the extra cars which are needed."

He went on to write: "In consequence, the limited power which will only allow fifty or sixty cars in excess to the ordinary traffic, the authorities are confronted with the risk of finding other means to carry the thousands of football enthusiasts. A large part of the increased traffic may devolve onto the Salford service, which runs cars to Trafford Bridge, not a great distance from the ground."

Traffic was particularly heavy in the Stretford area on the day of the Liverpool match, as all imaginable forms of transport headed towards Old Trafford, with those not fortunate enough to own, be able to pay for or be offered a lift on a vehicle of some sort, making their way on foot. Admission was sixpence (just over two pence) for the ground and one shilling (five pence), one shilling and six pence (just over seven pence) and two shillings (ten pence) for the covered stand. There were also a few reserved seats in the centre of the stand for those who could afford the five shillings (twenty-five pence). Those who could afford the luxury of a seat in the stand were pleasantly impressed upon their arrival, as the seats were no wooden benches, but plush, tip up affairs to which they were shown by attendants. It was, as one supporter commented, "more like the theatre than football".

With the prospect of thousands of people converging on the area every other week, local businesses were rubbing their hands in the anticipation of a vast increase in their turnover, with Mr J. H. Hargreaves, the

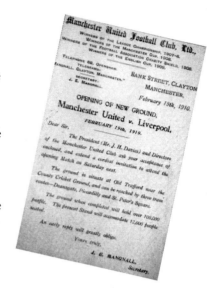

▲ **An invitation to Old Trafford's inaugural fixture:** *United v Liverpool on 19th February 1910.*

▼ **Lucky Escape:** *On February 17th, 1910, just after Manchester United moved out of the Bank Street ground, one of the stands blew down in a storm, damaging the houses opposite.*

LEAGUE DIVISION ONE - 19TH FEBRUARY 1910

UNITED 3 LIVERPOOL 4

As KICKOFF TIME approached, it was not easy to estimate the actual attendance inside, but outside, both around the ground and on the approach roads it was quite obvious that both the gatemen at the turnstiles and the Manchester Tramways were having difficulty in coping with the vast crowds. Today, the record books give an attendance at a rounded up 45,000, but it is to be believed that around 5,000 more managed to gain illegal entry by various means, including a small unfinished window fanlight.

So, the lush green turf, with its vivid white lines markings, looked immaculate as the sun shone down, with the red and white quartered corner flags fluttering in the afternoon breeze. The surroundings were all something of a dream for ever how many were indeed present, but they were soon brought back down to reality with a bump, as the visitors won 4-3, fighting back from 2-0 down.

Within fifteen minutes of the kick off, United were in front, Sandy Turnbull christening the new ground by latching onto a Dick Duckworth free kick to head the ball firmly past Hardy in the Liverpool goal. Or, as the correspondent from the Manchester Guardian seen it - "Duckworth took a free kick ... and skilfully dropped the ball some 10 yards or more from the goal-mouth. A Turnbull rushed in with lowered head. The ball was within a foot or two of the ground by the time he got it but he met it with that extra-durable head of his and drove it hard into the goal." A few minutes later, it was 2-0, Homer following through on a Harold Halse shot that the Liverpool goalkeeper failed to hold. It was the perfect start to life at the new venue.

United managed to maintain their advantage until the interval, but after the re-start, the visitors began to regain some of the play, keeping Stacey and Hayes, the two United full backs well occupied. Their pressure soon paid off and they pulled a goal back through outside right Goddard, his shot going in off the underside of the cross bar. The two goal advantage, however, was soon re-established, when George Wall scored with a fine shot from an oblique angle, blasting the ball past two defenders before it beat Hardy at his left hand post.

Despite this further setback, the white shirted Liverpool players refused to give in and their resilience was rewarded as they began to get the better of the United defence.

Goddard, with his second of the afternoon, soon made it 3-2. Stewart then not only equalized, but then a few minutes later scored what was to be the winner, as the rain began to fall on the by now subdued spectators.

It was certainly not the best of starts, but with the surroundings just as unfamiliar to the United players as they were to the visitors, it was not what could have been otherwise considered a shock defeat.

'Jacques', a correspondent in the 'Athletic News', the top football paper of the day, wrote: "Manchester United are a curious side. A week ago they defeated Newcastle United after being three goals to the bad at the interval, and now they open the finest ground in the country, before at least 45,000 people, by suffering defeat by four goals to three, after leading at the interval by two goals to none, and also leading midway through the second half by three goals to one."

He went on, "In many respects, it was an extraordinary match. The turf, which had been especially laid, and which looked a fit venue for a tennis tournament, was tremendously fast and, contrary to expectation, this proved more in favour of Liverpool."

owner of the Dog and Partridge Hotel (which could be found near to where the Bishop Blaize stands today), eager to have his slice of the cake. So much so, that he attempted to obtain a licence to sell alcohol at the new ground.

"Football and Drink" proclaimed the headline of an article in the *Manchester Evening News* of February 17th, with "Licence Sought for Manchester United New Ground. Application Refused."

The article read: "At Manchester County Police Court this morning, before Mr J. M. Yates KC, an application was made by Mr J. H. Hargreaves of the Dog and Partridge Hotel, for an occasional licence to sell drink at the new ground. The applicant explained that he wanted permission to sell at five bars on the ground between 3pm and 6pm.

Mr Yates: "They refuse to grant applications in other large towns. If you want anything of the sort, you must apply at the council meeting of licensing justices. It is a matter for them not me. The football public must be a curious lot, if they cannot watch for two hours without having a drink."

The stipendiary refused the application, so the landlord of the Dog and Partridge had to be content with the supporters passing through his doors prior to the game and then perhaps returning to debate the afternoon's entertainment after the final whistle (see match no.1).

Having got the initial fixture out of the way, things could now only become easier in the day to day running of the club. There was still a considerable amount of work to be done, but it was not long before the new stadium was being acknowledged as one of the best in the country.

Within months of the ground coming into use, United were honoured by the Football Association, who asked the club to stage the 1910 F. A. Cup semi-final tie between Barnsley and Everton, a game the Yorkshire side won 3-0 in front of a 40,000 crowd, while a year later, 56,657 (or 66,646, or even 58,000 depending where you obtain your figures from) packed into the ground, paying £3,487 to watch Bradford City defeat Newcastle United 1-0 in the F. A. Cup Final replay. This was the first time that the current F. A. Cup had been played for, as the previous one had been withdrawn by the Football Association when they found out that United had had a replica of it made following their cup win in 1909. The replay, on April 26th 1911, had produced rather hurried ticket sales and total chaos outside the ground on the day of the match, as thousands were reported to have been unable to gain admission, despite the attendance being 10,000 below the ground capacity.

These events were soon to become a common addition to the Old Trafford fixture list, with eight semi-finals and two Final

replays being played there prior to the Second World War. Such games provided an extra source of income for which the club were always grateful, although financial problems were not something which caused the management of the time any sleepless nights, with £12,000 of the ground debt paid off in 1912 and plans for further developments well in advance. Those developments were to see an entrance to the ground from the Salford side, with the building of a bridge at a total cost of £4,000, as well as a large car park next to the ground although it was to be season 1922-23 before this project was actually completed.

As for United, they finished their first season at their new home in fifth position, which was

certainly an improvement on the previous campaign, when the First Division league table found them occupying 13th spot. But twelve months further on, they had finally became accustomed to life in Trafford Park and lifted the First Division championship trophy for the second time in three years.

The visit of their newly promoted neighbours City on September 17th 1910, saw 60,000 click through the turnstiles, for an attendance record that would stand for ten years, when City's visit on November 20th 1920 saw it increased by 3,000. But the turnstiles didn't always click away merrily on match days, as only 7,000 witnessed the 3-2 victory over Bury on December 3rd and rather surprisingly, a mere 10,000 on the wet

Rocca's Brigade: *An early incarnation of the Red Army, they followed Edwardian United near and far.*

afternoon of April 29th to see the championship clinched against Sunderland with an emphatic 5-1 victory.

'Jacques' of the *Athletic News* was again present and below the headline of 'Hail the Champions', he wrote: "There were only about 12,000 people in the rain at Old Trafford, but they had a great day. They saw a splendid match, in which quick, strong, clever football was shown by both teams, and they saw Manchester United secure the championship of the League by a slashing victory over Sunderland. The crowd cheered at half time when the score at Anfield (where

PREPARING FOR CUP FINAL AT OLD TRAFFORD.

A workman breaking through the wall at Old Trafford for one of the extra entrances to the ground, in readiness for the Cup Final to-morrow. The turnstile can be seen through the opening, already fixed in position.

Liverpool were playing nearest rivals Aston Villa) was signalled on the telegraph-board, and at the finish there was a wonderful scene of enthusiasm, Mr. J. H. Davies, the president of the club, and the players being cheered to the echo."

Strangely enough, it was Sunderland who took the lead, Holley scoring with a fierce drive in the twenty-third minute, but having gone behind, the United players simply rolled up their sleeves and set about the job in hand. Within seven minutes,

United were level, Meredith sending a free-kick into the penalty area and Turnbull heading past Worrall in the Sunderland goal. The Welsh winger was also involved in the second goal five minutes before the interval, his corner kick falling to West, who back headed the ball home. The United defence kept the visitor's defence well-marshalled, allowing the rest of the team to keep Sunderland under almost constant pressure, with Meredith involved in practically every

move. Halse made it 3-1 before the interval.

In the second half, Meredith created goal number three, moving down the wing before crossing on the run for Halse, who controlled the ball before shooting past the 'keeper for his second. An own goal by Milton rounded off the scoring for the newly crowned Champions, whose success was in little danger, as the news from Liverpool filtered through, with the home side having beaten Aston Villa 3-1. United had secured the title by one point; fifty-two to Villa's fifty-one.

The title success, however, was not the start of exciting times for the club, but was in fact the opposite, as the following season they slipped to 13th, rallied twelve months later to climb back up to a creditable 4th, but went into free-fall, dropping to 14th in 1913-14 and then 18th in 1914-15, prior to the disruption of League football due to the outbreak of the First World War.

*

THE GAME ON April 2nd 1915, saw United play what was to be their most talked about fixture to date and, ironically, it was Liverpool who once again provided the opposition. On the morning of the match,

F. A. representatives, Mr Fredrick Wall and Mr Arthur Kingscott, visited the ground to discuss arrangements for the forthcoming F. A. Cup Final, to be held at Old Trafford on April 24th and it was fortunate that they left prior to the start of the match, as the events of that particular afternoon were to produce much controversial debate in the weeks ahead.

On a pouring wet afternoon, the 15,000 crowd had to endure more than adverse weather conditions, with performances best described as dubious (see match no.2). A couple of weeks after the match, a letter appeared in the *Sporting Chronicle*, signed 'Football King', on behalf of a firm of bookmakers, asking if anyone could help with information relating to several players betting on the United – Liverpool match ending in a 2-0 win for the home side? This opened a can of worms and although the finger of suspicion was pointed at several United players, they managed to keep their minds on playing, with relegation narrowly avoided.

In the meantime, a committee was assembled by the Football League to investigate the allegations arising from the match and the referee, John Sharpe, was even quoted as

LEAGUE DIVISION ONE - 2ND APRIL 1915
UNITED 2 LIVERPOOL 1

LIVERPOOL WERE EXPECTED to take both points from this encounter, as United were not enjoying the best of seasons, and sat in a precarious position third bottom of the league with only eight games remaining at kick-off. However, it was United who began the game more promisingly and opened the scoring with a goal from Anderson.

Strangely, as the first half progressed, the visitors showed little appetite for the game and play sluggishly dragged on until the interval. Half time opinion suggested that the second forty-five minutes would see the home side up against it. Liverpool had been runners-up in the FA Cup a season earlier before - surely they would commit themselves to attack and show their true form.

As it turned out, this was not to be the case and it soon became obvious to a large majority of the crowd that they were witnessing something a little more involved than a simple game of football. Voices of displeasure soon began to echo around the ground.

Play continued to be rather mundane, until a United attack on the visitors goal saw a Liverpool defender penalised and a penalty kick awarded. Much to the crowd's amazement, centre half O'Connell stepped up to take the spot-kick instead of the regular penalty taker Anderson. O'Connell's effort gave the goalkeeper no cause for concern, as it flew well wide of the post.

> ' Pagnam almost pulled a goal back... for his efforts, he received a severe reprimand from some of his team mates, as the crowd looked on in disbelief. '

Anderson eventually did secure the points for United with his second goal, although near the end, Liverpool's Pagnam almost pulled a goal back, but his shot rebounded off the crossbar, when it looked easier to score. For his effort, he received a severe reprimand from some of his team mates, as the crowd looked on in disbelief.

So United 'earned' two valuable points, but the press were not lacking in comment on the fixture. "the most uninteresting game ever seen at the ground" wrote the 'Sporting Chronicle' correspondent, while the 'Daily Dispatch' reporter penned "United's West was clearly employed in the second half in kicking the ball as far out of play as he could".

▲ **The Dog and Partridge hotel:** *Once a regular match day haunt for United supporters and the meeting place for the match fixing players prior to United – Liverpool match of April 2nd 1915..*

saying that following the penalty incident, he "suspected that something was amiss", but decided to continue with the game, although it was the most extraordinary match that he had ever officiated over. United manager John Robson, was also disgusted by the performances of both teams and had left the ground before the final whistle. Following many hours of questioning players from both sides, the investigating committee announced that four Liverpool players, along with A. Turnbull, West and Whalley of United were to be suspended *sine-die* from football.

Much was made of the case, and 'Knocker' West went to great lengths to declare his innocence in the matter. So incensed was he that he decided to take the matter to court. Prior to a home match during the First World War, he even stood outside Old Trafford, having made the short journey from his home in nearby Railway Road, handing

out leaflets which stated that he was prepared to give £50, quite a sum in those days, to any Red Cross Fund, if anyone could prove that he had placed a bet, or won any money, from the Good Friday fixture. No one ever came forward.

On July 5th 1917, some two years after the eventful confrontation, the court case opened and while some players denied all knowledge of any attempts to fix the outcome of the game, others, including Sheldon of Liverpool (and a former United player) suggested otherwise. It was revealed that on the morning of the match, he had journeyed to Manchester alone, meeting up with his former United team mates Turnbull, Whalley and West in the Dog and Partridge pub close to Old Trafford. After much conversation and debating, it was agreed that the result of the game would be 2-0 to United, with a goal in each half. Sheldon had been approached previously

1915 FA Cup final: *This became known as the Khaki Cup final because of the number of servicemen in attendance.* **Inset:** *the programme and teams on the day.*

When the First World War had broken out, it was assumed by many that it would be all over by Christmas 1914, so the football authorities went along with the politicians' theory and continued with a normal League and Cup programme. However, when it became clear that hostilities were going to be a little more prolonged, both competitions were postponed indefinitely, with clubs reverting to regional fixtures.

In the season following the end of the war, on March 29th 1919, the second last game of the season, a young twenty year-old Northumberland born forward, who had recently signed for the club, made his Old Trafford and Manchester United debut against Bury. It was to be a debut few could match. Joe Spence had previously played for Newburn and Scotswood in the Northern League and played a handful of games for Liverpool reserves as a guest player whilst serving with the Machine Gun Corps, before signing for United. Against Bury, playing at inside right, Spence got off to the best possible start, scoring four in United's 5-1 win. This was the start of a Manchester United career which would last until season 1932-33, during which time he would become a firm favourite with the supporters, producing the early terrace shout of 'Give It To Joe' during a career that would produce a record 481 League appearances, that was to stand for thirty-three years. He also continued to score goals, netting 158 in the League and a further

and had made arrangements with some of his Liverpool team mates regarding fixing the result and everything could be finalised. Few who used the Dog and Partridge in the years to come would be aware of the conspiracy which had been discussed between the four walls all those years ago.

With the First World War in its infancy, Old Trafford hosted what was to be the last F. A. Cup Final for four years, Sheffield United and Burnley had drawn 0-0 at the ground in the F. A. Cup semi-final the previous season, as competitive football took a back seat. On the afternoon of April 24th 1915, on what many people would call a typical rainy Manchester afternoon, Sheffield United, having enjoyed yet another favourable run in the competition, defeated Chelsea 3-0. in what was to become known as the 'Khaki Cup Final', due to the number of servicemen in uniform in the 49,557 crowd.

The game would normally have remained in the capital and played at the usual Crystal Palace venue, but in an effort to avoid any unnecessary disruption to traffic in and around London, it was decided to move the game to the next best venue or, as many would have suggested, the ideal ground for this prestige match. Unfortunately, the attendance was not in keeping with the Final and was around 40,000 less than expected. This was due mainly to the restrictions on war-time travel and also the fact that many had already been drafted into the armed forces. As for the match itself, some saw very little of the action at times, due to a thick fog that enveloped the ground, but it was the Yorkshire side who mastered the conditions best, taking the lead nine minutes before the interval and adding their two other goals in the final eight minutes of the game.

10 in twenty-nine F. A. Cup ties.

Following the First World War, when American servicemen had used the Old Trafford pitch for baseball, it took a while for life to return to normal, as the hostilities had affected everyone, but slowly, recreational activities began to regain importance in people's lives and football was soon to enjoy an increase in popularity. Some 258,000 spectators attended the eleven First Division fixtures on the opening day of season 1919-20, the first after the war and it was soon to prove a boom time for the vast majority of clubs, United included, as the turnstiles clicked merrily away on match days. The local derby against City on October 18th 1919, attracted a crowd of 49,360 compared to only 20,000 for the corresponding fixture in 1914-15. On February 14th 1920, a crowd of 58,661 watched United defeat Sunderland 2-0, when only 16,000 had been in attendance where United had won 3-0 five years previously.

On December 27th 1920, however, the Old Trafford turnstiles were put into overdrive, as some 70,504 passed through the gates (with thousands locked out), paying £4,824 to watch United play Aston Villa. One newspaper at the time gave a different attendance figure of 72,000, but this was not regarded as official and the lower of the two figures is that which appears

in the record books. It was certainly a busy festive period for the turnstile operators at Old Trafford, as the previous day, 15,000 had been at the ground to watch a reserve fixture between United and Villa, which had ended in a 0-0 draw. Twenty-four hours after the attendance record was set, United played host to Corinthians in a friendly. This fixture, however, attracted a mere 3,000.

Two days prior to Villa's visit to Manchester, United had won a seven goal thriller at Villa Park 4-3, but there was to be no League double, as Villa won the Old Trafford fixture 3-1. The visitors took a two-goal lead through Walker, with United failing to make the most of their chances, although they did hit the crossbar on a couple of occasions. Harrison managed to pull a goal back, but Villa took everything in their stride and Stephenson soon added a third.

On May 7th, towards the end of that 1920-21 season, another record attendance was set, when a crowd of thirteen paid to watch Stockport County play Leicester City in a Second Division fixture. Stockport's ground at the time was closed by the Football Association due to crowd disturbances, hence the reason for their appearance in Manchester. The attendance is, however, a little misleading, as the game was actually watched by a crowd of around 10,000, due

to United having been at home that afternoon, defeating Derby County 3-0 and many of the crowd stayed behind to watch a second ninety minutes for free.

The construction of Old Trafford had been something of a burden on the club's finances, with those at the helm having to juggle the pounds, shillings and pence off the pitch, while matters on it had not exactly kept the turnstiles clicking merrily away, as the club dropped from the First Division to the Second at the end of season 1921-22.

As 1921 had blended into 1922, a man who had played a major part in taking the club out of its severe financial predicament passed away. John Robson had been appointed manager on December 28th 1914 (the first with the club to actually carry that title) and although if League positions are taken into account, he would not be considered a major success, his influence on the club could not be dismissed.

Sadly, he suffered health problems and brought his seven year reign to an end in October 1921, but remained at the club, as his administrative skills were second to none, taking on the role of assistant manager. This appointment, however, was relatively short lived, as Robson died of pneumonia in January 1922.

Joe Spence: *A United legend in an era bereft of success.*

Robson, lived close to Old Trafford on Warwick Road, and many of those attending the first game after his death, against Newcastle United on January 14th, would have been well aware of this, whilst also knowing that the former manager's body was lying only a few yards away behind the drawn curtains. The attendance for the Newcastle match was 2,000 up on that of the previous some fixture, but there was to be no victory to honour the man, with the visitors returning to the north-east with both points following a 1-0 victory.

A couple of months later, on March 8th 1922, the gate receipts

Albert Pape: *The player behind one of the most bizarre transfers ever, who arrived at Old Trafford expecting to play against United, but ended up playing for them against his former team mates Clapham Orient.*

from an England international trial game played at the ground, a sum of £2,000, was donated to his benefit fund. Only one United player featured in the 1-1 draw, with Jack Mew in goal for the 'Whites'. In the 'Reds', however, were two former United players, Tommy Meehan of Chelsea and Fred Hopkins of Liverpool.

The ground record attendance, set against Aston Villa, did not last for long, as the estimated 73,000 became a reality on March 24th 1923, when Bolton Wanderers faced Sheffield United in an F. A. Cup semi-final, bringing in gate receipts of £7,600. By 2pm on the afternoon of the game, the Old

Trafford gates were firmly locked, with large numbers of the usual ticketless supporters, as well as many with tickets unable to get near the turnstiles, still milling around outside. One Sheffield United supporter rushing towards the turnstiles passed a friend and enquired which way he was going. "Home" came the unexpected reply.

Inside the ground, the scene was remarkable, with the popular side (where the North Stand is now) a mass of heaving, swaying bodies, moving in all directions like a human tide. Many were squashed against the barriers, while for others the heat was far too much to bear and having fainted, they were passed over the heads of fellow supporters to the sanctuary of the touchline.

Along the sidelines on other parts of the ground, were spectators who had suffered similar discomforts, but who had been forced bodily across the fencing at the front. The police had tried in desperation to force them back, but to no avail and many watched the game from a more comfortable spot. When all was considered, it was perhaps a little surprising that the game went ahead as scheduled and that there were no serious injuries amongst the spectators.

Sadly, the game itself could not compare to the pre-match excitement and was cautiously played, with neither side prepared to take any chances.

Bolton, perhaps, just deserved their 1-0 win and moved on to become one of the finalists in the first ever Wembley Final and many of their enthusiastic supporters invaded the pitch at full time, to carry their heroes off shoulder high.

The following year, 1924, produced a couple of interesting events in the history of Old Trafford, with United involved in neither. February of that year saw the ground become a guinea pig for an experiment which would later become something of a compulsion for thousands of people from all walks of life, and not just football supporters, making considerable sums of money for some of those fortunate individuals and a considerable amount more for the man behind it all.

John Moores, who later became chairman of Everton and was at one point listed as the second richest man in Britain, had picked up the idea of 'football pools' from a failed Birmingham entrepreneur and had persuaded two friends, Colin Askham and Bill Hughes, to put up £30 each for the first batch of his 'coupons'. Those coupons were then taken to Old Trafford, where Moores hired some local children to hand them out to supporters making their way to the ground to watch United. Much to his dismay, the idea was not an immediate success as only 35 out of the 4,000 coupons were returned. This, however,

was a much better return than that of a future attempt at Hull, when only 1 from 10,000 was returned. The second 1920's Old Trafford 'first' came a few months later, when Manchester County hired the stadium to play the New Zealand 'All Blacks' at rugby, an agreement which saw United receive 20% of the gross gate receipts. This was the first non-football match to be held at the ground.

1924-25 was also something of an eventful season for United, finishing runners-up in the Second Division, therefore securing promotion back to the top flight. Opening the campaign with eighteen points from their opening eleven games, whilst losing only twice between September 1st and December 20th, went a long way towards this success. United's main challengers in the first half of the season were Derby County and when the two sides clashed at Old Trafford on November 29th, in front of the biggest crowd of the season – 59,500, they certainly got their money's worth. The points were shared in a 1-1 draw, with the visitors taking the lead through Fairclough, who was later sent off for a somewhat reckless challenge as the game threatened to bubble over, and within minutes of Derby being reduced to ten men, United were level. A McPherson corner was punched up in the air by Olney the Derby 'keeper and as it dropped, the robust Barson took care of the goalkeeper as he attempted to re-gain possession of the ball

Programme for the Lancashire v New Zealand Rugby League match played during season 1924-25.

◀ **Manchester United 1924/25:** *Taken in front of Leitch's Main Stand*

and Hanson nudged the ball home. Despite protests from the irate Derby County players, the referee allowed the goal to stand. Even 'Jacques' in his *Athletic News* report, begged to differ with the match official

An F. A. enquiry was set-up to look into the game, following the rather unsavoury press reports that followed, with Barson, not a great favourite of the men who ran the game, summoned for the use of abusive language, found not guilty.

A year after that debut appearance of the football coupon came another surprise debut at the ground and this time United were very much involved. On February 7th 1925, Clapham Orient journeyed north to play a Second Division fixture and shortly after arriving at the ground, they found themselves involved in transfer negotiations, with United wanting to sign their centre forward Albert Pape. The player, and both clubs, agreed the transfer details, while the move was also approved by the Football League over the telephone. Pape therefore lined up against his colleagues with whom he had travelled north and went on to get his name on the score sheet, netting United's fourth in a 4-2 win.

Old Trafford must have formed a favourable impression with the Football Association (either that or they enjoyed days out 'up north') because on April 17th 1926, the 'Auld Enemy' – England and Scotland – faced each other in the ground's inaugural international fixture, and what was also the 50th meeting between the two countries. The occasion brought out the best in Manchester United, with the ground in immaculate condition, while Allied Newspapers, with the authority of the United directors, produced a 112-page souvenir brochure, detailing the history of the club in words and photographs. The club itself, as it had done for the F. A. Cup semi-finals and Finals, produced an excellent match programme.

As for the game itself, it certainly matched the occasion, with the atmosphere greatly enhanced by the estimated 10,000 Scots in the crowd creating more noise than the rest of the 40,000 present. Prior to kick off, a number of the tartan clad visitors invaded the pitch to embrace their favourites, staging a similar 'invasion' again at the end, as their enthusiasm got the better of them following the 1-0 Scottish victory. The only goal of the game came from Jackson, following a move with Hughie Gallagher, the former's shot going in off the upright.

The financial situation began to show something of an improvement, with the overdraft at the bank being reduced from £3,355 to zero by season 1926-27 mainly due to the fact that attendances had increased with the return of First Division football in 1925. A local 'derby' match with Manchester City on January 23rd 1926 attracted 48,657 and a 5th round F. A. Cup replay against Sunderland that same season was watched by 58,661, paying £4,823. On other occasions, there were some poor attendances, with the likes of 9,214 against Liverpool on March 10th 1926 and 9,974 on the final day of the season for the visit of West Bromwich Albion.

Nevertheless, the board of directors decided, after much debate, to take up the option which enabled the club to purchase the freehold of Old Trafford, which at the time was costing £1,300 per year in rent and rates. The Manchester

Brewery Company agreed to the proposed sale, as had been agreed in the lease dated December 30th 1914, with the price being £10,150 and a yearly ground rent of £48. United had also to pay the Brewery Company the sum of £11,199 18/8d, which was the sum agreed between the two parties as what was owed in rent up to March 25th 1927, when the deal would be completed.

Seven months later, the directors were perhaps regretting their decision, as J. H. Davies, the club President and benefactor with his huge investment and interest free loans, passed away. His presence and expertise was obviously greatly missed in the boardroom and once again, the club began to struggle.

One particular aspect of the ground enjoyed by the spectators of the day was the fact that they could move freely from one end of the ground to the other along the Popular side (United Road in more recent times). This was not so easy when the ground was packed, but on less busy days, it was not so much of a problem.

A perfect example of this was mentioned in a *Guardian* match report for the charity match against Motherwell on April 27th 1927, with the reporter writing "It was notable that the spectators crowded behind the end at which the Motherwell forwards could best be seen. They were well rewarded, for, displaying clever control of

the ball and exploiting the short pass." The reason for the interest in the Scottish side was due to the difference between Scottish and English football at that time, with the former considered much more entertaining to watch. Visits from Airdrie in May 1923, Celtic and Rangers within a seven day period in April 1924 and Third Lanark in February 1935 were all eagerly awaited fixtures by the Old Trafford regulars.

During the summer months, most football stadiums are deserted places, with repair and maintenance work the only action going on, but for Old Trafford, the summer of 1927 produced something completely different and certainly unique for any football ground. Hired by a Mr C. B. Cochran, there was a week of activity at the ground with an "Exhibition of Tennis by Madame Lenglen". Despite the star attraction, Suzanne Lenglen being a Wimbledon Champion, she was not in the same league as Joe Spence and co. and attracted disappointing attendances.

Overall, results between seasons 1927-28 and 1929-30 were poor, with 12th position the best that could be achieved, although it had to be said, that home form could be considered favourable at times.

Derby County were beaten 5-0, Aston Villa 5-1, Leicester City 5-2 and Liverpool 6-1 during 1927-28, while Newcastle conceded five without reply in both season 1928-29 and 1929-30. There were also a few 'let's leave early' score lines – 7-1 against Newcastle in 1927-28, 5-2 against Grimsby in 1929-30 and 5-1 against Sheffield United in the final match of that same season.

The following season, 1930-31, was nothing short of disastrous, with every one of the opening twelve fixtures being lost. Attendances dropped from 18,004 on the opening day against Aston Villa to 10,907 for the third home fixture against Newcastle United. Score lines such as the 6-2 defeat at Chelsea, the 6-0 defeat at home to Huddersfield and the 7-4 defeat, again at home, to Newcastle United, were not tolerated by the support and it was soon obvious to everyone that frustration was mounting.

Strangely, the directors decided to build a new road on the 'popular side' of the ground (the road under the North Stand today), for the "convenience of our patrons", something that could well have been considered a waste of money, as those patrons became fewer with each passing fixture. Leaflets were handed out at home games by members of

the Supporters Club, with many opinions put forward to the cause of the poor start, but the directors chose to keep their heads in the sand.

By mid-October, things were reaching boiling point and following the 5-1 defeat at West Ham, the Supporters Club called a meeting at Hulme Town Hall on the night of Friday October 17th, hours before the visit of Arsenal to Old Trafford. There had already been a handful of previous meetings at various venues across the city, with a few hundred supporters turning up to voice their concerns about the way the club was heading.

Some 3,000 attended the meeting and the board were unanimously given a vote of no confidence, while Mr Greenhough, the Supporters

◄ *Programme cover for the proposed 'Boycott Match' against Arsenal on October 18th 1930.*

▲ **A New Stand rising:** *Goalmouth action during a schoolboy match in the early 1930's with the construction of the United Road – "Popular" side cover in progress.*

► **The Main Stand:** *As viewed from Warwick Rd railway bridge shortly after the opening of the Old Trafford Foootball Ground halt, in this painting by Dave Weldon.*

◄ **British Rail leaflet:** *Advertising the opening of the Old Trafford Ground Station on September 4th 1935 - "Third Class Return fare 3d."*

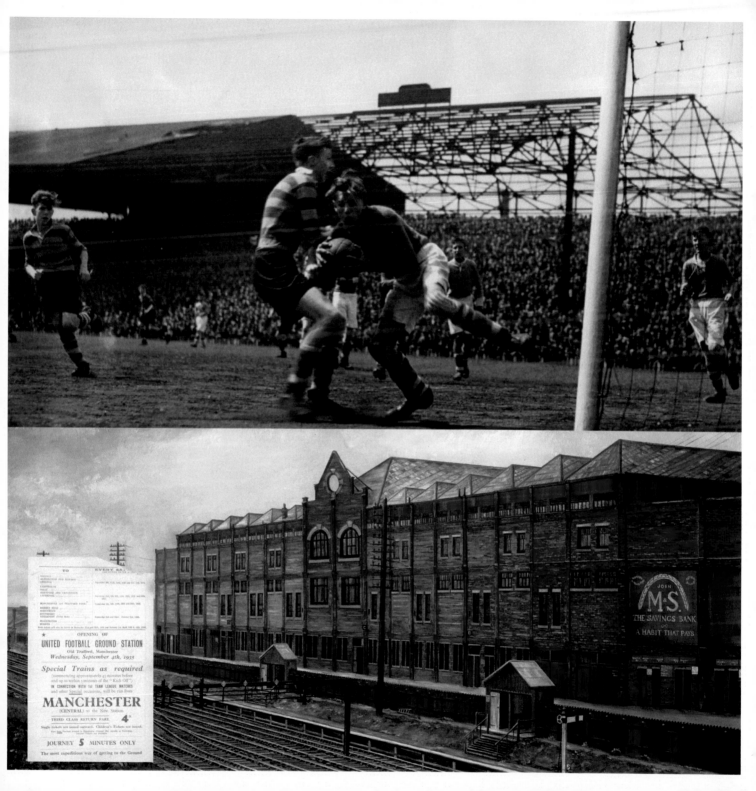

club secretary, proposed that the match the following day should be boycotted. Former United captain Charlie Roberts was one of those at the meeting, invited by the Supporters Club, as they wanted him elected to the board as their representative, but he was quick to speak out against the threat of a boycott. His opinion mattered little, as a show of hands decided otherwise.

So, armed with his soapbox, Mr Greenhough set off for Old Trafford on Saturday October 18th, hoping that the feelings of the meeting the previous night would be carried over and the board would pay attention to the most important people behind the club – its supporters. Extra police were on duty outside the ground to quell any unruly behaviour, but heavy rain seemed to dampen the spirits a little and the intended boycott was reported in the press as a failure, due to the attendance of 23,406, which was not only the highest of the season to date, but the highest for the entire season, except for the Manchester 'derby' against neighbours City, which had attracted 39,876. Many had

travelled to the ground to view the pre-match events, expecting considerable excitement, but after listening to what Mr Greenhough had to say, they simply paid their admission money at the turnstiles and watched United go down to yet another defeat, this time 1-2 to Arsenal.

Whilst mentioning attendances during season 1930-31, it is worth noting that every fixture played after January 1st, except one, was watched by less than 10,000 spectators, the exception being the visit of City. A mere 4,808 turned-up for that clash with Portsmouth on March 16th, 3,679 for the **visit of** Leicester City on March 25th and on the final day of the season, 3,969 against Middlesbrough.

It should also be stated that Mr Greenhough was far from being some sort of trouble seeker or self-centred individual. Rather he was a fervent supporter of United and was one of the initial forces behind the formation and establishing of the first Supporters Club in the mid 1920's. His dedication and that of fellow committee members and other willing hands, saw to it that the the terracing and stands were swept each week, as well as assisting with any other maintenance that was required.

The headquarters of the Supporters Club was at the Clowes Hotel, Trafford Road, Salford, but they also had a hut on what was the United Road side of the ground, where they catered for the spectators on match days with various refreshments. The hut was also put into use on Sunday mornings, when members and players met to discuss the previous afternoon's ninety-minutes and also enjoy a game of cards or darts.

The 1930's were troubled times for everyone, with rising unemployment and a lack of ready cash causing more than just a slight worry for businesses and individuals alike. It was no different for Manchester United, who were forced to approach the Brewery Company and ask for their mortgage interest payments to be suspended, along with a similar application to the Stretford Urban District Council for permission to pay road charges by instalments. With financial problems mounting at the Bank, a solution had to be found or the club would soon find themselves in very serious trouble.

Thankfully help did arrive, towards the end of 1931, in the form of Mr J. W. Gibson, a local clothing entrepreneur, who met the board, set out a plan for recovery and made an investment of £30,000 and became club Chairman. Ground improvements at this time, were few and far between, with the covering of the two corners of the ground on either side of the main stand the only work carried out between the mid 1920's and mid 1930's. Certainly, there was a lack of ready cash with which to fund any improvements, but the lack of interest given to the ground, despite hosting F. A. Cup semi-finals in 1928 (Sheffield United .v. Huddersfield), 1930 (Huddersfield .v. Sheffield Wednesday) and 1931 (Everton .v. West Bromwich Albion) added to the rumours, which began to circulate in 1932, that United

were going to move away from Old Trafford. These were firmly scotched, however, when plans were made and carried forward, in 1936, to cover the popular side.

It is more than a possibility though, that those plans would have have been put on hold, or more likely abandoned altogether, if the club had succumbed to relegation to the Third Division, in season 1933-34. Stability and consistency were certainly not to be found at Old Trafford during the 1930's, as the club called on the services of some sixty different individuals between seasons between 1932 and 1934, with 1933-34 almost bringing the ultimate embarrassment.

Everything that the club had achieved in the future hinged on just ninety minutes of football, with the journey to Millwall on Saturday May 5th 1934. That game, if it ended in defeat, would mean relegation to Division Three. The home side had a total of 33 points and sat second from bottom of the table, while United had one point less and occupied bottom place. With only one home defeat at the Den all season, the odds were stacked heavily against United, but goals from Cape and Manley gave the visitors a 2-0 win and ensured at least one more season in the top flight. Had the result gone the other way, who knows how United and Old Trafford would have fared in the years ahead.

Through those depressing times, Old Trafford was still one of the finest grounds in

the country, thanks mainly to its initial construction. In 1935, the station that Archibald Leitch had tried to persuade the Cheshire Lines Railway to become involved with some twenty-seven years previously, finally materialised. Over the years, delays had been frequent at Trafford Bar, coupled with countless traffic jams on the nearby roads, so at long last a train service was to run from Central Station direct to the ground. Strangely, the railway company had a written agreement with the club guaranteeing them compensation against any loss.

*

FOR THOSE FOOTBALL fans of the mid-1930's, with a curiosity as to what the interior of Old Trafford was really like, the *Football Weekly* of November 21st revealed all, with a visit to

the ground by new publication 'The Wanderer', who went behind the scenes with famous football clubs.

"Three years ago Manchester United were on the verge of bankruptcy. One Friday afternoon the players stood about waiting for their wages. None came – the club had no money! But those lads turned out the next day knowing that they would not be let down. And they weren't. United turned the corner, and to-day they're back in the First Division.

"I certainly found no signs of bankruptcy when I called at Old Trafford the other day. In fact, there's nothing wrong with United these days. Everything's spick and span about the ground – a great ground too. Since my last visit the main entrance at one corner of the huge stand has been remodelled with oak panelling and what not. Just inside is the office. Opposite

▲ **The Main Stand c.1938:**
*taken from the Stretford End
terracing c. 1938*

▶ **A section of the vast
crowd, at the Wolverhampton
Wanderers – Grimsby Town
FA Cup semi-final of 1939.**
*Photograph looks down on the
'Scoreboard End'.*

▶▼ *A break in play gives the
photographer the chance to
capture a last shot of Leitch's
main stand.*

– the boardroom.

"Old Trafford is a strange
ground. Under the big stand is
a long, rambling tunnel. Some
way along it, are the players'
quarters. I opened
a door marked
'Recreation Room'.
Empty – except for
the billiards table
and a whole host
of pictures on
the walls, photos
of great United
teams of the past.
A little farther on
is the dressing-
room."

Upon
meeting one of the United
coaches he knew, the 'Wanderer'
was invited for a kick-about

behind the stand and readily
agreed, continuing his
description of the ground as he
went.

"Walking along under the
stand we passed the
shooting-box
(whatever this
was, it was not
revealed) and
the heading ball
hanging from a
beam."

Crossing the
car park with
United manager
Scott Duncan to
the near-by railway
station, the man at
the helm told the
correspondent: "It's only used
on match-days, of course. Two-

pence each way from Manchester
Central (now the G-Mex) – a ten
minute's service, too, so you can
guess how many people can be
brought to our home games."

Prior to season 1938-39,
the wing terraces had been
re-roofed, giving cover to some
4,000 spectators. Beneath the
main stand, a new treatment
room was set up along with a
cobblers workshop, while the
dressing rooms were also re-
decorated, bringing in bills of
around £35,000, but keeping the
ground in contention to hold
'high profile matches', such as
the somewhat regular F. A. Cup
semi-finals and the Football
League .v. Irish League fixture of
November 1938.

The above mentioned Inter-
League fixture saw the 'home'
eleven turn in a memorable
display, with Stanley Matthews
at his masterly best, teasing and
tormenting the Irish defence,
whilst helping to provide
Tottenham Hotspur's Willie Hall
with five goals in the 7-0 victory.
Three of those goals came in a
five minute period and were all
provided by Matthews. It was
fitting, therefore, that the man
from the Potteries rounded
off a fine afternoon's work by
completing the rout with a fine
solo goal, much to the crowd's
delight.

Towards the end of that
1938-39 season, the Football
Association awarded Old
Trafford yet another semi-final
fixture, with Wolverhampton
Wanderers facing Grimsby
Town on March 25th. A League
fixture between the two today

would create little interest (or excitement), but on that distant Saturday afternoon, Old Trafford was filled as it had never been before, with a record 76,962 inside (paying £8,193), creating two new ground records. As a matter of interest, the Midlands side won 5-0, but the score line was a little misleading, as they were certainly not as superior as that would suggest.

To football followers August is the month of the year which heralds the start of yet another new season, with dreams of honours and excitement in the months ahead. 1939, however, was rather different, with the outbreak of the Second World War imminent, with the whole country on a state of war footing. The Football League decided to keep things as they were and prepared complete fixture lists for all divisions, despite the general unrest and the possibility of what might lie ahead.

As it was, Old Trafford was the venue for only one First Division fixture before hostilities got under way, with a crowd of 22,537 present on August 26th, to watch United beat Grimsby Town 4-0. On September 3rd war was declared, with only three fixtures having been completed. and Old Trafford was requisitioned as a temporary depot for the military, with the Cliff training ground (purchased a few years earlier)

being used by the RAF.

The government at first ordered clubs to refrain from playing, due to the threat of aerial attacks, but later they did an about turn as they felt that any form of recreation would help boost the morale of the people and transfer their thoughts to something else for a short period of time. The Football League in its current form, however, was disbanded and Divisional Leagues set up, with United in the Western Division, which was made up of northern

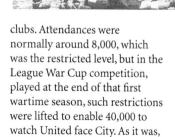

clubs. Attendances were normally around 8,000, which was the restricted level, but in the League War Cup competition, played at the end of that first wartime season, such restrictions were lifted to enable 40,000 to watch United face City. As it was, only 21,874 turned up for that 1st leg tie, with around 9,000 fewer turning up for the second leg of the second round against Blackburn Rovers, which United lost 3-1.

3 - FROM THE ASHES...

Blitzed: *A devastating attack on Old Trafford in March 1941 shattered the Main Stand.*

By the summer of 1940, Britain was under attack following the capitulation of France in July of that year. Despite this, the Football League once again decided to continue their War League fixtures for the forthcoming season, a decision which was to cause United numerous problems, some that would take almost a decade to overcome.

Christmas Day 1940 should have seen Stockport County visit Old Trafford for a North Regional League match, but on the night of Sunday December 22nd, German aircraft bombed Trafford Park, with the Old Trafford ground sustaining damage, as did the industrial area surrounding it. During those air raids, over 300 Mancunians were killed. As a result the Stockport match was hastily switched to County's ground and the scheduled Old Trafford fixture against Blackburn Rovers three days later on December 28th was also switched to Stockport. Playing those two home fixtures at Stockport did not have too much of an effect on attendances, with 1,500 watching the Blackburn fixture (a 5-5 draw), with home attendances having ranged between 700 and 3,000, although the 'derby' fixture brought 10,000.

Following the bomb damage, Old Trafford was tidied up and home fixtures were resumed at their rightful venue, in both the Lancashire Cup and the League War Cup. The North Regional League fixtures began again on March 8th with a match against Bury, when hat tricks from Rowley and Carey, along with a single Smith goal, brought a 7-3 victory, thrilling a 3,000 crowd. This, however, was to be the last competitive match to be played at Old Trafford until 1949, as on the night of March 11th further sustained German air attacks on Manchester causing yet more damage and devastation on Trafford Park. The stadium was once again caught in the line of fire and suffered severe damage, losing most of the main stand, dressing rooms and offices. This time, there could be no swift patch up job and the club moved to temporary office accommodation a short distance from the ground at Cornbrook Cold Stores, which were then owned by Mr J. W. Gibson, where club affairs were continued by secretary Walter Crickmer.

Manchester United Football Club were now homeless and while arrangements were being made with the Stretford Corporation to dismantle what was left of the stand and salvage the steel, along with demolishing other unsafe parts of the ground, claims for war damage to property were put forward to the authorities. This was all very well in the long term, but what was to happen in the meantime, with half a seasons fixtures still to fulfil?

Assistance came from neighbours City, who offered their rivals a helping hand suggesting that they used their Maine Road ground for 'home' fixtures until the time came when Old Trafford was playable again. It was a lifeline United grasped thankfully, as they were determined to continue with their fixtures as best they could. Following clearance from the Football League, Maine Road became 'home' for both the Blue and the Red fractions of Manchester, as Old Trafford lay dormant several miles away.

On November 17th 1944, the War Commission wrote to the club directors to say that after inspection Old Trafford was "not considered a total loss", but it was still some time before any repair work could be proposed. Local MP Ellis Smith, himself a keen United supporter and a man to whom United should be more than grateful, became very much involved in the club's attempts at obtaining grants towards the rebuilding of the ground. This involvement continuing for many years after the war ended in 1945, as United continued to seek help towards the rebuilding of the stadium.

So, with war in Europe finally over, servicemen were returning home, while throughout the country attempts were being made to try and regain some form of normality, United found themselves in a situation similar to that of days gone by – a ground in much need of repair, large debts and no manager. One third of those problems were solved on Monday February 19th 1945, when former Manchester City and Liverpool wing half Matt Busby was appointed manager. Standing on the rubble strewn terracing looking around the deserted ground, with a large bush growing on the pitch, most would have been put off. However with the total control of team affairs granted to him by the board Matt recognised United as the cleanest of slates.

In August 1945, the War Damage Commission granted the club a sum of £4,800 to clear the debris around the ground, with a further sum of £1,430 being granted in November 1946 for the demolition of the stand, or to be more precise, what was left of it. Another cheque, this time for £17,478 popped through the Old Trafford letter box some time later, as this was the figure granted towards the rebuilding of the stand. Those payments were made in instalments, with the final sum of just over

German Reconnaissance photograph over Trafford Park taken on 4th October 1939: *The main targets were Salford docks and the munitions factories of Trafford Park. Old Trafford can been seen towards the top right of the photograph.*

£710 for the demolition work not being paid until February 1947. Local youngsters earned themselves some extra pocket money by painstakingly walking up and down the pitch picking up broken glass.

Despite being uncertain as to what funds were being made available to them, the difficult job of pulling down the entire main stand, or what was left of it, along with the wall behind it, was carried out in April 1945 and during the summer of that year the wall was rebuilt and new dressing rooms were erected. Repair work on the covered section on the opposite side of the ground was also carried out, with the playing surface, although in reasonable and playable condition, being given 300 tons of special soil with new turf laid down its centre from one goalmouth to the other.

Devastated: *Old Trafford lay in ruins for years after the attack with re-construction delayed due to more urgent post-war re-construction.*

United had hoped to kick off season 1946-47 back in the familiar surroundings of Old Trafford, instead of the shared, rented accommodation at Maine Road, but the club accounts for season 1945-46 mention that "owing to the persistent acute shortage of building materials it had not been possible to reinstate the club premises and they would continue to use Manchester City's ground". Some 30,000 did squeeze into the ground in early August to watch a Reds .v. Blues practice match, which ended in a 3-3 draw, while both United and City reserve teams played their Central League fixtures there. The more serious business of League football, was however, still played a few miles away.

In the opening 'United Review' for 1946-47, Chairman Mr J. W. Gibson wrote, "A lump rises in my throat when I think of our premises at Old Trafford damaged beyond repair by fire and blast in March 1941 and still looking a sorry spectacle owing to government policy of issuing only limited licences for building materials whilst the housing problem is so manifest".

By December, plans had been drawn up for the proposed 'new look' Old Trafford once permission was given. The architect's drawing gave the impression of large covered stands, spacious terracing, accompanied by up-to-date facilities for the players. It was hoped the capacity could rise to around 125,000 with the railway station, now fully in operation alongside the ground providing quick and easy access to and from it. But could the ideas on paper be transferred onto brick and concrete?

"Old Trafford Exiles" was the heading above a full page article by Denzil Batchelor, which appeared in the January 11th edition of the *Leader Magazine*, "It cannot be said that the German bombs pulverised the cobbled streets, imposing squares and massive public buildings that make up Manchester. But fair and square, the incendiary bombs peppered the famous football ground at Old Trafford and reduced most of the seating accommodation

on one side of the ground to a desolation of rubble and a jungle of weeds. Down below, the workrooms in which the raw material used to be moulded into a team of footballers were reduced to a shambles. The gym, the room for electrical treatment, the players' dressing room, the recreation room – all were gone."

"All this happened years ago, and the scene of the disaster has been swept clear of rubble, but the essential repairs (except for one dressing room) have not been made, or even promised. The historic home of Manchester United is used by the reserve team nowadays who play before a handful of spectators in the barren stands: and the famous

Old Trafford roar that used to rouse like sudden thunder when Pearson or Rowley slashed home a goal, now echoes from the home-from-home that hospitable Manchester City have lent the First Division team on alternate Saturdays."

As Denzil Batchelor wrote, the reserve team fixtures at Old Trafford never produced 'ground full' notices or anywhere near it and Manchester City certainly enjoyed the extra income from the attendances that United attracted at Maine Road. However, on June 6th 1947, the Old Trafford gates were firmly locked, with 36,000 inside, having purchased their tickets weeks before, allowing them to

Reconstruction begins:
Workers begin to clear the rubble from the ground and **(inset)** *a tree that had grown during the years while Old Trafford stood dormant.*

watch Salford Schoolboys play Leicester Schoolboys, in the English Schools F. A. Final replay. The Salford boys had been more than happy with their 0-0 draw against the current holders in the first match, but a venue for the replay looked as though it might cause them a problem. Earlier round ties had been played at United's Cliff training ground, but such was the interest in the final, a larger venue was required and following consultation with the local constabulary, a 36,000 all-ticket limit was put on Old Trafford and a strong police presence was prominent at the ground to prevent spectators encroaching on the bomb damaged areas.

It had been a long time since vocal encouragement similar to that given to the Salford team had been heard in the vicinity and the youngsters provided excellent entertainment to those present, with the crowd certainly receiving their money's worth, as the match went into extra time, following a goalless ninety minutes. The local boys soon made the breakthrough and went on to add a second, to lift the trophy for the first time. Salford Schools were not the only people who wanted to use the bomb damaged Old Trafford as a look through the directors weekly meeting minutes show, with names such as the Cheshire Association,

Manchester Youth Organisation League, Manchester Schools and Christies Hospital all writing for permission to use the humble facilities.

MP Ellis Smith was now enthusiastically involved in assisting United with their attempts to get Old Trafford back to some sort of normality and in January 1948, he tried to rush things through by asking the Minister of Works if a light alloy could be used for the roofing of the stands. The reply was negative. A month later, following a speech from the Chancellor of the Exchequer, in which he said that "the government desired to encourage all forms of entertainment", Ellis Smith quickly pointed out that Manchester United Football Club wanted to "finish the building of the ground so that it would hold 120,000 people". Again the response was not favourable to United.

A somewhat frustrated Walter Crickmer kept in regular contact with the Member of Parliament and in one piece of correspondence bemoaned the state of affairs at the ground, in particular the failure to get the stand back to some sort of normality, almost pleading with the MP to try and get something done "if only as a compliment to this great industrial centre, whose people have certainly

made a magnificent effort in the export drive."

The lack of a roof on the seating area was all very well on a nice autumn afternoon, or in the springtime, but in the middle of winter or when the weather was what many would describe as being typically Mancunian, it was certainly far from enjoyable. So much so, that season ticket holders were advised "in their own interests to claim a seat 30 minutes before kick-off if a choice of position is desired. Ticket holders will, of course, be admitted at whatever time they care to present themselves, but those arriving later than the time recommended may find that the only seats available are situated in an exposed position."

Obviously, those who had held season tickets for a few years did not want to give them up simply because there was no cover above their heads, but it must have been slightly annoying on a wet afternoon that they were paying more than the man on the terracing and getting just as wet!

November 1948 saw City give United notice to quit Maine Road, as they were beginning to find it somewhat restricted with both clubs continued sharing of the ground. Whether or not United had suggested the idea to their neighbours, in order to help push forward their plans for the further re-construction of Old

Trafford, as they were becoming a little exasperated with the limited progress being made, is not recorded. The slow progress in refurbishing the ground also annoyed the United support, with one, a Mr H. S. Thompson of Stockport, going as far as to organise a petition, in the hope of persuading the Ministry of Works to expedite the issue of licences for the restoration of Old Trafford. Mr Thompson had already approached Members of Parliament and had between 200 and 300 fellow supporters standing by ready to help with any work involved at the ground.

The name of Manchester United Football Club was once again raised in the House of Commons on January 24th 1949, when a Mr Austin asked the Minister of Works if he was now in a position to make a statement in regards to United's application for a building licence for repairs to Old Trafford. Mr Key, the minister concerned replied, "As my Hon. Friend will now be aware, I have given instructions for a building licence to be issued to carry out the minimum work necessary to bring the Manchester United Football Club's ground back into full use." To which Mr Austin replied: "Is the Minister aware that that answer will give a great deal of satisfaction to the many thousands of supporters of the

finest team in the country?"

The tabloid press of today are quick to make headlines out of any comments made by anyone involved, or having been involved in the game, more so if they are directed at a rival club. Had reporting been at a similar level in February 1949, then the back pages and possibly even the front of some, would have given over as many column inches as possible to a comment made by the chairman of Manchester City in relation to United's tenancy of Maine Road. Back then, only the *Daily Mail* picked up on the comments of the City top man at a 'Hot-Pot Supper', when he said: "Eight years is ample time for a football club to put its house in order", having a clear dig at United for prolonging their stay across the city.

United then, as they would more than likely do today, diplomatically shrugged the matter off, although it was suggested that such suppers were always the occasion which

The Uncovered Main Stand:
Having cleared the rubble construction of the Main Stand began.

From the Ashes: *Work begins on re-roofing the Main Stand.*

"has an effect on oratory and of course a brief report never conveys the whole spirit of a speech."

The editor of the *United Review*, Mr Sidney F. Wicks, politely defended United in his column: "I dare say that there was a kindly smile on Mr Smith's face", while becoming slightly more irritated and defensive by continuing, "but asking the bare sentence as it stands in the necessary brief report it is unconvincing. Eight years! Yes, plenty of time to put one's house in order – in normal times! But for four years of that period, Britain was fighting for its very existence and had little time for rebuilding a bombed football ground.

"During the second four-year period the economic life of the nation has been subjected to severe controls over building and building material, and football grounds were given very low priority indeed. How could any club put itself in order when all efforts at self help were banned and barred by powers over which we had no control? One year of freedom would have been enough – but eight years unique in the history of our nation – is it fair to speak of them as normal years?

"Yet though we regard the words as unfair, actions speak louder than words. We shall never forget the hospitality of Manchester City and its directors. But now the

Government are allowing us to do a bit towards rehabilitating Old Trafford. Was it ever supposed by anybody that Manchester United did not want to return to the old home? Maine Road was kind but what housewife likes to share her kitchen with another woman? It never works, does it?"

By the end of April 1949, the final remnants of war damage had been removed and the levelling and concreting of the stand area begun. A section was made into concrete terracing and some wooden cinema type seats were procured to accommodate around 3,000, all without cover. But who would care? Being back home would be enough for club and supporters alike. Some cover

was eventually provided, but this was only for a select few, such as the directors and the press, with a corrugated iron awning constructed over their respective boxes in an attempt to keep out any inclement weather.

So, at 6.30pm on Wednesday August 24th 1949, United ran out onto Old Trafford's lush green turf, to face local Lancashire rivals Bolton Wanderers, for what was the first League fixture at the ground since 1939. In the club programme, which had "Welcome Home" emblazoned across a photograph of the ground, Chairman Mr J. W. Gibson wrote: "It grieves me to know that I cannot welcome you back to a properly restored ground, let alone the fully developed stadium which I had in mind many years ago. However, we must do something about the grandstand before next season and I hope the powers that be will see fit to grant the necessary permission. Surely a First Division club in such an important industrial area should, at least, have some covered seating accommodation? You know of course that plans are being formulated and when the work is finally carried out, your ground will compare with the best in the country. We are patiently waiting for that day." (see match no. 3).

But what of the spectators in those immediate post-war days? They could now arrive at the ground by car, but where parking was once allowed adjacent to the ground, they could no longer do so due to the lack of space. There

was also a more than adequate bus service to and from games, as well as the train, with the station beside the ground open for Saturday fixtures. So, there was no need now to leave your bicycle behind the ground or in the gardens of nearby houses, for four pence, as in the 1930's.

Once inside the ground, the place of the modern day stewards was taken up by members of the Ground Committee and seventy volunteer marshals, whose presence was certainly a big bonus on the day of the Bolton Wanderers game, when there was massive traffic congestion in the approaches to the ground. There were obviously early teething problems due to the return 'home' not having been something of a regular routine.

Overcrowding in particular was often something that caused problems, mainly due to latecomers being content to stand at the top of the terracing, often blocking gangways and not letting others through to the less populated front. In order to try and accommodate everyone comfortably, a flag system was adopted, with a white flag signalling that there was room in that particular section. This system was later to be replaced on the Popular Side by dividing that part of the ground into sections, each identifiable by means of metal discs, numbered 1-21. The idea behind it being that any part of the terracing could be identified as having space available and it would then be announced over

LEAGUE DIVISION ONE - 24TH AUGUST 1949

UNITED 3 BOLTON 0

WITH A KICK-OFF time of 6.30pm, many headed to the ground straight from work and such was the congestion around the stadium that many of the 41,748 spectators were late in arriving, therefore missing the kick-off. They did, however, celebrate the return 'home', with United recording a rather decisive 3-0 victory, in what was a rather untidy ninety minutes, both sides scorning easy opportunities to add to the score line.

It was not until the 40th minute that United took the lead, after seeing Downie come close with a shot against the post. A Lynn free kick was contested by Pearson and Gillies, with the latter reaching the ball first, only to see it glance off his head and past his own advancing goalkeeper. Mitten added a second from the penalty spot after Rowley had been obstructed in the box by Gillies and Roberts, with the third coming from a Rowley header following another free kick.

It was a game, however, not without incident. Midway through the second half, the referee awarded a free kick against United and as Bolton prepared to take the kick, a spectator walked onto the field of play, heading in the direction of the referee, who was standing near the centre circle. Players and officials stood still in amazement, while at the same time thinking that he might have an important message for the referee (other than what was actually on his mind). But before he reached the centre circle, the two trainers and a policeman caught up with him and escorted him off the pitch and out of the ground.

the loud speaker system where supporters could find space. Another familiar sight of old was also gone – the boy walking around the pitch side carrying a blackboard on which were chalked the team changes, as a new public address system had

Old Trafford c.1949:
An aerial shot of the ground as it prepares to welcome back first team football.

been installed.

A new relaxation of steel control by the Ministry of Works in May 1950, gave the United directors hope that they would finally be allowed to go ahead with the building of a new £75,000 stand. But it turned out to be false as the minister who looked at United's proposal refused them permission. This was mainly due to there still being a rigidly enforced ban on capital expenditure involving non-essential work. It wasn't

just the application for the new stand, which would have seen the seating capacity doubled from three to six thousand which was refused, the stops were also put on the plans to put up a temporary cover, costing around £18,000.

Eventually, permission to begin the re-construction of the stand was given and United wasted little time in going ahead with the building work, although it was the end of the season before supporters could enjoy

the home comforts,

Cover and seating in the new stand were available for the first visit to Old Trafford by a foreign club side on May 12th 1951, when Red Star Belgrade, from Yugoslavia, played a friendly as part of the Festival of Britain celebrations. Although the game ended 1-1, the visitors were by far the better team, playing some superb football to whet the appetite of the 41,000 crowd. Always a yard faster and more precise with their passing, Red

Star scored after only three minutes, with their first shot at goal, through centre forward Zincanovick. Surprisingly though, they failed to capitalise further on their superiority. United somehow manage to withstand the seemingly non-stop pressure, thanks mainly to Chilton and Redman and salvaged a draw eight minutes from time with a Rowley penalty, after Aston was brought down inside the area.

Improvements were slowly being made on and off the pitch. 1948 had seen the F. A. Cup won for the first time since 1909 and the semi-finals being were reached again the following year. In the First Division, the title was always within touching distance, but they had to be content with the runners-up spot in three consecutive seasons – 1946-7, 1947-8 and 1948-9. Off the field, ground development continued, with a laundry being built underneath the terracing at the Warwick Road end of the ground, and a half-time scoreboard also appearing at that end in 1950.

September 26th 1951 saw the first visit of a non-European team to Old Trafford, Hapoel of Tel Aviv. Due to the strange kick-off time of 5.25pm, the fixture only managed to attract a crowd of 12,000, but for those present, they were treated to a fine afternoon's football, with United winning 6-0. The visitors

had begun brightly, playing some attractive football, but they did not have the physical strength to break down the home defence. As the game progressed, United began to take command and in a thirty-five minute spell scored six without reply. The goals coming from Rowley (2), Pearson (2), Aston and Walton.

Scoring six in a friendly was all very well, but it was performances at League level that really mattered and as season 1951-52 began to unfold, it became clear that whatever improvements were made to the stadium, they would pass almost unnoticed to the supporters, as on the field of play the team at last began to look like winning the Championship.

It wasn't all plain sailing though, with early season form failing to reveal a hint of the silverware that was to eventually materialise. The visit of Preston to Old Trafford on September 29th saw the gates locked prior to kick-off, with an estimated 5,000 still outside. By the end of the ninety-minutes, the 53,454 inside might well have wished that they had arrived late at the ground and been one of those unable to gain entrance, as they had to suffer watching their team slide to a 2-1 defeat.

United continued to blow hot and cold, losing at home to Sunderland (1-0) and Portsmouth (3-1) before

LEAGUE DIVISION ONE - 26TH APRIL 1952

UNITED 6 ARSENAL 1

WITH ONLY EIGHT minutes gone, any fear of being overtaken on goal average disappeared, when Rowley opened the scoring following a defensive error. Eleven minutes later the Arsenal defence suffered a second early blow when centre-half Shaw had to leave the field with an injury. United showed the London side little clemency and kept them under constant pressure, with Rowley again coming close, his drive hitting the crossbar, bouncing on the goal line before being frantically cleared amid cries of "goal" from the United players and supporters on the terracing behind.

As the minutes ticked away towards the interval, United went further ahead with two goals in sixty seconds. First, Pearson's net bound shot went in courtesy of a deflection to make it 2-0, while Byrne made it 3-0 with what could be considered the best goal seen at Old Trafford all season. Rowley robbed Forbes and tricked Mercer, before passing the ball into Byrne's path for the winger to score. A Carey lob forward to Rowley was hooked over Swinburn's head for number four, while the man of the match gratefully accepted a penalty to complete his hat trick and United's fifth.

Arsenal were now well and truly defeated and United hit yet another nail into their coffin with Pearson scoring whilst in full stride from a Rowley through ball. The luckless Londoners did score between all the United action, but it was a mere consolation effort and did nothing to upset the rhythm of the Champions.

As the final whistle blew, many of the 53,651 crowd clambered over the fencing surrounding the pitch to congratulate their favourites, while the Beswick Prize Band struck up "See the Conquering Hero Comes" as the ecstatic supporters gathered in front of the main stand around the mouth of the tunnel chanting "We Want Carey". So, Champions at last, winning the trophy for the first time since 1911 and for only the third time in the club's history, and it was hoped that there would be more honours to follow in the not too distant future.

the end of November. From December, however, they set off on a run that would see them unbeaten until April 5th (although their F. A. campaign wasn't simply cut short, it just never got going, due to a 2-0 home defeat by Hull City), when Portsmouth did the double over the championship hopefuls. The

visit to Liverpool on April 12th produced a 4-0 victory which kept the momentum going and two days later, a 6-1 demolition of Burnley at Old Trafford put the championship within United's grasp with three games remaining.

On Monday April 21st, Chelsea visited Old Trafford

Match Day at Old Trafford in the 1950s:
◀ *Walking down Warwick Road; a queue to see 'Matt Busby's Aces';*
▼ *The scene on the forecourt outside the United Cafe.*

score one, in reply to United's six, with Jack Rowley the thorn in the Gunners side, with a notable hat trick (see match no. 4).

The first opportunity of adding to the League Championship trophy came as early as the following September, when as Champions, they faced F. A. Cup winners Newcastle United in the F. A. Charity Shield at Old Trafford on the 24th of the month. A big occasion, and one that the BBC felt worthy of a larger audience, as they decided to show live action from Old Trafford. Another first for the stadium.

"Television at the F. A. Charity Shield Match on Wednesday Evening" proclaimed the front page of the Radio Times for that particular week, while on page forty-seven there was an action shot from a previous Old Trafford encounter between the two sides, along with a photograph of the two captains, Carey and Harvey, underneath. Unfortunately, television coverage in the early 1950's was nothing like the broadcasting of today and coverage did not begin until 6pm, finishing at 6.50, providing viewers with only the second half. For those fortunate enough to own a television, the second forty-five minutes turned out to be the most entertaining

and on a heavy pitch could do little to prevent United's 3-0 victory, thanks to goals from Pearson, Carey and a McKnight own goal. There was now little chance of the First Division championship going anywhere other than Manchester and five days later, Arsenal journeyed north needing to win 7-0 to steal the championship crown from United's grasp. A nigh impossible task for any team.

Rather surprisingly, at the end of the ninety minutes, Old Trafford had indeed witnessed seven goals, but of these, the Londoners had only managed to

and exciting, with five of the six goals coming during this period.

United began the match in a flourish, with Byrne hitting the post after only two minutes, but Newcastle soon settled and opened the scoring through Keeble. Play proceeded to drift from end to end and shortly before the interval, Byrne once again came close to scoring, but his shot was cleared off the line by Stokoe.

With the television sets around the country switched on, United began to entertain the viewers. Three minutes after the break, they drew level through Rowley, following good work by Byrne and Downie and four minutes later were in front. Byrne was yet again in the heart of the action, interchanging passes with Gibson, before setting up Rowley to score his second. Play began to settle after the rather frantic start to the second half, but it was certainly providing absorbing viewing for those in front of the television sets, as well as providing value for money for those gathered on the Old Trafford terracing.

Half-time queues: *Certain aspects of match-day never change as the queue to get a cup of tea at this unknown reserve game testifies.*

The Wrong Side of the Tracks:
A view of Old Trafford from the other side of the railway line c. 1955

United's lead was increased in the sixty-third minute, as Newcastle began to have difficulty in containing the reigning Champions. Rowley found Downie, whose pass inside was collected by Byrne, who shot past Simpson, earning some reward for his earlier contribution to the game. Newcastle to their credit continued to press and were rewarded with a second goal from Keeble in the sixty-eighth minute. This seemed to give United a gentle nudge, reminding them that the game was not yet won and they subsequently proceeded to step up the play once again and Rowley, a constant threat to any defence, provided Downie with

goal number four. Unfortunately, Rowley was kicked as he headed the ball through to Downie and had to leave the field. But even against ten men, Newcastle could not pull back any further goals.

That Charity Shield victory over Newcastle was the only source of silverware at Old Trafford during season 1952-53, but for those who did not attend United's youth team fixtures, but were regulars on the Old Trafford terraces to watch First Division football, they saw something akin to a crock of gold in a red first team shirt on April 4th 1953.

There were dark clouds amid the Easter sunshine that Saturday afternoon, with Cardiff City inflicting a 4-1 defeat upon United. But the main topic of conversation amongst most supporters, was the emergence of a sixteen year old Wing-half by the name of Duncan Edwards. Dudley born Edwards was

already known by name and to a certain extent, reputation, beyond the confines of Old Trafford, due to his quite extraordinary displays in the United youth team. But his debut against Cardiff City was to push him into national spotlight. Having played only nine reserve games,

he was thrust into the hustle and bustle of First Division football by Matt Busby, unperturbed by his lack of experience, but he was not to enjoy a dream debut, as Cardiff City prevailed on their first Old Trafford appearance since 1928.

Edwards was certainly not overawed by the occasion, taking everything in his stride. One minute he was setting up his team mates with accurate passes, the next he was trying a shot at goal, whilst holding his own against seasoned professionals. His inexperience did tell on one occasion, however, when he held onto the ball for too long and was robbed of possession, with Cardiff moving forward to score their fourth. His subsequent performances on the Old Trafford turf were to thrill thousands, going on to become a legendary figure within the history of Manchester United. Yet his debut heralded a new era at the ground.

The rebuilding work in and around the stadium had finally brought it back to normality, much to the relief of directors and supporters alike. In manager Matt Busby's eyes, however, there were other plans and rebuilding work that would soon have to be implemented. This did not concern bricks, cement or any other type of construction material, but footballers. The players who had borne the brunt of resurrecting the club after the war, bringing it back into the spotlight and amongst the top honours in the English game, were now approaching the twilight of their careers. Busby, realising that such work would at some point have to be carried out, had continued the idea of the MUJAC (Manchester United Junior Athletic Club) which had been set up in 1939, but instead of relying solely on local talent had ordered his army of scouts to scour the whole of the Britain for the best schoolboy players.

Slowly the line-up changed, as the likes of Delaney, Pearson, Carey, Cockburn and goal machine Rowley made way for names such as Byrne, Pegg, Taylor, Berry, Viollet, Blanchflower and the cream of the United youth team, which included the previously mentioned Edwards, Whelan and Colman who were waiting on the sidelines ready for their opportunities. So, as the 1950's began to unfold it became obvious that an exciting period in the history of Manchester United was about to begin.

The 0-0 draw at Huddersfield on October 31st 1953, following a 3-0 victory at Kilmarnock three days previously, unofficially marked the birth of Matt Busby's new United, with the headline above Alf Clarke's *Manchester Evening Chronicle* report on the Huddersfield game reading – "Busby's Bouncing 'Babes' Keeping All Town Awake" – a name was born.

Football today can be a costly form of recreation, but what did the United supporter of the mid-fifties have to pay to watch his favourites? Admission to the ground was 2/- (10p), juniors 9d (4p). The covered terrace 3/6d (18p), juniors 2/- (10p). Unreserved seats in A and E blocks were 5/- (25p), while

reserved seats in B and C were 6/5d (33p). A season ticket for Stand 'B' would have put you back the grand sum of £6.10/- (£6.50p). For those parting with their hard earned cash at the turnstiles on the opening day of season 1955-56, grandstand patrons had the added bonus of some 3,000 extra seats after reconstruction work which also provided new refreshment bars below sections A and E.

Over the years, as this book illustrates, Old Trafford has been used on countless occasions as a neutral venue, be it for internationals, cup finals or semi-finals. It has also played host to replayed cup-ties, where more than a couple of games have been required to decided who would progress into the next round of whatever competition it was.

January 24th 1955 saw one such fixture take place at Old Trafford, when near neighbours Bury faced Stoke City in the fourth replay of a 3rd Round tie, a fixture that went on to claim the record of the longest running game in the competition proper. The teams met at Gigg Lane, Bury on 8th January and played out a 1-1 draw. Four days later, the replay at the Victoria Ground was edging towards another 1-1 draw, but the game was abandoned 22 minutes into extra-time. A second replay was

scheduled for Goodison Park on 17th January where, despite extra time again being played, the teams could not be separated at 3-3. A fourth encounter, two days later at Anfield, could still not separate the two after a further one hundred and twenty minutes, with the game finishing 2-2.

So, the cup saga moved to Old Trafford on 24th January, where Stoke City finally triumphed 3-2. It did, however, look as though the saga was going to run into a sixth meeting, as incredibly, Stoke's winning goal was not scored until the last minute of extra-time. Although a 4th qualifying round tie between Oxford City and Alvechurch in the 1971-72 competition dragged out to six games, the Bury – Stoke record encounter will last as an all-time record in the competition proper.

Around the ground, other work had been carried out during the summer break of 1955, leading to state of the art offices, reconditioned dressing rooms and recreational facilities for the players. The latter coming in for high praise when used for the first time on the opening day of the season for the match against Tottenham Hotspur. There was also a new main double wooden door entrance.

Writing in the 1956 'F A Book for Boys', manager Matt Busby, gave the reader an insider's view of what the new dressing room area, and indeed the rest of the new-look stand interior, was like. "Before reaching these (the dressing rooms) we come

to the medical room. This has some of the most modern electrical equipment available for treatment of various types of soccer injury.

"Next door is the referee and linesmen's room, and then come the two dressing-rooms – home and visitors. They contain the last word in football equipment – indeed we claim they are among the best in the country. They are divided into two parts: one for changing and dressing and the other for bathing. The latter has what we call a 'community' bath in which a full team can be accommodated in piping hot water. There are also several slipper baths and hot and cold showers. In both rooms the walls are brightly coloured as there is no doubt that cheerful surroundings are good for a team' morale".

As regards to the rest of the 'behind the scenes' facilities, the United manager wrote: "On the storey above the dressing-rooms are the boardroom, manager's office, refreshment room, ladies' retiring room, and players' recreation room which contains tables for both billiards and table tennis. An innovation in the large refreshment room is the electrically controlled score-board on which final scores in all English league matches are exhibited after the match." All of which may seem rather spartan and non-descript compared with the facilities available to both players and staff today.

The second home fixture, of season 1955-56, against West Bromwich Albion three days later

Old Trafford c.1952: *Before the completion of the new Main Stand..*

on August 27th, saw Old Trafford for a dry run by the BBC. They filmed the entire ninety minutes of the game and then rushed the film off to Ringway Airport to catch a flight for London, where it was then taken to their studios to be put through the processing labs. The recording, however, was never shown on television, as it had all been nothing more than a dummy run for a new Saturday night Sports programme entitled "Sports Special" which was due to begin on September 10th.

Manchester United's training ground at the Cliff in Lower Broughton had enjoyed the luxury of floodlights for some six years, but the directors had only given it the briefest consideration to installing them at Old Trafford. Writing in the *Manchester Evening Chronicle* on November 5th 1955, Matt Busby revealed that the installation of floodlights had been delayed due to more important work having to be carried out, but once the necessary work was completed then the directors would look closely at the need for floodlighting.

In his article, he wrote: "The type of floodlighting we plan for our ground is very expensive, and you can rest assured that when it is installed there will be no better in the country. Installation of floodlights at Old Trafford has been delayed by the necessity to re-build blitzed stands. This work is still not quite finished, but when it is there will be nothing to prevent us going ahead, at any given moment, with the lights plan. Had United's ground had floodlighting, I believe we should have been offered, through the Football Association, the chance of a game against the Moscow Dynamo, who arrive here today to play Wolverhampton Wanderers and Sunderland.

"You may say that United could have played Dynamo in the afternoon, and I admit we should have been willing to do so. But the industrial situation must be considered. A Wednesday afternoon match could lead to a lot of absenteeism, and neither the F. A. nor ourselves wish to hinder production. Although we are in no immediate hurry about erecting the pylons, we shall not be found wanting when the time comes to get equipped. We have one or two "revenge" games against Scottish sides who, I believe, would be great attractions at Old Trafford, and we should look forward to playing the Russians, Hungarians, Yugoslavians and the rest of the crack Continentals. These are the matches which would pack the ground.

"I believe that the Sheffield Wednesday lights cost about

£26,000, but at Easter Road Edinburgh, I understand that Hibernian paid only £10,000. These lights are reasonable enough, but when I recall the brilliance of the lighting systems in America comparison ends. We played some games starting just before midnight, and you could not see a player's shadow cast by the lighting. That is the kind of floodlighting we should want at Old Trafford, and we should put on two or three big games each season to help to reimburse us for the heavy outlay. So it may well be that in the near future Manchester United will join the increasing number of clubs who can put on games by night as well as by day."

The Manchester 'derby' on the last day of 1955 produced some amazing scenes outside and inside the ground. An hour before the kick-off, there were some 35,000 inside and by the time the teams ran

Admission Prices: *Always a source of consternation amongst supporters at the start of every season.*

Renovations to the Main Stand (1955): *These included a new main entrance, which can be seen in the centre of the photo at the end of the scaffolding.*

out onto the pitch, this had increased to 60,956, creating a post war record. The turnstiles, which had been completely operational with the queues forming and re-forming rapidly, had closed ten minutes before, with thousands still outside the stadium and chaos everywhere as masses of people, shoulder to

shoulder, tried to obtain entry. The scene looking towards Warwick Road Railway Bridge was just as dramatic, with the crowd so thick that it was almost impossible to get across.

Extra police had to be called out, as streets around the ground were a mass of bodies, resembling a sea of human

heads bobbling up and down. With all traffic having ground to a halt, coaches trapped in the traffic jam nearer to the ground dropped off their passengers and turned back from where they had come. Thousands of supporters, unable to gain entry, hung around Warwick Road in the hope that the gates would

re-open, which they eventually did, but only to let people out who could not see or who found the crush inside too much to bear. Those unfortunates outside could not even catch any of the empty buses home, as the drivers and conductors were inside at the match! As for the game itself, goals from Tommy Taylor and Dennis Viollet gave United a 2-1 victory, to end the year on a satisfactory note.

As 1956 unfolded, United clearly had their sights once again on the League Championship and with three games still to play, led the table with 55 points from their 39 games, with nearest rivals Blackpool sitting on 49 points from only 38 games. The title crunch was to come at Old Trafford on Saturday April 7th, when the Seasiders visited Manchester.

Every man and his dog wanted to be at this game and as could be expected, the gates were locked fifteen minutes before kick-off with 10,000 locked outside and a new post war record attendance of 62,277 inside. Upon arriving at the ground, thousands of supporters were annoyed to find the gates locked and began frantic attempts to gain entry (see match no. 5). This led to squads of policemen, some mounted, struggling to bring order to the melee of supporters.

Two weeks later, on April 21st, Old Trafford enjoyed something of a carnival atmosphere, as Portsmouth brought the curtain down on a triumphant season. The United players ran out to a tumultuous reception and gave their support a pleasant surprise when they walked to the centre circle and bowed to each section of the ground in turn, as a tribute to the support that

Season 1954-55: *United entertain Portsmouth on the opening day of the season (Pompey won 3-1). This is a supporter's view from the covered Old Trafford Paddock End adjacent to the Scoreboard End.*

LEAGUE DIVISION ONE - 7TH APRIL 1956

UNITED 2 BLACKPOOL 1

Inside, Blackpool's live duck mascot, accompanied by his 'eastern prince', who took to the field alongside the team, certainly brought them some early luck, as the visitors took a two minute lead through Durie, following a Mudie lob into the United goalmouth.

United were soon out for the equaliser, with both Viollet and Doherty coming close, the latter heading against the post, with play being mainly concentrated around the visitors goal. As the first half progressed, Berry was slowly beginning to have the better of the Blackpool defence and at one point beat five men before crossing to Doherty, whose shot evaded Farm in the Blackpool goal, but was cleared off the line by Firth. Blackpool held on for all they were worth, as the fervent Manchester support urged on the red shirts, but it was to no avail, as the half time whistle blew with the visitors still holding the advantage.

The second half resumed where the first left off and Pegg should have levelled the scoring in what was almost the first attack. Both sides were then reduced to ten men, following a clash of heads between Taylor and Wright and it was during this period that United finally drew level. Berry, again tantalizing the Blackpool defence found Doherty in a scoring position, but before he could make the most of the opportunity, he was brought down following a challenge by Farm. Byrne, the regular penalty taker, made no move to take this particular one, so it was Berry who strode up and despatched the ball firmly past the Blackpool 'keeper.

As the crowd went ecstatic, both teams returned to full strength and the remaining thirty-five minutes were obviously going to be a test of nerves, both on and off the field. Play drifted around the pitch as the minutes ticked away and with only ten remaining, it was that man Berry again, taking on the now exasperated Blackpool defence. His cross this time was too close to goalkeeper Farm, but the ball eluded his clutches and fell to Taylor a yard from the goal line, the United number nine managing to push the ball in with his knee, as a defender dived to try and prevent the goal.

United were Champions!

they had received throughout the campaign. Unfortunately, the match itself did not live up to the occasion and a solitary Viollet goal in the eighteenth minute was all that the 38,400 crowd saw.

Shortly before the end, the sound of the referee's whistle, blown for a free kick, was taken by some of the crowd as the signal for full time, thus creating a small pitch invasion. Play was held up while the police cleared the over jubilant fans from the field of play. Minutes later, when the final whistle eventually brought the game to a close, there was an even bigger invasion, as supporters surged forward to secure a better view of the League Championship trophy being presented to United captain Roger Byrne by Mr Joe Richards of the League Management Committee.

*

What then, was Old Trafford and its match day experience like some five decades ago? Tom Clare, who first set foot inside the ground in the autumn of 1950, looks back on those days of a bygone era.

"I first set foot inside Old Trafford for a reserve game in August 1950 when I was just five years old, accompanied by my brother Peter. We travelled from our home in Chorlton-upon-Medlock and even though almost sixty years have elapsed since that day, I can still remember it well. I suppose that for United supporters, from wherever they may hail, your first visit to Old Trafford is something that sticks in your memory for the rest of your life! Whenever I return to Old Trafford today, I always take time to look around the magnificent arena that stands before me, and then reflect upon how grand it has become since those old days many years ago. Today's magnificent showpiece bears no resemblance in any way, shape or form, to the old lady that once stood there and served the club so well. So let me take you on a trip down Memory Lane.

"There was a lot of football played at Old Trafford back then from First Division fixtures, Reserve team games, youth team games, amateur representative games, and even schoolboy representative games and cup finals. So the pitch got a lot of wear and tear. Although it always seemed to be in pristine condition for the opening game of the season in August each year, I think that it is true to say that by December the pitch was certainly only ever on nodding terms with a thing called grass! January and February would see the pitch cut up badly and at times, especially if there was inclement weather, the players would be playing on a sea of mud after ten minutes play.

"The first team match day experience was totally different in those days. Getting to the stadium would be either by bus (which most people preferred), electric train using the London Road – Altrincham line (now the Metro Link) or the steam train from London Road from which you could alight immediately outside United's main stand, or by car.

"If you were travelling by bus, Manchester Corporation Transport used to run "football specials" from Aytoun Street, and Piccadilly, in the city centre, to Old Trafford, and return after the match. There used to be lots of double-decker buses in line and the fans used to queue at the bus stop. A bus inspector would call the buses forward and load them to capacity before waving them off.

"Travelling on these buses was quite an experience. The lower deck seating was filled and then in the aisle between those seats there would be a lot of people jammed in standing up. The bus conductor would have to go around taking fares and issuing the bus tickets from what was a clipboard with different tickets on it. Travelling on the upstairs of these buses you could say that you risked permanently damaging your health in doing so! Upstairs was for smokers and within minutes of the bus moving off, thick, acrid cigarette smoke would permeate the air, and half way through the journey to Old Trafford, you would smell it from downstairs. The poor bus conductor having had to go upstairs to collect the fares would then descend when his job was done, eyes watering and more often than not, coughing his lungs clear. He would spend the rest of the journey stood on the bus platform trying to get as much clean air as possible as the bus meandered the rest of its way to its destination.

"Travelling by train, either the electric or steam mode, was far more sedate and comfortable. The electric train used to fill up,

Champions!: *A capacity crowd pour onto the pitch after United's final game of the 1955-56 season (a 1-0 win over Portsmouth) to get a better view of Roger Byrne lifting the trophy.*

but this was also a scheduled service that ran from London Road through to Altrincham and return. It also catered for the everyday traveller who wasn't going to a match, and on the occasion of the "bigger" match, you would often find people standing in the carriages once the seating was full. The train would arrive at the Old Trafford station and the fans would disembark and make their way down Warwick Road like an army of ants on the move. Past the Cricket ground, over Talbot Road, past Stretford Town Hall, over Chester Road, and down to the ground.

"Today, the Metro service has replaced what used to be the electric service, and the line has been expanded out eastwards to Bury. However, upon arrival at Old Trafford station, the scene back in those days was very different from the colourful scene that greets today's fan. Back then there were never any ticket touts waiting to greet you as you made your way out from the station. There were no vendor's stalls at all along the whole of the walk down Warwick road to the stadium. It wasn't until the late 1950's that hot dog/burger men in their white coats were seen at matches, but again, they were nothing like the giant mobile eateries that you see around the stadium today. Back then they were on tricycles!

"As you crossed over Chester Road the shop on the corner of

Warwick Road on the left hand side, used to be just a newsagents – there were no chip shops on that frontage at all. Over the other side of the road was Quick's motor dealership and their premises used to run down almost to the railway bridge. As you made your way down to the stadium, just before the bridge on the left hand side was the "United Café" and on match days this place was always overflowing with people.

"One of the most memorable match day scenes on that bridge was the band of buskers who played there for probably 20 years or more. The accordionist on many occasions was a man named Terry Foy who originated from Dundee in Scotland and was a good friend of my father's. Certainly, I can remember them still playing there in the early 1970's and maybe even later.

"Fans who travelled to the ground from London Road on the steam train, alighted right outside the main stand (South Stand today) and had not very far to walk upon their arrival. The forecourt of the ground at the Scoreboard End was what we used to commonly call a "croft". On the rebuilding of the ground after the war, the forecourt was originally all cinders and over the years these cinders became trodden down making a hard surface. On match days, both first team and reserve, fans travelling by car would park their vehicles

on the forecourt until it was full up. There was no charge, and no stewards organizing the parking! No vendors around that area, only newspaper boys from the *Manchester Evening News*, and *Manchester Evening Chronicle*, selling their latest editions.

"Whilst mentioning cars, I must add that not all the United players owned such a mode of transport and it was not unusual to see them alight from a bus and walk down to the ground with the supporters. I can also recall waiting patiently before games for Duncan Edwards to arrive and the big man would suddenly appear on the forecourt on his bicycle, which he would proceed to tie to a lamppost beside the Ticket Office with a piece of string.

"On the ground where the car park is today that faces the mega-store, used to be a mineral water firm named 'Aerowater'. Mineral used to be the common name back then for what is now termed pop! Going past the 'Aerowater' company's premises you came to the Canal Bridge and immediately across that was the large black castleated building and tower that was the Kilvert's Lard Company. This was a landmark that was there for years and instantly recognizable.

"As you walked past the Scoreboard End and went to the left, you came upon United Road and walked down by what

was termed then the 'Popular Stand'. On the right hand side was a large wall and behind that wall was the Glover's Cables factory with its huge imposing buildings and two tall chimneys that soared into the air like two tall guardsmen on sentry duty at Buckingham Palace. United Road came to a dead end as you got towards the Stretford End of the stadium. The Glovers wall finished at a gate which enabled employees and visitors into the works and also into their sports ground which was immediately at the back of the Stretford End. The Glovers wall carried on around there until you reached the railway line. Again, the area between the back wall of the Stretford End and the Glover's wall had been cinder and was trodden down. It was in this area that the players used to play 'killer ball' during training and kick hell out of each other. Jimmy Murphy used to cast a watching eye over a lot of those sessions because as he used to say, he learned a lot about the character and qualities of a lot of the young players who were coming through.

"Around the ground there was probably twenty–twenty-five entrances, that allowed the fans to enter the stadium, and going through them was by means of passing through the rickety turnstile. Exit from the stadium was by means of large wooden

gates and there were two each at both the Scoreboard and Stretford Ends, three along the United Road, and four smaller ones along the Main Stand. The only seating area in the stadium in those days was in the main stand. It wasn't until the Stretford End was modernized, and then the original Cantilever Stand was built that it really opened up the stadium to seating. There were also two Paddocks; the Old Trafford Paddock and the Stretford Paddock. The main stand and the two paddocks were covered from the elements. Both the Stretford and Scoreboard Ends were uncovered. Down along the 'Popular Side' there was a covered area that ran from approximately 18 yards line to 18 yards line.

"Once you had gained entrance to the stadium through the turnstiles, normally the

first person you saw was the man selling the official match programme. There were plenty of them and they were only on sale inside the ground. When I went to my first league game in September 1954, the cost of a programme was four pence (two pence in today's currency). In the areas immediately inside the ground, at various intervals were small wooden huts/sheds that sold refreshments. Mostly it was Oxo/Bovril or tea, minerals, crisps, sweets etc. I can't honestly recall if pies were sold then but I can say that I did start seeing them on sale around the 1960 time. Oxo/Bovril which was a hot beef drink, and was always welcome on those cold winter Saturdays throughout the football season.

"Entrance into the actual stadium once you had gained access to the ground was by

various avenues. There were three small tunnels which you could walk through – one each at both the Scorebaord and Stretford Ends, and one in the middle of the 'Popular Side'. As you cleared these tunnels, the stadium would open up in front of you in all of its glory. There were also a large number of stairways that went around the ground. Separating the stands from the running track and the actual playing pitch was a picket fence that went the whole way around the ground. Where each stairway was located, you would see a metal stanchion about six feet tall and at the top of the stanchion would be a metal circle with the number of that particular stairway painted upon it. These stanchions would be taken down by the ball boys and placed on the running track alongside the picket fence, just

The back of the Main Stand:
As seen from the Stretford Railway bridge.

before the game began.

"Prior to kick-off, you would see Jack Irons, the United mascot make his way round the track, dressed in his colourful bowler hat and tailed coat. there was also a one-legged man, wearing a red running vest and shorts, who would sprint towards the Stretford End amid the cheers from the crowd. The Stretford and Scoreboard Ends back in those days were just very small terraced areas. The Scoreboard End's main feature was the large Scoreboard at the top of the terrace. It was made of brick, wood and corrugated sheeting and was coloured for some reason black and yellow. There were twenty-six boxes marked

OT c. 1957: *The as yet uncovered Stretford End and United Road stand.*

with a letter of the alphabet. Below each individual letter was a door that opened and had the facility for two cards to be inserted, one in the top half, and one in the bottom half. On the back page of the match programme would be the day's football fixture and each game would have a letter of the alphabet adjoining it. These letters would be matched to the letters on the scoreboard and at half time, when the doors of the boxes on the scoreboard were opened and the cards inserted, the top number would show the home team's score and the bottom number would show the away team's score. At full time, the process would be repeated and fans would know the results of most matches that were played that day.

"The Stretford End was

nondescript back then, just a small standing terrace. However what did used to happen was that if you stood at the top of the Stretford End terracing, you could look down and over into the Glover's cables sports ground. You could see the whole of their football pitch. Hundreds of fans used to stand at the top watching the Glover's works team play whilst waiting for kick off time in the United game .You would see and hear them all stood up there and whenever a goal was scored in the Glover's match, a roar would go up.

"Back then United's gates fluctuated depending upon who they were playing. The end that the away team defended would always be packed with spectators. At half time it used to be funny to watch people moving from behind one goal to

the other at the opposite end of the ground. Again it was like an army of ants marching towards its prey!

"The players used to emerge from a tunnel in the centre of the Main Stand and either side of this were concrete dugouts for the home and away team staff and normally United's would be occupied by Tom Curry, and Bert Whalley. Behind the dug out was a small flight of stairs that led up to the seats in the Main Stand. Sir Matt and Jimmy Murphy had two seats on the front row where they would watch the game. It was a better vantage point than watching from the dugout as that was quite low and you didn't get a wider view of the game.

"After a game we youngsters would hang around outside the Old Trafford main entrance. Unlike today there were never

Winning the Championship brought an invitation to compete in the European Cup, a competition inaugurated the previous season by the editor of the French sports paper *L'Equipe* and involving the Champions of the various European countries. The Football League had thwarted the hopes of the 1955 League Champions, Chelsea, of competing in that first competition, but United, and Matt Busby especially, were determined to bring European football to Manchester and at the same time gain a wider knowledge of the game outside English shores. Encouraged by the backing of the Football Association, the invitation was accepted.

With all European ties being played mid-week, the United directors had to approach neighbours City once again for the loan of their Maine Road ground, as their local rivals were one step ahead when it came to this facility, with floodlights already having been installed. In the meantime, United unveiled their own plans for floodlights at Old Trafford in the *United Review* for the match against Portsmouth on September 1st 1956. Illustrated on the front page was a model of the stadium, complete with the pylons and the accompanying text read as follows, "According to electrical experts we should have a floodlighting system as good, if

any autocratic commissionaires or security men policing the door, and often we would go inside. The area immediately inside those solid wooden doors was quite open, and led to the stairway that went up to the directors' box and to the posh seats in the main stand. If you turned left once you were inside those main doors, there was the sliding door which led to the dressing rooms – Mecca for us, young starry eyed kids.

"Immediately inside the main door and facing it just 10 yards or more away, was the players' tunnel, a surprisingly steep and narrow concrete ramp that led down and out into the stadium and then onto the pitch. The number of times that I ran down that tunnel as a young boy,

imagining that I was carrying the ball and leading out my heroes to a full house – Oh! What a dream that used to be. We kids would fight to be first in the line to run down that tunnel, followed by the rest of the 'Ragged Arsed Rangers'! It must have been so funny for the ground staff, who after a game would be tending to the playing surface, replacing divots and forking areas around the goalmouths, to watch this assembly of scruffy street urchins emerging from that old tunnel. They never chastised us or interfered with our innocent play; usually they would just smile, or make a few witty remarks. The kids would wait for the players in the area immediately outside the dressing rooms. If you waited long

enough you could even travel home on the same bus with your hero. In those days there was a very close bond between the players and the fans, the community and the club.

"So that's how the old lady of a stadium used to be. Far, far, different than the magnificent arena that stands there today. However, the old stadium holds so many, many wonderful memories for people who saw it as it used to be. So much history was made there. As the centenary of Old Trafford being opened draws nearer, I get a little teary, as my Grandfather was present on February 19th, 1910 when the first ever match was played there."

*

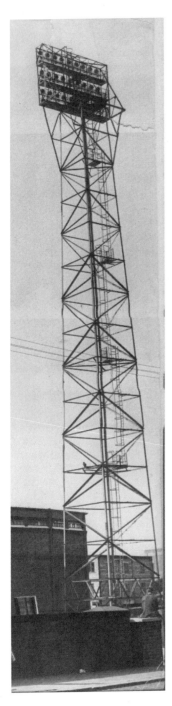

Floodlight Pylon: *One of the pylons situated outside the ground on the forecourt and the Warwick Road End.*

not better than any installation in the country! From the model photographed here you will see four pylons – each to be 160 feet high. At the top of each tower will be 54 floodlights – equal to millions of candle power – and the whole installation will be controlled by a single press-button. The work has been commissioned and completion is expected early in the New Year." The expected cost was to be over £40,000.

United began season 1956-57 where they finished the previous campaign, looking down on everyone else from the top of the table and even without first team regulars, they could overcome those below them without too much trouble. Such was the case on Saturday October 6th, when England required the services of Roger Byrne, Duncan Edwards and Tommy Taylor for their Home International fixture against Northern Ireland at Windsor Park, Belfast, forcing Matt Busby to field a team with the average age of twenty-two for the visit of Charlton Athletic to Manchester. Into the United line up came full-back Geoff Bent, wing- half Wilf McGuinness and at centre-forward, making his League debut, eighteen year old Bobby Charlton.

Up against the experienced Hewie, Ashington born Charlton kept the big South African on his toes in the opening stages,

but it was the visitors who took the lead in the twenty-fourth minute through Lucas. It was a lead, however, that was to last only sixty-seconds, as Berry equalised, shooting through a crowded goalmouth.

On the half hour, United took the lead, with Tom Jackson in the *Manchester Evening News* describing it as follows: "And exactly on the half hour the crowd rose to a magnificent goal by newcomer Bobby Charlton – a dream goal if ever there was one for a boy making his debut in first-class football. Charlton got his chance from a pass by Bent. He took the ball in his stride and a brilliant dribble saw him race past Hewie and finish with a low 25-yarder into the corner of the net. No wonder his team mates mobbed young Charlton! It was a brilliantly schemed goal."

Six minutes later, Tom Jackson was again scribbling furiously: "United were soon back on the attack and after 36 minutes they made it 3-1 and Bobbie (sic) Charlton was the marksman. Pegg and Colman both had a part in the move before Viollet, chasing out to the right wing, was put in possession. He quickly turned the ball into the goalmouth for Charlton, running in, to breast the ball down to his feet and then smack it home from close range."

Charlton Athletic pulled a goal back just before the interval to make it 3-2, but United added

a fourth through Whelan in the sixty-fifth minute to wrap up the scoring. As for the debutant, he went on to make a further thirteen appearances during the 1956-57 campaign, scoring another eight goals, in what was the beginning of a long and eventful career.

By the spring of 1957, United were challenging on three fronts – the League, F. A. Cup and the European Cup. In the latter, Anderlecht, Borussia Dortmund and Athletic Bilbao had all been brushed aside under the Maine Road lights with some of the best football Manchester had ever witnessed. Anderlecht had been trounced 10-0, while Bilbao, having won the 1st leg in Spain 5-3 were defeated 3-0 with a near perfect performance. Even on the domestic front performances took on a new perspective. Arsenal were thumped 6-2 on February 9th, with the press scrambling for new adjectives to describe the play of Matt Busby's team, with Frank Hallam of the *Sunday People* stating that United were "THE Greatest Show on Earth", having scored thirteen goals in three games watched by 188,000 spectators.

The erection of the floodlights at Old Trafford had gone according to plan and were to be used for the first time when Lancashire neighbours Bolton Wanderers visited on March 23rd. This gave Bolton the distinction of being the first visitors after the war and also the first to play under the new lights. The night sky around Old Trafford was bright in the evening air, with the illuminated glow from the new lights, (three of which were situated outside the stadium walls), as the supporters made their way towards the ground, attracted like moths, as they hurried on their way.

Once again, the 'house full' notices appeared, the gates again locked about half an hour before kick-off, with many still outside and traffic have already come to a standstill on Chester Road some thirty minutes previously. Seventy extra police had to be called to the ground to deal with the estimated 15,000 who were stranded outside, with 60,862 shoulder to shoulder inside.

Not only were the lights a first for United, but they made it two firsts on the night, surprising their supporters in the process, by taking the field in an all red strip. While the press hand out said that the lights would produce the effect of continuous sunlight, the ninety-minutes that followed produced nothing but gloom for United players and supporters alike. Twice in the opening stages, Gubbins came close as United struggled to put their game together and after thirty minutes, the visitors eventually took the lead. A cross-field pass from Lofthouse found

Gubbins, whose forward pass to Parry was blasted past Ray Wood. David Pegg came close to an equaliser, as did Johnny Berry and emergency centre-forward Duncan Edwards, but it was the visitors who continued to impress.

Within four minutes of the game resuming after the interval, it was 2-0 to Bolton, with a controversial goal. McGuinness was fouled and with the linesman flagging for the free kick, Bolton counter-attacked. Full back Hartle, still some distance from goal, decided to try his luck with a shot and was as surprised as anyone to see his effort fly past Wood via the head of Foulkes. Booing echoed around the ground, but the referee was unmoved and the goal stood. United proceeded to storm the Bolton goal, but to no avail, as the Burnden Park side held out until the final whistle.

So, with the installation of the Old Trafford floodlighting system, there was no journey to Maine Road needed to be made to host the home leg of the European Cup semi-final against reigning European champions, the world famous Real Madrid. Television rights were secured by Granada and this time there was to be no second half only broadcast, as the whole match was scheduled to be shown live, much to the disappointment of the BBC, who had been caught on the hop by

A model of how Old Trafford was to look once the floodlights were erected.

the move.

Granada's securing of those television rights, however, did give them a few problems in the run up to the match. They planned to use three cameras, but finding ideal positions for them proved to be difficult. Each side of the ground had covered accommodation and placing cameras near the half way line would mean blocking the view of a few spectators. Using either end of the ground behind the goals, would mean that, while they would be above the heads of the crowd, they would perhaps be too far from some of the midfield action. A camera in the main stand would mean the removal of some seats and as architects, along with stress and strain experts were called in, it was even suggested that part of the stand roof could be cut away

UNITED 2 REAL MADRID 2
25TH APRIL 1957
Real Madrid win 5-3 on aggregate.

This was always going to be a big test for United, against the experienced Spanish Champions, as they were already 3-1 down from the first leg in Madrid. It was a test that they failed, being slower in the tackle and being unable to raise the tempo of the game when necessary. Johnny Berry was fouled in the opening minute and a further four free kicks in the same number of minutes followed, three of those against Madrid, thus setting the pattern for the remainder of the evening.

It was eighteen minutes into the first half before United had their first shot on goal and after twenty-five minutes, the Spaniards advantage was increased when Di Stefano flummoxed three United defenders with a neat back heel before passing to Rial, who in turn pushed the ball through to Kopa. Up until that moment, the Frenchman had been shackled by Byrne, but he eluded the United captain to push the ball past Wood. Seven minutes later, Gento beat Foulkes by yards before slipping the ball across the goal to Rial who made it 2-0. United were now four goals behind.

After the interval, United came more into it with the wind behind them and began to put their game together, but it was to prove too late to change the course of the game. Tommy Taylor pulled a goal back in the sixty-fifth minute after his first shot had hit he post. This seemed to prompt United into action and for the first time looked like the team that had won the championship the previous season. It was, however, too little too late, as they had more or less given the Spaniards a forty-five minutes start and with a mere four minutes remaining, Bobby Charlton scored what was to prove nothing more than a consolation goal.

As the final whistle sounded, manager Matt Busby ran onto the field to confront the French referee, who it was thought had blown for full time early, an opinion shared by Liam Whelan. The United inside forward said after the match – "Soon after our second goal, I saw the Spanish trainer signalling that there was six minutes to go. Seconds later the final whistle went. I was surprised". How many more minutes Busby thought should have been played, certainly would not have been enough for his players to rescue the match.

to accommodate the necessary equipment. In the end, ideal positions were found behind the goals and along the side. Everyone seemed happy except, that is, the BBC!

Outside Old Trafford on the night of the match, the *Manchester Evening News* gave out thousands of red and white caps, along with red and white megaphones, in the hope that the crowd would make it the most colourful and noisiest night in United's history. Leading up to the kick-off, the police found themselves in the unusual position of giving away hundreds of tickets, as supporters with spares found it difficult to get rid of them and not wanting to hang about outside the ground gave them to the police. Even the ticket touts had difficulty selling their wares, offering £1 tickets for 4/- (20p).

The handing over of such cash could all have been for nothing, as unbeknown to those outside, there had been drama inside even before a ball had been kicked in anger. In the days running up to the game, United had kept the Old Trafford turf well watered, but upon inspection by Madrid on the morning of the game, they had informed their United counterparts that if the puddles which appeared on sections of the pitch were still there an hour before kick off, then they

would call the game off. As it was, the ground staff turned off the sprinklers and covered the soft, puddle areas with sand (see match no. 6).

*

The newspapers the following day contained much more than basic match reports. "I Was Ashamed" wrote George Follows of the *Daily Herald,* "A squalid show of one-eyed partisanship... a public display of bad manners... they wanted physical revenge." He continued by writing of the poor sportsmanship shown both on and off the pitch at Old Trafford, incidents such as the throwing of cartons at Spanish supporters who carried a Madrid banner around the pitch at half-time, and the crowd's incitement of Edwards and Byrne into actions that they would rather forget – the former trying to drag the injured Torres off the pitch, so the game could restart and the latter committing a bad foul on Mateos.

There was obviously disappointment in losing to Madrid, but the First Division championship was soon re-claimed, with half dozen games to go, a 0-0 draw at Old Trafford against Tottenham Hotspur, one of their nearest rivals, kept them in first place with fifty-three points. Preston North End sat in second spot on forty-nine, but having played one game more, with Tottenham third on forty seven. Only two defeats could prevent United from making it two titles in a row.

There was little chance of that, however, as five consecutive wins made sure that the championship trophy remained at Old Trafford, the sixth and final fixture, a 1-1 draw against West Bromwich Albion, being of no significance whatsoever, other than an afternoon of celebration, with the trophy presented to captain Roger Byrne at the end of the ninety minutes. Rather surprisingly, this game was watched by the smallest home crowd of the season – 20,357. Some 8,000 less than the second lowest.

As it was, United were to get a second bite at the European Cup cherry, as the First Division Championship was retained, with a League and Cup double denied them at Wembley mainly due to Peter McParland's robust (some may say reckless) challenge on goalkeeper Ray Wood when the score was still level at 0-0.

One unusual incident did occur at Old Trafford on December 22nd 1956, when United were scheduled to play West Bromwich Albion. At the ground and all ready and raring to go were the crowd, the United team, the referee and linesmen, but West Bromwich Albion and Matt Busby were absent. The United manager had travelled to Brussels to watch forthcoming European Cup opponents

Bilbao play Honved, but the train on which he was returning to Manchester from London was held up in the Midlands due to fog. He telephoned Sandy, asking him to come to Crewe to pick him up, so that it would enable him to make the game, but unbeknown to him, events at Old Trafford were not developing as expected. Kick-off had been put back from 2.15 to 2.30, but still no sign of the West Bromwich Albion team and officials. It was 4pm before they eventually arrived in Manchester, but by that time, the game had long since been postponed and everyone had gone home.

Early in September 1957, United held their annual AGM, announcing profits of £39,784 and also their intention to raise the capacity of the ground to 100,000. Some supporters had recently voiced their opinion that the club should consider covering the popular side of the ground, so they were more than happy with the news that the directors planned not only to cover that side of the ground, but at the same time to build a double-decker stand. Work, it was said, was scheduled to begin the following year.

On the field, the team were going from strength to strength. Their style of football was admired throughout the country, while the players, many of whom had gained international honours with their respective countries, were now household names, often travelling from their homes or their digs on the same bus as the supporters

travelling to the game.

Season 1957-58 was by now, progressing in a similar vein to that of the previous campaign and again, expectations were high for both domestic and European success. Wolverhampton Wanderers looked to be the main challengers for the First Division title, Sheffield Wednesday were the next opponents in the F. A. Cup, while a trip to Belgrade, to defend a 2-1 first leg lead against the Red Star club, was all that stood between United and a second consecutive semi-final appearance.

As it turned out, the first in that trio of fixtures, against Red Star, on February 5th, saw a creditable 3-3 achieve the required objective and as the players prepared for their journey back to Manchester, Old Trafford was a hive of activity. Out on the pitch, the ground staff were busy making preparations

Pre-match scene for the European Cup semi-final second leg against Real Madrid: *Above the terracing of the Scoreboard End the facilities constructed to accommodate the television cameras can be seen.*

for the Saturday League fixture against top of the table rivals Wolverhampton Wanderers, while office staff, on the other hand, were just as busy with that same Wolves fixture along with the ticket arrangements for the forthcoming Sheffield Wednesday F. A. Cup tie on February 13th.

▲ Old Trafford in mourning:
A Dave Weldon painting of fans gathered outside the ground in the aftermath of the Munich disaster and the club's championship pennant at half-mast.

▶ A menu from the reception before the first leg of United's ill-fated European Cup quarter-final against Red Star, Tuesday 14th January 1958.

*

Shortly after 3pm on Thursday February 6th, all the hustle and bustle around Old Trafford ceased, as a telephone call brought the news that the plane carrying the United players and staff had crashed whilst attempting to take off from Munich airport, following a re-fuelling stop. With only the briefest of details available, everyone's thoughts went into overdrive, all hoping that the accident would be exaggerated and would not turn out to be too serious.

Soon news that there were fatalities filtered through, although there were no names. The telephone lines were now red hot, with those in the Old Trafford offices ringing non-stop. Outside the ground, on the stadium forecourt, people were beginning to gather hoping for any snippet of news, as

the media began to break the news to Manchester and the rest of the country. Those who had been queuing for cup-tie tickets were among the first to hear of the crash, but for some, the opportunity to purchase a ticket never came, as sales were immediately suspended and the ticket office closed. Entry into the main office area was barred to all except club personnel, while the eager journalists, who had been quickly despatched to the ground, had to join the growing crowd outside. Inside, assistant manager Jimmy Murphy, who had been on international duty with Wales, sat devastated by the telephone, having arrived minutes after the news had come through, completely unaware of the unfolding drama, only to have the details broken to him by secretary Alma George.

As the crowds on the forecourt increased by the minute, making it begin to look like a match day, police were called to try and disperse them, their job made increasing more difficult as workers from the nearby factories emerged

following the five o'clock hooters, rushing through the gates quicker than normal, eager to hear more about the rumours that had swept through their buildings earlier. Their breaks and lunchtimes had been passed debating the draw in Belgrade and the chances of beating Wolves on Saturday, now it was all past memories.

The following day saw Manchester in mourning and like the previous afternoon and evening, Old Trafford was swarming with people, desperate for any news from Germany, as the Championship flag flew at half mast from the stand roof. Earlier preparations for the games against Wolves and Sheffield Wednesday had been in vain, as both were postponed, with the Sheffield cup-tie re-arranged for February 19th.

On the night of February 10th, the tears and memories began to flow once again, with the bodies of the 'Babes' coming home from Munich. At 9.35 pm, a BEA Viscount landed at Ringway Airport, seventy minutes late and one by one

the brown coffins, along with fifty-eight wreaths, were carried from the plane to the waiting seventeen hearses. Above the terminal building, the League Championship flag, brought from Old Trafford, flew at half mast.

At 11.15 pm, the coffins were ready to begin the solemn journey to their various destinations. Those of Roger Byrne, Eddie Colman, Geoff Bent, Mark Jones and Tommy Taylor, along with Bert Whalley, Walter Crickmer, Tom Curry, Alf Clarke and Tom Jackson were taken to Old Trafford to lie in the gymnasium, while the bodies of the other journalists and local businessman Willie Satinoff were taken to private addresses. The coffins of Liam Whelan and David Pegg had been off loaded during a stop at London.

Despite the late hour and ignoring the rain that had begun to fall, thousands lined the ten mile route to Old Trafford, with many kneeling in prayer as the cortege passed slowly by. The largest crowd in the club's history had turned out to pay its respects

to the dead Red Devils who had come back home. By the time Old Trafford was reached, the crowds had thickened and it was difficult to tell if it was tears or rain that dampened the faces of both young and old who huddled together.

In silence, apart from the muffled sobs, the coffins were carried one by one through the large wooden doors of the main entrance towards their resting place for the night. A room that only a few days previously had been full of laughter, as those who lay there had trained. Slowly, the crowds began to disperse, as the empty hearses turned away from the stadium. By 2.00am all was silent around the shadowed stadium, with a dim light sneaking out from underneath the gymnasium door where the bodies lay at rest.

As a new dawn broke over Manchester and the first streaks of daylight filtered through the gymnasium windows overlooking the railway line along the side of the main stand, the coffins lay on black cloth topped tables, with numerous

▼ The game that never was: *A programme for the postponed match against Wolverhampton Wanderers on Saturday 8th February 1958.*

▶ Chaotic scenes: *Queues snaked round the ground as the demand for tickets in the aftermath of Munich oustripped supply.*

wreaths and flowers placed along the wall-bars, while outside, the supporters began to re-appear on the forecourt, some stopping momentarily on their way to work, others with their own reasons for being there. Club officials and players who had not made the trip to Belgrade through injury or because they were only juniors or members of the reserve team, arrived at the ground later that dismal morning, to gather in the gym, where for several silent moments they stood with heads bowed and with their thoughts elsewhere. As the morning passed, relatives of those who lay in the gym arrived to take the coffins to various destinations for their final journey, with the coffin of the boy from up the road, Eddie Colman, the first to leave.

Life had to go on, but around Old Trafford everything seemed to be moving at half pace, however, the Sheffield Wednesday F. A. Cup tie was drawing closer and Jimmy Murphy, now in charge of the day to day affairs at the club, still had a lot of work to do.

It was one of those fixtures that everyone, not only Manchester United supporters, wanted to attend and on the night of February 15th, people began to assemble outside the ground beside the ticket office to make sure they were there when the ticket office opened at 10 o'clock the following morning. As night turned into day, those supporters who had braved the cold were soon joined by many others, and in what seemed to be no time at all, there was a crowd of around 20,000, six deep in places, around the ground. By 10.am, Warwick Road North was blocked with cars. Police tried to keep control of both crowds and the traffic, but it was proving a thankless and hopeless task, prompting the ticket office to open for business an hour earlier, in order to keep the crowds moving. Many of those who had been there for hours left disappointed.

Limited to one ticket per person, the 18,000, 2/- (10p), tickets were sold within four hours. Some, however, much to the annoyance of the genuine supporters, had managed to evade the scrutiny of the mounted and foot police, making second visits to the office windows to obtain additional tickets, which were later sold at more than double the face value. Even on the night of the match, the occasion did not deter the unscrupulous ticket touts who were now asking £1 for 6/6d (33p) tickets in the city centre. Outside the ground as the minutes to kick off ticked away, it was 30/- (£1.50p) for a 2/- (10p) ticket and £5 for a 7/6d (38p) seat in the stand.

Old Trafford, on the evening of February 19th, was experiencing a match day like no other, with the forecourt a hive of activity with supporters arriving early to savour the dramatic occasion. Black ties, armbands, red, and black rosettes, red and white scarves with a black cross sewn beside the names of the players that had been laboriously embroidered on them months before, seemed to be the dress of the day as all approach roads to the stadium filled with people.

The scenes around Old Trafford soon became chaotic. United supporter George Watson, then a twenty-three year old from Flixton, remembers the scenes vividly. "I worked in the industrial area of Trafford Park and when the works hooter blew at 5.30pm, I was out of the factory gates like a sprinter from the starting blocks and I must have covered the two miles or so to the ground in record time.

"I had arranged to meet up with a couple of mates on the stadium forecourt, but the closer I got to the ground, the more congested the pavements and roads became. When I eventually

reached the ground, it became obvious that I would never find my friends, as cars were now bumper to bumper and there were thousands milling around. Many of those did not have tickets, as I received numerous requests for any going spare from emotional fans anxious to

be inside. There were also a few ticket touts hovering around, unconcerned about the abuse shouted in their direction by passing supporters, with others only happy to relieve them of their wares at the required price. Once inside the ground, it seemed to be filled with more

people than normal. You didn't seem to remain in the same spot for more than a minute or two."

Three hours before kick-off the ground was packed. The player's tunnel was bathed with the lights of the newsreel and television cameras, alongside press photographers jostling

United Will Rise Again:
A grim-faced Bill Foulkes leading out Manchester United in the re-arranged FA Cup 5th round tie against Sheffield Wednesday and (inset) the famous programme of the game with blank spaces on the team sheet.

The gymnasium under the Main Stand: *Where the coffins of the Munich victims were placed for the night upon their return.*

for the best camera angles. In the United dressing room, the minutes leading up to the kick-off provided the players with time to reflect. For the survivors, Bill Foulkes and Harry Gregg, a glance around them must have provoked strange feelings without the likes of Roger Byrne, Eddie Colman or Duncan Edwards involved in the pre-match preparations. There was even a late arrival, claiming a vacant peg, with Stan Crowther having only joined United at 6.45 that evening, signing from Aston Villa for a fee of £18,000. In the

Sheffield Wednesday dressing room, a few yards along the corridor, just what thoughts were running through their minds it would have been difficult to imagine. They were preparing for a match that no-one, maybe even their own supporters, wanted them to win.

George Watson, now well and truly caught up in the emotions of the evening recalled, "I remember the match programme contained eleven blank spaces where the names of the United players should have been and on the terracing, we eagerly waited for the teams to be announced over the tannoy. As the names were read out, each received a loud cheer, with the loudest following that of Stan Crowther's. A minutes silence

followed and many around me cried unashamedly as they remembered those who had graced the empty pitch in front of us."

That silence was soon to be broken and amid a barrage of noise and camera flashbulbs, Bill Foulkes led the red-shirted United team onto the pitch, as the tumultuous roar of the crowd reached an unbelievable level, acting as a signal for those outside with tickets that they had not much time left to get inside, and for those without, that the long awaited match was near to starting and they would not be able to relate to their children and grandchildren that 'they were there' (see match no. 7).

*

The tears of joy following United's 3-0 success, were soon to turn to tears of sadness, as two days later, on February 21st, Duncan Edwards died. The colossus from Dudley had suffered multiple injuries in the crash and had put up a spirited fight as he struggled to survive in the Munich hospital, but after fifteen days, defeat finally came.

The following day, Nottingham Forest visited Old Trafford and possibly, if time had permitted, this fixture should also have been all-ticket affair. With a vast number of supporters outside the ground as early as eleven o'clock, it became obvious that problems would arise and with an estimated 20,000 outside by 1 pm and still two hours to go before kick-off, it was decided to open the gates. Despite the vast numbers, there was something of a subdued atmosphere both inside and outside the ground, as they were there just as much to pay tribute to their lost heroes in the memorial service due to be held prior to the kick off, as they were to cheer on the new United.

As the kick-off drew nearer, with the buses and trains off-loading their passengers, things became even more frantic, as one by one the turnstiles began to shut as different sections of the ground became full. Stewards were quickly despatched around the outside of the ground in an attempt to guide the late comers towards the few gates where admission could be obtained. Around 2.30, snow began to fall, but by then Old Trafford was full.

UNITED 3 SHEFFIELD WEDNESDAY 0

Around 30 cameramen invaded the pitch as captains Bill Foulkes and Albert Quixall tossed for ends, and then quickly scurried off to vantage points behind the goals so as not to miss any of the action. They had to be quick, as the game began at a frantic pace, with the unfamiliar United eleven showing no signs of nerves or inexperience, as for the most seasoned professional within the Wednesday ranks, the atmosphere that evening must have had a considerable effect. The opening minutes, however, saw them have the best of the play, coming close to scoring on three occasions, with centre forward Johnson shooting wide, Harry Gregg saving from Cargill and Ronnie Cope clearing off the line after Wilkinson had placed a header beyond the United keeper's reach.

Once United had established their rhythm, the youthful side were quick to show that they were not simply there to make up the numbers. They began to string a few passes together and their confidence increased with the veteran Ernie Taylor the pivot of every move. The former Newcastle United and Blackpool star almost succeeded in breaking the deadlock in the twenty-second minute, when he shot through a crowd of players only to see his effort thud against a post.

With the early nerves behind them, the red shirts were growing in confidence, with Taylor the midfield general, producing some sparkling football, spraying passes down either flank for Brennan and Webster to chase, or prodding the ball forward for the battling Dawson or Pearson.

United continued to press home their advantage, as a Foulkes free kick was punched round the post by Ryalls in the Wednesday goal. From the resulting corner, the Wednesday 'keeper could only grasp at the Manchester evening air, as Brennan's cunningly flighted corner swirled in the breeze and dipped below the bar and into the net. It was 7.58pm. United were reborn and the huge crowd saluted the breakthrough with an ear-splitting noise, a noise from the 59,848 crowd that matched that at the start of the game and seemed to give United an extra man as Wednesday crumpled under the sheer passion of the occasion and the fervent play of the red-shirted unfamiliar eleven.

In later years, Shay Brennan looked back on his first entry into the Manchester United history books and recalled, "I went to take the corner and tried for an in-swinger by hitting the ball with my right foot. It swung beautifully under the glaring floodlights, wafted even further towards goal by a gust of wind and curled over the 'keepers head into the net".

"A strange goal in many ways" recalled George Watson. "The ball seemed to hang in the air for a moment and as the Wednesday goalkeeper jumped to grasp it, it dropped over his outstretched arms. You seemed to get the impression that the crowd behind the goal, opposite to where I stood, had sucked it into the net. There was silence for a split second, before the stadium erupted. Hats and scarves flew into the air, never to return to their owners, but who cared? There were tears too, as never before could a solitary goal have meant so much to so many".

The visitors managed to subdue the red tide for the reminder of the first half and the opening stages after the interval, but in the seventieth minute, their hopes of obtaining anything from this particular fixture became little more than a pipe dream as they went further behind.

A Mark Pearson shot was only blocked by the legs of Ryalls, following some good work by Dawson, but the scoring opportunity did not go amiss, as the ever alert Brennan darted forward to control the lose ball and bang it into the net, to claim his second goal of the night. If Wednesday felt beaten at the start then they knew they were now and could only wish for the final whistle to arrive. However, a third goal was still to come, six minutes from the end, when Pearson set up Alex Dawson to score with a fine drive. The result not only gave United a passage into the next round of the F. A. Cup, but it brought some life back into the club, giving everyone a lift. Maybe United could go on.

Prayers for the fallen:
An inter-denominational service takes place prior to the match with Nottingham Forest on February 22nd.

United in Memory

The gates were firmly shut, with thousands still rushing about frantically outside, hoping to find a turnstile still open, which would enable them to gain entry. Their attempts were to prove fruitless.

Inside was a post-war record crowd of 66,123, who stood silently for the one minute silence during the inter-denominational service conducted out on the muddy Old Trafford turf by the Dean of Manchester, the Very Rev. Herbert A. Jones. A service also attended by the lord Mayor of Manchester, Alderman Leslie Lever and the Mayors of Salford and Stretford.

There were more than a few tears shed during the service, as short prayers were said for the dead, the injured, the mourning families and those connected with the club. Missing were the United and Nottingham Forest teams, who remained in the dressing rooms, shut away from the emotions of the events taking place not far from where they sat deep in their own thoughts. Relatives of some of the deceased players were amongst the silent crowd, but for one, Molly Leach, Duncan's fiancée, it proved too much and she left the ground in tears.

The silence was soon broken as the two teams made their way onto the pitch, but could United

match their performance of three days previously, or was the Sheffield Wednesday result little more than a one-off?

As the ninety minutes unfolded, the make-shift United side proved that the cup-tie performance was no fluke and that Sheffield Wednesday had not simply stood aside and allowed the mis-shapen United side a victory in order to ease their sorrows. Forest, like their Sheffield counterparts, were on a hiding to nothing and the young United side once again found themselves elevated to a level superior to their experience and their visitors were to find themselves on the end of a hammering and were indeed fortunate to leave Manchester with a point.

It was one-way traffic for the majority of the ninety minutes and had the United youngsters been a little more composed in front of goal, the 1-1 score line would certainly have been much different. Thomson in the Forest goal was called into action

as early as the ninth minute, doing well to save a powerful Dawson header. A minute later, the 'keeper was again tested, this time stretching to push a Pearson lob over the cross-bar, although he was rather fortunate soon afterwards, when Brennan, through on goal, shot directly at him.

But it was Forest, in a quick movement that Robin Hood himself would have been proud of, who snatched the lead on the half hour mark. Wilson gained possession out on the right and as he moved forward, he spotted the upraised arm of centre-forward Stewart Imlach. An inch perfect cross picked out the Scot and before any United defenders could re-act, the ball was sent beyond Gregg into the United net from twenty yards.

The second-half opened in identical fashion to the first, with United throwing everything at the Forest goal. Dawson shot on the turn, but Thomson was once again equal to the effort, pushing the ball round the post

for a corner. Sixty seconds later, the Forest 'keeper knew little as Pearson's shot cannoned off his chest and bounced to safety. The 'keeper was beaten by Dawson in the fifty-sixth minute, but Thomas was on the line to kick clear. No matter what United tried, they just could not break down the visitors defence, or beat the fortunate Thomson standing between the posts, but their all-out attacking play almost cost them a second goal, as a break by Gray saw Gregg brought into the action, pulling of a superb save to keep United in the game.

Forest were more mature, confident and systematic about their play as the game wore on, but there was little they could do to prevent the equaliser when it finally materialised. With fifteen minutes remaining, United gained a corner and from Brennan's kick, Dawson lunged as the ball eluded two Forest defenders and the ball flew past Thomson into the net. There were, however, to be no last minute heroics, although it was not without trying on United's part. But in reality, this and subsequent games were not about results, they were about survival against the odds and rebuilding a team when all seemed lost. The necessity to win games and success were for another day.

An away 6th round F. A. Cup tie at West Bromwich Albion followed on March 1st, and yet again United defied the odds, earning a creditable 2-2 draw in a game described at the time by

Daily Express reporter Desmond Hackett as "The greatest game I have ever seen". Little did he know what drama was going to unfold in the Old Trafford replay four days later.

Not for the first time in a matter of weeks did Manchester United command the front as well as the back pages of the national press. "90,000 in Cup Storm – Locked Out Fans Miss Last Minute Victory" proclaimed the *Daily Express*, while "Chaos for a Mile Around Manchester United Ground" appeared on the front of the *News Chronicle* and *Daily Despatch*.

Beneath the *Express* headlines, a photograph, taken outside the ground prior to the game, showed little more than a sea of heads, with the caption beneath reading - "Still an hour to kick-off last night, the gates are shut and 60,000 are INSIDE Old Trafford. But OUTSIDE – a milling 30,000 crowd turned away."

Alongside, however, there is a more dramatic story, with the 'Express Staff Reporter' who had witnessed the scenes writing – "A near riot flared in Manchester last night before the city's Busby Boys shot themselves into the F. A. Cup semi-finals with a dramatic last seconds goal. It was Manchester's most heated sports scene for years. But three cool policemen on horseback put a damper on the trouble which sparked half an hour before the kick off at Old Trafford

"Two men were arrested at the height of the trouble And early today a police spokesman

said, "They have been bailed, but will appear in court at a date to be fixed, accused of conduct likely to cause a breach of the peace. Inside – a 60,000 crowd. Outside, locked out – 30,000 disappointed fans. They were stunned. They had rushed from work – and they found they had no chance of seeing the match."

The article continued with 'The Timetable of Tempers': 6.25pm." The gates were closed with more than 60,000 people – the police limit for a floodlit evening match, inside. Spivs offering 7/6d (38p) reserved stand seats for £7 sold out. Police loudspeaker vans warned the traffic packed roads within a two mile radius of Old Trafford ground – "The gates are closed. The ground is full." But still the crowd converged on the ground – including coaches of West Brom supporters who had travelled 100 miles."

6.55pm "Youths began

climbing up the 10ft high glass topped wall to get into the 2/- (10p) parapets. Two police constables caught one and led him away struggling, his arms pinioned behind his back, in front of the 2/- entrance. The booing crowd surged forward – hurling bottles, tin cans and half-eaten oranges at the two policemen. A sergeant on a chestnut horse galloped forward and spurred his mount round and round the two policemen and the struggling youth to protect them from the crowd. Then a man grabbed the sergeant's arm and half pulled him from his saddle. Another mounted constable galloped his horse at the crowd, clearing a 50ft path. One man in the crowd complained that he had been trodden on."

7.05pm "A police officer climbed 75ft up a floodlight pylon to order down a youth perched more than three-

Locked Out: *The chaotic scenes at the ground continued before the FA Cup quarter-final replay against West Bromwich Albion.*

quarters of the way up. Again the crowd booed. But this time they made no move forward, and mounted policemen edged a path for the constable and the youth."

7.15pm "Ringleaders of the mob started to batter the locked turnstiled doors. Two doors were torn off their hinges, but policemen inside the ground turned back the crowd. One of the peak-capped "Mounties" was hit in the face by an orange. Good naturedly, he touched his cap and joked with the crowd: "Keep it to oranges". The other two mounted policemen as they edged the crowd away from the entrances repeatedly said: "Do you mind please

A hero's reception:

Professor Maurer accepts the thanks of the crowd before United's third meeting with West Bromwich Albion in the space of 8 days

lads". None of the police on duty lost their temper. And no batons were drawn. Three police horses moved the crowd – now numbering about 10,000 – away from the entrances to stop more attempts to batter in. Twelve police officers under a superintendent stayed on throughout the game at 15t intervals to prevent spectators getting within 30ft of the entrance."

Chief Superintendent Frederick Waddington head of the Manchester Division of the Lancashire County police said:

- "In 22 years controlling crowds at Old Trafford I have never seen anything like it. My officers tell me the trouble was caused by youths and a few hotheads. There was no need for drastic action and all of the men, I believe, handled themselves extremely well in what could have been difficult circumstances."

In the *News Chronicle*, a similar photograph to that in the *Express* was to be found on the front page, while their readers were given a similar story of the evenings events, although more can be added to the mental picture of crowd chaos. Under a minor heading of "60,000 crowded out of Old Trafford Cup tie" was the following – "And at Central Station (the G Mex Centre today) 6,000 people, waiting on two queues stretching round the forecourt of the station, shouted angrily when a loudspeaker announcement told them at 6.35 – "We are very sorry, but the gates have now closed at Old Trafford and British Railways are running no more trains to the ground. Your money will be refunded at the special ticket offices". At the Warwick Road Station on the Altrincham electric line, the huge numbers getting off the trains were caught in a bottle neck at the ticket barrier."

The *News Chronicle* also carried an interesting "Contrast Note" at the end of the front page article. It read – "At the other night game in Manchester – City .v. Birmingham – the crowd was estimated at 40,000. Half of them had come from Old Trafford after the closing of the gates there. Scores of buses had been diverted there to take to Maine Road people unable to get in at Old Trafford."

Back at Old Trafford, West Bromwich Albion almost took a surprise lead in the first minute when Bill Foulkes made a hash of a pass back to Harry Gregg, but the United 'keeper spared his captains blushes, catching the ball in mid-air, under threat from two Albion forwards. Three minutes later, Gregg rescued United again, making another fine save, this time from a Whitehouse cross.

Play switched to the opposite end and Charlton sent debutant Harrop through, but his drive hit Kennedy on the arm. Calls for a penalty were ignored by the referee. As the noise level rose, United continued to press and again came close, this time through Dawson, whose header hit goalkeeper Sanders before being scrambled away to safety. Back in the United goalmouth, it was once again thanks to Harry Gregg that Albion were kept at bay, with the Irishman somehow clutching a threatening shot from Robson.

Webster was brought down by Kennedy on the edge of the Albion area, but Taylor's free kick was easily blocked. Shortly afterwards, Dawson fired against an Albion defender, while

Charlton, seizing the rebound, could only stand with his head in his hands as Sanders pushed his shot against the post.

Three times in the first five minutes of the second half United prised the West

Bromwich defence apart, but Taylor, Dawson and Goodwin all failed just to find the net. As the game wore on, the visitor's attacks on Gregg's goal became less frequent, as the crowd began top sense that a goal would soon materialise. As it was, they began to have their doubts, as the minutes ticked away.

With only seconds of normal time remaining, centre half Ronnie Cope shoulder charged Horobin off the ball, before threading a pass forward to Ernie Taylor. United's midfield general prodded the ball out to the right, towards Bobby Charlton, who took it on the run. It looked, however, as if the United winger had pushed the ball too far in front of him before being blocked by Kennedy, but with the linesman signalling for a free kick to United, Charlton regained possession, crossed the ball into the Albion area and there was Webster to tap the ball into the net. The cheers that greeted the goal must have been heard by those supporters who had journeyed to Maine Road. United were in the F. A. Cup semi-finals.

Every match at Old Trafford seemed to conjure up an occasion to remember and West Bromwich Albion's second visit in a matter of days, this time on League business was little different, although the drama of the previous encounter was replaced with a wave of emotion. Old Trafford was again full to capacity, with many once more locked out, as a blizzard blew over the stadium. But the weather was of little concern to the crowd, as their thoughts lingered elsewhere, to a hospital in Munich to be exact. Silence enveloped the ground, as the words of manager Matt Busby echoed around the ground in a recorded message from his hospital bedside.

"Ladies and gentlemen" it began, "I am speaking from my bed in the Isar Hospital, Munich, where I have been since the tragic accident of just over a month ago. You will be glad, I am sure, that the remaining players here, and myself, are now considered out of danger, and this can be attributed to the wonderful treatment and attention given to us by Professor Maurer and his wonderful staff, who are with you today as guests of the club.

"I am obliged to the *Empire News* for giving me this opportunity to speak to you, for it is only in these last two or three days that I have been able to be told anything about football, and I am delighted to hear of the success and united effort made by all at Old Trafford. Again it is wonderful to hear that the club have reached the semi-final of the F.A. Cup, and I extend my best wishes to everyone. Finally, may I just say God bless you all".

Tears were unashamedly shed as the soft Scottish brogue drifted around the ground, but as the message came to an end, loud vibrant cheering took over, as the packed stadium roared its appreciation to the doctors and nurses of the Rechts der Isar

EUROPEAN CUP SEMI-FINAL, FIRST LEG
8TH MAY 1958

UNITED 2 AC MILAN 1

In the opening forty-five minutes, it was backs to the wall stuff for the United defence, as Milan began in a determined mood and it took the Italians only twenty-four minutes to gain the advantage. Crowther tried to find Greaves, but his pass was intercepted by Bredesen with the inside-right quickly finding Schiaffino, who easily beat Gregg.

Much to the Italians annoyance, some of the United tackling seemed to be a little too enthusiastic, but it was enough to unsettle the visitors, and with only five minutes to the interval, Viollet snapped at a Maldini mis-hit clearance to put the scores level.

If Milan had the better of the first half, United took the initiative after the restart, and goalkeeper Buffon pulled off fine saves from Goodwin and Taylor, while Webster shot over the bar. With only eleven minutes left to play and the tie looking more like remaining on level terms, an innocuous shoulder charge from Maldini on Viollet, brought a penalty decision from the Danish referee. Inside-right Ernie Taylor placed the ball on the spot, and after much protesting from the Italians, he beat goalkeeper Buffon, with the ball going in off the underside of the bar.

Old Trafford erupted and the noise threatened to shake its foundations as the crowd kept up their vocal encouragement up until the final whistle.

hospital in Munich, who had travelled to Manchester as guests of the city.

Led by Professor Maurer, they walked out of the tunnel onto the pitch, accompanied by Chairman Harold Hardman, the Lord Mayor of Stretford and the deputy Mayor of Munich, as the snow shower gave way to sunshine, as if on cue. The whole ground rose, every man, woman and child, to pay their own tribute to the 'Angels of Munich'. Wave after wave of applause accompanied their walk onto the pitch, where once in the centre circle, Bill Foulkes and Harry Gregg presented bouquets of flowers to Mrs Maurer and the youngest of the nurses.

With cheers of "For He's a Jolly Good Fellow" echoing around the ground, Professor Maurer took the microphone and speaking haltingly said – "I thank you all for your wonderful welcome. Manchester United leads every time."

The third meeting against West Bromwich Albion in eight days saw the amazing run of success finally come to an end, as the Midland visitors won 4-0.

An injury to midfield general Ernie Taylor after half an hour could be considered something of a major factor in the defeat, as the former Blackpool player had been instrumental in United's recent performances and without his expertise, Murphy's side were a shadow of their cup form.

Albion, however, were a goal in front before the injury to the former Blackpool player, a simple strike in the ninth minute from Ronnie Allen. It was Allen again, who was very much involved in the visitors second goal nine minutes before the interval, his shot being deflected past Harry Gregg by Ian Greaves. Almost on the half time whistle, Bobby Charlton hit the post from thirty-yards and that was the closest that United were going to get to scoring. The second forty-five minutes was almost all West Bromwich, with the Midlands side giving United a football lesson and they increased their lead through Derek Kevan in the fifty-sixth minute, with Allen making it 4-0 in the eighty-second minute from the penalty spot after Goodwin had brought

down Kevan. It could well have been more, as United were lucky not to have conceded an earlier penalty, when Gregg upended Kevan as he bore down on goal and it was sometimes little more than luck that the United defence manage to keep the visiting attack at bay.

This defeat did not knock the United youngsters off their stride, as they overcame Fulham in the F. A. Cup semi-final (after a replay) to reach Wembley on a wave of national emotion. Lancashire neighbours Bolton Wanderers, however, spoilt a fairy tale ending to the season by snatching the Cup with a 2-0 victory. As had been the case twelve months previously, the game was lost following a controversial incident, both times involving the Manchester United goalkeeper. This time, it was Harry Gregg on the receiving end, bundled into the net by Lofthouse for Bolton's second goal.

The Cup Final normally brought down the curtain on each season, but 1957-58 had been no ordinary one and Old Trafford still had to prepare for one final match. When the campaign had begun, hopes of success in Europe had been high in everyone's mind, after narrowly losing out to Real Madrid the previous term and now only AC Milan stood between United and the Final, with Old Trafford hosting the semi-final first leg on May 8th (see match no. 8). Sadly, it was all in vain, as the return leg in Milan brought little joy, as in front of

an 80,000 crowd, the one goal advantage was quickly wiped out, with Milan cruising to a 4-0 victory, thus ending another bid for European success.

＊

If United's performances following the disaster at Munich were considered nothing short of remarkable, then season 1958-59 must go down as one of the most inspired in the history of the club, with Jimmy Murphy deserving much more credit than he ultimately received. It was a campaign that many felt would really test United, stretching them to their utmost. But, rather surprisingly, amid a number of sterling performances, they finished runners-up spot in the First Division, only six points behind Wolves.

The season had opened with a 5-2 victory over Chelsea at Old Trafford, with the home crowd enjoying further enthralling ninety-minutes against Blackburn and Portsmouth, both of which ended 6-1 to United.

The former, on September 6th, brought an end to Blackburn's unbeaten opening run, with some "most spectacular football", while against Portsmouth on March 27th, Derek Hodgson of the *Daily Express* wrote: "This could have been the greatest massacre in First division history. Instead this pitifully poor Pompey team were allowed to get away with no more than a severe drubbing."

Despite not having been crowned First Division

champions, United were invited by the organisers of the European Cup to take part in the 1958-59 competition as a gesture of sympathy. It was an invitation that the club gratefully accepted and went into the draw for the opening round of the competition where they were paired with Swiss club Young Boys of Berne.

United, however, soon found themselves involved in controversy, with the Football Association back tracking on their original letter to Old Trafford on July 5th, which stated that they had no objections to the club entering the competition. The Football League had already written to the club telling them that they could not give their consent. Upon receiving the letter from the Football League, United went to the Board of Appeal, which upheld the appeal. In the rules of the game, this decision should have been final, with the Football League unable to interfere but the Football Association then denied United the opportunity to compete.

Berne were given a bye into the next round, but the two clubs decided to play the two fixtures as friendlies and on September 24th United travelled to Switzerland, where they lost 2-0. In the 'return leg', the Old Trafford European Cup tie that never was, on Wednesday October 1st, United won 3-0, thus would have gone through on aggregate had this been a competitive fixture.

On a pouring wet night, the

"rough, tough free for all" was certainly played in a competitive spirit, with W.R. Taylor of the *Manchester Guardian* writing: "It was a good thing that it was only a friendly match instead of a European Cup tie – imagination boggles about what might have happened otherwise. The description of 'friendly match' was as laughable as calling the Berne players "Young Boys" for they have certainly nothing to learn."

United went in front through Ernie Taylor after sixteen minutes, but the red shirts and yellow shorts of the Swiss were frequently seen around Gregg's goal as the opening half progressed. But after the interval, it was an entirely different game. The longer the second half went on, the tougher it became. Crowther was booked, much to the crowd's disapproval and shortly afterwards, they were even more voracious when the referee sent off Colin Webster for an alleged kick at an opponent. The Welshman departing to sympathetic cheers. Almost immediately, Alex Dawson ran onto the pitch, in an effort to take Webster's place, but was obviously chancing his luck, as there was no way that he was going to be allowed to replace a sent off player. Quixall came in for some undeserved punishment at the hands of the visitors, as Gregg stood a virtual spectator, with his

Matt Busby unveils the plaque on 25th February 1960: *Just over two years after the crash.*

The original Munich Memorial plaque: *situated above the Main entrance to the ground, where the directors entrance is today.*

opposite number under constant siege. Eventually a second goal materialised, Viollet scoring from Pearson's pass. Quixall added a third from the penalty spot.

On November 5th 1958, the Old Trafford goal posts were altered to accommodate the Rugby League match between Salford and Leeds. The local Salford club had hired the ground on an experimental basis, wanting to try a match under floodlights and much to their delight, a crowd of over 8,000 people turned up. Sadly the evening did not quite go as planned, with the visiting Yorkshire side winning 22-17.

During season 1958-59, more junior turnstiles were opened at the Stretford End, as there had been an increase in the number of youngsters attending games and the additional entrances made it easier for them to gain entry. That particular end of the ground came in for more alterations during the summer of 1959, when work began on a new covered stand which would hold over 12,000 supporters. This improvement would also provide cover for the 22,000 who stood in this section. Admission to this new stand would be 2/- (10p). It was also during this season that all seating at the ground was made bookable in advance for first team fixtures.

Numerous suggestions had been put forward for the erection of a lasting memorial at the ground to those who had lost their lives at Munich. Some supporters had gone as far as to suggest that sections of the ground should be called after individual players, but this

particular idea was turned down by the board. In the end, a large memorial plaque was decided upon, which was to be sited outside the main entrance on the railway side of the ground, while the ground committee were to have a special clock made for a site at the Warwick Road end. In the Press-Box, small plaques bearing the names of the journalists who died was to be installed by the Football Writers Association.

On February 25th 1960, the rain poured down from a dark Manchester sky, as some 1250 invited guests, including United players and directors, along with parents, relatives and friends of those who had died in the disaster, stood silently outside the main entrance, as manager Matt Busby pulled back the purple drapes which hung over the Munich Memorial Plaque, situated above the large wooden doors. Clearly moved by the occasion, the United manager said in a brief speech, "I know that those who are near and dear have a memorial in their hearts which will last for all time. But now our many friends will also have an everlasting memorial here to the lads who helped make this such a great club."

The plaque, designed by local architect M. I. Vipond, and constructed by Messrs Jaconello Ltd. of Manchester, showed a complete plan of the ground measuring 7'9" by 6'. Green slabs of faience marked out the pitch incised with black and gold glass letters forming an

inscription and names of those who lost their lives. The terraces, gangways and steps were also in faience to scale, and were in a memorial colour of mauve and grey. The stand roofs and perimeter path had been worked from solid quartzite, enclosed by red Barmoral granite forming the boundary wall of the ground. Two teak figures representing a player and spectator stood either side of a laurel wreath and ball, inscribed 1958.

The second of the memorials, a clock, was sited at the Warwick Road end of the ground, facing the main approach to the stadium. Above and below the two faced dial was the inscription - February 6th 1958, Munich. This was unveiled by Mr Dan Marsden the chairman of the ground committee, while the bronze plaque in the press box, bearing the names of the eight journalists who died was unveiled by the only surviving journalist, Mr Frank Taylor.

An interesting inclusion was found in the *United Review* for the match against Wolves on March 5th. 1960. Under the heading - "Important Notice", the article which followed stated that "a small boy had suffered a serious eye injury due to another boy firing an air pistol or rifle into the crowd at a previous game." Obviously this was a matter which concerned the United directors very much and was something that was clearly an early sign of things to come.

4 THE PERFECT MATCH

George Best dazzles in front of a new look Old Trafford: *The cantilever stand represented a landmark in football stadium design, fully equipped with executve boxes, unobstructed views and a clear view of one of the finest teams British football has ever produced.*

AS THE PITCH enjoyed a well-earned rest during the summer of 1960, further ground improvements were carried out as contractors battled to beat deadlines set and have the stadium ready for the opening match of 1960-61 against Blackburn Rovers on August 20th. Rebuilding and repairs were carried out at the Stretford End and neighbouring Paddock, at a cost of between £20,000 and £25,000. This gave the ground a capacity of 66,500, with admission prices for the new section of 3/- (15p) for adults and 1/6d (8p) for juniors. The following season it would be the turn of the United Road section of the ground for improvements, with this section being re-roofed.

In the club accounts for the year ending May 31st 1961, Chairman Harold Hardman reported that "during the year the club were faced with heavy commitments for repairs and maintenance. In the close season the outer wall and internal

▲ **Pre-season 1959-60.** *Matt Busby and his players out on the pitch with the construction of the new Stretford End stand taking place in the background.*

▶ **The Inner Sanctum:** *Matt Busby's office.*

buildings at the Stretford End Terraces were completely rebuilt and the old roof replaced by new sheeting." Looking at the expenditure account for that year, it shows that 'Repairs and Renewals' came to £27,026 16/-. A rather trivial sum by today's figures.

Whilst looking through those accounts, it is interesting to note that under the 'Balance Sheet', the 'Fixed Assets', which included 'Land, Stands, Buildings and Ground Equipment at cost, less depreciations and realisations at May 31st 1947 came to £71,911 4/5d, but with the additions to date, it rose to £111,590 12/8d.

But besides the actual ground itself; the stands, terracing and scoreboard, what was life like in the inner sanctums of the club, the places hidden from supporters' view, behind the

brick facade of the stadium? One man, who began working at the ground in 1960, as a fifteen year-old office boy, and is therefore better placed than most to take us through the inner sanctums of Old Trafford at this time is current club secretary Ken Ramsden.

"Turning onto the forecourt, having crossed the Warwick Road railway bridge", Ken began his flashback tour, "there was access to the stadium through a door situated just to the left below where the Munich clock is today. Going through this door, you would find the ticket office to the left and the general office and switch-board to the right. There was also what could be described as little more than a cupboard really, which was home to the club book-keeper. Access to the Scoreboard Paddock

area of the stadium could also be made through a door in this area. It must also be remembered that at this particular time, the number of people employed by the club was minimal and I could probably still name them all today. There was also another small office in a 'cubby hole' on the ground floor level, not far from the main offices, which housed the club computer then used for checking the number of spectators passing through the turnstiles in each area of the ground on a match-day.

"Taking the stairs, you would find the boardroom, assistant secretary and the secretary's office. The latter was set immediately below the Scoreboard Paddock terracing and had a barred window, which overlooked the ground. Those offices later moved to above the Development Association offices, when they were built in 1963. Coming back outside the stadium, there was also an outbuilding connected to the outer wall of the ground and this was sometimes used for the selling of match tickets, although this small building disappeared in 1963 when the Development Association offices were built. Walking down towards the Stretford End, we come to the players' entrance, which was then nothing more than a wooden door, perhaps about half-way between where the away fans go in today and the main entrance.

"The main entrance was the director's entrance of today and consisted of two large wooden doors, above which could be

found the original Munich Memorial. Going through these, on the right, was the gymnasium, which would later become the Players' Lounge, while to the left, going past the top of the tunnel which led down onto the pitch, were the dressing rooms, referee's room and the boot room. Tracing your steps backwards towards the gym, there were stairs up to the left, which took you to Sir Matt's office and the player's games room. Sir Matt's original office was in the same area as the other offices accessed from the forecourt. Opposite Sir Matt's office, and again, little more than a cupboard, was the stadium announcer's room. It was very small, but it had a

window, which overlooked the inside of the ground.

"Moving from the dressing room area, there was access to a basement area, below the old 'D' Stand, which housed the club laundry. This was where my mother and aunt worked and where conditions could become rather wet underfoot due to flooding. The laundry also housed the only radio in the stadium and could become quite packed on the Monday afternoons when the F A Cup draws were made. The laundry was later to move to the Scoreboard End of the ground."

There was also something of an outbuilding joined on to the wall of the main building, next

to the entrance into the office area. This, according to Ken, was occasionally used for the sale of tickets. It is certainly difficult for many present day supporters to imagine, that when Ken joined the club there was little or no money in the bank, a staff of around eleven, with three of those in administration and also, almost everything was bought second hand.

Season 1960-61 had also seen Old Trafford commemorate yet another milestone in its notable history, when, on Wednesday October 26th, the first Football League cup-tie was played at the ground. The visitors were Exeter City, for a First Round Replay, following a 1-1 draw at St. James

Park the previous week. A mere 15,662 turned up, with United showing their lesser rivals little mercy in a 4-1 win, thus sparing any further blushes. The goals coming from Albert Quixall with two (one a penalty), Johnny Giles and Mark Pearson.

The club were now beginning to find that the costs of ground improvements and refurbishments were becoming increasingly hard to bear, as despite the recent success, money was not exactly flowing into the club's bank account. Discussions took place at boardroom level regarding ways and means of improving revenue in order to keep the ground up to date and in pristine condition. It was those discussions which prompted a visit, in March 1961, to Edgbaston cricket ground in Birmingham, the home of Warwickshire County Cricket Club, who had set up a football pools competition, which had proved highly successful and made a profit of over £70,000 per year. Following the visit, further discussions took place at Old Trafford and it was decided to set up something similar, entitled the Manchester United Development Association, an organisation which, whilst offering the supporters an opportunity to win sums of money through a football pools style operation, would also help finance further ground improvements. As time would tell, it would prove to have been an invaluable innovation.

Not only did United take the idea of the pools competition

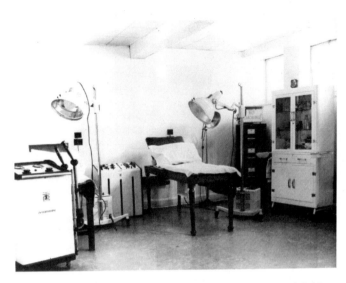

State of the Art:
*The Physiotherapist's Room
beneath the Main Stand.*

from their visit to Warwickshire, they also prized away the assistant organiser of the cricket club's pools, Bill Burke. Under his guidance, and from his small office inside Old Trafford, he began bringing in much needed revenue, with the weekly pools beginning in August 1961, with prize money of £240. It was not long before the enterprise bore fruit, with the Development Association's first contribution to ground improvement being the installation of seven hundred wooden seats at the back of the Stretford End terrace, which became Stand E. These seats were used for the first time on September 25th 1962, when Portuguese club Benfica, the current European Cup holders, visited Manchester for a friendly fixture.

The following season, 1962-63, relegation looked a real possibility, although rather surprisingly, Matt Busby's team managed to claw their way through to the F. A. Cup Final at Wembley. Four days after having beaten Southampton 1-0 at Villa Park to earn that Cup Final place, Sheffield Wednesday visited Old Trafford and tore United apart, winning 3-1. Now with just six games left, United faced a scrap to stay in the top flight.

"The Muddle and Mess! United Slip to the Brink" proclaimed the *Daily Mirror*, with its correspondent Derek Wallis writing: "Manchester United's most deplorable failures this season must have looked positively brilliant compared with their appalling performances at Old Trafford last night. I did not think a team with so much talent could sink so low. Wembley and the Cup final may be in sight, but the Second Division is nearer. Even the optimists who were relying on the mistakes of other teams must now be changing their opinions."

There was some reprieve at Turf Moor, Burnley three days later, when a solitary Denis Law goal went some way in the attempt to change the course of history, but a 3-2 defeat at home to Arsenal, followed by a 2-1 defeat at Birmingham made relegation once again more than a mere possibility.

With three games remaining, United needed three points to be safe. A visit to Maine Road on May 15th would prove pivotal as the Sky Blues were in an even worse position. The reds trailed 1-0 until ex-City star Denis Law won a last minute penalty to earn a vital point.

In the second of the three games, already doomed Leyton Orient journeyed north with nothing to lose. Before the interval, with United still trailing 1-0 to Dunmore's eighth minute goal, the sound of slow hand claps filled the Old Trafford air, with sections of the crowd taking out their frustrations on certain players. That tension lifted slightly, however, in the fifty-third minute, thanks to a goal by Charlton. Stan that is, not Bobby, as the Orient defender headed past his own 'keeper. Minutes later, the news filtered through that City were losing 4-0 meaning that victory would keep United in the top flight. Play, and time, dragged on and with only nine minutes remaining, the Orient 'keeper dropped the ball whilst under pressure from Charlton and the ever alert Law nipped in to score. Four minutes later, Charlton, Bobby this time, secured United's safety with a third.

Despite the dismal League campaign, Matt Busby's restructured team, which included recent signings Pat Crerand (from Celtic) and Denis Law (from Torino), inspired a memorable F. A. Cup run which saw Leicester City defeated at Wembley. Although it was only at the end of the season that any sense of direction was achieved on the playing front, off the pitch saw ground development begin on the outside of the stadium, on the section facing the forecourt. The construction consisted of new administration, ticket and development association offices, and it took a local contractor just six months to complete the work, at a cost of £14,000.

1963 brought the announcement that England was to host the 1966 World Cup Finals and United were honoured when Old Trafford was selected as a venue for some of the fixtures. The stadium were to be given some of the fixtures in Group C. This prompted the board to put their plans for further ground development into motion and it was announced in December that the club was to build a £250,000 cantilever stand along the United Road side of the ground. "New Trafford – as it will be after the £250,000 investment in soccer's future" proclaimed the *Daily Mail*, with a Sportsmail's artist's impression of the new stand superimposed onto an aerial view of the present ground.

Although prompting enthusiastic comments from the United support, the illustration of the architect's drawing which had appeared in the *Manchester Evening News and Chronicle* the previous day, made the new construction look even more imposing. Alongside this, David Meek, the newspaper's United correspondent wrote – "Manchester United are to have an elegant, £250,000 cantilever stand at Old Trafford. Work will start at the end of the season on what will be the longest and most advanced stand in the country. It will go up opposite the main stand in place of the

old covering over the terracing. There will be 10,500 seats and covered standing room for 10,000 more.

"The cantilever roof will project to the front of the terracing where it will be 48ft high. It will be suspended from steel tubes retained from concrete yokes projecting 30ft above the rear of the stand. All seats will have a clear, uninterrupted view of the game. The architects, Mather and Nutter, of Manchester, have prepared a preliminary scheme and are starting ground investigation immediately. Building will start next summer and be completed in 15 months, they hope, for the start of the 1965-66 season.

"This will give United use of the stand in good time for the World Cup in 1966. It is, in fact, the plan for this new stand that clinched Old Trafford as a choice of venue for the World Cup in favour of Maine Road. The stand, which will be 660ft long, will run the whole length of the ground and will turn at the corners. At the Streford end it will link up with the existing stand extension, though there will be a slight gap for the floodlighting pylon. At the Streford End, the corner will also be included in the stand.

"The new development will not mean a reduction in the capacity of Old Trafford. New techniques will be used to take the stand further back so that spectators will be sitting over the entrances."

The building of this new stand was a matter of careful

consideration, as it left no funds for strengthening the playing squad, which obviously took priority over any structural matters. Manager Matt Busby, however, felt that his squad was strong enough to challenge for the game's highest honours and gave the go-ahead for the money to be spent on the stand instead of being left in the bank in case he wanted to make any new signings.

Perhaps the most prominent feature of this new construction, but one that was not mentioned in David Meek's article, would be the installation of thirty-four private boxes, which could each hold up to six people. The reason for there being no mention in David's article was that they were not a feature of the original plans and it was only after Bill Burke managed to persuade United directors to visit Manchester racecourse to see a previous Mather and Nutter construction containing private boxes and then view the pitch from the back of the semi-constructed stand at Old Trafford, that the board decided to go along with the idea. Whether the added bonus of each director being given three boxes each swung the matter is not recorded... For those who were interested in the new facilities, centre boxes were to be let at £300 for a season, with those at the side £250. The rental secured admission to all home games and needless to say, all boxes were over-subscribed from the start.

In a rare article at the time, United's secretary, Les Olive,

spoke of the "One new and interesting feature which will be the installation of 34 private boxes, each of which will hold six people." Going on to describe the facilities that would be available he said: "These have been taken up by business houses in the city to entertain their clients in the best possible surroundings – a sort of Soccer-Ascot if you like.

"There will be a waiter service available for refreshments, and a private lift will transfer spectators from ground level to the boxes, which will be approached via a luxuriously carpeted lounge. The boxes will be heated and high class refreshment bars will be installed.

"When all is done, it will indeed be a far cry from the old-time conception of the football fan standing in the open in all kinds of weather, shouting himself hoarse. In fact, it will be the equal of anything that the world soccer traveller will find no matter where he goes."

Mr Olive, was also quick to add that there was to be much more to Old Trafford's World Cup facilities than one new stand, continuing, "When completed, our stand will have cost more than £300,000, but by 1966, we will have spent in all, more than £500,000 over the past 15 years on improvements at Old Trafford.

"Two corner paddocks have been rebuilt and cover has been erected behind the Stretford End goal. Our main stand has been rebuilt and its design will prove a tremendous boon

Model of the proposed new cantilever stand which would run along United Road.

in accommodating visiting radio, television and press representatives. We will have to remove seats to extend the press-box to take at least 400 soccer writers and we shall have to provide them with working and rest rooms.

"We will require at least 300 telephone lines, a communications room, radio and TV interview rooms and platforms for TV and film cameras which will show pictures of matches in all parts of the world. Luckily, we have sufficient space in which to erect these temporary structures on the first-floor level underneath our "A" and "D" stands."

The United secretary mentioned a cost of more than £300,000 for the new stand, but an early estimated cost for the construction was £175,000. A closer examination then took the figure up to £250,000. The final cost, however, was nearer to £320,000, and with only around £75,000 in the bank at this time, it was a major undertaking, putting the club well into the red, although most of the costs were eventually paid by the Development Association.

Construction work on the new stand was not as straight forward as had first been planned, as during the early work, cracking appeared in some of the concrete support columns and tests had to carried out to correct this. An article by Mr. R. M. Trelfall, a group engineer with Ove Arup and Partners, the consulting engineers on the project, in the *BSI News* of April 1966 revealed further problems. "The most difficult design problem lay in turning the cantilever over vertically into its stabilizing beam. In all stands, space and good viewing are at a premium so that little space is generally available at the back. In this case, where the stand is carried right out to the building line alongside United Road, there was little enough room to start with but the difficulty was compounded by the introduction of private viewing boxes with a rear entrance corridor. Again, various alternative designs were considered in detail, and it was found that the cheapest and constructionally most simple way came by changing the structural material from steelwork to reinforced concrete".

The sixties were beginning to swing, and popular music was taking on a completely different style as the outlook on life was beginning to change. Crowds at football matches were becoming more vocal in their support, with those at Old Trafford - especially at the Stretford End - no different from others up and down the country. This vocal participation in the game was greatly encouraged by the United management and on Saturday October 26th 1963, pre-match entertainment took on a whole new meaning, with the Ray Bradley troupe of drum majorettes, under the name of the 'Unitedettes' introduced the new 'United Song' to the supporters. With the supporters singing their own words to the popular tune 'When the Saints Go Marching In', words were composed and printed in the programme for the new song to that particular tune.

"Taking some hesitant but ominous steps into the sun-drenched Old Trafford football pitch, Manchester, on Saturday were eight leggy prototypes of what is, surely, the latest outrageous American graft on a British institution. Drum majorettes had come to soccer." Wrote "our own Reporter" in *The Guardian* on Monday October 28th, continuing with, "A trifle self conscious in red cloaks and tunics, the eight girls, called the Unitedettes made their hesitant first appearance 15 minutes before the kick-off of the Manchester United .v. West Ham United match. From their improvised dressing room in the players' gymnasium, the girls, who received a mixed reception, quick-marched on to the centre of the pitch.

"The terraces were struck dumb by the sight. In the 9/- seats, someone said: 'Football doesn't need it'. The girls were still marching when the teams entered the ground. In spite of the girls amplifying system their song was completely drowned out and the new words for what could become Manchester United's rallying song were forgotten."

How many joined in the pre-match community singing is not recorded, but it continued for a few weeks. This was a far cry from the more recent renderings from the Beswick Prize Band and the 1920's when pre-match and half-time entertainment was provided by the 'Manchester United Prize Band'!

In his report of the West Ham game, Derek Hodgson of the *Daily Express* wrote: "Fiasco is the only word to describe happenings at Old Trafford. It was a theatrical disaster even Rogers and Hammerstein would have been hard put to overcome. The drum majorettes turned out to be not cheerleaders at all, but poorly drilled formation marchers. The grand new rallying song fluttered and died under thin, squeaky amplification. Worse was to follow. Out trotted a United team who had no more idea of breaking West Ham's defence than infants have of opening a safe."

One of the main reasons behind Busby's decision to agree that the money in the club coffers should go towards ground improvement rather than into a transfer kitty, was the emergence of one talented youngster, already causing ripples of approval from regular reserve team watchers. His talents were soon to be paraded on a bigger stage and the majority in the 50,453 at Old Trafford on Saturday September 14th 1963 for the match against West Bromwich Albion, knew nothing of the debutant they were about to witness. The match itself was little more than a run of the mill First Division match, but the 1-0 United victory marked the first appearance of George Best, a seventeen year-old Belfast boy at outside right.

The 'Special Correspondent' covering the match for *The Guardian* wrote, "Young Best came in for some stern treatment by that splendid back Williams and twice sought refuge for short spells on the opposite wing. Best's football was occasionally of a high quality but he also showed his immaturity and it says much for his spirit that he twice returned to the right wing to take on Williams again who seemed intent on showing a disapproving crowd that there is no sentiment in football. Best started the move which brought the goal after 65 minutes when he directed a short pass inside to Stiles. The inside right's square pass across the penalty area found Sadler unmarked and, as Potter despairingly advanced, Sadler coolly slammed the ball past him."

In the *Daily Telegraph*, Denis Lowe wrote: "Best, a slim, dark haired lad of 17, had a promising first League game as Moir's outside-right deputy. He showed good ball control and had a subtle body-swerve, but will be happy to learn that few First Division left backs tackle with the power and accuracy of Welsh international, Graham Williams." Following his debut, Best returned to the reserves, but it was not long before the big stage would welcome him back for an extended run and in the years ahead he would become one of the Old Trafford legends.

Due to the construction of the new cantilever stand, whilst also assisting in crowd control, two separate sections were created at the Stretford End in early 1965, by erecting a barrier at the United Road side. This prevented spectators from entering the ground on Warwick Road and walking round to the Stretford End, thus causing crowding in this area, when it was still assumed that there was sufficient space going by the numbers having past through the turnstiles. On completion of the new stand, a further barrier would be erected at the Old Trafford end, to make these distinct sections, each with its own turnstiles and exits. Capacity would then be 64,000, with 18,500 seated and 52,000 under cover.

On the pitch, United had maintained their challenge for the First Division title throughout the 1964/65 season, with Chelsea and Leeds United also in contention. As the games became fewer, the confidence of Matt Busby's team never wavered, setting up a nail-biting finale to the campaign. Easter Monday saw Birmingham City beaten 4-2 at St Andrew's to send United top, a point clear of their two challengers, who had both lost that afternoon. A 3-0 home win over Liverpool on April 24th (with many supporters enjoying the facilities of the cantilever stand in a section nearest to the Stretford End of the ground) and a 6-2 defeat for Chelsea at Burnley, meant that the destination of the First Division Championship was now between United and Leeds, with only two games remaining and United still one point in front. Two days later, there was to be a night of high football drama, as Arsenal travelled to Manchester and Leeds made the journey to Birmingham. Defeat for either could prove costly (see match

no. 9).

At the final whistle the crowd thronged onto the pitch, a thin line of policemen were swept aside, helmets flying into the night air, with the area at the mouth of the tunnel a mass of humanity, as the supporters shouted for their heroes to make an appearance. Ten minutes later their cries were answered.

✳

On Wednesday May 19th, twenty minutes prior to the Inter Cities Fairs Cup quarter-final tie against Strasbourg, United were presented with the League Championship trophy. On a perfect spring evening, with the sun shining down on the colourful Old Trafford terraces, the trophy was brought onto the pitch and placed on a small table in front of the main stand. The cheering, which had begun at the sight of the trophy, erupted as Denis Law walked alone from the tunnel dressed in a red tracksuit top, to receive the coveted trophy from Mr Joe Richards, the Football League President. Each player then appeared individually to receive his medal and the adoration from the crowd, with George Best bringing up the rear. The biggest cheer, however, was reserved for Matt Busby who followed his team out onto the pitch to receive his medal.

After this presentation, the spotlight drifted back to Denis Law, who had to step forward for a second time, to receive his European Player of the

Year award from Max Urbini of *France Football*. Off the players then went on a lap of honour and the excitement for the night was over as United and Strasbourg played out a boring 0-0 draw. The score-line actually mattered little, as United had won the first-leg in France 5-0. Rather surprisingly, there were only 34,188 at Old Trafford for that European tie!

Throughout the summer, work continued around Old Trafford, with the World Cup now less than a year away and becoming much more of a priority to United. By the time season 1965-66 arrived, a large section of the new cantilever stand was ready for occupation, with the final section at the Warwick Road end scheduled to be available in October. Work also had to be carried out below the stand, with alterations to the toilet and refreshment areas adding to the expenditure. Better facilities for the supporters, but what sort of prices did the United fan of the mid-sixties have to pay to sit in what would be known as Stands G and H, or stand in the United Road Paddock, in front of this new construction? To sit in sections G and H, it would cost 10/- (50p) and 12/6 (63p), bookable two weeks in advance, while the Paddock was 5/- (25p), with no reductions for juniors!

Vocal encouragement was becoming more than just enthusiastic cheering, with many club's supporters beginning to compose numerous songs and chants to popular

View from above the Stretford End tunnel c.1963: *With the Popular Side to the left and the Main Stand to the right.*

tunes. Liverpool's Kop played a prominent part in this, jumping onto the 'Mersey Sound' bandwagon, but United's Stretford End became just as noted for its vocal participation and soon became the main section of the ground for the standing supporter who was proud to be known as a Stretford-Ender. Unfortunately, some of the crowd participation became a little too boisterous, (no better or worse than that at most other grounds around the country it must be added), and the club were forced on numerous occasions to publish notices asking those responsible to refrain from the throwing of toilet rolls and other objects on to the pitch.

The Inter Cities Fairs Cup-tie against Ferencvaros at the end of the 1964-65 season, had witnessed behaviour which had greatly upset the United directors, with manager Matt Busby being forced to mention the subject in the club programme at the start of the following season.

He wrote: "As League Champions we can expect all the other teams to be trying even harder than usual to lower our colours and we will need the help of our supporters at all times. I would like to say here and now that this assistance must be in a proper manner: as will be seen in another part of the programme we have been instructed to post warning notices as a result of the behaviour of a small minority during the match against Ferencvaros last season. I hope this will bring home to those responsible for throwing toilet rolls and other objects on to the field that they achieve nothing except to bring the good name of the club into disrepute. Such actions are not typical of the large majority of Manchester United supporters, and I appeal to those responsible to stop this practice."

Warning notices were also posted around the ground, but those, and the manager's programme notes, were generally ignored. This led to a further warning notice in the programme for the match against Newcastle United on September 15th 1965, referring to the obscene chanting at the referee at the previous home match against Stoke City.

"We don't need this kind of support…" was the heading of the notice on page four of the Newcastle United match programme and it went on to read – "Following the obscene remarks chanted at the referee during the match versus Stoke City eight youths aged from 15 to 21 have been banned from entering the ground for the remainder of the season. In giving this information the directors wish it to be known

LEAGUE DIVISION ONE
APRIL 26TH 1965

UNITED 3 ARSENAL 1

WITH 51,625 PACKED INTO *Old Trafford it took United only seven minutes to open the scoring through George Best. Denis Law, bandages covering a cut knee sustained against Liverpool, collected a pass from Connelly on the left and moved forward. Beating Howe, he looked or a team mate to pass to, but with no-one in space, he had little option but to beat the Arsenal man again before releasing the ball to Best. The Irishman, in front of goal, calmly controlled the ball before shooting home, off the goalkeepers legs.*

The roar saluting the goal was matched fifteen minutes later, as the Old Trafford loudspeakers echoed out that Birmingham had taken the lead, but by now, Arsenal had began to creep back into the game with McLintock, Eastham and Sammels all coming close.

It wasn't until the news came through in the sixty-sixth minute that Leeds were 3-0 down that United finally began to settle. Charlton threatened the Gunners defence with a forty yard run, while another United attack earned a free kick. Taken by Stiles, the ball was despatched towards the Arsenal penalty area where Herd's header looked destined for the back of the net, only for Furnell to palm the ball on to the crossbar. Quickest to react was Denis Law, who fired the ball past a helpless goalkeeper.

With twenty-three minutes remaining, everything looked to be in United's favour, but a tackle by Crerand on Baker inside the United penalty area saw Eastham score from the spot, despite Pat Dunne stopping the Arsenal player's initial kick. Everything was back on a knife edge, more so when the loudspeakers silenced the crowd when it announced that Leeds had pulled two goals back.

Two minutes later an even louder groan was heard, as a Law – Best move ended with Furnell tipping the formers header over for a corner. From Best's hard and low corner kick, the Arsenal goalkeeper, for once, failed to get near the ball and Law accepted an easy opportunity to score. 3-1 to United, but there was still five minutes to play, along with the agonising wait for confirmation of the Birmingham – Leeds score.

Eventually, the final whistle blew at Old Trafford and the two teams left the field, as many of the supporters invaded the pitch, while others remained rooted to their places, awaiting the all important score line from the Midlands. After what seemed an eternity, the loudspeaker crackled into life. "The final score from St Andrew's is Birmingham City 3 Leeds (pause) 3" and Old Trafford went wild. United were Champions, unless Aston Villa beat them 19-0 in the final game of the season!

that they are prepared to take these and other measures if the young fans at the Stretford End will not co-operate. They must be made to realise that they are a disgrace to the club they pretend to support and if they cannot behave as true supporters then they are not wanted in the ground. We do not wish to stop the singing but it should be beyond the wit of the leaders to make their choruses a humorous commentary instead of using obscene language. It is a sad reflection on their capabilities if they are unable to be topical without resorting to filth. Other clubs' supporters sing their choruses and these are enjoyed by all present. Part of the attraction of football matches for the spectator are the witty and comical remarks which are heard, some clubs' supporters include these in their choruses so that they become part of the entertainment. There is no reason why the young fans concerned cannot do this and do it better than anyone else, so what about it you Stretford Enders? Cut out the obscenities and let us hear some comedy?"

Such problems continued as season 1965-66 progressed, "Violence flares at Old Trafford" declared the headlines following the visit of Liverpool to Old Trafford on October 9th, something that was picked up on by most of the journalists covering the game. In the *Sunday Times*, Brian Glanville wrote: "It all got rather rough now (in the second half, with United leading 2-0 through Best and Law) , perhaps in response to the violent goings-on on the terrace behind the goal, which led to the usual stream of Liverpool (and perhaps some Manchester) supporters being hauled away by the police. Towards the end, a youth even ran on to the field, and later still, Stiles, who had been booed from the first whistle by the Liverpool throng, appeared to be hit by an object thrown from those boiling terraces."

In the *Guardian*, Eric Todd penned similar notes – "Manchester United beat Liverpool 2-0 on Saturday at Old Trafford in the presence of 58,161 spectators. Perhaps 58,150 would be nearer the mark by the time the local constabulary had finished its reaping. The arrests while necessary were regrettable as was the smashing of windows on the United premises as the crowd squeezed its way home. Appearances in court will reveal the miscreants identity and home addresses if any; until then judgement must be suspended because supporters of both sides favour the same colours. It did seem unlikely that United's followers would express their pleasure with the result by throwing stones at anybody and anything."

The stone throwing at the end of United's 2-0 victory came from disgruntled visiting fans gathered outside the main entrance of the ground, who immediately began throwing missiles at the windows. A pint mug shattered Matt Busby's office window, while a bottle

Fans celebrate on the pitch after victory over Arsenal clinches the 1965 Championship. *Note the development of the cantilever stand in the background in preparation for the 1966 World Cup.*

did likewise to the office of chief scout Joe Armstrong. The boardroom windows were also targeted, with directors of both clubs inside.

A month later, the visit of Blackburn Rovers on November 6th also made the headlines for all the wrong reasons. "This Is Vandal Vengeance" proclaimed the *Sunday People*, while the *Guardian* carried an article headed "Violent scenes at World Cup grounds".

The headline in the 'People' appeared above a photograph of some of the Blackburn Rovers players looking through a shattered window on their coach following the 2-2 draw. The report alongside read: "This (the photograph) was the Blackburn Rovers team coach when it arrived home after the Old Trafford game against Manchester United – a casualty of vandal vengeance which erupted after a sensational finish to the match.

"Blackburn directors and players were lucky to escape injury after wild young fans – including girls – stoned the coach, denting the bodywork and splintering the window which later shattered. "It was frightening to see the faces of those fans" said Blackburn manager Jack Marshall.

"The bitter finale came after Manchester United 'keeper Harry Gregg, playing his first home game in 18 months, had been given his marching orders seven minutes from time. The sequels: Gregg is certain to seek a personal hearing by a disciplinary committee – and call Blackburn players to his defence; and Blackburn's board may send a full report of the vandalism outside Old Trafford to the Football League.

Gregg, who had been subjected throughout the afternoon, to a hail of glass and stones from a large number of Blackburn supporters, had gone up for a high ball with Blackburn centre-half Mike England and both players had fallen in a tangle and then simply got up to carry on with the game. The big 'keeper was astounded at the referee's decision to send him off for what the official regarded as a kick at his opponent and spent the remaining seven minutes of the game crouched shirtless on the touch-line with a towel draped over his shoulders. An ideal position to watch the visitors equalise from the resulting spot kick, United to regain the lead three minutes later and Blackburn to snatch a point with seconds remaining when a Harrison free kick from thirty yards out was deflected past stand-in 'keeper David Herd. Rather surprisingly, there was no mention of the incidents from the Liverpool or Blackburn games in the club programme!

▲ Aerial view of the Cantilever Stand c.1967.
This radical design ended supporter's complaints about obstructed views.

▶ Disgrace: *Denis Law and Ian Ure troop from the field having been sent off during a league match in 1966. The incendiary nature of United-Arsenal fixtures has continued down the years.*

The building work at the ground caused some congestion in the United Road at the end of games, bringing the club numerous complaints, forcing them in the end to take some action. Two gates were therefore placed into the barrier which separated the United Road Paddock and the Scoreboard End, giving the spectators additional exits. A further improvement towards the easing of congestion after the final whistle was the erection of a footbridge at the Stretford End of the ground following the granting of permission by Stretford Council.

When the floodlighting was installed at the ground, the United management must have thought that the problems of staging evening games had at last been resolved. They were soon to find that this was not the case. The fixture against West Bromwich Albion on December 27th 1965, originally an evening kick off, had to be changed to a 2 o'clock start, as the North Western Electricity Board would not give permission to allow the floodlights to be used, as the match would be played during a 'peak demand' period. Today it is not unusual for television to 'call the tune' as regards to kick-off times, but for an Electricity Board to do so...

As 1966 unfolded, the final preparations for the World Cup were put into place, with United hosting three games in group C between Portugal, Hungary and Bulgaria, with the tickets for those fixtures being made available in books of three and graded into two prices for seating £6-6/- (£6.30p) and £3. Similar arrangements were available for those wishing to stand, with those tickets priced at £1-17-6d (£.88p) and £1-2-6d (£1.13p). To attend one match, standing on the Stretford End would cost 7/6d (37p). Some of the stars from the Portuguese and Hungarian sides had already graced the Old Trafford turf with their club sides, which perhaps had something to do with the rather poor attendances for the three games, although the cost might also have played a more decisive factor.

The opening match on July 13th, between Hungary and Portugal attracted the best of the three attendances with 29,886, while three days later Bulgaria and Portugal was watched by 25,438. The final match in the group attracted slightly less, with only 24,129 passing through the gates. Disappointing, considering the amount of time and effort put into the preparations, but it was, however, hailed as a success by the club, with many compliments received from the visiting media, teams and supporters. At least with the financial outlay for the new stand would be recouped many times over in the years ahead.

Not everything evolving from

the World Cup Finals received five stars, as prior to Manchester City's visit to Old Trafford on September 17th, the club issued a statement declaring a ban on banner-waving supporters, a craze which had developed from the recent finals.

The statement read: "The club have decided that supporters carrying banners or flags on poles will not be admitted to the ground at future matches. Complaints have been received of spectators being struck in the face when these have been waved, and as long as they are being brought along in increasing numbers they have become a source of danger, and are spoiling the enjoyment of many other spectators. The police have been asked to rigidly enforce this ban, and the co-operation of supporters of both clubs attending the derby match on Saturday is requested."

This, however, could be considered as a very minor irritation, as there was a much more serious problem simmering away and one that would not go away for a considerable period of time, with United well to the fore, much

to the disappointment of club officials.

Rivalry between supporters in the previous decades had generally been good natured. There had obviously been the odd over-heated differences of opinions, but nothing on the scale of what was about to hit the sport. Fans would more often than not share the same terracing, with no designated areas for home and away supporters. This was soon to change for good.

The first real hint at Old Trafford of what was about to happen on a regular basis up and down the country came on the evening of August 31st 1966, when Everton visited Old Trafford. The Stretford End was now confirmed as the congregation point for the most vocal of the United support, having taken over from the Popular Side of old and on the night in question, huge numbers of Everton supporters paid their admission money at the turnstiles and made their way to the front of the packed terracing with one thing and one thing only on their mind.

United took the lead a

minute prior to the interval with Foulkes heading home a Connelly cross and inadvertently lit the blue touch paper, with Eric Todd's *Guardian* match report recording the events that followed – "During the interval great gaps appeared among the throng at the Stretford end of the ground. Some people had elected to faint, and others to fight. Whatever the causes, police and ambulancemen were kept fully occupied and they missed United's second goal in the 55th minute."

How many also missed the third and final goal, "a goal that he and Old Trafford will remember for a long, long time" is not recorded, but for the record, Herd delivered a cross, high and fast, from the right touchline and Law, with the ball looking as though it would go out of play, twisted his head and body to a nigh impossible position to head home. This violence prompted the erection

of extra barriers being added on the Stretford End, with lateral passageways for the use of the police also being installed.

Season 1966-67 soon saw United up amongst the pack at the top of the table and in the post World Cup boom, crowds flocked to Old Trafford to enjoy the free flowing, entertaining football produced by Messrs. Best, Law, Charlton and company. But it was not always a glowing advert for the game, as on October 29th, Arsenal travelled north to Manchester and took part in one of the most ill-tempered matches ever seen at the ground.

On no less than four occasions, players from both sides squared up to one another as play drifted on around them. George Best and Peter Storey were the first, in the early stages of the game and after twenty-four minutes it was Law and Ure at loggerheads. The head-to-head confrontations continued

Player of the Tournament:
Eusebio proved himself the best player in the world in the summer of 1966. Here he evades the attentions of the Hungarians in a group game at Old Trafford.

six minutes later as Crerand and Simpson locked horns, with McLintock and Kidd having a similar set to, not so long afterwards.

But it was two tempestuous Scots, Denis Law and Ian Ure, who provided most of the venom in this somewhat embarrassing confrontation. Their initial twenty-fourth minute feud flared up in the middle of the park following an ugly tackle by the Arsenal defender which prompted Law into retaliation, earning both a booking. As the game progressed, Ure continued to keep Law under close scrutiny, with the United man's temper continuing to rise with every

tackle and with only seven minutes remaining everything eventually came to a head.

With play at the opposite end of the park, Ure aimed a kick at Law for one reason or another, who in return threw a punch at his international team mate. Numerous players moved in to try and separate the two, and when things had quietened down, both were sent off. Best was lucky not to follow them, when he too threw a couple of punches at an Arsenal player in the melee which followed.

Another memorable game from the early months of this season was against Sunderland on November 26th. It produced something of a record at Old Trafford, whilst also conjuring up a trivia question for the years to come. It was not the 5-0 score line, nor was it any activity similar to the previously mentioned encounter against

Arsenal that made this game stand out above others. It was the fact that David Herd scored against three different Sunderland goalkeepers!

Sunderland's regular goalkeeper, Jim Montgomery, already having been beaten by Herd in the eighth minute, collided with Tony Dunne twenty-three minutes later and was carried off. He was replaced by centre half Charlie Hurley until half-time, but by then United's centre forward had made it 2-0. After the interval, John Parke took over, but fared little better with David Herd netting twice as United scored a further three, with one of Herd's shots being measured at 72mph.

Friday March 3rd saw another first for Old Trafford, even though United were playing away at Highbury against Arsenal. The match, originally scheduled for the following day, was re-arranged, as the League Cup Final between Queens Park Rangers and West Bromwich Albion was being played at Wembley and it was decided to experiment with closed circuit TV and beam the pictures back to Manchester, making it the first Division One match to be shown in this way. It also created a 'record attendance' for a First Division fixture, with 91,423 watching the ninety minutes at

the two different venues, with over 63,000 packed into the north London ground for the real thing.

The images from Highbury were projected onto seven screens, measuring some 40 feet wide by 30 feet high, situated around the pitch, giving the 28,423 spectators a panoramic view of the match in London. Opinions on the night's viewing were varied, especially as one of the screens was blown down, but the quality of the camerawork was acceptable, and on the night the crowd soon became involved in the game, which gave the sponsors encouragement for the future. The match itself saw no repetition of the unsavoury incidents which marred the meeting between the two clubs at Old Trafford earlier in the season.

Familiar scenes were once again in evidence at the final match of the season against Stoke City, when 61,071 spectators saw Sir Joe Richards, President of the Football League, present Denis Law with the League Championship trophy prior to the kick off, the title having been secured the previous Saturday with an emphatic 6-1 victory at West Ham. "We are the champions" echoed around the ground as the United captain, attired in a red tracksuit lifted the trophy above

his head, with loud cheers for each United player who followed to receive his medal, with a special cheer for David Herd, who had broken his leg against Leicester City on March 18th.

An hour and a half before the kick off, there were already 13,000 in the ground, many carrying bottles of champagne and brown ale, but there was little to celebrate other than the championship, as the match against Stoke City, was itself something of a non-starter, finishing 0-0.

With the championship trophy having already been presented to Denis Law, the visitors formed a guard of honour as United took to the field prior to the kick-off and with the lack of real entertainment out on the pitch, it was down to the majority of the 61,071 fans to make their own afternoon's entertainment and dispose of their remaining toilet rolls.

As the final whistle blew, around two hundred supporters invaded the pitch from the Stretford End and were immediately warned via the loudspeaker system that if they did not clear the pitch that the players would not come out for a lap of honour. Slowly, the police regained control and the pitch was cleared, allowing the players to re-emerge, Matt Busby joining them as they reached the Stretford End. All previous misdemeanours were momentarily forgotten as they stood and applauded their most vocal and controversial supporters.

Having spent about five minutes out on the pitch, with the police continuing what was slowly becoming a losing battle in attempting to stop spectators from encroaching on the pitch, the players returned to the sanctuary of the dressing rooms, as more and more fans scrambled onto the pitch, many throwing the numerous toilet rolls back into the swaying crowd, some dug lumps out of the turf for souvenirs, while others swung from the cross-bar at the Stretford End until removed by police. Eventually, as they began to get fed up they began to drift away at their own accord, much to the relief of the Manchester constabulary.

Having won the Championship, season 1967-68 kicked off with the F. A. Charity Shield fixture bringing the curtain up at Old Trafford. Tottenham Hotspur (the F. A. Cup winners of the previous season) providing the opposition. Nothing very notable neither in that, nor in the 3-3 score line, but the manner in which one of the Tottenham goals was scored is certainly worth a mention, going down as one of the most unusual of the bizarre goals ever scored at the ground.

On a rain swept pitch and Tottenham already a goal in front through Roberson, Alan Mullery tapped a free-kick back into the area and into the arms of Pat Jennings and having gathered the ball, with his back to the Stretford End, he launched a long kick from his hands and

The programme for the closed circuit tv showing of United's game against Arsenal.

Supporters follow the action from Highbury on large cinema big screens.

watched as the ball soared into the United half. Bouncing twice on the soft slippery surface, as Foulkes and Gilzean jostled in an attempt to reach it, the second of the two bounces took it towards United goalkeeper Alex Stepney who had surprisingly advanced fifteen yards from his goal line. Unfortunately for the United No.1, this was a few yards too far, as the bounce carried the ball over his head and into the vacant goal.

Ground development had come to something of a halt following the dramatic transformation of the stadium prior to the World Cup. However, in September 1967 a simple construction, out on the Old Trafford forecourt, heralded the beginning of the United Souvenir shop. During the club tour of Australia that summer, the board discussed the possibilities of the club shop and upon returning home it was decided to invest in such a venture, to the sum of £1,000. A small wooden hut was erected, and under the management of Mr Frank Gidley (assisted by his wife, daughter and another female), he began selling badges, ties, pennants, photos, bags and key rings to the United supporters eager for anything with the club name or that of its players on it.

One visitor to the ground who did not stop to view the goods on sale at the hut, was the Rt. Hon. Harold Wilson OBE, the Prime Minister, who was a guest at the match against West Bromwich Albion on December 2nd 1967. Over the years, many thousands have visited Old Trafford to enjoy an afternoon, or evening's entertainment, but this occasion was the first time that such a prominent figure had been present to watch United and the occasion was marked with a full page mention in the programme.

As reigning Champions, United were once again involved in the European Cup, with Matt Busby's opportunities of claiming the ultimate prize becoming fewer with each passing year. Hibernians of Malta, Sarajevo of Yugoslavia and Gornik of Poland were all beaten as they progressed into the semi-finals, where awaiting them were old foes Real Madrid. With the first leg at Old Trafford, it was imperative that a lead was secured that would make the visit to the cauldron of the Bernabeu Stadium slightly less daunting (see report).

Towards the end of the season, on April 29th, the club staged the F. A. Cup Semi-Final between Everton and Leeds United, the first such fixture to be held at the ground in post-war years, although it had regularly been the venue prior to the hostilities. A full house of 63,200 was present, producing record receipts for an F. A. Cup Semi-Final of £51,000. Everton fans turned the Stretford End into a mass of blue and while for the day and it was the Merseysiders who went home singing, following a narrow 1-0 victory.

Before everyone connected with the club could concentrate on that second leg of the European Cup semi-final, there was still the small matter of the First Division championship to bring to a close and in something of a mirror image to that of three years previously, United found themselves again in contention, with the destination of the trophy not being known until that last Saturday of the season.

On this occasion, by a strange quirk of fate, the team challenging United for the title was neighbours City, with the

First Division table on that final Saturday showing both United and City on fifty-six points from their forty-one games. Although it was the Maine Road side who sat in top spot, courtesy of a better goal average. United, despite having scored six more, had conceded fifty-three to City's forty.

There was also a third party with more than a slight interest in the proceedings, as Liverpool lurked in the background should either of the two slip up, as the Merseyside club had played only forty games and were three points behind. So defeats for United and City and two victories for Liverpool, would see the handsome trophy disappear down the East Lancs Road.

With United at home to Sunderland and City having to travel to Newcastle, a team that United had thrashed 6-0 at Old Trafford the previous week, United had, on paper, the easiest fixture, as Sunderland had not won there for some sixteen years. It was a strange afternoon at Old Trafford, as United were a shadow of themselves and Arthur Hopcraft wrote in *The Observer*: "With the championship hanging on the result here and at St James's Park, this match was bound to be taut with tension. Yet even the most pessimistic spectator could not have anticipated the degrees of wretchedness in the football, and of ugly belligerence in the ill-temper."

United found themselves two goals behind after little more than half an hour, due to

their "stuttering confusion and their wholly uncharacteristic incoherence." Suggett scoring the first from a Sharkey cross, taking advantage of Dunne being off the field for some attention to a cut eye and Mullhall adding the second with a header after both Foulkes and Brennan missed the ball.

One minute before the interval, Best, not for the first time, clawed United back into the game, with a shot from all of thirty yards. Newcastle also scored prior to the interval, giving United and their supporters hope. The second half saw too much tension creep into the game, with Best's frustrations seeing him booked for arguing with the referee. The game threatened to boil over, with Crerand getting himself involved with Harris, and later Ashurst, after the latter had clashed with Best, as news filtered through for the north-east that City were winning 4-2.

United surged forward at every opportunity, spurred on by the majority of the 62,963 crowd and only a timely header off the goal line by Charlie Hurley cleared Tony Dunne's effort to safety. Busby threw on Gowling for Foulkes and within sixty seconds the gangly forward had the ball in the net, but was pulled up for off-side. On Tyneside, Newcastle had scored a third, but City had added another two to their total and as the final result was announced at Old Trafford, the crowd treated the news with a commendable round of applause.

APRIL 24TH 1968
EUROPEAN CUP SEMI-FINAL, FIRST LEG

UNITED 1 REAL MADRID 0

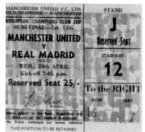

On the evening of April 24th, the Spanish champions visited Manchester, playing their part in a game which flowed and throbbed with pulsating football, the hosts considered rather more dominant than their illustrious visitors. However, as the game wore on, the missed opportunities by Brian Kidd and John Aston looked as though they were going to be rued, while the creative play of Bobby Charlton and Denis Law, along with the mesmerising skill of George Best were all to no avail.

In the end, the 63,500 crowd had to be content with one goal, a 35th minute effort from George Best. Aston, often bearing the brunt of the crowd's frustration, got the better of Gonzalez at the second attempt. From the bye line on the left at the Scoreboard End, his cross found the Irishman, who hit the ball on the half volley from around fifteen yards out, sending it past a helpless Betancort in the Madrid goal.

The Spaniards had obviously came to Manchester looking for a draw and their goalkeeper played a major part in keeping United down to that solitary strike, but some poor finishing (Stiles hit the roof of the Stretford End in the second half), along with the previously mentioned misses, left the United supporters wondering if the chance of European glory was once again going to pass them by.

As it was, an even more dramatic night in Madrid saw United shock the majority in the 125,000 crowd, earning a 3-3 draw and thus claiming a place in the Final due to be played at Wembley. And as they say, the rest is history.

Interest in the club had always been high, but following the European Cup victory things began to escalate, with the recently opened Souvenir Shop becoming an overwhelming success and a magnet for United supporters. So much so, that it was soon obvious that new premises would have to be found to accommodate this runaway business and it eventually moved into the offices of the Development Association, (just to the left of where the Munich clock stands today), who in turn moved across the forecourt to a completely new home costing

£40,000.

To the stadium itself, there was little in the way of changes, but on the field of play there was much to write about, with the visit of Estudiantes from Argentina producing another 'first', in the way of a World Championship Cup-Tie, a competition for the winners of the European Cup and the South American equivalent, the Copa Libertadores. The first leg, in Buenos Aries, was not without incident and United returned home with only a 1-0 defeat to turn around, but the second leg at Old Trafford caused concern with the United directors even before a ball was kicked and it was also to produce a tempestuous evening as the game unfolded.

Eleven days prior to the second leg of the Estudiantes fixture, United had faced Arsenal at Old Trafford, a fixture, which perhaps more than any other on the domestic front over the years commanded newspaper coverage on more than the actual football played. This particular ninety-minutes on October 5th, a 0-0 draw, brought a warning from the referee Ken Burns mid-way through the second half, with an announcement over the loudspeaker system – "If any more objects are thrown into the

The White Picket Fence:
Bobby Charlton takes a corner before an adoring Old Trafford Paddock. The fence, a symbol of more innocent times, was a distinctive feature of the ground.

Arsenal goalmouth the referee will abandon the game". This announcement followed the hail of coins and other objects that had flown towards Arsenal goalkeeper Bob Wilson. Wilson was later to say: "I was showered with hundreds of pennies, aspirin bottles, conkers, apple cores and everything else these fans could get their hands on. Coins could blind you if they caught you in the eye. It was frightening. And this was no ordinary League match."

In *The Guardian*, Albert Barham wrote : "Judging by their attitude during the game against Arsenal, the Stretford Enders – admittedly only a small part of this vociferous, fevered crowd – is not as it should be. Yet their behaviour 10 days hence could decide the out come of the game (against Estudiantes). On Saturday, their aim, ill directed, was against Wilson, in the Arsenal goal, with a shower of pennies. There was a threat to call the match off – broadcast on the referee's instructions – because of this.

"Between now and October 16th, the unruly element might do well to ponder on whether continental officials – Lo Bello from Sicily, Bakhramov of Russia or Zecevic of Czechoslovakia – would tolerate such irresponsible and potentially dangerous actions, remembering

it was a missile which struck Simpson, in goal, and sparked off much of the ill-feeling in the infamous matches between Racing and Celtic last year in South America."

In the programme for the Arsenal match, Matt Busby had pleaded for tolerance against Estudiantes, writing – "I ask that all spectators should support them (the players) by not misbehaving in any way. Failure to do this can bring disaster to the club and our hopes of becoming world champions". Busby also wrote to the sports editors of the principal newspapers to help try and create a calm atmosphere. While the consequences of any trouble were made very clear, with the confirmation that the game could simply be awarded to Estudiantes and Old Trafford could be banned from hosting games against foreign opposition for three years.

There was a brief hint that United might switch the game to Wembley, with a stadium official saying: "It would be a rush – but we could do it. We could have the pitch ready at 24 hours notice." While erecting barriers at the Stretford End of the ground was also considered, but considered something of a panic measure.

It had been a worrying

season for United regarding crowd trouble, as it had been a thorn in their side since the early weeks of the campaign. Prior to West Ham's visit to Old Trafford on September 7th, United sent a letter to their next visitors outlining two steps that the London side should take in an effort to help stamp out the possible threat of crowd trouble. The Hammers were asked to be first out onto the pitch prior to kick off and that they should use the Scoreboard End goal for their pre-match warm up. It was felt that if the opposition went to the Stretford End to warm up, then the fans could quickly get into an unsettled mood. It wasn't just West Ham who were asked to do this, as the club sent letters to all teams in the First Division.

Hopes of becoming the first British club to win the trophy were high, but were dashed after only six minutes of the second leg when the South Americans, who conceded three fouls in the opening four minutes, went 2-0 in front on aggregate following their first attack. A Dunne tackle on Veron gave away a throw in, which in turn saw Foulkes being pulled up for a foul. Madero took the free kick and Veron popped up to head past Stepney.

United's chances were

further hampered in the 36th minute when Denis Law was carried off with a gashed knee as United pressed forward as they continuously tried to create an opening and get back into the game. But with tempers running high after the numerous unsavoury incidents in the 1st leg, which had seen Nobby Stiles sent off, the match always looked like boiling over.

Numerous opportunities were squandered and as the match moved into the final minutes, with United still trailing, George Best and Medina were ordered off following a fist-throwing melee on the touchline. With the crowd on their toes, Morgan scored in the dying seconds, but it was too late to save the game. Both legs will probably be remembered more for the unsavoury incidents than the football that the World Club Championship brought. An interesting footnote to this game was that the *United Review* sold a record 74,680 copies on the night, when record ground receipts of £63,438 were taken.

Whilst mentioning programme sales at the ground, the League match against Arsenal on October 5th, saw an incredible 64,772 copies sold, while in December, an open letter appeared in the "United

Review" relating, once again, to recent obscene chanting by large numbers of the spectators in the Stretford End. Whether or not this had any effect on the overall behaviour of these supporters is doubtful, as events later in the season would show.

A re-arranged First Division fixture against Queens Park Rangers on March 19th 1969 saw another club record set, when the 8-1 score line was the highest recorded by the club since changing its name to Manchester United. Morgan had begun the rout on the half hour, scoring his first League goal for the club after Aston headed on a short corner by Best, but it was not until the second half that the floodgates were well and truly opened. Best made it 2-0 within five minutes of the re-start, with a shot from twelve yards, but Rangers pulled it back to 2-1 through Marsh after sixty-two minutes. Three minutes later, however, the two goal advantage was restored when Best scored with a typical effort, taking the ball from Stiles before firing home. A fourth followed from Morgan, after Kidd hit the bar from an Aston corner.

That left four in the final six minutes, with many missing those last few goals having left before the final whistle, thinking that the evening's entertainment was more or less over. As it

was, Morgan completed his hat trick from another Best corner and further goals from a Stiles header, Kidd and Aston made it a night to remember.

Although struggling in the League, the assault on Europe was more productive with the semi-final stage once again reached, following victories over Waterford, Anderlecht and Rapid Vienna, with AC Milan standing between United and a place in the Final for a second consecutive season. The first leg in Milan on April 23rd was transmitted live to Old Trafford on six giant screens and was a vast improvement on the previous closed circuit showing against Arsenal a couple of years previously. A crowd of 22,429 supporters, paying between 6/- (30p) and 15/- (75p), watched the game on the 40 foot square screens, preparing themselves for the real thing in the return leg, twenty-two days later.

As far as those standing on the Stretford End were concerned, the match could

▶ **Under Seige:**
United in their white change strip, throw everything at AC Milan in the 1969 European Cup semi-final, 2nd leg. Sadly their combined talents could not force a way through.

have been unfolding down on the pitch in front of them, such was the noise they made. They sang, chanted and hurled abuse at the Czechoslovakian referee, although the final ten minutes or so was watched in relative silence following the two late Milan goals.

Although the second leg saw United two goals behind, they were confident that they could still obtain a satisfactory result on the night. With the goalless first half presenting little in the way of scoring opportunities for United, all was set for an enthralling second forty-five minute period. However, with only a few minutes of this played, drama unfolded in front of the Stretford End.

With play at the opposite end of the ground, a missile was thrown from the crowd, hitting the Milan goalkeeper Cudicini on the back of the head and knocking him to the ground. Play was soon stopped, with the 'keeper flat out in the

goalmouth, and as he received attention from the Milan trainer, the hooligan element in the Stretford End cheered and bayed "we want a riot". A loudspeaker announcement was made to warn the crowd that any further throwing of objects would result in the game being abandoned. This was something United did not need as they were just beginning to inflict some pressure on the Italians goal. Play resumed after five minutes, but United had lost that little bit of momentum, allowing the Italians to re-group and keep the home attack at bay.

In the sixty-fifth minute, with United now attacking the Stretford End, George Best broke away, bravely avoiding five lunging Italian challenges, before prodding the ball through to Charlton to score a remarkable goal, bringing revived hopes as the ground erupted. The wall of noise gave United inspiration as both the crowd and the players sensed that the goal required

to force a play-off would surely come. For six minutes, the ball hardly went out of the Milan penalty area, as Morgan headed inches wide, Foulkes came close to repeating his semi-final strike of twelve months previously, while in the seventy-eighth minute, with United playing at a frantic pace Pat Crerand, forever the midfield inspiration

of United's attacks, once again set things in motion. His cross, low from the right, found Law lurking in his familiar position close to goal and his side-footed shot crept slowly towards the Milan net with the 'keeper beaten.

Full back Anquillietti managed to get back and scrambled the ball out of the

vacant goalmouth, while Law, with arm raised in salute, was already claiming the goal as were fellow team mates. "The ball was a good six inches over the line" declared Law later, but the referee, a little behind play, did not share that opinion. Their protests were waved away and United's chances of making the Final evaporated in the evening

View from the Cantilever: *The Stretford End and Main Stand as seen from the new stand prior to the 1966 World Cup.*

▲ The Cantilever stand:
Above the new stand about to be completed with F Stand (adjacent to the Stretford End) still under construction.

▶ *The completed stand with United Road terracing beneath. The cantilever was a landmark for football grounds in Britain - no obstructed views and clear sightlines for all spectators.*

air. The repercussions from this match were to be felt for some considerable time.

The hooliganism which had sprung to life in the mid-sixties was now common at many grounds around the country, Old Trafford included, and was beginning to cause concern. Due to the missile throwing incident during the Milan match, the board considered erecting fences of some sort behind the Stretford End goal, but prior to the start of season 1969-70 they decided against it, although it was something that they would keep in mind if any similar incidents occurred in the future.

Never a club to sit back and wait for things to happen, with the opening of the souvenir shop a classic example, (a small kiosk selling souvenirs was also opened that season in the cantilever stand), United began to plan ahead with further improvements. Chairman Louis Edwards revealed in October 1969 that the board had studied several ideas of constructing a sliding roof over the ground, similar to the Houston Astrodome in Texas, which was fully enclosed and had cost £11 million to build in 1965.

The United retractable dome was estimated to cost £700,000

and the United chairman said, "This is essentially a long term project. It is one of many ideas we have discussed. There are other things to do before we get to this ultimate stage in the development of Old Trafford. Yet it is something to aim at for the future and we regard it as a logical step towards creating perfect conditions for football and for the fans who watch it". He went on to say that two plans had already been submitted by architects and had been carefully considered by the board. Like the earlier dreams of a 100,000 capacity stadium, it was something which failed to

materialise.

Other alterations to the ground were also mooted around this time, with the erection of a 15 foot wire fence behind the Streford End goal, one short term measure being considered. One other long term plan under consideration, in an effort to combat hooliganism, was to develop the stadium along "continental lines" by building cantilever stands at both ends of the ground.

The Old Trafford of the late sixties, early seventies, was still one of the best in the country, which was proven when, for the first time since 1911, the ground was chosen to stage an F.A. Cup Final. The 1970 Final between Leeds United and Chelsea had ended in a 2-2 draw at Wembley, so it was decided that the replay would come north to Manchester. United had actually lost to Leeds in the semi-final and on the eve of the Final at Wembley, had beaten Watford in the first ever third place play-off match.

Under the Old Trafford lights, on April 29th, the Londoners defeated United's Yorkshire rivals 2-1 after extra time, in front of 62,070, who paid ground record receipts of £88,000. The game was also watched by a television audience of some 28 million, a then record for an F. A. Cup Final. Over 75,000 programmes were sold for this match creating yet another record.

The replay was one of the most physical ever to be played at the ground, when a recording of the game was replayed by former referee David Elleray, he said that in the modern day game, there would have been six red and 20 yellow cards given out to players on either side. Amongst the numerous incidents were Ron Harris kicking Eddie Gray out of the game, Jack Charlton head-butting Peter Osgood, Mick Jones bundling Peter Bonetti into the back of the net and Norman Hunter and Ian Hutchison trading punches, while Eddie McCreadie and Johnny Giles lunged at anyone in opposition colours who came near them – Chelsea going on to triumph 2-1 in extra-time.

Earlier in season 1969-70, the ground was also selected as the venue for a minor representative match between England and Russia at under-23 level, but it was watched by a disappointing crowd of only 19,404.

5 - NOTORIOUS

▲ **Caged in:** *The notoriety of the Stretford End led to the club fencing the area in.*

▶ **The development of the Scoreboard End:** *and the erection of the later to be famous K Stand in 1971.*

OLD TRAFFORD WAS once again under construction as the 1970s dawned. Along with the disappearance of a familiar land mark, it was decided that the cantilever stand along the United Road would be extended round behind the Scoreboard End at a cost of £400,000, costs which would be met by the Development Association. This would create 5,000 new seats with further executive boxes

behind, and a paddock for standing supporters in front. Work was scheduled to start before the end of the 1970-71 season.

Slight alterations were also made at the Stretford End during 1970-71, but these had certainly not been planned, but were forced upon the club and as a result, reduced the capacity of the ground by around 1,500. Since the mid-sixties and despite

the repeated warnings from the club, police and match officials before, during and after matches a number of individuals in that section of the ground failed to take any heed regarding the throwing objects onto the pitch or at opposing players, forcing the club into taking action.

On his first day back in the manager's chair, following the demotion of Wilf McGuinness, Sir Matt Busby announced that

because of the past behaviour and two recent incidents when missiles were thrown at opposition players, the club were to erect special barriers behind the goal at the Stretford End. A pair of heavy-bladed scissors and a sharpened piece of metal were handed to the referee during the match with Manchester City on December 12th, while a week later, Arsenal goalkeeper Bob Wilson had to have a stitch to his head after being hit by an object.

The third round F. A. Cup tie against Middlesbrough on January 2nd 1971, was the first match following the alterations, which featured a buffer zone around the Stretford End goal extending as far up the terrace as the now infamous tunnel. In his programme notes for that game, Sir Matt Busby wrote: "Today you will all see the changes that have been made to the terracing behind the Stretford End goals. This has had to be done because spectators in that section have failed to respond to appeals not to throw objects on to the pitch or at visiting players, and my directors and I are most concerned about the possibility of serious injury to either players or innocent spectators who happen to be standing in the vicinity. We are particularly sad that this should become necessary and I never thought I would see the day when Manchester United spectators (I refuse to call the persons responsible supporters) would bring such action upon themselves and such disgrace upon our Club and the many loyal and well behaved supporters who enter the Stretford End groundside. We at Old Trafford are determined that these actions must be eliminated and again appeal to all supporters at that end to try and influence those near by them who are responsible and get them to see the error of their ways. We shall continue to work in close liaison with the police who have done a magnificent job throughout and these steps will make it easier and the culprits will be more easily spotted. If the behaviour does not improve, further steps will be taken but we sincerely hope that good sense will prevail and the barriers can be removed at some future date."

Sadly, Sir Matt's plea in the *United Review* was to prove futile, as during the game against Newcastle United on February 27th 1971, a knife was thrown onto the pitch and although match reports following the game failed to give the incident much in the way of column inches, the club were called before the F. A. Disciplinary Committee under a charge of gross misbehaviour, but the first hearing was adjourned so that further evidence could be obtained, as exact details of the incident were unclear.

Once again Sir Matt spoke out in the *United Review*, "I experienced one of my most embarrassing moments of the season recently. I had to stand before the Disciplinary Committee of the Football

Association in an effort to try and explain the lunatic behaviour of a tiny minority of our supporters." Relating to the adjournment of the hearing because of the lack of any exact details as to how the knife actually arrived on the pitch, he wrote: "The assumption was made that it had been thrown from among the crowd in the Stretford End, but no-one could be precisely sure. Had it been hurled at a player for instance? Or had it been dropped there before the game had started? Nobody knew for sure and so the matter was held over."

The second hearing did not take place until Friday July 16th and began with a ninety minute session in a Manchester hotel, where the Association Commission heard evidence from the match official, Mr Ken Wynn and Newcastle United defender Ron Guthrie, who had picked up the knife as it landed on the pitch. Sir Matt Busby, now general manager, following the appointment of Frank O'Farrell, and Secretary Les Olive, spoke on behalf of the club. They then drove to Old Trafford, where they studied the Stretford End and steps that the club had already taken, before meeting for a further forty-five minutes before releasing their findings.

The thoughts, opinions

and pleas of the United duo were of little avail as the F .A. Commission verdict was to fine the club a sum of £7,000 and ban them from playing at home between August 14th and August 28th inclusive, in effect, making them play their first two fixtures scheduled for Old Trafford at the start of season 1971-72 on neutral grounds. It was also stated that the venues were to be not less than twelve miles away from Manchester and they had also to pay the costs of staging both games along with compensation payable to the opposition club if the match drew less than last season's average attendance.

The search for suitable temporary accommodation to host the games against Arsenal and West Bromwich Albion proved a little difficult at first as on the day of the opening fixture against the Gunners, Burnley, Preston North End, Stoke and Everton were all at home. Blackburn showed some early interest in staging one or both fixtures, while the idea of holding the first of the two fixtures, against Arsenal, at Wembley, was soon cast aside, as the playing surface at the national stadium was being re-laid.

In the end, Liverpool's Anfield and Stoke City's Victoria Ground were decided as venues

for the 'home' games against Arsenal and West Bromwich Albion, with the first of the two being played on a Friday night. The first 1971-72 fixture at Old Trafford was now scheduled to take place on September 4th against Ipswich Town.

Perhaps it is of no surprise to note that several youths and young girls were ejected from Anfield, with the start of the game held up when hundreds decided to leave the Kop and head for the opposite end of the ground via the pitch. At Stoke, there were no reports of trouble or incidents during the ninety minutes.

*

It is fair to say that some of the football played by United in the early to mid 1970's wasn't the best in recent history. There were few great games to be recalled. However one possible exception was on Saturday October 2nd 1971.

A visit to Old Trafford by Sheffield United is not something that would normally stir the emotions or insight much excitement in the supporters, but on that autumn afternoon and with the First Division season only ten games old, the newly promoted Yorkshire side sat at the top of the table with eighteen points with United, in thrall to an all too brief Best rennaissance, second on fifteen.

On a fine, sunny afternoon, over 72,000 flocked to Old Trafford, of which 20,000 failed to gain admission as the gates were firmly closed forty minutes before kick-off, With the ground capacity, due to the building work at the scoreboard end, down to around 54,000, scenes outside were described as "chaotic". In the chaos a Sheffield United supporter was stabbed in the ribs as he tried to go through the turnstiles.

The visitors took the game to United, who were slow to settle down, with both teams having opportunities to score during the first forty-five minutes, Gowling coming closest for United with a shot that went narrowly past the post. In the second half, play again moved from end-to-end and with the game looking like ending 0-0, with only eight minutes remaining, a flash of genius edged the game United's way. The ball was played out to George Best wide on the left, with five Sheffield United defenders between him and the scoreboard end goal thirty yards away, but, as only the wayward Irishman could, he left them all for dead. Running parallel with the goal, he twisted and turned his way past Hockey, Salmons and Reece before swerving into the penalty area, conjuring up a gap as other defenders attempted to close him down, before

stabbing the ball past an equally helpless Hope in the Sheffield goal. Thankfully the goal was captured by the television cameras as it was undoubtedly one of the best witnessed at Old Trafford and one which is still re-played today. Gowling added a second for United two minutes later, with the visitors still in shock from Best's stunning strike.

The colossal shambles outside the ground prior to kick-off prompted the club into making their next two home fixtures all-ticket. In *The Sun*, reporter Frank Clough wrote: "It may have been fine inside Old Trafford, but outside it was a nightmare of confusion and chaos. I was trapped for fifteen minutes in the middle of it and it was the most un-nerving experience of my life. United are a lucky club indeed not to have a death or a serious injury on their conscience this morning. If ever a game should have been made all-ticket at least a fortnight before it was due to be played, this was the obvious one."

Wth work beginning on the extension of the cantilever stand, the familiar half-time scoreboard soon disappeared from the back of the terracing at the Warwick Road end of the ground. No longer would the supporters pass the ten minute break in the action watching the numbers appear against the corresponding letters. In its place, came the 63 character

Paying the price: *Look beyond this typically acrobatic Denis Law effort and the restrictions on standing room at the Stretford End are apparent.*

addicater - a new electronic scoreboard, placed in the top corner of the cantilever stand J section. This first came into operation towards the end of 1971-72, although many would say that the old manual scoreboard was better, and more reliable, than the new replacement. New floodlights were also installed under UEFA requirements and a necessary change due to colour television coverage.

The building work caused some upheaval to supporters who used the 'Scoreboard' end of the ground, as it had done to those on the United Road some years before. New turnstiles were opened on the United Road corner of the ground, with the toilet, exit and catering facilities below standard until some progress was made.

The cleared area behind the Stretford End goal remained as it was, even though it was brought up at the AGM when a shareholder complained that it was rather silly turning people away from games when there was accommodation available for some 1,500. It was suggested that wire fencing could be erected as an alternative, but the area remained vacant. It was re-opened, however, for the start of season 1972-73, and with the cantilever stand at the Scoreboard End now complete, Old Trafford now had seating on all four sides and

MANCHESTER UNITED FOOTBALL CLUB LTD.

OLD TRAFFORD · MANCHESTER · M16 0RA

13th October, 1973

Dear Supporter,

This is a short note firstly to thank you for your magnificent support and encouragement and secondly to ask for your co-operation with regard to the increasing numbers of young supporters who are running on to the field before, during and after the game and also the obscene language directed at the match officials and the Visiting Team.

The vocal encouragement we have received again this season has been very much appreciated by myself and the players and I am sure this plays a big part in lifting the team to even greater efforts. It is very heartening to know that we have our supporters behind us in this practical way and especially when things are not going right for us which is the time we need it the most.

I would now like to ask for your help in two other directions, firstly to stop running on the playing pitch at any time, whether before, during or after the game. This in itself is an offence which makes the people responsible liable to prosecution and the Police will not hesitate to take whatever action they feel necessary. This means amongst other things that the offenders will not see the rest of the match. The fact that supporters are on the pitch is wrong and potentially dangerous and I would ask you to help the Club by not causing difficulties in this way. We do not want to see the ground closed because of any incident or complaint that may arise, nor do we wish to put up wire fences around the terraces.

I also take this opportunity to refer to the use of bad language with the chanting and singing. After a period when this was much improved we now hear obscene words being used much more often and this is very distasteful and offensive to those within hearing. It certainly will not persuade the referee to change any decision he has made and the Board and myself would be grateful if this is eliminated.

I feel sure I can rely upon the good sense and pride of you all to help the Club in these ways and that we may all work together to enhance the reputation of the Club both on and off the field.

Tommy Docherty

Manager.

The Doc's plea: *Seemed to fall on deaf ears as events surrounding the Derby in April 1974 would indicate.*

was undoubtedly the best club ground in the country. For a second consecutive season an F. A. Cup semi-final was held at the ground. Liverpool defeated their Merseyside rivals Everton 2-1, while the previous year, Arsenal made a long haul up from London to defeat Stoke City 2-1.

Although the stadium was a superb sight, the playing surface left a lot to be desired. A couple of games had to be postponed due to its muddy state and the failure of the grass growing properly gave groundsman Joe Royle nightmares. Bingley Turf Institute were called in, and following a survey, discovered the newly built stand was preventing a drying wind from circulating around the pitch. This was considered to be only a minor problem, with the real cause producing the poor condition of the playing surface being a layer of compact soil a few inches below ground level. The job of solving the problem was given to the Cambridge Soil Service, who cut slits in the ground and injected sand into them. This went a long way to improving the condition of the pitch.

Monday April 23rd saw the curtain come down on not only another season, but it also the Old Trafford career of one of the greats - Bobby Charlton. Season 1972-73, had been a testing time for all connected with the club, but for the second time in those traumatic days, the man who had begun his United career on the same ground, scoring twice in a 4-2 victory over Charlton Athletic on October 6th 1956, helped create lingering memories for the supporters.

The first of the two occasions was on September 18th 1972, when 60,538 people, a British record for a testimonial match, turned up to watch United draw 0-0 with Celtic in his testimonial match, a game describe by Charlton as "....like the old days in Europe. It was a real football match and this is what delighted me so much. I wanted all these people to see a real game and they got it. Unfortunately, the goals didn't come, but that's football isn't it. I didn't want there to be gimmicks or anything like that and when I lapped the pitch at the end it was a spontaneous gesture. Actually, I hadn't planned to run that last lap so quickly but all the youngsters pushed me along. It was a wonderful, unforgettable night for me and it proves what wonderful supporters we have in Manchester."

Many of those supporters were again present on April 23rd to watch the balding figure emerge from the tunnel and

walk between the players of his beloved United and Sheffield United to receive presentations from both club's. Sadly, the visitors had not read the script properly and recorded a 2-1 victory.

Charlton did show glimpses from his halcyon days, with a long right footed pass sending Morgan scurrying down the wing, while also setting up Kidd to open the scoring in the twelfth minute. From then on, however, it was downhill. Dearden ran through the United defence, dispossessed Stepney and scored the equaliser and later, Eddy drove home a goal that Charlton himself would have been proud of. At full time, the crowd surged onto the pitch and congregated in front of the main stand. Charlton did make a fleeting appearance and speech in answer to their shouts, but his words were barely audible and in a flash he was gone, as some of the crowd swung from the cross bars.

Building work during season 1973-74 concentrated on the club training ground at the Cliff in Lower Broughton instead of the more familiar surroundings of Manchester 16. At Old Trafford, however, there was some upheaval, as Government restrictions, due to power strikes saw the club office hours alter with kick off times having to be brought forward to 2 o'clock, as floodlights could not be used.

UNITED 0 CITY 1

The game itself was never going to be a spectacle, but in the early exchanges United looked the better side. Corrigan was tested with a cross from Morgan, while Stepney did well to hold one at the opposite end from Summerbee. After 13 minutes, it was United who almost took the lead as Corrigan made a mess of a McIlroy lob, while Donnachie had to head off the line

MANCHESTER UNITED F.C. Ltd. OLD TRAFFORD, MANCHESTER	PADDOCK STRETFORD
FOOTBALL LEAGUE **UNITED** v **MANCHESTER CITY** SAT. 27th April, 1974 Kick-off 3 p.m.	Nº 3613
L. Oliver Secretary	Admission **45p**
Issued subject to the Rules, Regulations and Bye-Laws of the Football Association. No Ticket exchanged nor money returned. **This portion to be Retained**	As a capacity attendance is expected, it is strongly recommended that persons ENTER THE GROUND not less than 30 minutes before kick-off.

from McCalliog. Another fumble from the big City 'keeper almost let in Daly as United continued to press. With the visitors beginning to exert a little pressure, United were glad to hear the half-time whistle, but the second half resumed where the first had left off although it took United a few minutes to regain their composure, once again they came close to opening the scoring, with a McIlroy shot being cleared off the line by Barrett.

During this second period, the Old Trafford cauldron was boiling over and a flare was lit in the Stretford End behind Corrigan in the City goal. A number of people strayed onto the pitch, causing the referee to take the players over to the touchline until they were removed. It was later revealed that Corrigan had more than a flare behind him to contend with, as he had been hit with a dart while a knife had narrowly missed him during the opening forty-five minutes.

As the minutes ticked away eager fans spent more time looking at their watches and listening to other scores on the radio than the match unfolding in front of them. City were beginning to take the upper hand, with Booth heading narrowly over and Oakes shooting wide, both being supplied by crosses from the ever dangerous Tueart.

With only eight minutes remaining and a goalless draw beginning to look a likely outcome, City once again moved towards the United goal. A cross from Lee into the crowded goalmouth reached former United hero Law a few yards out, but with his back to goal. Casually he back-heeled the ball and to his eternal grief saw it trickle past the wrong footed Stepney into the net. Manchester United's days as a First Division club were now closer than ever before of coming to an end. Law, shunning all congratulations, was immediately substituted, and minutes later all hell was let loose as hundreds invaded the pitch, some attacking City players and the police.

Since winning the European Cup in 1968 and reaching the semi-Finals the following season, team performances had varied from memorable to downright dismal, with the latter being more frequent during season 1973-74. So much so, that a glance at the League tables saw the name of Manchester United flirting with relegation as the final fixtures of the campaign were played out.

Consecutive home wins, against Newcastle United, on April 13th and Everton two days later, gave United a glimmer of hope in surviving the drop. Jim McCalliog netting the only goal of the game, his first for the club, against the Geordies, before trebling his tally against Everton, with Houston adding the other in the 3-0 win over the Goodison Park side amid something of a carnival atmosphere.

A 1-1 draw at Southampton and a 1-0 defeat at Goodison Park undid the good work and with only two fixtures remaining, it was obvious to all that the result of the penultimate match, against local rivals Manchester City at Old Trafford on April 27th, could decide United's fate.

As the sun rose on Manchester that Saturday morning, it brought to life a city divided in its favours, the tension and importance of the match was obvious everywhere. To the City contingent it was an opportunity to send their dearest rivals into the Second Division, giving them more pleasure than any previous victory. Meanwhile, the red and white clad followers winding their way towards Old Trafford hoped that City would perhaps show a little clemency for their struggling neighbours and not give this particular 'derby' match the fire an enthusiasm of past encounters.

Before the kick off, hundreds of youngsters invaded the pitch on several occasions, mainly coming from the Stretford End,

▲ Relegation: *United fans invade the pitch in a vain attempt to get the 1974 derby abandoned having seen their team lose 1-0 thanks to a Denis Law backheel.*

▶ The madhouse of the Stretford End: *was a real concern for the authorities in the early 1970s. United were banned from playing at home on several occasions in the 70s, with the end packed well before kick-off, a contrast to the often funereal atmosphere at home games nowadays.*

keeping the numerous police officers busier than usual, as they attempted to keep the rival factions apart and the pitch clear. As the United players ran out onto the pitch, however, another mini invasion took place, as a non-descript voice crackled over the loudspeaker system "Please keep off the pitch" it was not to be the last such incident on an infamous afternoon (see report).

*

The remarkable events of that Saturday prompted Eric Todd, in his *Guardian* match report to write: "Law, you may remember, used to play for Manchester United whose subjects elected him to their exclusive monarchy and lauded him in such excerpts as 'We'd walk a million miles for one of your goals our De-he-he-nis'. They gave him a generous

encore when he returned from exile as captain for the day. They cheered him again when he trotted up for the spin of the coin." A couple of paragraphs later Todd wrote, "Eight minutes from time, Bell passed to Lee, and Lee to Law who back heeled the ball brilliantly past Stepney. Law did look a bit sheepish – 'Oh now you weep and I perceive you feel the dint of pity' – but being Law he just had to score. The Stretford Ender had only a few yards, never mind a million miles, to walk after this goal and reinforced by an auxiliary army from the old scoreboard end, they swarmed over the pitch in their hundreds. Mr Smith (the referee) led the players to the touchline while the police, hopelessly outnumbered as they were, managed to repel boarders in a three minute counter attack.

"The game was re-started,

and the Stretford End started a fire of toilet paper and programmes, hoping perhaps that a smoke screen would help towards the abandonment for which obviously they were hoping. Sir Matt Busby, another of the Stretford End unofficial kings, appealed for order when a second invasion got under way, but it was useless. According to the referee, four minutes remained when he abandoned the match. By that time, results had come through – they were not announced publicly which perhaps was as well- and United were down."

As more and more people found their way onto the pitch, it became obvious that the game would not re-start, and an announcement to this effect followed soon after, with the police inspector in charge advising the referee that it would be unwise to let the game continue. This led to even more spectators coming onto the pitch and they began to assemble in front of the main stand at the mouth of the tunnel, where a line of twenty policemen prevented anyone from going any further.

During the pitch invasion, some of the City players were unable to escape the attention of the invaders. "I was struck several times on the side of the head" claimed Willie Donachie, while Mike Doyle, never one to flinch at physical contact said: "I wasn't worried when the fans came on because I expected a few whacks." Denis Tueart, on the other hand admitted to being "terrified".

Over two hundred had been ejected from the ground before and during the match on a shameful day in the club's history, and it was they - along with those who had on several occasions invaded the pitch - who made the newspaper headlines in the days that followed. Calls were made to close the ground and a record punishment looked to be coming United's way as the afternoon's events began to be digested. Sir Matt Busby said that perhaps cages of some kind would be a solution. The final match of the season, at Stoke a few days later, saw further trouble from United supporters and club officials began a nervous close season waiting to see what punishment would be handed out.

"Clear the Terraces" proclaimed Frank McGhie in the *Daily Mirror*, "The Football Association should not close Manchester United's ground for a couple of matches at the start of next season. The FA should close the Stretford End of the ground for the whole of next season. And they also should make it clear that if there is any further trouble from loutish, mindless, moronic scum at Old Trafford than all the terraces there will be kept empty of customers and only seated fans allowed in the ground.

"I do not feel the Manchester United club should resent this suggestion. They - and football –will be healthier without some of the United fans, who are notorious as the very worst in the game, the dregs, causing

trouble wherever they go."

In *The Sun*, Peter Batt was not as to the point as his *Mirror* counterpart, writing: "Now that the Sunday morning sermonisers have had time to adjust their petticoats and climb down from their self-erected pulpits, let us get the Manchester United mayhem into perspective. A second look at the television yesterday only confirmed what we already know – that the 'villains, thugs and mobsters' we are being urged to get hysterical about are simply a bunch of children with microscopic minds. And when the rest of us are hemmed in by fences and barbed-wire, let us remember that we have been imprisoned by the reactions of the wise men to pathetic, pimply adolescents in

big boots and braces.

"The simplest solution is to put the old fashioned bar up – refuse them admission without their dads or a responsible adult guardian (the kids I mean, not the wise men). Your average gateman can pick out the trouble makers. That way the police will be able to deal with them outside the grounds rather than having to waste time and energy chasing them off the pitches."

One of those 'pimply adolescents' involved in the pitch invasion was actually a fresh-faced seventeen year old from North London, called Roy Coldham, who was quick to admit in the press that he had punched a police sergeant on the back and confessed "I only wish I could have kicked him in the head."

Having spent the night in custody and fined £50, Coldham spoke upon leaving court, saying: "I was standing in the paddock when the City supporters in the Scoreboard End started to take the mickey out of United. So when the United supporters jumped over the railings and went after the City fans, I joined in. I just couldn't take the slag from Manchester City fans. To me City is a swearword. I hate their lot.

"When Law scored against us and they started crowing about it, I felt like belting everyone of them in the mouth. I honestly didn't realise that I was kicking hell out of a copper. He was on the ground, and I thought he was a City fan. It felt great as I put the boot in. it gave me a lot of relief." Strangely, he predicted that "next season is going to be really rough."

The Football League later confirmed that the 1-0 scoreline would stand, and in June the United directors decided to take matters into their own hands rather than await the F. A's decision, and announced that they would be erecting nine foot high spiked fences behind each goal, which would stand nine feet above the supporters standing at the front and they would be seven feet six inches from the pitch. The total cost would be £4,500.

A five man F. A. disciplinary commission visited Old Trafford and were shown two specimen sections of the fencing with safety gates added in case of an emergency. The commission were satisfied with United's move and simply ordered the club to pay their costs, which amounted to less than £200. In effect, it was the supporters who received the punishment and not the club, although the commission did add that no games could be played at the ground until the fencing had been completed.

So, those attending the opening fixture of 1974-75 at Old Trafford were greeted with the unfamiliar sight of the metal fencing behind either goal. It was perhaps a deterrent of sorts at Old Trafford, but trouble continued at away games, something which United could do little to prevent.

United's flirtation with the Second Division lasted only one season and rather surprisingly attendances during that period were actually better than those of that fateful last term in the top flight. The opening six home games averaged 43,285, which was more than 500 a match better than they had averaged last season when, despite relegation, they were still the best supported club in the land.

At times, life in the Second Division did not go all United's way, but the supporters were treated to some excellent football, with perhaps the best performance coming at Old Trafford on November 30th, when promotion rivals Sunderland were defeated 3-2 (see report). Nor could they do anything to prevent United from taking the Second Division title some five months later.

*

Despite the more or less constant trouble at away fixtures, one type of supporter that United were happy to accommodate at Old Trafford, were the blind. In order to be of more assistance to such supporters, headphones were fitted to six seats in the main stand, beside the hospital commentary position, with the prospect of more to follow. Before the turn of the year, work began on rebuilding the main stand which was going to incorporate an executive suite with two restaurants. This plush construction would cost in the region of £500,000 which the club were confident would soon be recouped in membership fees. The interior decoration, including genuine rosewood panelling, luxurious carpeting and concealed lighting, was reported to be costing around a further £70,000.

A large window offered a panoramic view of the stadium, but games would have to be watched from a seat in the stand, which now had a cantilever roof in the centre section. While a separate section, reserved for the executive members, provided electrically heated seats during winter games. More private boxes were also installed and could be hired at £1,000, while other minor alterations included an area cleared in front of the Old Trafford Paddock (in front of the main stand) to accommodate wheel chair supporters. The television gantry on the roof of the main stand was also enlarged and improved in an effort to give cameras a better angle.

Hooliganism was by now a major problem facing every club and although outbreaks of trouble at Old Trafford were limited to minor scuffles on odd occasions, when the team played away from home it was a completely different story. Many clubs found their ground under siege when the 'Red Army' paid a visit and every away fixture seemed to cause problems of some sort. So frequent were the problems, a Member of Parliament called for Old Trafford to be closed for a year following one such outbreak of trouble at Carrow Road, Norwich, following the 1975 League Cup semi-final defeat.

A year after the embarrassing scenes that accompanied the match against Manchester City, 58,769 packed Old Trafford to salute captain Martin Buchan

and his team mates, as they received the Second Division Championship trophy prior to the final fixture of the season against Blackpool. As the players did a lap of honour, one or two over enthusiastic youngsters managed to get onto the pitch to run alongside the players, but as the players disappeared down the tunnel, the youngsters ran back to the terracing. Thousands were locked out of the ground with more than forty minutes to kick-off and one or two, either brave or foolish, or perhaps a bit of both, found their way on to the roof of the main stand in an effort to say that "I was there".

The match itself was something of an ordinary affair, with United winning 4-0 with goals from Pearson (2), Macari and Greenhoff and following the final whistle, the now seemingly 'annual' pitch invasion was very light hearted compared to that of twelve months previously, with the jubilant supporters breaking through the police cordon, clambering over the railings which were designed to keep them on the terracing and dodging the police dogs. The players, had already made a hasty exit, but re-appeared in the stand to take the salute of their fans.

By the beginning of season 1975-76, the Executive Suite Restaurant and Grill Room were catering for members of the public as well as supplying a superb a la carte menu on match days in the former, while the latter catered for those with more simple tastes. The same facilities were also available at lunch times during the week as well as non-match weekends, whilst they could also be hired for banquets, conferences and any other private function. This provided the club with extra revenue, with the Executive Suite having a limited membership of three hundred, at a cost of £135, which soon over subscribed.

In September 1976, an article appeared in the Scottish edition of *The Weekly News*, under the heading – "Why Old Trafford Is More Like The London Palladium", and it went on to say: "When a team has the charisma, not to mention the drawing power, sufficient to attract 56,352 people – 7,705 more than the combined attendances of the Rangers and Celtic cup-ties last Saturday – to watch them play a Third Division side (Brentford in the Football League Cup), that's what I call the success story of the season.

"And who else could it be than the club who have attained cult status by the murky waters of the Manchester Ship Canal, Manchester United. There, amid the cranes and warehouses of dockland, the magnificent cantilever stands of Old Trafford tower as a defiant answer to the doom watchers of modern football. But this great stadium and those 'house full' notices, are built on the vision and drive of a man who is the giant of post war football in Great Britain. Today, Sir matt Busby CBE slips quietly into the Directors' Box on match days to look out over the crowds packed into the vast stands….. and to remember the bomb

FOOTBALL LEAGUE DIVISION TWO
NOVEMBER 30TH 1974

UNITED 3 SUNDERLAND 2

This top of the table clash saw 60,585 click through the turnstiles that particular afternoon, with thousands more locked out, creating a tremendous atmosphere as United kicked off attacking the Scoreboard End goal. An early attack saw Malone clear a Houston free kick following a foul on McIlroy, while Halom tangled with both Greenhoff and Holton as the verbal (and sometimes physical) exchanges on the terracing bubbled over onto the pitch.

With only eleven minutes gone, the deadlock in the frantically paced game was finally broken. Watson mistimed a headed clearance and the ball fell to Macari, whose pin point pass found Pearson. The United number nine cleverly beat two defenders before scoring his ninth goal of the season. Four minutes later, having momentarily rested on their laurels, United were to find themselves 2-1 down, as Billy Hughes quickly took charge of the proceedings. Immediately after the restart, Sunderland moved towards the United goal and from a low Kerr cross, Hughes touched the ball home. Two minutes later, a fine solo effort by the same individual gave the visitors the lead.

United missed the opportunity to equalise in the twenty-fifth minute when Morgan's cross hit McIlroy in the face, with the Irishman only yards from goal, while at the opposite end, Stepney prevented United from falling further behind with two magnificent saves from Robson and Watson. At the opposite end, Robson should have put Sunderland in the driving seat with a third goal, but with an open goal to shoot at, he hesitated and the opportunity was lost.

Ten minutes after the interval, United were level. A poor clearance by Montgomery in the Sunderland goal was headed to Pearson, wide on the left, by Macari. The centre-forward's cross into the goal-mouth was steered home by Willie Morgan, amid cries of offside against McIlroy from the visiting defenders. Poised on a knife edge, the game could have gone either way. Tommy Docherty replaced Brian Greenhoff with Ron Davies and having had little time to ease himself into the game, the big Welshman's first touch set up what proved to be the winning goal. Swinging a pass out to the unmarked Forsyth, the full back's long ball forward found Daly, who in turn crossed to McIlroy who beat Montgomery from eight yards. United had to weather a few Sunderland attacks before the end, but the Wearsiders could do little to prevent United from holding on to their 3-2 advantage.

▲ *Looking towards the Main Stand, with the old players tunnel in the centre.*

▼ *Looking towards the packed, volatile Stretford End.*

was to build a team. Then if we did well, maybe a couple of stands would give the ground character'"

"'The cantilever idea came from abroad. Sheffield Wednesday were the first to try it in this country. I got the idea for the boxes from a visit to the old Manchester racecourse. I was invited into one of the private boxes they had there in front of the grandstand. It struck me this could be an idea for football. Now, of course, Old Trafford has plush glass-fronted vantage points right round the back of the cantilever stands on two sides of the ground. At the moment, the centre of the main stand is also converted to the new style roofing. The two wings of the stand will follow.

"'Wembley went for uniformity all around the stadium. I think we would lose something if we did the same. The Stretford End is part of the history of the club. It helps create, too, the special atmosphere of Old Trafford. There is no doubt there is a special atmosphere about this place. People come from so far away to see us play. To be here.'"

He then recalled going to watch Rangers play Celtic in a cup final at Hampden in front of 130,000 and how it was like a dream to go to a place like that, before adding: "I think Old Trafford has

become just such an experience for many people. It is a Mecca, if you like. Rather like a golfer going to St Andrews, because it is steeped in golfing history .I think our continuity of success has seen Old Trafford grow to that sort of status."

An interesting view by the man who was responsible for the way both club and stadium had developed over the years, but one wonders what he would have made of the present day stadium? He was certainly correct when he said that he thought United would lose something if they opted for uniformity.

In 1977, the Executive Suite was extended with the opening of the Jubilee Room next to the Grill Room. This area saw the beginning of match sponsorship packages, with the sponsors and up to 50 guests receiving a champagne buffet prior to a match. On weekdays, the room was used for meetings, small exhibitions and private lunches.

The building of the Executive Suite had involved extending out from behind the main stand, still enabling vehicles to be driven down that side of the ground. It did, however, destroy a familiar landmark - the Munich Memorial Plaque, which had been situated above the main entrance. Upon

devastated wilderness of 1945 when he took over as manager.

"'I often sit there now and recall that scene,' says Sir Matt, 'I sometimes wish I had a picture to show to people who only know the ground as it is today. I don't think they would believe the scene. The place was on the floor. For a start, we bought a wooden hut to work from in those days. We actually played a few games at Old Trafford when the fans had to sit out in the open exposed to rain. Obviously at that time I had no thoughts of building anything like the stands we have today. My first priority

◄ **The second Souvenir Shop:** *The excitement of badly dressed youths peering at early United merchandise is palpable.*

▼ **The back of the Stretford End:** *and the wooden hut which served as an off-shoot of the Souvenir Shop.*

the completion of the new extension, only part of the plaque was still visible. It had been originally planned to remove the plaque and relocate it, but when attempts were made to do so it was discovered to be to firmly attached to the outer wall and could not be removed in one piece. So, with only one alternative, the club commissioned a new memorial, identical to the original, which would be sited on the brick wall of K stand at the Scoreboard End of the ground in full view of anyone approaching the ground.

United's final League position in season 1975-76 gained them a place in the following seasons UEFA Cup and with the hooligan element still causing problems it was decided to extend the existing fencing right round the ground to prevent any crowd invasions and stem punishment from UEFA should any occur during their competition. The eight foot high fencing would cost £20,000 but it was considered a cheap price to pay to prevent any unnecessary enroachments on the pitch. Chairman Louis Edwards commented, "This fencing scheme has been considered for some time. It could cost us up to £20,000, but it's the right sort of insurance now we are back in Europe. We fully realise what damage a few stray fans could do, and we want to stay in Europe. Having fought our way back we do not want to jeopardise anything with the risk of over-enthusiasm from a small element."

With the prospect of European football returning to the ground, the club installed a new £50,000 floodlighting system, as the old lights had deteriorated over the years and the new system was a vast improvement. The reserves were the first to enjoy the benefits of the new system in a Central League fixture against Coventry, while the first senior match under the new lights was against Tranmere Rovers in the League Cup a few days later.

Due to the ongoing improvements, the Munich clock, the other memorial to those who died in 1958, was also soon to be moved from its original site, whilst at the same time, being replaced with a new one. This took up a position above the memorial plaque, a few yards around the corner from its original position.

The 1977 F. A. Cup Final victory over Liverpool kept United on the European stage for the second consecutive season and a better performance than that of the previous campaign

was hoped for, when a 2-1 aggregate victory over Ajax (2-0 at home) had been followed by a 3-1 aggregate defeat to Juventus, despite a 1-0 home victory. But as it turned out, this was not to be.

In the first round, a 1-1 draw in France against St. Etienne was overshadowed by trouble in and around the stadium prior to kick off, with rival fans involved in vicious exchanges. UEFA acted quickly and strongly, banning United from the competition, but following an appeal the sentence was reduced to a fine of £7,500 and a ruling that the return leg against the French side must be played at least 125 miles from Manchester. Following this announcement, there were no shortages of offers from clubs willing to host the game, despite the reputation of United's following.

From Sunderland to Bristol and Aberdeen to Glentoran, it was soon a case of take your pick for the United directors. Even Norway came under consideration. In the end, however, Plymouth was confirmed as the venue, with the match being shown live on closed circuit TV at Old Trafford, although there would be a crowd limit of 50,000. A figure that the club did not expect to reach.

The transmission of the match from Plymouth was certainly a big improvement

on the last closed circuit match at Old Trafford in 1969 against AC Milan. The BBC replayed the pictures from Home Park by land line and microwave link to a receiving dish outside the ground, before it was beamed onto six 30' x 40' 'weatherproof' screens. These would be situated so that every section of the ground had a clear and unobstructed view. Although the pictures would still be in black and white, there were the benefit of action replays. Admission was £1.50 to sit and 80p for the standing enclosures.

As the action unfolded at Plymouth, a crowd of 27,000 followed every kick of the ball back on the familiar territory of Old Trafford, chanting and singing throughout the ninety minutes. At the end of the ninety minutes, they all filed out of the ground and headed for home, without a hint of trouble. Television executives were enthusiastic about the way the evening had gone, declaring that it was the way ahead and the answer to the problems surrounding the travelling supporter.

Despite the inconvenience of playing at unfamiliar Plymouth, St Etienne were beaten 2-0, giving United an aggregate 3-1 victory, with FC Porto being paired with United in Round Two. However a 4-0, 1st leg defeat in Portugal

left Dave Sexton's team with a mountain to climb in the Old Trafford second leg.

With so many goals required, United employed an all-out attacking policy and it almost paid off on another memorable European night. Porto were swept aside in midfield for long periods and it took United only eight minutes to open the scoring. The somewhat nervous Fonseca, in the Porto goal, placed a goal kick at the feet of McGrath, who returned it into the penalty area for Coppell to hammer home. A better start could not have been asked for, but United were soon to find themselves back at square one, when Albiston misplaced a clearance and Gabriel put Seninho through to beat Stepney in the United goal.

In the thirty-ninth minute, a Hill centre was misjudged by both Pearson and Fonesca and the ball bounced off defender Murca's shoulder and into the net. On the stroke of half time, United went 3-1 in front, when McGrath's corner was punched out, but only as far as Jimmy Nicholl who shot home just inside the post. Old Trafford was alive as the teams walked off, with the question of "can they do it?" on everyone's lips.

The answer seemed to be "yes" twenty minutes after the re-start, when Pearson headed

forward another inch perfect Hill corner, for Coppell to score and make it 4-1. Only one more goal would level the scores on aggregate, but when the next goal came in the eighty-second minute, it was to the Portuguese, with Seninho scoring with ease, after dribbling round a stranded Stepney. Murca added a second own goal for United in the dying seconds of the game to make the score on the night 5-2, but everyone in the ground knew by then that United were out of the competition despite a memorable effort.

In the summer of 1978, on the eve of the club's one hundredth birthday celebrations, Bobby Charlton posed a question which led to much debate – 'Are United too big For Old Trafford?' With a certain amount of foresight, Charlton thought that United might not even be at Old Trafford in twenty years time, going on to say: "Naturally I am biased, but the thing that has made Manchester United great, and will keep them great, is there uncanny ability to be first. Old Trafford is something special. The atmosphere there is like no other football ground on earth – and that includes Wembley, Hampden, the Bernabeu Stadium in Madrid or the Maracana Stadium in Brazil. But with only a reasonable amount of success from the team, the Old Trafford stage won't be big enough in another ten or twenty years.

"They'll have to introduce the first two-tier all covered stadium in the country – or even move to a completely new stadium. And knowing United as I do, I'm sure they've even considered that possibility already. They already have a stadium that is streets ahead of everyone else as far as facilities are concerned. But in ten or at the most twenty years, even that will be out of date – and Manchester United are never out of date. They are a club who are never short of ideas. When sponsorship really comes in, the face of football will change, and Manchester United will."

With the club celebrating its centenary, a special fixture was arranged against old European rivals Real Madrid at the start of the 1978-79 campaign and it was decided by the board of directors that admission to all regular supporters would be free. Those to benefit from this decision would be all season ticket and League match ticket book holders, plus all other supporters who had between 18 and 22 programme tokens from the previous season. This was a kind gesture by the club, at a time when there was not exactly thousands in the bank.

The match itself was a nostalgic night, as members of past United teams filed onto the pitch prior to kick-off. Famous names such as Carey, Pearson, Rowley, Delaney, Blanchflower, Connelly and Charlton appeared on the pitch along with Jimmy Murphy and Sir Matt Busby, to warm applause from the 49,000 crowd. Representatives from every United Supporters Club also marched around the ground before the action got under way, with United making sure that their visitors did not spoil the party by winning 4-0. The goals coming from Sammy McIlroy and Jimmy Greenhoff, scoring two each, with goalkeeper Alex Stepney saving a penalty.

Although the club welcomed their supporters through the turnstiles with open arms for the visit of Real Madrid, they slammed the Old Trafford doors firmly shut into the face of former manager Tommy Docherty, banning him from attending a Lions Club dinner at the ground as guest speaker! Plans were almost finalised for the dinner in one of the suites, with the booking confirmed and tickets and posters produced, but the directors, upon finding out who the guest speaker would be, informed the organisers that Docherty was not welcome and the event was re-scheduled for the nearby cricket ground.

During the summer of 1978, there had been little peace and quiet around the ground, due to the constant noise of machinery as various improvements and alterations were carried out. The major work was carried out on the pitch by E. A. Yates and Sons of Sandbach, who set about trying to improve the drainage system. Three inch wide trenches were slit across the length and breadth of the pitch, to a depth of fourteen inches, and 230 tons of sand and gravel were injected, in a bid to try and find a solution to what was once a quality playing surface.

Elsewhere around the stadium additional safety barriers were erected, whilst the public address system was improved so that it now included the areas below the stands. Safety was perhaps the main area of improvement with a police and fire control room being built, along with emergency lighting, a new fire alarm system, fire proofing of the snack bars and a better communication system all adding to better facilities, at a cost of £300,000.

Since the mid-sixties, hooliganism had been a problem that the club, unlike most opponents, could not overcome and although it had been a little subdued as of late, it was reported that the worst case of such activity at the stadium for a number of seasons reared its head against Everton on September 2nd.

Taunts relating to the Munich air disaster from rival supporters had been around since the late 1950's, but on this particular afternoon, the visiting Everton fans inflamed the situation by unveiling a blue 'Munich '58' banner, which was obviously worse than waving a red rag at a bull. With the home support enraged, those nearest to the visitors began to throw whatever came to hand into their section.

This eventually developed into a pitched battle, which the police had much difficulty in controlling. When they went into the crowd, the banner was quickly passed around, making it impossible for the original culprit to be arrested.

In total, twenty seven fans were arrested, with many more ejected, and fines of £3,600 were imposed on eighteen of those at a hearing of Trafford magistrates. One of those in court was fined £250 for throwing a half brick at the Everton fans, while another was fined £200 for shouting obscenities at the Everton manager after being given first aid on the cinder track at the side of the pitch. A deaf and dumb United supporter from Scunthrope who "threw a meat pie at an Everton supporter"

failed to appear and a warrant was issued for his arrest.

In October, at the clubs' AGM, plans were revealed for a £500,000 social club next to the ground. Negotiations were made with a brewery towards such a venture which it was hoped would rival that of Manchester City and their Junior Blues set up. Chairman Louis Edwards said that the proposed club would feature a lounge room capable of holding between 500 and 600 people, and one of the objectives would be to invite parties from local schools to come and watch films of United games. The initial idea was certainly welcomed by supporters, who were without any real form of a headquarters or match day meeting place, but it was some time before anything

further was heard on the matter.

Unexpected refurbishing work had to be carried out on the Souvenir Shop, following a fire at the start of the season. Hundreds of pounds worth of stock was destroyed and the shop interior was severely damaged, causing the outlet to close. It was the end of September before it was re-opened, with investigations into the cause of the fire being carried out.

The condition of the Old Trafford pitch continued to cause concern, although hard frost also contributed to fixtures being postponed, as well as playing conditions being far from ideal when games were actually played. Drainage was also becoming a major problem. Soil in the trenches, which were cut the previous summer in an attempt to help drain the pitch, had become loose due to the frost, causing the pitch to cut up and the actual trenches becoming visible as dark streaks running the length of the pitch. Something clearly had to be done, but the board seemed to shy away from spending money on the matter.

The dawn of the 1979-80 season saw further mention of the proposed social club, which was now called a 'supporters club' with Chairman Louis Edwards announcing the new plans while the club were abroad on their pre-season tour. He revealed that a new £1m extension would be built alongside the existing Executive Suite in the middle of the main stand, with the cantilever roofing extending

round to the Stretford End. It would feature more private boxes with the main development providing two rooms capable of holding almost 1,000 people and would be given over to the ordinary fans, with supporter's club branches using the facilities on match days. With numerous branches from all over the country arriving at the ground early on match days, this was widely welcomed.

Upon returning from the pre-season tour of Germany and Denmark, the club staged a new venture at Old Trafford in the form of the first Open Day. This was attended by some 8,000 people and they watched trainer Tommy Cavanagh put the players through their paces, with bands, hot air balloons, police dog displays and other activities adding to the afternoon entertainment. Proceeds from the event went to the Variety Club of Great Britain.

Not for the first time, George Best put United on the spot. This time, he had asked the club if they would stage a testimonial match on his behalf at Old Trafford. A request that had the support divided in their answer. Many felt that the Irishman had a cheek in requesting such a thing after the way he had treated the club towards the end of his time there, on the other hand, others felt that his match winning genius deserved to be repaid. Having discussed the matter, the board rejected the idea.

The new £1m stand development, involving the previously mentioned plans, was given the go-ahead in October. This venture, which would cost around £750,000 and would be paid for from the Development Association operations, would double the accommodation of the existing suite, helping to reduce the extensive waiting list, whilst at the same time also make an improvement on the existing facilities. Although the major part of the work would be carried out during the close season, initial work would begin as soon as possible.

This announcement put shareholders attending the AGM a few days later in a happier mood, but did little to prepare them for a surprising revelation at the meeting. Following an influx of new shareholders, which helped towards the club announcing record profits of £2m, more interest than ever before was paid to the AGM, with many of those new shareholders in attendance. One of these shareholders, a Mr Frank Holt, a fervent supporter who at times seemed to have a weekly column in the *Manchester Evening News Football Pink* letters page and who had been thrown out of Old Trafford last year for barracking Mr Louis Edwards, asked why the profits from the Souvenir Shop were not shown in the accounts. Chairman Louis Edwards replied that he could not answer that question, and amid shouts of "why not", Sir Matt Busby stood up and said that the shop was, and always

had been his.

"Some years ago, probably ten or twelve, I had the idea of starting a souvenir shop" said the former United manager. "I started it quite apart from the club, and it is actually Matt Busby Limited. The club were kind enough to give me the facilities. That is the situation.

Does that satisfy you?"

Less than a couple of months after announcing their ambitious plans for the £1m redevelopment, incorporating the new supporters club, the Trafford Council Planning Committee blew the whistle on the idea by turning down the planning application. This was

due to numerous complaints by residents living nearby who thought that the new club would bring trouble from rowdy supporters.

One Councillor, a United season ticket holder, spoke of "an outcry by people living near the ground since the plans had been made public" and claimed that since the executive suite had been built, there had on occasions been trouble and the new venture would give youngsters the opportunity to obtain drink and cause further trouble. A noise problem and litter problem would also add to the resident's worries, in Railway Road and Warwick Road. The councillor went on to suggest that the club should build on the opposite side of the ground away from the residential properties. United counterclaimed that there had been no trouble since the executive suite was opened and

▲ **The cantilevered Main Stand c. 1979:**
Now featuring a state of the art television gantry and executive facilities.

◀ **The floodlight pylon behind the Stretford Paddock c. 1979**

they would certainly protest against the decision. Protests which never happened, with the idea falling by the wayside.

The club was later to come under further fire from the Trafford Planning Committee, when it was claimed that they had begun work on their new development without receiving the necessary permission. Councillor Marland, who had already spoken out about the plans said that pile driving and excavation work had begun, something that he had witnessed, as he lived near to the stadium. In reply, the club stated that they had only been having some work carried out on the drainage system!

United then proceeded to submit amended plans which would give a better view to some 3,000 spectators, a new restaurant and lounge for three hundred and fifty people, and a buffet room for entertaining supporters clubs. After much debate, the new plans received the go ahead and work could begin. The only remaining doubt seemed to be regarding the television reception in surrounding homes and the club agreed to ensure, at their own expense, that there would be no interference and they would give written assurances regarding this as well as on the subject of crowd control.

The re-development of the ground was all very well, but a more pressing necessity was the state of the pitch during the winter months, when games were often postponed due to it being frozen. Numerous matches had been called off over the years and cries had gone out time and time again for the club to install undersoil heating, but the club had always pushed all considerations to the side, preferring nature to take its course. It was now felt, however, that it was time to do something, and a special study was set up in the hope that a system could be found that would not endanger the playing surface.

On Monday February 26th 1980, Mr Louis Edwards, the club Chairman, died at his home in Alderley Edge Cheshire. He had recently been the subject of an ITV 'World In Action' programme - 'The Man Who Bought United', and the club had come under the spotlight for all the wrong reasons following the broadcast. Since he became a director, and Chairman in 1965, he had played a major part in transforming Old Trafford into the 'Wembley Of The North', and following his retirement from his meat business he had been an almost daily visitor to the ground and had recently moved into a newly built office beside the executive suite. His ambition had always been to generate the same sort of income through off the field activities as that which came through the turnstiles, and who was to say that he would not have succeeded?

March 22nd 1980 marked the date of the 100th Manchester 'derby' match, and prior to the kick-off it was announced that Martin Edwards was to succeed his father as club Chairman. His first appearance as chairman was soon to follow, when along with his City counterpart, Peter Swales, they walked onto the pitch to exchange gifts. As for the match itself, it was only memorable for the occasion, with the record books showing a 1-0 United victory. Neither side had scored in their previous three games, so the pre-match prospects of an outstanding match were rather dim. United goalkeeper Bailey was troubled only a couple of times in the entire first-half, while at the opposite end there was little more activity, with a Thomas shot bringing out the best in Corrigan. The second forty-five minutes, however, began with a bang. Jordan found McIlroy on the left. He in turn moved the ball wide to Albiston, who pushed it on to Thomas moving into the penalty area. The quick shot from the little Welshman struck Henry on the toe and spiralled over the helpless City 'keeper into the net. One nil to United, and that was it really. City did try and press forward, but they just did not have the players to break down the United defence, who on the other hand failed to take control and continually gave the ball away, much to the home crowd's disappointment and annoyance. The remainder of the game produced little and the 100th 'derby' match would be remembered simply as just another match (and victory) against City.

Fixtures against Manchester City are always high profile affairs attracting capacity crowds, with this latest being watched by 56,387. But such attendances at Old Trafford are nothing out of the ordinary and therefore each fixture is well policed as a major operation is put in force. Policing Old Trafford around 25 times per season was an expensive business, costing United a minimum £3,700 a match for crowd control, with the tax-payer having to payout another £2,600 towards traffic control and street patrols.

The whole match-day operation was run by a chief superintendent who had everything at the ground, except the director's lounge, at his disposal. The Old Trafford layout, with its fencing and small manageable paddocks, helped make crowd control a little easier, but from the mouth of the players' tunnel he controlled his 120 or so officers around the ground, (who would be earning £14-39p less tax for their four hour shift), with an exercise of tact and experienced organisation. The officers worked in commando type units, in positions where they could see and be seen clearly. One would be on the roof with binoculars while in close communication through radio with others, while outside the stadium foot patrols, mounted police, and dog patrols would escort opposition supporters from their coaches down by the cricket ground up Warwick Road, keeping United infiltrators at bay. A similar operation was carried out at full time.

The Stretford End, once the nerve centre of the United support, didn't cause as much trouble as it used to, with troublemakers having moved into the Paddocks at the opposite end, to be nearer to the opposition fans, where they could exchange insults and throw items such as coins, belts and the occasional dart. With the Old Trafford crowds being larger and at that time potentially more violent, the success of the police operations were shown by the average of only one and a half arrests per match.

6 - THE EIGHTIES

It HAD BEEN some time since an International fixture had been played at Old Trafford, but with season 1980-81 only a couple of months old the England 'B' team faced the United States under floodlights. It was the first visit to this country by the U.S. national side since the 1948 Olympic Games and they put up a spirited performance, losing only 1-0 to a strong England XI, with United's twenty-two year old goalkeeper, Gary Bailey, in the side.

Building work was progressing on the new extension to the executive suite. The stand roof had been further cantilevered, with the old roof support pillars removed as part of that area of ground development. This now gave Old Trafford five specialist function rooms - the Grill Room, Stretford Suite, Trafford Suite, Europa Suite and Jubilee Room and on the afternoon of December 13th 1980, for the match against Stoke City, the £ l.5m development was opened. It

now enabled over seven hundred members, each paying £360 plus VAT per season, to enjoy the dining and wining facilities along with a special seat in the stand to watch the game.

The Grill Room, which was situated on the ground floor of the complex, was open weekdays, 12 - 2.30pm and on home match days, but then only available to executive suite members until 6.30pm. The Stretford Suite, on the upper floor of the new extension

▲ Forecourt Portakabins:
The Manchester United offices in the early 80s would not have won many architectural awards.

next to the restaurant complex, offered an *a la carte* menu with window tables overlooking the pitch. The Trafford Suite, situated above the Grill Room, again had window seating with the additional attraction of an impressive showcase of club trophies and memorabilia. This was mainly an evening function room and could be adapted to hold two events at the same time. The Europa Suite, the latest addition, was possibly the most versatile, and was used by the Development Association agents on match days. Finally, the Jubilee Room, adjacent to the Grill Room, was also used on match days, but by sponsors, whilst also doubling as a small function room for special occasions.

Further alterations at the end of the season actually brought people swarming to the ground and they all went home happy without seeing a ball being kicked or any of the United players. It was decided by the club to rip up the pitch, taking off the top six inches of soil and then work in around 1,200 tons of sand before preparing a seed bed and sowing new grass. The scheme would cost around £40,000, but it was hoped it would create a much better playing surface and improve the drainage system. It was the first time for twenty years that the pitch had been completely torn up. Word soon got round that the turf was being dug up and piled outside the ground. In next to no time, cars and vans began appearing with eager supporters filling whatever came to hand with sections of the hallowed turf to take home

and relay in their gardens. Some were happy with a mere square of turf, while one fan from Timperley completely replaced his lawn, even incorporating the penalty spot!

The playing surface soon returned to normal, much to everyone's relief, but on the 17th September 1981, minor adjustments were made to the regular pitch markings with black sight screens also installed, as cricket moved a few hundred yards up Warwick Road from one Old Trafford to the other. On the night, just over 3,000 spectators paid to watch the Lambert and Butler seven-a-side tournament, with Lancashire taking on Yorkshire, and Nottinghamshire facing Derbyshire. The two winners then faced each other for the right to play in the Final of the competition at Stamford Bridge.

Under the lights, with yellow pads and a white ball, it was the likes of Clive Lloyd and Graeme Fowler instead of Steve Coppell and Ray Wilkins being cheered on. As the evening progressed, it was Nottinghamshire and Lancashire competing against each other in the ten overs, one innings, decider and it was the 'local' team that progressed through to the Final in London. Football, tennis, rugby, cricket

- what would be next to be seen at Old Trafford?

With the success of the Family Open Days, the third having been held in the summer, it was decided to begin behind the scenes tours of the stadium, as such things were impossible to attempt on the open days due to the numbers they attracted. A tour guide was appointed and supporters could book their tour on any day except Sunday (and of course match days). With supporters always on the look out for something different, they were quick to take advantage of this new feature, as it took you behind the scenes, giving access to areas that only a select few were privileged to.

Spectators at the ground on Saturday October 3rd 1981 for the match against Wolverhampton Wanderers also witnessed something a little different with the signing of a player on the pitch before the kick-off. This was normally something that was carried out in the confines of the chairman's office, with the press sometimes in attendance, however, on this occasion some 46,837 witnessed West Bromwich Albion's midfielder Bryan Robson put pen to paper at a table in front of the main stand, signing a contract which made him a United player for a fee of £1.7m.

His signing had something of an immediate effect on the man he was widely tipped to replace, Sammy McIlroy. The Irishman proved to everyone that he had no intention of making way for the new signing, by scoring a

memorable hat-trick in a 5-0 victory. The other United goals came from Stapleton and Birtles, in what was at times a stunning display of football.

The cost of watching football will always be debated, with prices seemingly ever-increasing and United taking as much criticism as anyone. However, Wednesday November 4th 1981 saw the gates at Old Trafford thrown open to anyone who cared to come along and watch a United XI play Sydney Olympic in a friendly fixture. The reason for the free admission was due to the fact that United were unsure how many people would turn up for the 2pm kick-off and the expense of gatemen might not be justified. Schoolmasters and employers were the only ones to complain and around 3,000 attended the match which United won 2-1.

Calls for the club to invest in an undersoil heating system had grown in the last few years and, following another winter of postponed fixtures, Chairman Martin Edwards finally announced that the board were to discuss the installation of a system. With the complete overhaul of the pitch during the previous summer, it was now felt that things could be taken a step further as the playing surface was in excellent condition. Money for such a venture would be no problem as attendances were excellent, with the 'derby' match against City on February 27th attracting 57,872 and most of the previous fixtures achieving figures of around 45,000 or more.

Despite the upsurge in attendances, avenues to bring in additional revenue were always being looked at and the United board soon released plans for a rock concert at the ground. This could bring in profits of around £50,000, but unfortunately in the end, all it brought was a lot of complaints from residents near the ground and the club considering what might have been.

The concert had been pencilled in for Saturday May 29th and was to feature Queen, with a crowd of some 46,000 having been expected. The gates were expected to have opened at around 9am, with the music from a DJ beginning at 2pm. Two support bands would then have played from 4.30pm, with Queen taking the stage in the evening. The concert finishing at around 10pm. However, all the plans were hit on the head by Trafford Council who refused to grant the club an entertainment license due to the noise and nuisance the concert would cause local residents. United protested against the decision, but to no avail and the concert was later switched to Leeds United's Elland Road ground, much to the local's delight and United's disappointment.

The only market that United had ever had shown any interest in to this point was the transfer one, but with running a football club becoming more like a business, any source of income

was worth considering, as the ill-fated concert had shown. A company called Kavanger approached the club with the suggestion of holding Sunday Markets in one of the large car parks adjacent to the ground, and United showed an interest. Like the concert, plans were drawn up and it was announced that from Sunday October 3rd 1982, between 9am and 2pm there would be hundreds of stalls in the main car park selling a wide variety of goods and it was hope it would become a regular occurrence. Much to Kavanger and United's dismay, however, it was not that simple. Both Manchester City Council and Trafford District Council opposed the plans and twenty-four hours before the

scheme was due to take off, an injunction was brought out against the holding of the market. United and Kavanger could have pursued the matter further, but after much discussion it was agreed to forget about the whole idea.

On Saturday February 12th 1983, when thousands of supporters should have been at the ground for the match against Luton Town and to remember those who had lost their lives at Munich twenty

five-years previously, the ground stood empty as not for the first time, a heavy frost brought the postponement of yet another fixture. As *Manchester Evening News* correspondent Paul Hince wrote: "It is really quite unbelievable in these days of high technology that Manchester United, one of the most influential clubs in world soccer, cannot protect their pitch from something as simple as frost. But why are a rich and powerful cub like United at the mercy of the English winter when only a few miles away, Oldham Athletic were enjoying a perfect playing surface for the visit of Middlesbrough?

"United's chairman Martin Edwards is aware of the mounting pressure on his club to move into the 80's by investing in some sort of pitch-heating system. He counters that the reds also have a duty to their fans and points out the dangers of having 45,000 fans trying to get to Old Trafford along snow bound streets and standing on treacherously slippy terraces.

"Clearly, the head of the Old Trafford empire has a point. But the streets and terraces were free of ice and frost last Saturday. In fact, the only place in Manchester still affected by the cold snap seemed to be Old Trafford itself. The Reds of course might be reluctant to spend the amount of money needed for an efficient pitch-heating system. But there are still good 'old fashioned'

ways of protecting a pitch from frost at very little expense." Hince went on to mention that Widnes Rugby League, with a fixture that same day and not wanting to loose the income from a Saturday fixture, covered their pitch with plastic sheeting, which was not removed until just before kick off, with the cost being less than £200.

United clearly had to do something about this on going problem, but it was to be a couple of years down the line before anything would be done. With the installation of under-soil heating pencilled in for the coming winter, contractors run into early problems, forcing the operation to be temporarily postponed due to the £80,000 drainage system leaving the grass little time to develop. The £60,000 heating system was to be the main project for the following summer, although it was disappointing to see it put back a year. To be fair, however, if the club had gone ahead with it as planned it would have caused problems with the playing surface in the immediate months ahead.

United came under fire again a couple of weeks later, following the fixture against Liverpool on February 26th 1983. With the teams holding the top two places in the First Division and also Milk Cup Finalists, many were surprised that the match was not an all-ticket affair. United, however, explained that when the decision was made, the average attendance at Old Trafford was around 40,000 and Liverpool were only expected to bring between two and three thousand supporters, which would leave a margin of 15,000 before the capacity would be reached. This was considered enough to keep the game a pay at the turnstile fixture.

On match day it was found to be a big mistake, as any fixture against the red shirted side from the other end of the East Lancs Road is no ordinary affair, and as kick-off approached the scenes outside the ground brought chaos and howls of protest. The gates had to be shut some forty-five minutes before the start, with thousands still outside and ugly scenes developing. Children and adults were crushed, while others collapsed due to the pressure of those behind trying to reach the already locked gates. Control was in total disarray with the mounted police being unable to restore immediate calm. Fighting also broke out as tempers became frayed. With a club such as United having such good organisation, scenes like this should have been easy to avoid. Inside the ground there was an attendance of 57,397 and a crowd the size of an average Third Division match outside listening to the noise from the game that produced a 1-1 draw.

Following the shambolic events outside the ground prior to the Liverpool fixture, there were countless letters from irate supporters sent to the *Manchester Evening News*. "Manchester United should be publicly pilloried for the utter stupidity and lack of foresight in not making the Liverpool match all ticket last Saturday" wrote Martin Watkins of Timperley, "well aware of the potential problems the day could bring, my friends and I made a point of arriving at the ground early. Queuing fifteen minutes only to see doors slammed in our faces forty minutes before kick off. The scenes I saw in that forty minutes were horrific – children crushed, adults collapsing, fainting, fighting, someone in a wheelchair turned over and trampled on and fans getting tangled up with mounted police."

Another letter, from P. Stone of Moston contained – "...having arrived at the ground around 2.15, thinking I was giving myself ample time to get in, I had to barge through the crowds to try to find a turnstile queue. This was impossible as we were all being herded like sheep."

On the same letters page, United apologised for the events and stated that they would obviously looking at future games in the light of the dramatic increase in attendance levels.

Following the F. A. Cup success against Brighton and an F. A. Charity Shield victory over Liverpool at the start of 1983-84, the new campaign, with the treat of European football once again at Old Trafford, was eagerly anticipated. During the summer, around £800,000 had been spent on various sections of the stadium, with everyone from the ordinary fan on the terraces to those fortunate enough to be Executive Suite members, able to enjoy the improved facilities. The latter were now given a view overlooking the pitch from the bar and dining room following a re-arrangement of the restaurant. A further £100,000 was earmarked for future improvement of this section. Catering facilities were also improved around the stadium, with twenty sites receiving a facelift over a two-year period at a cost of £150,000. New caterers were to be employed and a bigger and better variety of food and refreshments would be available on match days. The private boxes, an important part of the club's revenue, were also in line for improvement at a cost of £500,000.

Early September saw the club stage a successful Open Day at

ATT: -54,900
UNITED V NEWCASTLE UNITED
STRACHAN (2), OLSEN, HUGHES, MOSES
LEAGUE DIV 1   KICK OFF 3-00
STAIR STAND   BLOCK 53
170811304

the ground, with around 15,000 turning up for the charity fund raising event. Queues for a tour behind the scenes, at 50p a time, stretched back over the Warwick Road railway bridge, while more than 2,000 supporters paid £1 to have their photograph taken with the F. A. Cup. The day also incorporated a five mile fun run, in which Chairman Martin Edwards took part, and should have seen the ground close at 5pm, but it was nearer to 8.30pm before the last of the fans made their way home.

The amount raised for charity through the Open Day was minute compared with the sum that the club expected to earn during the months ahead, as a new League ruling now allowed the home side to keep all the money they took through the turnstiles, making a gate of 42,000 worth around £105,000 to United. With their involvement in three cup competitions added to the League fixtures, a figure of well over £3 million could be pulled in.

The business side of the club was now becoming even more important, and the previously ill-fated Sunday Market finally got off the ground, if only for a short while, with around seventy stalls present. Early in 1984 Martin Edwards announced that he had agreed in principle to stage an American Football match at Old Trafford, "If the teams are right and provided we can get permission from the local council. If it doesn't go ahead this summer, then perhaps next". It was hoped to bring together the Los Angeles Raiders and Dallas Cowboys over, but whether anything further would develop was open to debate and, as with numerous ideas in the past, nothing more was heard.

Friday December 16th 1983, was another date for the United history books, with the first live television showing of a League match from Old Trafford. The

Around the ground c.1982:

▲ *United Road and Cantilever Stand turnstiles.*

▶▲ *Approaching the ground over the canal bridge.*

▶ *Fans gather pre-match at the back of the Stretford End.*

fixture, against Tottenham Hotspur, was shown on BBC between 7.05pm and 9.00pm and was presented by Jimmy Hill with John Motson the match commentator. The ninety minutes were also shown live in Scotland, Italy and Poland, with edited highlights being shown in at least another 40 countries, adding up to the biggest worldwide audience for an English League fixture.

The game itself, a thrilling 4-2 victory for United with goals from Arthur Graham and Kevin Moran netting two apiece, (Alan Brazil and Mark Falco scoring for Spurs), only attracted 33,616 spectators, forcing the Football League to pay United compensation of around £50,000 for loss of revenue, as a 50,000 gate could normally have been expected for this fixture.

In the early weeks of 1983, attention drifted from the pitch to the boardroom, with talks of a takeover beginning to drift around Manchester. A £10 million figure was put on the club as millionaire publisher Robert Maxwell moved to the forefront of the take-over deal. Cheap at the price? His £10 million deal would bring him control of the club which began in a six shillings a week rented cottage, with a handful of players and staff, and now had the splendid surroundings of Old

Trafford to call home. A stadium which also incorporated eight chefs, twenty-seven catering staff, twenty-seven workers in the development association office, twenty in the club administration, six stadium crew plus players and management, along with a £70,000 a year rates bill. There was also the lure of a thriving commercial side, which had declared a trading profit of £600,000 the previous year.

The takeover soon snowballed and began to attract more newspaper coverage than the team's exploits on the pitch, as the price began to creep up towards the £15 million mark. In the end, Chairman Martin Edwards remained in charge and all thoughts of selling were soon forgotten as a European date with Spanish giants Barcelona loomed on the horizon.

The visit to the Nou Camp stadium in Barcelona on the evening of March 7th left United with a 2-0 deficit to make up in the return leg at Old Trafford. Although they had not been outclassed, an own goal by Graeme Hogg in his first European appearance and a last minute goal from Rojo gave United plenty to think about on the journey home. In the *Manchester Evening News* the following day, their United correspondent David

Meek seemed to sum it all up by writing that "United need a football miracle if they are to reach the semi-finals of the European Cup Winners Cup." A fortnight later, on Wednesday March 21st, a 58,350 full house at Old Trafford (paying record receipts of £180,000) witnessed one of those magical nights, conjuring up an atmosphere that can only be created at a midweek game under the floodlights (see match no. 13).

November 1984 saw plans put before the Trafford Borough Council's Planning Committee to re-develop the old Scoreboard Paddock section of the ground. This project, which would create stand L, would provide a further 1800 seats and fifteen executive boxes inside the stadium, with a new ticket office on the outside. It was also hoped to incorporate a form of club museum in this section, but the plans were still at a very early stage.

A few weeks later, on December 12th, an ideal quiz question for the future was conjured up - "Which European tie at Old Trafford did United not play in?", when Glasgow Celtic played Rapid Vienna in a highly controversial UEFA Cup second round second leg tie. Following dramatic scenes in the original second leg tie in Glasgow, when a bottle was thrown onto the

pitch amongst other incidents, Celtic were ordered to replay the game, which they had won 3-0 (winning the tie 4-3 on aggregate), at a neutral venue a certain distance from Glasgow, with Old Trafford being the chosen venue.

Further controversy loomed. Around 50,000 Scottish invaders took over the ground, (and indeed Manchester itself), but many brought disgrace to the Glasgow club and its vast majority of well-behaved supporters, who had in the past enjoyed testimonial games at Old Trafford. Trailing 1-0 on the night, and 4-1 on aggregate, trouble flared in the 63rd minute, shortly after a penalty claim for a foul on Brian McClair had been turned down. A spectator managed to find his way onto the pitch and with play at the  opposite end of the ground, punched the Austrian goalkeeper into the back of the net before Rapid players and six policemen intervened. As the minutes ticked away towards full-time, another fan encroached onto the pitch only to be tackled by five policemen, and with attention for the moment diverted, another fan found his way onto the pitch and managed to kick an Austrian player before being apprehended. It was later revealed that both assailants were in fact English-based supporters.

The plans for the new development at the Scoreboard end of the ground were passed and work soon began, causing a disruption to the running of the club and to the supporters. Temporary measures had to be taken and the ticket office found new accommodation in the vicinity of K stand in what was the Supporters Club office, while the Souvenir Shop was moved into temporary premises in the form of a large portacabin on the forecourt. The Supporters Club office, in turn moved alongside the Development Office beside the railway, while a new site had to be found for the Munich clock. After much consideration, it was decided to put it on the wall of the lift tower at the front of the stadium.

As 1984 moved into 1985, with the 75th anniversary of the opening of the stadium drawing near, opinions were being voiced that the ground should be re-named 'Busby Stadium' after the man who had done so much for the club. As modest as ever Sir Matt would not have been too eager for such an innovation to be considered, as he was always content to have the three great teams he created as his memorial. This suggestion had reached the ears of the United directors and had been carefully noted. Although they did not go as far as agreeing to the opinions, they pleased everyone, including Sir Matt, by commissioning a bust of the great man, which would proudly stand at the entrance to the planned

UNITED 3 BARCELONA 0
UNITED WON 3-2 ON AGGREGATE

Judging from the opening minutes of the game, it looked as though United would struggle against Barcelona's defensive blanket and regimented offside trap. So much so, that they managed only one goal scoring opportunity in the opening twenty minutes. That had come when Whiteside, reacting quickly to a mix up between Urruti and Alexanco on the edge of their penalty area, struck the top of the bar with a neat lob which ended up on the roof of the unguarded net.

With Remi Moses keeping a close watch on Argentinian danger man Maradona, Schuster and Victor poised the biggest threat to the home defence, but Moran and Hogg stood against anything that came their way. United though, kept their minds on the task in front of them and finally got the opening they were looking for in the twenty-second minute. Stapleton won a corner and the swinging, dipping flag kick from Wilkins was headed on by Whiteside and at the far post Bryan Robson headed past Urruti from close range, sending the crowd wild.

Wilkins, the playmaker in midfield, should have done better with a shot after thirty-five minutes, but put the ball wide from fifteen yards out, while a counter-attack by Barcelona saw Marcos also driving wide. Shortly after this, Bailey saved well from Maradona, as the Spaniards searched for the equaliser. At the half-time whistle the score remained 2-1 to Barcelona on aggregate, leaving the crowd a short period in which to regain their breath and contemplate the exciting forty-five minutes ahead.

Within seven minutes of the restart, United were 3-0 ahead on the night and now held the aggregate advantage, through a second goal by Robson and one from Stapleton. In the fiftieth minute, a back pass by Alonso created problems and allowed Moses to centre from the right. A shot from Wilkins was fumbled by the Barcelona 'keeper and Robson gratefully accepted a close range opportunity to level the scores on aggregate. Two minutes later, a stunned Barcelona found themselves further behind. Albiston's penetrating run and cross was headed goalwards by Whiteside, and Stapleton, lurking at the far post, sent the ball past Urruti in front of a rapturous Stretford End.

The volume of noise rose to a crescendo as the game went into overdrive, with Barcelona searching for the away goal which would possibly swing the tie in their favour. The Spaniards made a double substitution, while United replaced Whiteside with Hughes. Schuster was booked for a foul on Wilkins, Bailey pulled off a couple of excellent saves, while at the other end Robson once again came close to scoring. United, however, held on and as the final whistle echoed around the ground.

Sections of the crowd soon scaled the fences to salute their heroes and within seconds the pitch was a mass of bodies. Most of the players managed to find the sanctuary of the dressing rooms without too much of a problem, but the hero of the evening, Bryan Robson, was lifted shoulder high and carried from the field of play by the United supporters. Unfortunately, hopes of glory in Europe were dashed in the semi-finals by Juventus, who reached the Final with a 3-2 aggregate win.

museum, scheduled to be opened at the ground the following season. In addition to the bust, a Sir Matt Busby Suite would be incorporated into the new stand construction on the Warwick Road end of the ground. This suite would be for the ordinary supporters on match days and would be able to accommodate around three hundred people.

The early rounds of the F. A. Cup has produced numerous upsets and red faces amongst the 'big names' of the top division over the years, with the third round of the 1985 competition almost bringing embarrassment to United without a ball being kicked. Having pondered the installation of under-soil heating for so long and finally gone ahead during the previous summer, the winter temperatures should have created little problem for Old Trafford. However, upon the system's 'debut' prior to the third round tie against Bournemouth on January 5th, things did not go quite to plan.

The thermostats on the system proved faulty and had to be replaced on the Thursday prior to the match, leaving a couple of sixty yard sections of the pitch to be thawed out in a short period of time, with heavy overnight frost forecast. On the Friday the match referee, a Mr Brazier from Northampton, decided the pitch was unplayable in parts, but agreed to leave the final decision until 10.15 am on the Saturday morning. Thankfully the red faces (and the wrath of the travelling

supporters) were spared and at the end of the day the heating system caused more problems than the Third Division opposition, with United winning 3-0.

The 49,443 spectators who arrived at the ground for the opening fixture of season 1985-86, against Aston Villa, saw the further development of the ground for the first time. New seating had been installed in the main stand sections of A, B, C, and D, with a few of the forty year old wooden seats finding their way to new homes, as supporters prized a few away for souvenirs as they lay outside the ground during the installation. At one point, it looked as though they might be asked to return them, as the installation of these new seats fell a little behind schedule, with the last few of them being screwed into place just an hour before the match. Incorporated into the new stand section L was a 'Family Stand', exclusively for the use of families, with adults only gaining admission if accompanied by a child.

The 'Family Stand' was officially opened as season 1986-87 got underway, against Charlton Athletic, on August 30th, by F. A. Chairman Mr Bert Millerchip, who was accompanied by F. A. Secretary

Ted Croker and Graham Kelly the Secretary of the Football League. At a time when hooliganism was still causing a problem, it was a notable move by United to promote good feeling between young supporters, with families of visiting clubs often receiving an allocation of tickets.

Thursday August 29th 1985 saw Sir Matt Busby officially open the new suite named after him and this facility, housed on ground level at the front of the new-look main stand, was the first phase of the 'United Visitors Centre'. Its luxurious surroundings provided the supporter with a fine range of food and drink as well as an ideal meeting place, although to begin with it was restricted to Development Agents only. One of the unique features of the suite was a magnificent mural along one wall, painted by local artist Walter Kershaw. The 30ft long mural depicted the history of United from the early days of Newton Heath, right through to the previous season's F. A. Cup winning goal by Norman Whiteside against Everton.

Re-developing the ground with its Europa, Stretford, Trafford and Warwick suites and other excellent facilities, along with the changing faces

of playing personnel, gave the impression that the club had a bottomless piggy bank. However, as football in general began to feel something of a tug on its purse strings, United decided that after spending £2.5 million on the ground and in the wake of the European ban on British clubs following the Heysel Stadium disaster the previous season, a close watch had to be kept on the financial situation at the club, forcing them to shelve an ambitious scheme to build a £3 million, 8,000 seater, sports hall beside the ground. The club's adoption of a basketball team played a big part in the original idea of such a venue, but Chairman Martin Edwards decided that an indoor complex was something that could be done without at present.

The ban following the Heysel tragedy was not the only loss of revenue the club. A subsequent ban on alcohol at grounds also created a decrease in revenue. The law, banning the sale of alcohol at points which overlooked the pitch, prompted United to raise the matter with Trafford magistrates, as the main bars at the ground were out of sight of the playing area and as long as the supporters drank at them it was felt that there was no problem.

The success on the field, with the club hitting their seventh straight win at the start of season 1985-86 against Oxford United, seemed to boost affairs off the pitch with the club successful in its appeal to serve alcohol at the twenty-nine bars scattered around the stadium on match days. Worth around £500,000 a year in income, it was a welcome result, but it was not a 100% victory as a ban remained on a bar in the main stand overlooking the pitch and also in two 250 seater restaurants with similar viewing facilities. The magistrates also granted an application to the club to serve drinks for the hours prior to home matches and in some executive areas for an hour after evening games. It was also good news for fifty of the catering staff who had earlier lost their jobs due to the ban, as they would now be re-instated.

League, F. A. Cup, Football League Cup and various European competitions had been contested at Old Trafford in the past, but on September 18th 1985 came yet another first with a match against Everton in the newly created Football League Super Cup. Unfortunately United's outstanding League form (which had now stretched to eight straight wins) stuttered on the night and the champions recorded a 4-2 victory. This was actually the first time United had lost an initial competition appearance at home since that inaugural League game against Liverpool back in 1910.

As the winter nights began to close in, the evening sky around the ground was lit up a little brighter from November 16th, by a new 'Manchester United' neon sign on the cantilever roof, above what was once the Old Trafford Paddock section of the ground. This cantilever

roof now extended around three quarters of the stadium providing an uninterrupted view for spectators in those sections. Just around the corner from the new neon sign a completely new main entrance, with a reception area, had been included as part of the new office complex which straddled the road down the railway side of the stadium.

For United officials and supporters it was not entirely a satisfactory start to 1986, as a similar situation occurred to that of twelve months previously, with the under soil heating system failing to live up to expectations. On the Friday afternoon prior to the January 4th third round F. A. Cup-tie against near neighbours Rochdale, it became noticeable that the system was not functioning properly. Cold overnight weather did not help the situation and a 9am Saturday morning inspection brought little hope of the game taking place. A further inspection two hours later brought the expected

"match off" announcement. A team of experts later dug up part of the pitch and discovered that sections were corroded or burnt out, a mere fifteen months after they had been installed. It was quite ironic that having debated under-soil heating for so long before going ahead and actually installing it, the directors had made something of a bad decision with the system they chose.

Plans for a United Museum had been revealed some time before, but in the *United Review* of February 22nd 1986, supporters were given their first look at those plans and in the following five issues of the programme, an artist's impression of how the concept might look was included. Since the idea was first mentioned, numerous items had been handed in to swell the already large collection of trophies and memorabilia assembled by the club over the years. Obviously there would not be enough room to display everything, but

The re-designed forecourt:
Now without portakabins but with ticket office on the left and entrance to the Museum next door.

the showcases in the museum would cover the complete history of the club from the days as Newton Heath to the present, and would include everything from shirts and contracts to medals and match tickets. Interactive displays featuring videos and computers were early suggestions for sections of the museum, but the sheer volume of items made this impractical if as much as possible was going to be displayed. The Aladdin's cave of United memorabilia was eagerly awaited by those supporters who could not get enough of the club.

The doors of the museum, situated above the Sir Matt Busby Suite, eventually opened on Thursday May 1st 1986, when club President Sir Matt Busby, along with local civic dignitaries, present and former players, plus other special guests, including Duncan Edwards' mother, watched club Chairman Martin Edwards cut the ribbon on the £100,000 development, a concept originally suggested by the late director Denzil Haroun.

*

The frequency with which new goal posts have been installed at Old Trafford is not on record, but on October 25th 1986, the posts were altered to accommodate enthusiasts of the oval ball for

Two views of Old Trafford c. 1982:
The Stretford End as viewed from the Main Stand and the new cantilevered Main Stand and tunnel area.

the Whitbread Trophy Bitter 1st Rugby League Test between Great Britain and Australia. The prestigious event had captured the imagination of the Rugby League world and the BBC considered it important enough to broadcast their 'Grandstand' programme live from one of the luxury boxes at the ground, while their Radio Two counterparts used the box next door. Unfortunately the weather did not match the occasion, but a crowd of 50,583 (with many others locked out) braved the elements to watch the exciting confrontation which the visitors won 38 -16.

A week prior to the rugby fixture, Luton Town's League visit to Old Trafford saw the new floodlighting system being switched on for part of the match. The first full match played under the new lights was a Littlewoods Cup-tie against Southampton on October 20th. Gone now were the pylons, landmarks eagerly looked out for by those travelling to the ground for the first time, which had been erected in 1957. In their place were 216 fittings, with 2500 watt lamps, situated along the roofs of both touchline stands. Costing around £170,000 (not including the dismantling of the old lights), compared with £40,000 for the old 1957 version, the Thorn EMI system took just over five months to be installed by contractors Piggot and Whitfield of Stockport.

The F. A. Cup once again brought cold weather, and the annual disappointment of the under-soil heating failing to live up to its expectations. In place for less than three years, the board decided that enough was enough and that it would be ripped out during the coming summer, but thankfully the threatened Cup-tie went ahead, as it was no ordinary third round match, but a local 'derby' against Manchester City. Manager Alex Ferguson's first Cup-tie in the United hot-seat was only saved from embarrassment with the hire of a line of industrial heaters which pumped hot air onto the frozen areas of the playing surface prior to a 1-0 home victory.

April 1987 brought a significant announcement from Chairman Martin Edwards, and one which would change the match day arrangements of many supporters, with the introduction of a club membership scheme. United were the first to react on a government demand for football clubs to have greater control over their own supporters and the following season saw the introduction of a members only scheme for supporters wishing to watch games from either the Stretford End or the United Road Paddock. The proposed scheme cost £5 to join, but there would be additional benefits, such as reduced admission to League games, priority cup tickets and discount on souvenirs. The need to become a member would also apply to Season Ticket and League Match Ticket book holders in both sections.

With the ground capacity then standing at 56,000, the membership scheme would initially attract around 28,000, but it was hoped that the other sections of the ground, which were available to non-members and visiting supporters, might also become members only areas. That season had only seen five arrests at the ground, so trouble prevention certainly wasn't the motive behind the introduction of the scheme, which was not received too favourably by a large majority of the supporters.

Despite the concern and disapproval of many supporters regarding the new scheme, the close season saw the newly established membership office at the ground being kept busy with around 200 applications per day, as supporters not wanting to find themselves locked out of the ground once the season got under way, eagerly parting with their £5.

With Arsenal the first visitors to Old Trafford for 1987-88, a side who regularly produce one of the better fixtures each season, the *Manchester Evening News* United correspondent David Meek wrote on the day of the match that he hoped "United supporters had got the message that it was members only in the Stretford

End and United Road Paddock, or there could be chaotic scenes outside the ground". In an attempt to avoid this problem, United had the membership office open prior to the match and also a portacabin in the forecourt for supporters wishing to join on the night. However, such warnings went unheeded, with hundreds still queuing at the turnstiles when United kicked off, many of whom were not members. The Stretford End causing the biggest problem.

Following the match, United claimed that they had everyone inside the ground by 8pm, half an hour after the kick-off, but by then many had given up all hope of gaining entry and gone home, with the official attendance later given as only 42,890. This was well below the expected 50,000, and following the game, numerous complaints were made to the club by irate supporters. But thankfully, those early teething problems were overcome and the match going United supporters realised that the membership scheme was here to stay.

Scotsmen have always played a major part in the history of Manchester United and in the summer of 1987, the signing of Brian McClair from Celtic made him the latest in a long line to join the ranks. However, the part-time recruitment of Sauters of Stirling had the possibility of turning out to be yet another important acquisition for their ability on the Old Trafford turf. Whilst not bringing the club anything advantageous on the playing front, the Scottish company laid a completely new playing surface, along with the installation of twenty miles of plastic piping situated ten inches below the surface. This would provide what was hoped to be the perfect under soil heating system at long last.

A 1-1 televised match against Liverpool on November 15th 1987 provided the normal fever pitch atmosphere, whilst also producing some severe after match comments from the visiting goalkeeper Bruce Grobbelaar. The Liverpool custodian claimed that he was subjected to an endless stream of missiles for forty-five minutes of the match, having to endure everything from eggs and coins to bananas descending into his goalmouth. Fortunately for the club no action was taken, nor were Grobbelaar's suggestions that large perspex screens should be erected at the Stretford End to protect all visiting goalkeepers taken too seriously. The Liverpool match also created something of a record on the catering side, with 864 meals served on the day!

Three days later, on November 18th 1987, United had the unusual situation of playing an away match at home.

The 4th round draw for the Littlewoods Cup paired the club with Bury at Gigg Lane, but the near neighbours felt that it would be more profitable to switch the tie to Old Trafford. This fixture also produced the first senior football match at the ground when the *United Review* match programme was not on sale for a United game, as Bury produced 35,000 of their own programmes to be sold on the night. For the record, United won 2-1, away at home.

While mentioning the *United Review*, an interesting article appeared in the issue for the match against Oxford United on December 12th, stating the United Executive Suite had recently completed its largest single function since the opening in 1975. The event, held by the Electrical Contractors Association, was a two day exhibition in the Europa and Trafford Suites, with the Warwick Suite and private boxes used for catering, with some 2,125 meals being served.

As season 1987-88 drew to a close, it was decided that there would be no work carried out on the stadium during the summer months, as it was considered more important and productive to improve the playing staff and that any money available should be made available to manager Alex Ferguson. But, before the curtain came down on yet another season, giant Sumo wrestlers, jugglers and other forms of entertainment took over the ground on the 15th May

1988 when, for the second season running, the Rugby League Premiership Finals were held there. Extended posts and the oval ball were becoming regular accessories to the Old Trafford equipment stores, bringing in further funds for the manager's team building plans.

Midway through season

MANCHESTER UNITED FOOTBALL CLUB

ADMIT ADULT TO MUSEUM AND VISITORS CENTRE, VIA SIR MATT BUSBY SUITE

TICKET NUMBER 3,922

Price £1.50

SHARP ELECTRONICS (UK) LTD.

1988-89, the government began to make it known that they felt strongly regarding the introduction of an ID card for all football supporters, a move that United were very much against. So strongly did United feel about the matter, that they produced a detailed brochure - 'Football: National Membership Scheme. A United Perspective'.

This publication explained the club policy regarding crowd control, with the section on 'Background and Club Policy' reading as follows: "The impending legislation to bring about a National Membership Scheme for football will have a far-reaching and possibly devastating effect on our national game. It is widely recognised that the presence of hooligans in and around our stadia has, for many years, been a very real deterrent to the vast majority of the general

public who want nothing more than an enjoyable afternoon out. Consequently, clubs like Manchester United have invested huge amounts of money, time and energy in creating an environment which provides safety and comfort for spectators whilst at the same time offering every assistance to police officers responsible for crowd control.

"No-one would deny that in any large gathering there is a potential for public disorder. The way clubs like Manchester United deal with that potential offers, perhaps a more acceptable way forward than does a compulsory membership scheme which would effectively deter, or at least seriously inconvenience, a huge number of people who are perfectly law-abiding and respectable. Manchester United positively and actively encourages school groups and youth associations to attend matches. Indeed, by the way of an example, much good has stemmed from accommodating joint visits of youngsters from Ulster and Eire.

"Leaders see this as a most effective way of harmonising the different factions. Furthermore, a National Membership scheme could be seen by both public and media as totally unfair in that it would appear to discriminate against football when there is a background of incidents, too numerous to list, at other venues or occasions where serious disorders take place. As part of its policy Manchester United makes tickets available to supporters of the opposition

club. These are for specially segregated areas where buffer zones of empty paddocks and rows of seats (at considerable cost in lost revenue) are employed to ensure that there is no contact between rival groups. The police presence is appropriate and supporters are supervised to and from their transport. The Old Trafford stadium is extensively covered both internally and externally by Closed Circuit TV system operated by the police.

"There is a long history of total co-operation and liaison with the local police and no decisions on crowd control or match arrangements are taken without full consultation with senior officers. The implementation of internal polices plus the wider use of Closed Circuit TV together with the increased level of police intelligence gathering has shown remarkable achievements. Successful stadium management is also an integral part of the overall scheme and the falling arrest and ejection figures for Old Trafford over the years support this contention.

"Football, at top club level, has long ceased to be merely a game. It is a multi-national business, a fact which is supported by the type of companies which use the one hundred and three Private Boxes and Executive Suite areas which cater for over 1,000 patrons. Those responsible for entertaining clients from both home and abroad would not do so if the atmosphere in and around the stadium was anything like that described by certain sections of the media."

On the subject of the United Membership Scheme, the brochure stated that the target of 40,000 was easily reached and that the club had actually lost money "through the added complication of restricting entry to certain areas of the stadium to members only." The sections of the stadium that the United Membership Scheme took in was J Stand – 1,601 members, G and H Stand – 6,746 members, United Road Paddock – 7,118 members and the Stretford End – 8,767. The Private Boxes behind stands G and H and the Executive Suite added a further 539 and 1,040 members respectively.

Turning to Appendix B, this showed a chart which detailed the flow of spectators through the turnstiles for an evening match, with the Sheffield Wednesday fixture on November 23rd taken as the example. For the 7.30pm kick off, the gates opened at 6.30pm ("the earliest possible time for all the gatemen to be present") with 2% entering between then and 6.45pm, followed by 14% in the next five minutes. The highest percentage gained admission between 7.20 and 7.25. This was 23%, while rather surprisingly, 10% passed through the turnstiles between 7.30pm and 7.35pm, 8% between 7.35 and 7.40 and 3% between 7.40 and 7.45!

Appendix C showed a detailed season by season list of ejections and arrests compared

▶ The Scoreboard End:
K Stand became infamous during the 1980s for occasional outbreaks of fighting with away supporters penned in behind the goal at the Scoreboard End.
▼ The view from K Stand to the Stretford End.
▼▼ The Cantilever Stand as seen from the Stretord End.

with the average attendances between 1978-79 and 1987-88. 9,217,944 people passed through the turnstiles in those ten seasons, with a total of 752 arrests and 2,034 ejected. The season that showed the highest number of arrests was 1984-85 with 124, with the highest number of ejections coming in season 1978-79 with 430. Perhaps at that particular time the membership scheme was not profitable, although most if not all who joined did attend games. But as the years passed by, it slowly became a vastly profitable venture, with a high percentage of those who are members today never venturing anywhere near Old Trafford.

At the beginning of April 1989, United announced that they planned to hold a Pop Concert on July 18th, with American stars Daryl Hall and John Oates as the main act. If they were not available then replacements such as Womack and Womack or Chris Rea would be approached. The United commercial manager explained that it was an ideal way to bring in some revenue during the close season, but everything would hinge on the local residents supporting the plans, as previous attempts to hold a concert had always fallen through due to the local opposition. Once again, however, the residents in the vicinity of the stadium overcame United's challenge and the concert became a non-event.

With the end of yet another season on the near horizon, tragedy struck at an English League ground for the second time in recent seasons. On May 11th 1985, fifty-six people had died and around two hundred were injured as fire swept through the main stand at Bradford City's Valley Parade ground during their Third Division match against Lincoln City. Prior to the match, the 3,500 to 4,000 spectators who were in the old wooden stand had been in a party mood celebrating Bradford's promotion to the Second Division, but the fire claimed 52 lives.

This time, it was perhaps much closer to home, as on Saturday April 15th 1989, disaster struck at Sheffield Wednesday's Hillsborough ground not long after the start of the F. A. Cup Semi-Final tie between Nottingham Forest and Liverpool, producing events that the thousands who attended football matches up and down the country every week never give a moments thought to.

At the Leppings Lane end of the ground, (an area occupied by United supporters on several similar occasions in the past), where the Liverpool contingent were massed, a late surge of

supporters determined not to miss the action pressed towards the gates. Such was the pressure on the exit gates beside the turnstiles that a senior police officer felt it safer to open them, even though it allowed many without tickets to gain entry. This resulted in a massive tide of bodies pushing into those already congregated on the terracing watching the opening minutes of the game. The steel perimeter fencing,

familiar at many grounds (but missing from Bradford's Valley Parade thus saving many lives due to the easy access onto the pitch) prevented those at the front of the terracing from escaping the crush. Many were trampled underfoot in the chaos that followed, and a total of ninety-six died and a further one hundred and seventy were injured. Could such a disaster ever occur at Old Trafford? It is easy to write no, but one can never tell what might happen, however, with the layout of the stadium as it was, such a disaster would be extremely doubtful.

With twenty-nine safety gates around the perimeter fencing, access onto the pitch was at hand for every section.

The Scoreboard End, with a capacity for 4,500 standing spectators, was divided into two sections, each with its separate entrance and exits with stewards and police well in control. At the opposite end of the ground, the Stretford End with an 8,700 capacity, there is one large tunnel behind the goal, but with additional access from the turnstiles at one of the sides. Control of the crowd is monitored from a police operations room, while the club has its own control point with computers registering the number of people in each section of the ground.

With the fateful semi-final still to be played, Old Trafford was selected as the new venue, a popular choice with both competing clubs, as it had already been chosen as a venue for any required replay. So, Saturday April 29th saw Liverpool face Forest in the F. A. Cup semi-final, which resulted in the Merseyside club marching to Wembley on a wave of emotion and a 3-1 victory, to face local rivals Everton in the Final.

It is worth noting that had United not lost 1-0 at home to Nottingham Forest in the quarter-finals then the Red Army may well have been caught up in the events of the Sheffield semi-final. Merseyside had already triumphed at Old Trafford the week prior to the F. A. Cup match when Leasowe Pacific defeated Friends of Fulham 3-2

in the Womens F. A. Cup Final. A meagre crowd of around 1,000 watched the match, which some present said produced the best ninety minutes football they had seen at the ground all season.

It was something of a busy spell for the United ground staff, with the two fixtures previously mentioned, together with United's first and second team League games, a Schoolboy International (between England and Scotland), an English Schools' Trophy Semi-Final between Salford and Plymouth, and the subsequent Final between Salford and St. Helens, as well as the Rugby League Premiership Finals. While mentioning the above schoolboy fixtures, it is worth nothing that a youngster by the name of Ryan Wilson represented England and Salford in those games, and he would in the years to come play again at Old Trafford on a more regular basis, in front of many more spectators, under the surname of Giggs.

Attendances at Old Trafford have always been around the best in the country, but the 1-0 victory over Wimbledon, on May 2nd 1989, produced the stadium's smallest attendance for a Manchester United fixture since May 9th 1966, with only 23,368 in attendance. This was only slightly better than the previous number of 23,069, when United had defeated Aston Villa 6-1.

In the wake of the Hillsborough Disaster, United unveiled ambitious new plans for an £8 million re-development of the Stretford End. Early suggestions were to build a design similar to that at the Scoreboard End, with executive boxes at the rear and seating and a standing paddock in front. Although in the red at the bank, Chairman Martin Edwards felt that this was the way ahead.

Prior to the start of season 1989-90, United made something of a shock statement, announcing that the club had decided to reduce the ground capacity by 5,646 as a safety measure. The new capacity would now be 50,837, made up as follows: Stretford End 7,168, United Road Paddock 6,292 (both members only), Old Trafford Paddock 1,520, Stretford Paddock 6,357, Scoreboard Paddock 3,742 (visitors section). The remainder consisting of the seating sections. Much should be made of this decision, as the income that those 5,000 supporters could generate was not to be sniffed at, but for once, United proved that they did think about their supporters and in particular their safety, when watching football at Old Trafford.

Over the years, Old Trafford has not produced much in the way of pre-match entertainment, having to drift back to the fifties for anything on a regular basis, this coming from the Beswick Prize Band. However, such pre-match entertainment will never be the same again following the events that preceded the United .v. Arsenal opening day fixture on Saturday August 19th 1989, when both sets of supporters stood open mouthed as a figure in a United track suit top and shorts emerged from the tunnel and proceeded to juggle a football towards the Stretford End goal, before smashing the ball into the back of the net and saluting the crowd. The sun-drenched 47,245 spectators had never witnessed anything like it, and the name of Michael Knighton was soon to be on everyone's lips.

Knighton's name appeared from nowhere and surfaced in relation to a proposed takeover of the club. This eventually fell through amid acres of newsprint and speculation, with Knighton obtaining a seat on the board and eventually taking over another United – Carlisle. If he had succeeded with his plans for becoming the United supremo, who knows what would have happened. One of his early proposals was a one hundred and sixty bed hotel adjoining the Stretford End as part of £10 million ground improvements, part of the reason behind Martin Edwards agreeing to sell the club for £20 million!

The Hillsborough disaster had repercussions throughout football, with every club having to deal with ground alterations and developments in a different manner, United being no exception. Following a visit from the Greater Manchester Fire and Civil Defence Authorities, after fans disappointed with United's performance against Norwich City on August 30th 1990 (a 2-0 defeat), tried to leave the ground earlier then normal, they found themselves locked in. Apparently, the gates were normally opened midway through the second half, but on this occasion they had been missed and it took some time to find the keys. United were asked to unlock all the gates or face the prospects of matches being postponed. The local authorities hoped that the club might be prepared to consider installing hi-tech electronic gates, at a cost of around £400,000. The club acted quickly and while not intending to install the electronic gates for the time being, it was agreed to have each exit gate individually supervised throughout each fixture, with all the gates being unlocked shortly after kick-off.

For many players, a visit to Old Trafford could prove a nervous, daunting affair, so what was it like for a supporter of the visiting team. Although there were still occasional confrontations between groups of rival fans, it was nothing like the 'wild-west' days of the previous decades. On December 8th, Leeds United visited Manchester for what is one of the most troublesome fixtures of the season. United had already taken the precaution of suspending the club membership scheme in order to stop any Leeds United supporter from joining and gaining entry to an area occupied by home supporters.

A total of 3,500 visiting supporters would already be in attendance, in their own segregated area and they would be well policed due to their well known reputation. Because of this, the Leeds directors had decided to attend games with the normal fans, forgoing the comfort, not to mention safety, with Peter Ridsdale going into the lions' den of Old Trafford. So, what did he make of the experience?

"I was delighted with the whole afternoon and I thought the police handled themselves impeccably. I can only say that apart from one very brief incident, when coins were thrown down at us from Manchester fans, that the terraces were safe."

It was suggested that a potential catalyst for disorder was prevented because seventy-five policemen positioned themselves at the front and sides of the seated area, while the front three rows of seats were left empty, as the visiting fans have massed ranks of home supporters sitting above and behind them

Ridsdale went on: "The police were objective especially in the second half when a few coins were thrown. They quickly stepped in behind us to stamp it out, whoever was misbehaving. I also liked the way the policemen made sure the youngsters present had the opportunity to get to the front where they could see everything. I spotted a couple of occasions when the fans became over-excited and gave the police reason to intervene. They sensibly gave the lads a warning, told them to behave themselves and they did that." Such measures did not come cheap, however, as that season's police bill for games at Old Trafford came to £172,841.

A hostile shareholders meeting on January 10th 1991, disrupted by a bomb scare and much heckling (directed at the top table), brought cries for Chairman Martin Edwards to sell his 57% holding in the club. Surprisingly it was something that he admitted he would consider. A consortium, made up of United directors Amer Midani, Nigel Burrows and Michael Edelson soon became firm favourites to gain control of the troubled club, but as deadlock loomed between the two parties, a group of property developers began to show their interest. They were, however, not interested in the club as a footballing concern, but had an eye for the ground and the surrounding area owned by United, with nearby Salford Docks and Trafford Park already earmarked for re-development, the potential of the Old Trafford site was obvious. The prospect of buying the ground and leasing it back to the club just did not bear thinking about. Speculation raged for some

time over the future of the club, but at the end of the day, the pressure which had been on manager Alex Ferguson as well as Chairman Martin Edwards waned considerably, and the running of the club returned to a form of normality as results and performances improved.

In mid-March, with the Wembley bandwagon gathering momentum as United strode towards the semi-finals, supporters were taken aback with the announcement of plans for a new Manchester 'super stadium' at a cost of around £200 million. With the city hoping to stage the 1996 Olympic Games, such a stadium would be a major requirement, and a site at Barton Cross was seen as ideal for the 80,000 all-seated venue. What upset supporters so much was the suggestion that the new stadium would be shared by both City and United, with their present homes being vacated. Was this indeed something for the future?

Meanwhile, at Old Trafford the fencing surrounding the pitch was reduced in height to 2.1m following just one of the forty-three recommendations in the Lord Justice Taylor's Hillsborough report. This was no easy job, as the specialist cutting gear brought in to do the job failed to cut through the extremely tough fencing, as fire crews looked on in amazement. New electronically controlled exit gates, costing around £140,000, were also installed, which would be of help with the movement of supporters in any

emergency.

After winning the F. A. Cup, following a replay against Crystal Palace, manager Alex Ferguson now had a close season break to assess the playing squad for the European campaign ahead, while the directors announced their plans for further re-development of the stadium. With Lord Justice Taylor's Report being endorsed by the government, all First and Second Division stadiums were required to be all-seated. This meant that the Stretford End, the main standing area of the ground, with a capacity of 7,168, would soon become a mere memory to generations of United supporters.

While some clubs' in the lower division would be quite content just to install wooden bench seating to the existing terracing, United decided to progress as had been originally intended, way back in 1965, and continue the cantilever roof right round the ground, resulting in the complete re-development of the Stretford End. Due to the huge cost involved, and there being no immediate rush into this major undertaking, the close season of 1990 saw only a little step along the way to making the ground all-seated, with the United Road Paddock being converted to accommodate 6,292 seated spectators.

7 - TERRACING'S LAST STAND

UNITED'S MEMBERSHIP SCHEME still experienced difficulties, with the non-arrival of membership cards at the start of season 1990-91 resulting in about seven hundred supporters being locked out of the opening fixture against Coventry City on August 25th. Temporary memberships were issued, but failed to ease the problem, with many clearly unhappy at having paid £7 to join the scheme only to miss the opening match of the season.

Following the dramatic Lee Martin winner in the F.A. Cup Final replay against Crystal Palace, United looked forward to competing in European football again, in the Cup-Winners Cup, as the ban on English clubs in all European competitions was now lifted. The first European fixture at Old Trafford since Videoton's visit in 1984-85 brought another unknown Hungarian side to Manchester, in the form of Pecsi Munkas and for some supporters in the newly named North Stand Lower it was watched from behind higher than normal fences, as UEFA regulations forced United to put the new safety fence at full height for all European fixtures. This did little to spoil the supporter's enjoyment as United celebrated their return to Europe with a 2-0 victory. The attendance, however, was a disappointing 28,411, the lowest to attend a European match, a record which stretched to some thirty-eight home ties.

Live screening of the match by ITV certainly affected the

The Stretford Groundside and Paddock - 9th February 1991
▲ *A year before they were bulldozed the old terraces, decked out with yellow safety paint, await their sad fate.*

numbers, which in normal circumstances would have brought a passionate full house to Old Trafford as had similar nights in the past. A night, thought by many as a typical Manchester autumn evening of driving rain and blustery winds, did not help much either, in persuading many to leave their armchairs, but the £300,000 offered by ITV for the live showing of both legs was enough for United.

Seventeen days later, on October 20th 1990, hooligan type behaviour reared its ugly head again before 47,232 spectators at Old Trafford plus thousands more on ITV's football highlights programme. The fighting dominated news programmes later that evening but it was the United and Arsenal players who went toe-to-toe rather than rival supporters as a mass twenty-one man brawl began in front of the main stand; what is it about United – Arsenal fixtures at Old Trafford?

In the 60th minute of the match, with Arsenal leading 1-0, a touchline clash between Anders Limpar and Dennis Irwin prompted the involvement of Brian McClair and Nigel Winterburn (who had a personal enmity dating back to a cup tie at Highbury a few seasons before), as referee Keith Hackett moved in to quell their anger. Within a minute, a further challenge by both Limpar and Winterburn on Irwin, brought not only McClair back into the fray, but also every

other player on the pitch, with the exception of Seaman the Arsenal goalkeeper. Despite the attempted intervention of both benches, the squabble continued for some two minutes before calm was restored. Surprisingly, the only action taken by the referee was to book Limpar and Winterburn. The resulting F.A. Commission proved costly to both clubs' with a £50,000 fine and the loss of two points to Arsenal and a similar fine but with only a one point deduction

◄ **An original Archibald Leitch crash barrier**: One of the last remnants of the famous football architect's legacy at Old Trafford. The Glaswegian was prolific designing the likes of Ibrox, Goodison, Stamford Bridge and Anfield to name but a few.

for United.

With Christmas on the horizon, United would soon raise the money to pay their fine through the takings from the revamped Souvenir Shop, with around one thousand supporters per hour passing through the doors on a match day, keeping the staff on their toes. The shop, a far cry from the small wooden hut which first sold a handful of United Souvenirs in the mid-sixties, now contained a vast catalogue of goods and catered for every taste and pocket, pushing United to the forefront of merchandising.

Although money once again seemed to be no problem for the club, they always welcomed the lump sums available in the forms of grants for ground improvements. In early February, the Football Trust awarded the club £132,000 to help pay for the installation of seats in the North Stand Lower. It was hoped the sum of around £2 million would follow at a later date when the Stretford End would be turned into an all-seated section, at a cost of around £13 million. An additional £1 million was also paid out in the summer of 1991 to install seating in front of stands B and C (the main stand)

and replace existing seating in F, G, H and J (the United Road stand). The latter would be done in red and white making the word Manchester, with the United on the seats in the lower section.

The European campaign, which had begun back in September, ended in triumph against Spanish giants Barcelona in Rotterdam. This third Cup Final appearance in a year, following the Rumbellow's Cup defeat against Sheffield Wednesday a few weeks previously and the F. A. Cup victory the previous May, helped towards the announcement of a £5.5 million profit and played a major part in the decision to go float the clubs shares on the Stock Exchange. Shares would be sold at £3.85 valuing the club at £47 million.

The visit of Everton on March 2nd 1991, a 2-0 defeat, brought further complaints regarding the state of the Old Trafford playing surface. In his match summary, John Roberts of *The Independent* wrote: "During the club's pioneering days in Europe, the Busby Babes would hone their skills by practising on the Old Trafford pitch. The groundsman's objections ceased after he was asked whether it was better to have the best pitch and the worst team or the best team and the worst pitch. These days United do not have the best team, as the League table shows, and their pitch must be among the worst in top-flight football."

Colin Malam in the *Daily Telegraph* was also critical of

the conditions, "Manchester United's pitch is now a disgrace and should be dug up as soon as possible." While Everton manager Howard Kendall said: "The pitch is awful. The surface moves. Derby did win the championship on a muddy pitch, but this one actually moves under your feet."

But despite the condition of the playing surface, and the defeat, there was one ray of sunshine relating to this particular match, with the debut of seventeen year old Ryan Giggs. For many, an Old Trafford debut can mark the start of a promising playing career, but for others, like Albert Kinsey, against Chester in an F.A. Cup tie in 1965 and Peter Beardsley in 1982 their initial Old Trafford appearances were their one and only in the famous red shirt. For Giggs, making his debut as a replacement for Denis Irwin, few in the 45,656 crowd could have imagined the path his career would follow in the years ahead.

The playing surface was surprisingly still causing problems, but although United brought the curtain down on a memorable season on May 29th with the visit of Tottenham Hotspur, some of the necessary work could not be carried out for almost three weeks due to the England Challenge Cup match between Argentina and USSR, and after numerous attempts over the years, a rock concert, starring football loving superstar Rod Stewart backed by Status Quo and Joe Cocker. Earlier in the month United had also

hosted the Rugby Premiership Finals.

A crowd of 39,900 attended the concert on Friday June 7th to listen to the gravel voiced singer and the support acts churn out their hits from the stage built in front of the Stretford End. Entrance on the night was through the turnstiles on the Warwick Road End of the ground with the hallowed turf accommodating much of the crowd.

Pre-season friendlies are normally rather meaningless affairs and used merely as workouts for the months ahead. Included in the fixtures arranged for the summer of 1991, however, was one that meant much more to anyone with an interest in United and a game that would not simply be dismissed - a testimonial match for Sir Matt Busby, against the Republic of Ireland on August 11th. A pre-match curtain raiser saw some of the players who enabled Sir Matt to achieve his dream of lifting the European Cup in 1968, take on a team of former Manchester City players. A little thinner on top and broader around the waist perhaps, but the 33,410 crowd still warmed to the talents of Brian Kidd, David Sadler, Pat Crerand, Bobby Charlton and the still enigmatic George Best, before Sir Matt appeared on the touchline to a tremendous ovation and was presented to the crowd and both teams. Sadly United could not produce a victory for the club President, being held to a 1-1 draw by a strong Republic team.

▲ From the Stretford End to the Executive Box.

Following the visit of Arsenal to Old Trafford on October 19th, many United supporters were up in arms not because of Peter Schmeichel's own goal giving the Londoners a share of the points, but because hundreds were locked out, leading to the fear that similar situations could become commonplace next season. Back in those halcyon days of Messrs Best, Law and co., Old Trafford could safely accommodate some 60,000 odd spectators, but by now, the capacity had shrunk to nearer 40,000, with 43,000 being the limit when the ground would become all seated with the reconstruction of the Stretford End.

One fanzine editor commented that "the club should be thinking of making Old Trafford bigger, not smaller," with chairman Martin Edwards replying: "It's financially unrealistic, short of knocking the entire stadium down and starting all over again, which would cost £60m. And where would we play in the meantime? The problem is the insistence of the government through the Justice Taylor Report that every ground must be all-seater.

"Our initial strategy for a 53,000 ground was sound, but in a stroke Taylor destroyed our plans. We have been back repeatedly to our architects for ways of holding our capacity. We have considered a double-decker stand at the Stretford End but it would cost a fortune for the addition of relatively few seats. We have looked at a gallery or upper tier balcony at the Stretford End, but it would cost £4m for the addition of only 1,800 seats. We have thought about raising the roof all around the ground, but that would cost £30m for an extra 8-10,000 seats."

The point of the reduction in the size of the stadium due to the implementation of seating was emphasised by Colin Gibson in his *Daily Telegraph* article of October 21st. Under the heading 'United may have to grace smaller stage' he wrote, "There were 46,594 fans packed into Old Trafford on Saturday. It was the biggest crowd of the season in the Barclays League. It will probably not be matched in this or in any season in the future. With considerable reluctance, on the same Saturday, Manchester United were forced to concede that the ground they herald as the 'Theatre of Dreams' was being reduced in size again. Old Trafford will tumble to a 43,000 capacity and with the restraints imposed by crowd segregation it is unlikely that figure will be achieved. The theatre is being reduced to the size of a provincial playhouse. English football is rapidly losing its most impressive arenas.

"As a supporter, I was one of the 65,000 people watching United in the European cup against Benfica back in 1966. It was a magical evening. Gradually Old Trafford has decreased in size to the point where it is no longer capable of holding all the fans who want to be there. When Notts County arrive and more than 15,000 are locked out it is a clear indication that you have a problem. United, as much as anyone, are aware of that. They have been attacked continually by their supporters for the reduction in capacity but Chairman Martin Edwards has explained that a bigger ground is now 'financially unrealistic'. United started, before the full and sensible recommendations by Lord Justice Taylor, with plans for a 53,000 ground. That has been destroyed."

Fans began to voice their opinions at the government enforced changes and numerous suggestions were made in an attempt to maintain the Old Trafford capacity at a level on par with the support enjoyed by the club. Amongst those suggestions thrown into the debate was lowering the level of the pitch to enable more seating to be installed. This was considered impractical by Martin Edwards who said: "We wouldn't be able to get in many extra seats because UEFA rules limit how near you can take the spectators to the pitch. There is also a problem of unsighting people at the back of the stands. The whole situation is fraught with difficulties", as he repeated his previous response: "The costs are prohibitive. For instance it would cost between £25m and £30m to raise the roof round the ground for the provision of 10,000 extra seats and each side would be out of commission for a year while we did it.

If we did it at just the Stretford End when that end is converted into an all-seater it would cost an extra £4m for 1,800 seats. That works out at about £2,000 a seat. It would never pay back.

"Believe me, if we could increase the capacity we would. We understand the concern of our supporters, but really it is all down to the government's insistence that we go all-seater following the Taylor report. Otherwise we would have had a 53,000 capacity and that is how our stadium was first planned.

We have the biggest club stadium in the country and we will continue to study ways and means of making Old Trafford bigger, but supporters will have to understand the problems."

While the debate raged about the reduction in capacity of the ground, plans were being put in place regarding the construction of a Euro freight terminal, providing UK imports and exports with direct rail routes to the continent. One of the possible sites was on the land beyond the Stretford End of the ground, where a rail link was already in place, but thankfully for United, the area was passed by in British Rail's £400 million investment plans, as in years to come the club would take over the identified area to create parking facilities.

On November 19th 1991, the European Super Cup was contested at Old Trafford between United - holders of the European Cup Winners' Cup - and a familiar name from the past, Red Star Belgrade, holders of the European Cup. Normally played on a home and away basis, this season was to see the tie played as a one off due to the civil war in Yugoslavia making a second leg impossible. United, however, agreed to split the gate receipts with Red Star after suggestions were made by UEFA to play the match in Bari, Italy, and selling the match to television. The attendance attracted in the neutral country would have been minimal and so Old Trafford hosted its first Super Cup match. As it was, a share of the gate money and further revenue from Sportscast who were to show the game live in pubs and clubs across the north west and to homes in Europe, made it more profitable.

A 7.15 kick off to accommodate the television coverage was slightly earlier than normal for the United supporters and a chilly November evening saw only 22,110 turn up (an attendance that was more than 11,000 down on the Rumbellow's Cup-tie against Cambridge the previous month). The small band of visiting supporters helped create something of an atmosphere in keeping with the fixture, with smoke bombs exploding into the night air as the game got off to a vibrant start. After only two minutes, Belodedic handled Martin's cross inside the area, but the usually dependable Steve Bruce saw his spot kick saved by Milojevic.

The European Cup holders treated the Manchester crowd to some entertaining football, but failed to turn the chances into goals. A fine save from Schmeichel, followed by a goal line clearance from Blackmore kept Pancev out, while at the other end the Yugoslav 'keeper did not give his defence the greatest of confidence with some of his actions. Savicevic should have given the visitors the lead early in the second half with a fifteen yard run followed by a shot which went narrowly wide.

Against the run of play, the deadlock was finally broken in the sixty-seventh minute. A twenty yard drive from Webb, who had dispossessed Savicevic, hit an upright and Brian McClair was on hand to tap the ball home from close range. United managed to keep the visitors at bay for the remainder of the match and it was Steve Bruce and his red shirted team-mates who took the applause on the lap of honour.

At the annual AGM on Friday November 22nd 1991, despite announcements that Manchester United were the richest club in English football with £14m in the bank following the previous seasons record profits of £5.3m, shareholders called for the club to rethink its plans on the development of the stadium. One supporter went as far as to call for an extraordinary general meeting to discuss the future plans, while another two went as far as to hand out a protest sheet to arriving shareholders, which expressed the alarm of the reduction in capacity.

The board was also warned

that they were alienating supporters by reducing the capacity, as "there have been too many lock-outs this season, with supporters arriving from Belfast, the south of England and Scotland and then not being be to get in. Once they lose the habit of coming to Old Trafford, they will never return."

The lock-out warning came too late for the club to prevent such scenes occurring once again with West Ham United's visit the following afternoon. A West Ham ticket tout was reportedly stabbed outside the ground as Greater Manchester Police struggled with the thousands who failed to gain entry, with a police helicopter hovering overhead until well after kick-off time. All a police spokesman would add was: "In a lock-out, there could have been problems." Problems there certainly were going to be, with the club's announcement that from next season there would only be a ground capacity of 34,000 due to the re-development of the Stretford End and with the team challenging once again for the games major honours, a scramble for tickets would unfold with thousands missing out.

Martin Edwards announced; "The Stretford End will be out of action for fifteen months while the development work is carried out and it poses tremendous difficulties. We could be down to 34,000 though we hope to make it 38,000 if we can get a safety licence to allow part of the stand to be used while work is carried out." What part, it was unclear, as the whole end was due to be demolished!

Within his United pages in the *Manchester Evening News* Saturday 'Pink' edition, David Meek suggested that the board should "Give the fans the facts", admitting that he understood the supporters suspicions regarding the club argument that a smaller ground is unavoidable. He went on to say that he had spoken to Sir Roland Smith (the new PLC chairman) after the AGM and the man at the helm admitted that he had been surprised at the strong emotive feeling over the size of the ground.

"There is clearly great concern about the size of the ground" Meek continued, "we mustn't let anyone believe that there is a division between the board and the supporters on this because we would also like to see Old Trafford accommodate as many people as possible. It is no use coming up with some grandiose £60m scheme because you won't find too many banks willing to find that kind of money at the moment."

Robin Maunders, the financial director, also spoke to David Meek and explained the problem in more detail: "It has taken twenty-five years to develop the ground with good sight lines, no pillars, decent facilities and a fair proportion of seats. The proposed development of the Stretford End was seen as a continuation of that strategy and would have given us 53,000 which would be ideal.

"We have looked to increase the number of seats in the Stretford End by going further back and even building a double-decker, but we cannot find a plan without a problem of either cost or difficulty still seeing the pitch. That is not to say we aren't looking beyond the development of the Stretford End. There will be a next phase as we look to strategic options for the future."

Whether or not it was simply a ploy to appease the United support, Bobby Charlton was quoted as saying that "It may mean spending millions of pounds to create a double-decker stadium, it is something that must be done. This is a problem we have to address quickly and the rest of the board feel the same as I do. We should not be turning customers away." A change of tune?

As well as the Taylor Report, UEFA also declared that they were going to ban standing at all European competition fixtures, another reason for United's intentions in going ahead with their plans to create as much seating as possible. Another, much less important matter, which irked the supporters was the constant failure of the scoreboard system, as it was felt that with the club sponsored by Sharp, arguably the biggest electronics company in the world, they should have a slightly less erratic scoreboard. So, it was a "not before time" reaction, when it was announced that although the club had held off installing a new one. They did admit to having looked into the possibility of installing video screens similar to the likes off PSV Eindhoven and Eintracht Frankfurt, but they would have cost around £2m each and they would have been required for each end. The installation of such screens would also have proved difficult, as they would have needed to have been suspended from the roof and would have been too heavy to do so. Putting them at ground level, would certainly not have gone down well, as the capacity would have been reduced even further.

One worry the supporters need not have had, was on the safety aspect of the ground. Along with the club doctor and forty St. John's Ambulance staff, there were also seven other doctors and fourteen nurses situated at various points around the stadium in case of any emergency. This followed a plea in the club programme the previous season for any supporters who were regular attendees and were also doctors or nurses, in the hope of forming a unique in-house disaster unit.

"It is the first of its kind in the country" said stadium safety officer Arthur Roberts, who went on to add, "The bottom line is, we are convinced that because of this extra cover, Old Trafford is one of the safest grounds in the country." As part of their training they had taken part in a 'mock disaster' at the ground, involving 'crushed and burned fans' following a stimulated fire in one of the stands. This had apparently gone very well.

Perhaps psychiatrists and psychologists would also have

been worth giving facilities to, if reports in the American *National Enquirer* newspaper were anything to go by. In its November issue, it was reported that, "at a recent Manchester United home fixture, 47,000 fans were scared out of their wits and screamed in terror, when a UFO hovered above them. Within seconds, they were shrieking in panic and pointing to the sky. Players were running in a frantic daze, aware that they were being watched by aliens" (!) A photographer had supplied the newspaper with four photographs and a supporter gave an eye witness account, but surprisingly nothing appeared in the British press. However, a fixture against Wimbledon could produce anything, I suppose.

Around the same time as the 'UFO visit', the pitch was coming in for further criticism from both United and visiting teams and was considered to be "a nightmare to play on". It was in better condition than the previous season, but was still some way from being ideal following the laying of under soil heading.

Fan fury ignited again in mid-December, following an announcement that due to the reduced capacity for season 1992-93, admission prices would increase by 50%. "We have lost 10,000 places and we have to maintain revenue. People elsewhere are paying a lot more for their football." declared Martin Edwards following the announcement.

"It's a joke" said one

supporter, "The cheapest seat now is £11, they are talking about £15 for next season. How can you afford that and take kids?" Another looked at the bigger picture, stating: "I can understand why the club are doing it but I'm not sure most of the fans will agree. They have to make these improvements to keep up with the other big clubs but the scale of the rises is a disgrace."

If supporters were stunned by the *Manchester Evening News* revelations regarding the ticket price increases, the front page headline on edition of the same newspaper for Tuesday

December 17th would also take them by surprise, as David Meek revealed that the club were considering banning away supporters for the following season.

This idea was put forward in an attempt to keep supporters happy due to the threats of countless lock-outs brought about during the reduction in ground capacity. It could, however, create a few problems, with opposition clubs deciding to do likewise when United were due to visit. But even if the plan did not go ahead, there would certainly be a reduction in away supporters at the ground next

A packed Stretford End: *In the era before the Taylor Report was fully implemented.*

season for League fixtures, but cup-ties would still be governed by the twenty-five percent ruling.

The proposed actions were spread across all the national newspapers the following day, when it was revealed that the idea of the proposed ban was that of Martin Edwards, as the chairman told William Johnson of *Daily Telegraph*; "I've not yet discussed the matter with my board. I've no doubt, though that they will go along with the idea." Neither was the 'ban' on the agenda for that evenings board meeting, with the plan leaked while the director's meeting was taking place.

Edwards also said: "If you ask the 10,000 supporters who are regularly locked out of our home games whether they would prefer to watch twenty-one matches at Old Trafford or the odd big one away from home I'm sure that they would take the first option." He went on, "There are two main advantages of that (banning away fans) policy: reduced police costs and the elimination of segregation which has often left us with 1,000 empty spaces."

Club secretary Ken Merrett added "If we proceed and it goes well we may feel we want to continue it, even when the gate is back up to 43,000. But we wouldn't take that decision until next season is over."

While many outside the confines of Manchester 16 condemned United's proposed action, Colin Gibson of the *Daily Telegraph* was quick to support the idea, writing that the club's decision was based on pure logistics and that they were simply being loyal to the United support. "I for one applaud them" said Gibson.

A survey carried out by the *Independent on Sunday* newspaper and published in their edition for February 2nd, revealed that two years after the Taylor report and with two years to go before it had to be implemented, there was a crisis within the game as to how the changes would be paid for. The survey also mentioned that there was no agreement that the all-seated stadiums would even be safer, with the police and local councils concerned that there was a tendency for supporters to stand on seats built in shallow terracing which could prove dangerous.

Within the survey, was a club-by-club survey of plans, work done and the likes, with the United one as follows:
Work to be done : Stretford End (current capacity 14,000) to be replaced by approximately 10,500 seats.; Terraces at the east end of ground (current capacity 3,556) to be replaced by seating for roughly 2,450.
Time scale: Stretford End to be demolished during the forthcoming close season. All works scheduled for completion by start of 1993-94 season.
Interim plans: Capacity for 1992-93 to be reduced by 14,000. Cost - £10-£12m.
Funding: Share flotation, Development Association, Football Trust, own resources.

There was a night of drama at the ground on Wednesday 5th February, with the visit of Southampton for an F. A. Cup 4th round replay, one which ended in another 'first' for the stadium. Trailing 2-1 with only one minute of ordinary time remaining, the Southampton defence made a hash of clearing Lee Sharpe's left wing cross and Brian McClair headed home the equaliser at the far post.

United had gone behind after seven minutes, when Peter Schmeichel, instead of kicking clear, dived at the ball, only for it to evade his grasp and roll into the net. Thirteen minutes later, it was 2-0, Alan Shearer scoring with a header. United pulled one back two minutes prior to half time when Kanchelskis followed up after Flowers had blocked an effort from Giggs. There was no further scoring in the additional thirty minutes and so it was down to penalties, a first at the ground.

Ruddock scored from the spot, but Neil Webb fired over. Shearer made it 2-0 to the visitors, but Irwin pulled one back for United. Horne made it 3-1, with Sharpe reducing the advantage. Adams made it 4-2. Ryan Giggs coolly juggled the ball towards the penalty spot at the Stretford end goal, but Tim Flowers stood firm and saved his effort to send Southampton through to the next round and United out of the competition, as the first team to do so at this level of the F. A. Cup.

In the meantime, the stadium was on the list of venues confirmed by the Football Association as one of those that would be used if their bid to host the 1996 European Championships was successful. Having been one of the host grounds for the World Cup ties thirty years earlier, it was an obvious choice.

Despite the fans' reservations regarding ticket pricing and reduction of ground capacity, they could always be guaranteed to get behind the team and produce the magical Old Trafford atmosphere. The evening of March 11th 1992 brought Second Division Middlesbrough to Manchester for the 2nd leg of the Rumbelow's Cup Semi-Final, with the teams having played a goalless first leg up in the North East. The match produced one of those memorable Old Trafford occasions, despite the rain and driving wind, with the Second Division side giving a good account of themselves and almost producing a shock (see match no. 14).

In the League campaign, United maintained a strong challenge up until the final few games of the season, only to see their Yorkshire rivals Leeds move in and snatch the trophy from their grasp. With the tears of despair still being wiped away, the club revealed plans for the £12m new look Stretford End, a complex which would take Old Trafford into the next century and maintain its position as the best ground in the country.

The complete end of the ground would be re-developed and when completed, would house 10,500 spectators with the inclusion of a new family section, forty-six executive boxes, lounges and restaurants. For the VIP supporter, 864 seats in the centre of the stand were earmarked for executive suite members, with lifts to ferry them to and from the three new lounge areas below. The Family Stand was to be moved into one corner of the Stretford End, with 4,000 seats given over to this section and thereby doubling the seating capacity. A purpose-built TV studio would also be incorporated into the construction, to the rear of which would be the new family area.

Despite the money that the club was putting into the rebuilding and the up-dating of the stadium with an eye for the future, many supporters found cause to complain as regards to the new plans, but Chairman Martin Edwards said he was proud of what the club had achieved and he felt that United had the finest stadium in the country. And so, on Saturday May 2nd 1992, the League curtain came down on the Stretford End, with the visit of Tottenham Hotspur. Synonymous with the name of Manchester United, it had for years been the vocal section of the stadium, with many of those seated in the stands and in the comfort of the private boxes having watched United many years before from their favourite spot on the concrete terracing. Everyone who had stood on this, sometimes notorious, section of the ground had a favourite

memory and many of those were recalled in the pages of the *United Review* for the Tottenham match.

The penultimate fixture in front of the Stretford End saw one of it's heroes, Norman Whiteside, enjoy a testimonial against Everton, but the final match of the season would not see a packed, swaying mass on the much favoured terracing, as it was the United youth team who enjoyed the honour of bringing the curtain down on a piece of Old Trafford history, with their second leg Final tie against Crystal Palace on May 15th. 3-1 in front from the first leg in London, the youngsters, who included Gary Neville, David Beckham, Nicky Butt and Ryan Giggs, made no mistake with a 3-2 win, to lift the trophy for the first time in twenty-eight years, watched by a crowd of 14,681.

By the end of the month, the Stretford End was gone, flattened by the demolition firm of Connell and Finnigan of Dukinfield, who had reduced the entire end to little more than a few heaps of soil and the odd pile of rubble. The terrace anthems had given way to the grinding drone of machinery, but it didn't keep the loyal supporters away, as many made a point of visiting the ground to obtain a brick or two from the old walls, as a reminder of the part of the ground that was for many the heart of Manchester United. Unfortunately, during the demolition work, one workman died in a fifty foot feet fall from

In the opening minutes, Middlesbrough almost took a surprise lead, when Wilkinson moved in ahead of Steve Bruce to send Slavin's cross narrowly over. Irwin came equally close at the opposite end, firing a fisted clearance by Pears, following Webb's free kick, just wide. The saturated surface tested both sets of players and clear-cut chances were few, but a flowing move combining Ince, Robson, Giggs and McClair produced the first breakthrough for United, when Webb supplied the final pass for Sharpe to place an angled shot beyond the reach of former United 'keeper Pears, after half an hour.*

Five minutes into the second half, the visitors were level when Slaven left-footed a low cross into the United net. As the Middlesbrough fans voiced their encouragement, taunting the United fans with "You're supposed to be at home." United almost regained the lead, with Irwin, once again supporting his colleagues, coming close. As play went from end to end, Schmeichel had to be alert, to save at the feet of Wilkinson. Pallister cleared off the line from Hendrie and with the visitors pressing, Falconer just failed to meet a Slavin cross. Neither side, however, could provide the necessary breakthrough and the match drifted into extra-time, which, considering the conditions, was going to be a test for both teams.

A minute into the second period of extra time, a cross from Webb was headed into the path of Giggs by Bryan Robson and the young Welshman volleyed home. There was now no coming back for 'Boro. as United held onto their lead to reach the Final, where a 1-0 victory over Nottingham Forest saw the League Cup displayed in the Old Trafford museum trophy cabinet for the first time.

Reflecting on the drama of the Middlesborough match, as he caught his breath at full-time, Alex Ferguson was to say: It was a memorable occasion for the club and one of my greatest nights at Old Trafford – I'll remember it forever."

the roof.

Work was also carried out on the other sections of the stadium during the summer, with part of the main stand roof

being stripped off and replaced by translucent sheets which would allow the sunshine to filter through and improve the growing of the grass. Many had

▲ **The end of The End:** *Two cranes dominate the Old Trafford skyline as a monument to the passing of the great terrace.*

seen the condition of the pitch as an additional handicap in the title chase of the previous season, and anything was worth considering if it helped improve the surface. Another attempt to save the wear and tear of the pitch was to switch reserve team fixture for the forthcoming 1992-93 season to Gigg Lane, Bury. Additionally, in the main stand at the rear of section A, a police control room had been constructed. Containing a bank of monitors and other electronic equipment, it would enable the stadium safety officer and the

police to keep a closer watch on the situation both inside and outside the stadium.

Around £275,000 was spent on a new public address system, which involved some ten miles of cable, five hundred loudspeakers and an amplifier weighing one ton. The benefit would be heard by spectators in all sections of the ground. The new electronic scoreboard was also installed, but would there be an improvement many wondered?

One new development which would not be seen or be of any benefit to the supporter, was a press conference centre underneath the main stand. This auditorium, which would feature in the ground tours, and was to contain comfortable seating on a

sloping floor like a cinema with a raised platform at one end. This would be used for the after match press conference and on other occasions, such as player signings when there was a large media turn out.

Two areas which had always been situated below the main stand were scheduled to move with the completion of the new Stretford End stand - the players lounge and the dressing rooms. The former could be considered rather plain and little different from a lounge bar in a hotel, although one distinctive feature was a large honours board containing the names of all the players who had represented the club at international level in the post war years. On the

other hand, the dressing rooms, although not identical, would be of an impressively high standard and would be able to accommodate twenty-two players and managerial team comfortably. To one side were toilets, spa pool (in the 'home' area only), baths and showers. The home dressing room was also equipped with a small warm up room. Televisions were also included in both rooms.

From the dressing rooms, the players would approach the pitch down a wide tunnel with extending covering for their protection from the crowd. One interesting feature would be the hydraulic lifting equipment at the mouth of the tunnel which would enable the roof to be raised twenty-five feet in order to allow large screens or other equipment to be moved onto the pitch for closed circuit TV showing or other events. At the opposite end of the ground, a further sixty seats had been installed in the visiting supporters section in L stand, the old Scoreboard Paddock, while stand C (a section of the main stand) was enlarged with a further two hundred seats. The old player's tunnel, in the centre of the main stand was to remain as it was and it is worth noting that it is the only part of the original stadium still in existence.

Outside the stadium, close season work was also evident. Toilets had been constructed outside the museum entrance, while the Souvenir Shop was now around 3,000 square feet in size, after taking over the Development Association premises next door, with the latter moving to a new building across the railway bridge on Warwick Road. The cost of all these additions and alterations? A mere £1m!

October 1992 brought supporters an opportunity to take the new one hour tour of the stadium. For £4.95 adults and £2.95 juniors and OAP's, visitors could see for themselves all the alterations to the ground in addition to the museum and trophy room.

*

Hundreds of players have worn the famous red shirt of United since Old Trafford became the club home and many have played their first senior game on the hallowed turf, having progressed through the junior and reserve side. Others have run out to be greeted by the fans for the first time after joining United from another club. Johnny Carey, captain of the 1948 F.A. Cup winning side made his first United appearance against Southampton on September 25th 1937, while the debuts of the legendary Duncan Edwards, on April 4th 1953 against Cardiff City, Bobby Charlton against Charlton Athletic on October 6th 1956 and his team-mate George Best against West Bromwich Albion on September 14th 1963 have all been noted within these pages. However, on December 6th 1992, the visit of Manchester City for the 117th derby match

saw another debutant added to the long illustrious list.

His signing, just over a week earlier, had caused a few eyebrows to be raised and had come as something of a shock and a surprise to the Old Trafford faithful. But, in the years ahead he was going to claim just as many headlines, front and back pages, as George Best, and become one of the United all-time greats. His name of course was Eric Cantona. Sadly, the Frenchman could not begin his career with a goal after coming on as substitute after the interval for the injured Ryan Giggs, but goals from Paul Ince and Mark Hughes gave United a 2-1 victory. There was, however, plenty of time for the new signing to etch his name into the Manchester United history books.

Work on the new Stretford End stand continued to schedule and by the end of 1992 the lower section was available to supporters, although there was no protection from the elements, other than free plastic macs. when it rained. Despite the progress going to plan, the construction of this new section of the ground wasn't all smooth sailing, as in mid-January, a workman was unfortunately severely injured in a horrific accident. A concrete girder, weighing a ton, was being off-loaded and fell, crushing the workman who was immediately rushed to hospital. Unfortunately, nine months later he died.

Following the furore of the

increase in ticket prices for the 1992-93 season, no one really knew what to expect attendance wise, but the men behind the club thought that there would be little change, with the faithful turning up no matter what. They received something of a shock, however, when a meagre 19,998 turned up for the UEFA cup tie against Torpedo Moscow on September 16th, the lowest ever attendance at the ground for a European tie.

Attendances did improve, with mid-November bringing news that many of the supporters had been waiting on for months, that the Stretford End was about to re-open. Obviously, it was only a small section of the new development, but it was better than nothing. The completion of the first stage of the major development, allowed 2,500 supporters to access the area for the game against Oldham Athletic on November 21st, with the uncovered seats priced at £8. If it rained, umbrellas were banned under ground regulations!

Friday February 12th 1993 saw a significant change take place a short pass from the Old Trafford turnstiles, when Trafford Borough Council officials changed the name of Warwick Road North - which ran from Trafford Park Road on the north side, past the ground to Chester Road on the south side - to 'Sir Matt Busby Way'. A brief unveiling ceremony of one of the new road side signs took place, with the man himself doing the honours, accompanied

by the Mayor of Trafford, Councillor Ray Tully, United Chairman Martin Edwards, and manager Alex Ferguson.

On the pitch, United steadily climbed the Premier League having found themselves anchored at the foot of the table on August 19th, after two games. By January 9th, they occupied top spot, a position that they continued to hold on to despite Aston Villa's challenge. Could the twenty-six year old jinx finally be at an end?

Things were beginning to hot up as the fixtures became fewer and with a local 'derby' against City at Maine Road on March 20th taking on an extra dimension, the decision was made to show the game live on closed circuit TV at Old Trafford. It had been over fifteen years since the last televised match at the ground, and despite the 11am kick off, a crowd of 10,462 surprised United officials by turning up to watch on the big 25' x 19' screen which had been erected in front of the North Stand.

With six games of the 1992-93 season remaining, Sheffield Wednesday visited Old Trafford on April 10th and as the match moved into the final stages, it looked as if the ghosts of seasons past were about to re-appear. Wednesday matched United stride for stride throughout the first half, and midway through the second they stunned the packed stadium into silence when they took the lead through a John Sheridan penalty, awarded by John Hilditch who had begun the game as a linesman but had replaced injured referee Michael Peck only minutes before. United replaced Paul Parker with Bryan Robson almost immediately in an attempt to rescue something from the game and keep their title hopes alive. The United supporters in the 40,102 crowd became increasingly unsettled as the minutes ticked away with their watches being constantly checked.

With six minutes to go, and attacking the old Stretford End, now a magnificent sight with every seat occupied, United won yet another corner and from Denis Irwin's kick, captain Steve Bruce headed home to level the score and send the crowd ecstatic. So often the scorer of vital goals, the big defender had once again saved United from the throes of defeat. A draw would have been acceptable, but the United faithful pumped up the volume in the hope that a further goal might be there, even though the final whistle beckoned.

No one, however, had reckoned on the amount of injury time that was still to be played due to the referee's injury, and with 97 minutes 14 seconds played, with every ball being thumped into the Wednesday penalty area, Gary Pallister flicked the ball over his head into the path of the oncoming Steve Bruce, who once again headed past Woods. The noise was deafening and must have been heard in Piccadilly Gardens as the red contingent in the ground

went delirious. Alex Ferguson and his assistant Brian Kidd staged a mini pitch invasion, as the usually serene supporters in the quieter stands embraced in the kind of fevered embrace, usually reserved for more intimate moments with members of the opposite sex. Seconds later it was all over, United had turned, what at one time had looked like a certain defeat, into a vital three points in one of the most memorable games seen at the ground.

On April 21st, with United at Crystal Palace, Old Trafford once again showed the match on closed circuit TV. A staggering 15,009 turned up, which was actually larger than Wimbledon's biggest gate of the season

at that time! Once again, the club was caught out by the number of people who were keen to watch the match on the big screen and additional gates had to be opened. Some people arriving at the ground found the queues along Sir Matt Busby Way and four hundred yards down Chester Road just a bit too much, and many decided to about turn and go home. Those who did take the time to queue enjoyed a good evening's entertainment, and admitted afterwards that the

atmosphere made it seem like a normal home fixture.

There were perhaps not quite as many people at Old Trafford on the afternoon and evening of Sunday May 2nd, although that may be open to debate, but they certainly made more noise, as they celebrated United's first Championship success since 1967, holding an impromptu party on the forecourt, following the defeat of nearest rivals Aston Villa by Oldham Athletic earlier that evening. Supporters began arriving at the ground once the outcome of the match at Villa Park was known and champagne corks popped in unison to the car horns of passing motorists, as the complete United songbook received an airing. At one point even Lee Sharpe appeared to join in the celebrations before heading off to join his team mates at the home of Steve Bruce.

And so it continued, with the pre-match scenes outside the ground on the Monday evening taking on a new level with flags and supporters everywhere, and tickets changing hands at Cup Final prices, making Monday May 3rd yet another of those memorable Old Trafford occasions, with visitors Blackburn Rovers playing a mere bit-part, as the long awaited Championship, now a new trophy for the inaugural Premier League season was to be presented following the now meaningless fixture.

The Old Trafford forecourt resembled a giant conga as scenes similar to those of

The progress of work on The new West Stand:

▲ *The Stretford End is bulldozed with a piece of the old terracing still on show* ▶
▼▼ *The new West Stand rises to meet the other Cantilever Stands.*

the previous afternoon and evening were repeated inside the stadium and didn't even let up when Blackburn took an eight minute lead through Kevin Gallagher. The sun drenched stadium continued to party. Thirteen minutes later a tremendous Ryan Giggs free kick got things back on the right track, and further goals from Paul Ince and Gary Pallister emphasised the superiority of the Champions. For once, there were no early departures before the final whistle, as no one had any intention of missing the presentation of the glistening trophy to team and club captains Steve Bruce and Bryan Robson. Tina Turner's 'Simply The Best' boomed out yet again from the public address system as the players went on their lap of honour, something that many present had never witnessed at the ground before, and all hoped to see again with nothing like the wait since the last triumph.

Success on the pitch also brought spin-offs elsewhere, with the Souvenir shop on the day of the Blackburn match recording record receipts. Although exact figures were not made available, it was believed that around £100,000 was taken over the

20TH OCTOBER 1993
EUROPEAN CUP SECOND ROUND, FIRST LEG

UNITED 3 GALATASARAY 3

As early as the third minute, Bryan Robson opened the scoring, finishing off a Keane, Cantona move. Ten minutes later, it was 2-0, Hakan putting a Giggs corner past his own goalkeeper while under pressure from Pallister. This goal settled the Old Trafford crowd, who now carried little thoughts of defeat, but within twenty minutes, Galatasaray were on level terms. Firstly, Erdem fired a twenty-five yard shot past Schmeichel and then in the thirty-second minute a mistimed Lee Martin pass back evaded the big Danish 'keeper, with Turkyilmaz slipping the ball into an empty United net as the majority of Old Trafford looked on dumbstruck. With sixty-three minutes on the clock, Turkyilmaz scored again to put the visitors 3-2 in front.

With the game now turned dramatically on its head, the Old Trafford crowd once again had cause to stand in amazement, but on this occasion, there was no goal or near miss to gaze agonisingly at, but the sight of two Kurdish students evaded touchline security and ran onto the pitch carrying a burning Turkish flag, in what turned out to be a human rights protest. As police and stewards moved towards the trespassers, Peter Schmeichel sprinted from his goalmouth and unceremoniously began to remove one of the invaders from the pitch, much to the concern of the Turkish players and to the delight of the home support. A second incident later followed, when a soft drinks can was thrown at, and narrowly missed, a Turkish player. Fortunately there were no severe repercussions for United regarding either incidents.

United, in the meantime, were still 3-2 down and the minutes were ticking away and with only eight minutes remaining, it looked as if United's proud home record of never having lost a European tie at Old Trafford was about to be brought to an end, but in hope and desperation, more than anything else, Roy Keane lofted a high ball towards the visitors goal, where Eric Cantona managed to evade his marker to stab the ball home in front of a relieved Stretford End. The record was safe, for the time being at least.

counter.

With the new Premier League trophy as top attraction in the United museum, all sights were set on its retention as season 1993-94 drew near. The Old Trafford curtain-raiser was a match against old adversaries Benfica, a fixture arranged as part of the 25th anniversary celebrations of winning the European Cup in 1968. On the day of the match the stadium had never looked better, with the new Stretford End stand setting it off perfectly, with its red and white seating showing the word 'Umbro' along the lower section and their diamond shape trade mark on the upper.

There was some concern, however, regarding the renovations in the South Stand, as the contractors struggled to complete the £2.5m facelift which included the installation of six hundred new seats and the re-alignment of the gangways. Thankfully the club's embarrassment was spared as the unfinished section was not required, with only a disappointing 20,800 turning up for the Benfica match, to watch an uneventful ninety minutes which the visitors won 1-0.

By August 18th, and the opening home League fixture of season 1993-94 against Sheffield United, United had paid out almost £15m in fifteen months. Most of this outlay, approximately £10m, had gone on the new Stretford End development, with around £5m on the South Stand and other areas. The Sheffield fixture also

saw for the first time, the ground fully operational after all the close season work, and a crowd of 41,949 watched a pre-match presentation of the Premier League Championship flag to manager Alex Ferguson and Chairman Martin Edwards. The giant flag would be flown from the pole on top of the North Stand on match days.

Prior to the European Cup-tie against Honved on September 29th, Frank Taylor, the only surviving journalist from the Munich Air Disaster, unveiled a new Memorial Plaque in the press lounge, in memory of his fellow newspapermen who had lost their lives. The original plaque, which had been stolen some years previously, used to be situated above the entrance into the press box, but the replacement plaque had been removed during the summer renovations and it was decided to find a new place for it.

Over the years many hardened professionals have both angered and inspired the Old Trafford crowds. Men like Frank Barson, Nobby Stiles, Mark Hughes, Bryan Robson and Roy Keane in the red of United, along with opponents such as Norman Hunter, Dave Mackay, Ron Harris and Tommy Smith, but two real hard men faced each other on the Old Trafford pitch on the evening of Saturday October 9th, when Nigel Benn faced Chris Eubank for the World Super-Middleweight Boxing Championship of the World. The famous hallowed turf was completely covered over, with the ring erected in the centre, for what had become known as 'Judgement Day'. Over 40,000 fight fans turned up for the confrontation between the two deadly rivals, breaking the boxing post-war gate record, set when Henry Cooper took on Cassius Clay at Highbury in 1964. After twelve uneventful rounds, which must have disappointed the likes of Sir Matt Busby and the other spectators, the judges declared the outcome a draw!

Following the fight, however, there were numerous complaints from those in attendance. Many of the ringside spectators, who had paid £250 to watch the fight, were upset because their area had been infiltrated by others, while another complaint arose from there only being five, instead of seven bouts. After the event, many were also left stranded at the ground, when the expected late night transport failed to turn up. Perhaps a football ground is, after all, just for football.

Restricted by UEFA from fielding the team which brought the Premier League title to the club in the European Cup, due to new regulations over the number of non-English players that a club could field, United's European dreams were shattered by the relatively unknown Turkish side Galatasaray in the second round, having defeated Honved 5-3 in round one (see match no. 15). A 0-0 draw in second leg in Turkey was enough to take the home side through on

the away goals rule, as they had stunned the Old Trafford crowd by scoring three in a dramatic first leg. Due to the 'foreigners' ruling, Alex Ferguson omitted Irwin, McClair and Kanchelskis, using Keane, Cantona and Schmeichel as his 'foreigners', with Hughes and Giggs being able to play as 'assimilated players' having came through the ranks.

*

On the evening of Thursday January 20th, the football world was stunned by the announcement that Sir Matt Busby had died. The man who more than any other was responsible for the worldwide adoration of the club and the magnificent stadium it called home, would no more be seen on a match day, walking slowly across the forecourt with members of his family to the acknowledgement of the supporters, as he went to watch his beloved team. For many, Sir Matt was Manchester United, and vice versa, and as the news broke across the city, supporters began to arrive at the ground to pay their respects. Some laid bunches of flowers against the wall of the stadium and underneath the Munich memorial, while others left their scarves and other items of memorabilia. The following day saw countless others make the same pilgrimage and the forecourt was soon a carpet of flowers, scarves and memorabilia. A book of

remembrance was opened in the museum for the fans to sign, and there was also a small area given over to a large photograph of Sir Matt along with numerous flowers and wreaths.

Saturday January 22nd, was match day at Old Trafford and it had been obvious over the last couple of days that it would be no ordinary one.

From early morning, there are always people scattered around the ground, but that day there were more than usual. Television crews mingled with

The House that Matt Built:
Scarves and other memorabilia left by supporters underneath the Munich Memorial following the death of Sir Matt Busby.

the increasing numbers on the forecourt as the carpet of scarves, flowers, photographs and the like, took on new dimensions. As 3pm approached, those with match tickets were already inside, determined for once not to be late, while outside there were still around an estimated 15,000, content at

▲ A final look at the Cantiliver: *Once the most advanced football stand in the country, the United Road awaited a similar fate to the Stretford End as demand for tickets outstripped supply.*

simply just being there on the day Manchester United paid its last respects to its President.

As an announcement from the public address system asked the crowd to stand, the first strains of the bagpipes could be heard from the mouth of the player's tunnel in the corner of the Stretford End. The haunting melody of 'A Scottish Soldier' grew louder as the lone piper led the players of United and Everton onto the pitch, followed by officials of both clubs. There were lumps in many throats and numerous tears were unashamedly shed as the scene unfolded before them. With the piper now silent, and both teams lined up in the centre of the pitch, an eerie silence enveloped the ground.

In the ninety minutes of football that followed the impeccably observed minute's silence for which the United support in the 44,750 crowd applauded their Everton counterparts, United played some vintage stuff, which Sir Matt would have certainly enjoyed, but could only win by a solitary Ryan Giggs goal. The young Welshman displayed his wide array of skills, accompanied by Cantona, who displayed his usual panache in midfield. The day, however, would always be remembered for only one reason.

A week after his death, on Thursday January 27th, came Sir Matt's funeral at Our Lady and St. Johns Church in Chorlton-cum-Hardy. Following a moving service, attended by some ninety former players, the funeral procession made its way towards the lasting memorial to Sir Matt - Old Trafford. Sir Matt Busby Way, and beyond, was lined with over 5,000 supporters caring nothing for the rain which fell, and with the Munich clock showing 12.06, the hearse, followed by fourteen cars and three coaches, came to a halt outside the ground.

For two silent, tear-jerking minutes, the crowd bowed their heads, remembered 'the Boss', and the three fabulous sides that he created, before a horn blew and the hearse pulled away from the ground towards Southern Cemetery. Inside, the stadium stood empty and one seat, number B122 in Row 25, would remain so as a mark of respect.

✷

With Old Trafford already chosen as one of the venues for the Euro '96 competition, the stadium was also put forward as the new home for England international games as a row between Wembley and the F.A. simmered. Although with a smaller capacity than the national stadium - 45,000 as opposed to 75,000 - United argued that at least everyone at Old Trafford could see, and the overall facilities were better. Such a move would of course be well received in the north if it ever came to pass, but time would only tell if future internationals would be played away from Wembley.

Over the years, many clubs have found it difficult to obtain a result against United at Old Trafford, but perhaps the best record in recent times is held by Chelsea, with the fixture between the two on March 5th 1994 proving the point, with the Londoners bringing the treble chasing United side to a temporary halt with a 1-0 victory. Although not a result, or a performance for the record books, it was still a notable day in the life of the stadium.

Prior to the match, a record number of people (1,148) paid to enjoy the memorabilia in the United museum, a number that some lower division clubs have to survive on passing through their turnstiles. The previous museum record had been 980. On the same day, Manchester United Radio was launched providing news and views and match commentary to those living within a five mile radius of the ground. Broadcasting on 1413 AM, the station would transmit for eight hours on match days, beginning at 10.30am, from a custom built studio under the main stand. It would be linked to the ground PA system, with the match commentary being transmitted to blind supporters within the stadium. Sponsored by greetings card company 'Birthdays', advertising would also help contribute to the running costs. The club itself paid out more than £40,000 to equip the studio.

Music of a different kind echoed around the stadium on Sunday April 24th when a memorial service for Sir Matt Busby was held at the ground. All the flags flew at half mast, as the 10,000 crowd assembled, along with past and present United players, show-business stars, and members of Sir Matt's family.

The moving, hour long service combined singing with spoken tributes from famous names of the past, such as Harry Gregg, Bobby Charlton, Charlie Mitten and Kenneth Wolstenholme. Denis Law and community signing leader Vince Millar sang one of Sir Matt's favourite songs, 'I Belong to Glasgow', while the tears flowed openly as the strains of 'Abide With Me', followed by the Old Trafford anthem 'Walking Down the Warwick Road' drifted into the afternoon air.

The spirit of Sir Matt Busby will always remain around the ground and his memory seemed to inspire the team as the final weeks of the season approached. With the games left to play slowly decreasing, United's retention of the Championship looked highly probable, and as Blackburn Rovers stuttered at Coventry, everyone with Old Trafford connections began to celebrate. The F. A. Cup had also

been contested determinedly, and on May 14th the Red Army headed for Wembley, where Chelsea provided little in the way of opposition as United joined the elite list of double winners.

On the eve of the penultimate match of the season, against

Southampton at Old Trafford, with the club scaling unforeseen heights, the *Manchester Evening News* carried an article on United's plans for increasing the ground capacity to 64,000 by building a second tier onto one of the stands, a development which would eventually continue around the ground. Each stage would depend on the money available as well as the demand for more seating from the increasing interest from supporters. The club, however, said that there would be no statement regarding such a development until plans had been finalised, and a decision made as to whereabouts it would begin. Once the ground had been completely seated then an announcement would be made.

So, the visit of Coventry City, four days later on May 8th saw another day of celebrations around the ground, despite the 0-0 draw, with the presentation of the Championship trophy at the end of the ninety minutes. The celebrations were perhaps not on the same scale as twelve months previously, but it was still an enjoyable and eventful afternoon. Despite the thrill of seeing and celebrating another

Championship victory, the afternoon was also tinged with sadness, as it marked the final competitive appearance in the red shirt of club captain Bryan Robson, with many present casting their minds back to his signing on the pitch over a decade earlier.

But as one United name made his farewell appearance, another red shirted figure was making his first, as the club unveiled its new mascot, Fred the Red. This was actually the second 'Red Devil' mascot to show face at Old Trafford, as a similar figure would parade around the pitch in the '80's, occasionally taunting the opposition supporters with some of his antics. Hopefully the current 'Devil' would also be better behaved than the mascot associated with the club during the time at Bank Street. This particular mascot was a goat named Billy, who apparently was given to captain Charlie Roberts and after each home match it would follow the supporters to a nearby public house and drink all the beer bought him until he collapsed on the floor!

In the 1950's – 1960's period, the United mascot was a gentleman called Jack Irons who, dressed in his red and white costume with accompanying umbrella, could be found at Old Trafford and other grounds around the country cheering the team on. Another 'human' mascot, although not in the same sense as Billy the goat or Fred The Red, was William 'Hoppy' Thorne, who was a regular feature at Old Trafford during the thirties and forties.

'Hoppy', was a First World War casualty, who had lost his leg during the hostilities and upon returning to Britain, having been fitted out with a false leg, would find odd jobs to do around the stadium. On match days, however, he took on a different role as crowd entertainer, removing his false limb, donning a running outfit and hopping around the perimeter of the pitch.

With United fans still on the crest of a wave following the double success, they received something of a jolt when stories began to surface involving neighbours City, who were considering renting Old Trafford while building work was carried out on the Kippax Street section of their Maine Road ground. City chairman Francis Lee later shrugged off the idea as a tongue in the cheek remark, and stated that there was little chance of the war time ground share being reversed.

Whether or not such a plan would ever have been accepted by United is debatable, as football had changed so dramatically from the time when supporters thought nothing off going to either Maine Road or Old Trafford when their favourites were playing away from home. Today, with the game played in a totally different environment, with the threat of damage to the stadium, especially after the final game there, it would have been best to avoid such a scenario altogether.

Interest in the club now seemed to be at an all time high, with official membership figures approaching 103,000. Stadium tours and museum visitors (which had reached 100,000 in the first six months of the year) were also on the up. The Super Store also had a constant ringing of tills, making the name 'Gold Trafford' seem much more appropriate and a ready made title for the tabloid press.

Sell-outs and over demand for tickets were therefore regular occurrences and Sunday September 25th 1994 saw yet another 40,000 full house at the ground with a further 10,000 ticket applicants having been unsuccessful in their bid to be in attendance. A look at the United fixture list for 1994-95, however, might lead many people to think that a mistake has been made, as on that particular afternoon, the red shirts were nowhere in sight. Instead the stadium had been taken over by BBC television to record their popular Sunday programme - 'Songs of Praise'. Worshippers flocked to the ground from all over the country and made just as colourful a scene as any match day, with numerous banners scattered around the ground, as the air filled with singing and music as the programme was recorded for a future screening. What next for the stadium?

Always alert to any breach of safety regulations, United officials banned a huge 130' x 60' red, black and white flag from the ground in early October 1995. Owned by supporter Mike Edroff, the flag was unfurled and passed over the heads of the supporters as it made its way around the ground, but the fear of it igniting and going up in flames forced the club to ban it. They did say, however, that if Mike could obtain a safety certificate for his flag then they would allow it back into the ground.

The suggestion of a second tier around the ground, that had been made towards the end of the previous season, took on a completely new meaning in early October, when a David Meek "exclusive" in the *Manchester Evening News* revealed that the club planned to 'Reach for the Sky', with a triple-decker stand to take the place of the existing cantilever one that ran along the United Road, which had been built back in 1966.

A feasibility study had been commissioned and Sir Roland Smith, chairman of the main board of directors admitted that "there were quite a number of options to consider". Much would depend on the continued success on the playing side and also the availability of the land owned by the Trafford Park Estates adjacent to the United Road, which would be required if such a development was to take place. There was also an alternative option being muted. With Manchester looking to build a new stadium in order to host major sports events such as the Olympic Games, or perhaps more realistically the Commonwealth Games, there was also a possibility of moving away from Old Trafford altogether, to a brand new custom built home. Supporters, however, were very much against such a move even being considered.

*

Football memorabilia today is big business, with collectors paying hundreds of pound for programmes, autographs and other items relating to the club and the players who have pulled on the famous red jersey over the years. At a tribute dinner to Bryan Robson, perhaps one of the most unusual items to become available appeared during a charity auction held as part of the evening. Hidden behind a curtain was an old hoarding from the ground, which dated back to the early seventies, and depicted a diagram of the stadium. United players at the dinner, as well as supporters, were speechless as the curtain was drawn back to reveal the sign, which had mysteriously disappeared during renovations some years previously and had not been seen since. It had came into the possession of a United supporter who thought that it would be ideal to use as a means for raising money for charity, and subsequently it appeared at the auction where it was bought by a company boss who intended to give it pride of place in his offices, but refused to admit to the press what he had paid for it.

By mid-November 1995, the plans for the new towering second and third tier to be added onto the North Stand were on show at Trafford Borough Council. The construction, which would dwarf the rest of the stadium, would reach almost one hundred and sixty feet in height, making it around ninety-four feet higher than the existing stand. In order to build such a structure, the United Road would have to be altered, as it would extend some sixty feet outwards. A new access road would need to be built, and a further ninety full and part-time jobs would be created to service the new

construction. Club secretary, Ken Ramsden confirmed that United were in negotiations with Trafford Park Estates to purchase the land required to implement the plans. Two months later, the Trafford Park Development Corporation had approved the plans and the Trafford Council were in agreement towards the triple-decker development.

The plans, once again, had not been straightforward for the club, as some angry clashes had occurred between rival factions on the council, who felt that local residents were perhaps not being considered as the club was increasing its capacity and bringing more people into the area on match days. With planning permission now secured, funding of the venture was now the main concern.

As the imagination of the supporters ran riot with thoughts of what the new stand would look like, the stadium, as it then stood, received the seal of approval from the UEFA stadium inspectors who were visiting all the proposed Euro '96 venues. Chairman of the committee, Mr Ernie Walker, gave the ground the supreme accolade of the 'Best in Britain'. "I know that Wembley is bigger", he said, "but it is not better than Old Trafford". Along with fellow committee members, the ground was inspected for security and facilities for the media, along with segregation arrangements.

December 3rd saw Norwich City visit Old Trafford and manager Alex Ferguson had to break away from his normal

UNITED 9 IPSWICH TOWN 0

Certain fixtures provide the supporter with ninety minutes to remember and the opportunity to say "I was there", when the game is recalled on various occasions in the future. Such a match occurred at the ground on March 3rd 1995, when Ipswich Town journeyed north. Most visiting players enjoy their seasonal visit to Old Trafford, but for the Ipswich goalkeeper Craig Forrest it was one to forget as United recorded a 9-0 victory. Forrest, it must be said, did not play badly, it was simply a case that along with his team mates, he came up against United on a day when everything clicked together.

The day undoubtedly belonged to Andy Cole, signed from Newcastle United in January for £7m, who claimed five goals (although one could be considered an own goal), the highest number ever scored by a United player in a League match. Attacking right from the start, United had the Ipswich goal under pressure on a few occasions before Keane opened the scoring in the fifteenth minute. The second followed four minutes later as Cole claimed his first from a Giggs cross. It wasn't until eight minutes before the interval, however, that the third goal was scored, although the visitors could have pulled one back before then. A McClair - Kanchelskis move created an opportunity for Hughes, who was unlucky to see his bicycle kick hit the bar. With the crowd still on their feet, Cole nipped in to score with the rebound.

After the interval, the floodgates opened, and three goals in six minutes finished the game as a contest. The 'Cole/own goal' made it four in the fifty-third minute. Hughes fired home two minutes later to make it five and the same player made it six in the fifty-ninth minute with a header. It was now a case of how many, as Ipswich gave up. Cole netted the seventh in the sixty-fifth minute as McClair's shot was pushed out by Forrest, while a cheeky free kick by Ince, as the Ipswich 'keeper stood stranded outside his area after conceding the kick, dropped into the unguarded goal. With the Ipswich players and their supporters longing for the final whistle, the scoreboard (thankfully working that afternoon) changed to 9-0 as Cole hit his fifth, to rewrite the history books. It was the highest League victory since the 9-0 defeat of Darwen in a Second Division fixture on December 24th 1898.

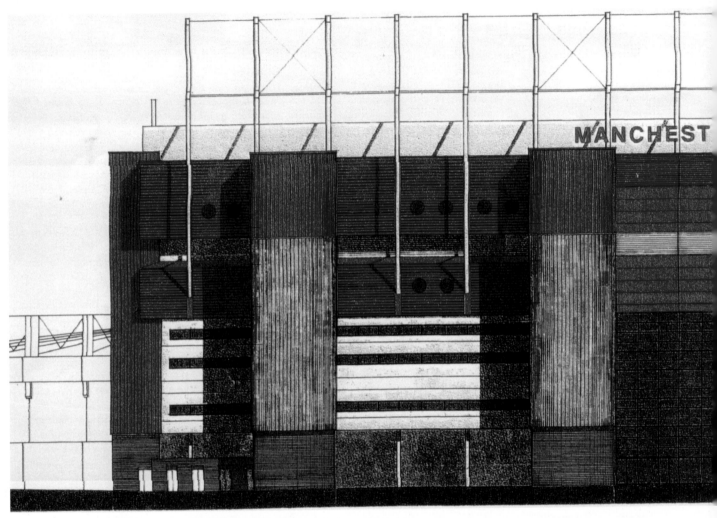

match day routine to officially open the new United Mega Store, situated behind the Stretford End of the ground, where the illustrious names of the club's past used to play five-a-side as part of their training routine. At 10.30am, the former goalscoring centre-forward kicked a ball through a paper net to declare the store open, as the queues

stretched back towards the spot where the original wooden hut stood which first sold United souvenirs. Crammed with everything from tiny strips for babies, curtains and bedding, to wallpaper and a United Trivial Pursuit game with 4,000 questions, the Mega Store could be considered every parents nightmare. The new store

closed at one minute to three, re-opened at half time for those without tickets for the match, and again at full time. As the last supporters drifted home with their carrier bags bulging, the day's takings were reported at an astonishing £250,000!

*

The imagination of local based

supporters could at last ease back to normality, as on Tuesday March 17th the front page of the *Manchester Evening News* carried a photograph of the scale model of the new super stadium, following Chairman Martin Edwards' announcement that, "the biggest, most costly and the most ambitious development ever undertaken by Manchester

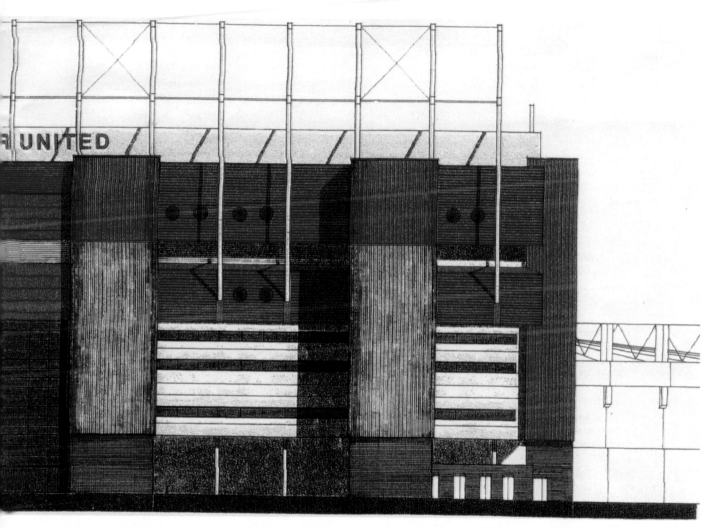

R UNITED

United", would go ahead eight days after planning permission had been given.

With the club given the green light, the project team was put together, consisting of construction managers Hilstone Laurie, architect Atherden Fuller, structural engineer Campbell Reith Hill, mechanical engineer W. E. Hannan, and electrical engineer Piggot and Whitfield. The team had been together for the Stretford End development, with the architects having been responsible for the original cantilever stand on United Road in 1965.

Tim Laycock, regional director of Hilstone Laurie, revealed that the company's original proposals were to construct a new two tier stand, cantilevered over the top of the existing North Stand, simply to increase the ground capacity, but they were concerned that the thirty year old construction would prove too expensive to re-design to modern standards. With United very much concerned on providing first class amenities for their

Architectural Plans: *The New North Stand takes shape.*

supporters and improving safety, the company decided to put forward a proposal to demolish the whole stand and replace it with a new steel construction. Even that was not completely straightforward, as thirteen different proposals were considered before the final decision was made.

For those interested in the merest detail, the stand would measure 114m long by 60m wide, rising 45m above the pitch at its highest point. The roof would be constructed in tubular sections, made up into sixteen main roof trusses measuring 66m long and tapering in depth from 9.8m to 2m. Some 3,500 tonnes of steel would be used, along with 4,500 tonnes of concrete in the form of 10,000 square meters of pre-cast seating units which would take one hundred and eighty five wagons to deliver. A total of 14,800 individual pieces of steel were to be incorporated!

The three tiers would be divided into eight seating levels, with 10,000 square meters earmarked for restaurants and a new museum. Fans in the top tier would sit at a steep thirty-four degree angle above the horizontal, while the second tier would be a mere thirty degrees. The cost of the development was expected to be around £28m, with some £9.1m of that total going towards the purchase of land along the United Road which would be straddled by the new stand. This was actually almost £3m more than the market value. Seating 25,111, the Old Trafford capacity would rise to 55,300, thus becoming the largest club stadium in the country. This would include thirty-two private boxes, with increased seating in the lower sections. The only minus points about the plans was that the next season would see a reduced ground capacity to a mere 33,000, with almost all of those being Season Ticket and League Match Ticket holders, leaving little or no space for the ordinary club member.

As well as increasing the seating capacity, a look at the early plans for the new construction showed that it would also incorporate numerous other facilities. On level one, there would be a bar dining area, along with part of the new club museum, although the main part of the museum would be on level two and would incorporate a classroom and a cinema. There will also be another dining area with kitchen. Level three would also house part of the museum, an executive suite, box-holders lounge and bar, another kitchen and the Red Café - a theme restaurant. The final, fourth level would also provide further dining facilities. The Hilstone Laurie contract would be dictated by five stages, and as each stage was completed it was hoped to be able to release further seating to the supporters, with the entire job scheduled for completion in April 1996.

The home fixture, against Arsenal, shortly after the record breaking defeat of Ipswich (see report), brought further talking points amongst the supporters, with notification that if they stood during the game then they could face ejection from the ground. Many during the course of the match continued the habits of a lifetime, and stood when the excitement got the better of them and goal scoring opportunities arose. Sadly, they found themselves being escorted from the ground by the stewards who had taken over the responsibility from the police for most aspects of crowd control inside the stadium. The fans, and many others, were not amused and meetings were held in protest. It was hoped that the United board would try and create special areas in the ground where like minded-supporters could sit (or stand) and encourage the team, like the vocal centred Stretford End of the past.

At the end of what proved to be a disappointing season by United's recent standards - runners up in both the League and F. A. Cup, the bulldozers moved in to demolish the United Road stand or 'North Stand' which was now its official name. First the seats were removed from both sections, with a state-of-the-art mechanical digger which punched the concrete to pieces, moving in on June 1st. It took just three days to reduce the former 12,500 seated stand to a pile of rubble and by the second week in June the site was completely clear and ready for the pile driving to begin and the new foundations to be laid. By early August, the lower terracing was in place and it was planned to admit fans into the first tier by the turn of the year.

Due to the progress made on the site, two thousand additional seats were made available for the opening home fixture of 1995-96 against West Ham. These seats were in the

▶ **Bulldozers begin to demolish the old cantilever stand.**

▶▶ **North Stand:** *The area where the cantilever stand once stood is ready for work to begin on the new development.*

▼ **Two views of the impressive East Stand that took the ground's capacity up to 55,000**

corner sections beside the open site. Wimbledon's visit in the following fixture saw a further five hundred available as work progressed ahead of schedule. Such seats only became available a day or two prior to the game due to the necessity of a site inspection to ensure total safety in either area.

✳

Numerous memorable goals have been scored at Old Trafford since its opening back in February 1910. Players in every position and from almost every position on the pitch, have found the back of the net, but we have to go back to season 1973-74 and an Alex Stepney penalty against Birmingham City to recall one by a goalkeeper. Competing in the UEFA Cup, the 1st round draw paired United with the unfamiliar Rotor Volgograd from Russia, and having obtained what was considered a creditable 0-0 draw in the first leg away from home, the return was considered a mere formality. The 29,724 crowd, like the United team and management, received

something of a shock as the visitors earned a 2-2 draw and progressed into the next round on the away goal ruling.

Some of the supporters (those who did not leave early in disgust) had the satisfaction of witnessing the first goal scored at the ground by a goalkeeper as a result of an out field move. With the game, like United's proud European home record, looking lost, (Volgograd had taken a 2-0 lead after 24 minutes, with Paul Scholes pulling one back in the 58th minute), a corner at the old Scoreboard End in the shadows of the construction work, saw the awesome figure of Peter Schmeichel amble up field to take a threatening position in the Russian area. This was not his first foray forward, but it proved to be the most profitable, as the green clad figure of the big Dane rose above the opposition defence to head strongly into the back of the net via a defender. A memorable goal on a disappointing night. The Russians, ecstatic with their performance, were also impressed by the Old Trafford pitch and managed to obtain eight bags of grass seed and two bags of fertiliser from United groundsman Keith Kent!

October 1st 1995, a day that had been marked in red within countless diaries around Britain and beyond, saw Old Trafford resemble Paris on Bastille Day, as the French tricolour fluttered in uncountable numbers the autumn air. The occasion? The return of Eric Cantona to the United side for the

first time since his evening of misadventure at Selhurst Park way back in January when he extracted his own form of justice on a supporter who decided to become too vocal in his thoughts. The opponents on the day were arch-rivals Liverpool, but it would not have mattered if it had been the likes of Hartlepool, as it was an occasion not to be missed, as never since the sixties had one man meant so much to the United supporters.

The volatile Frenchman did not disappoint his adoring fans and with only sixty-seven seconds gone, his cross was placed beyond Liverpool goalkeeper James, by Nicky Butt, to give United the lead. The tricolours were raised and the anthems sung a little louder. Liverpool did not lie down and went on to take a 2-1 lead, but the day was always going to belong to one man and, significantly, he had the last word. In the sixty-ninth minute, Giggs was brought down in the box by Redknapp as he moved through on goal, and without a moment's hesitation, Cantona collected the ball, placed it on the spot and proceeded to send James the wrong way, to level the scores. A draw in any other match against Liverpool would have been a disappointment, but the 'King' was back and he had scored. Stallholders scattered

along Sir Matt Busby Way were just as happy, with a few more T-shirts and flags being sold as the fans streamed out of the stadium at full time.

Due to the reduced capacity, United were allowed to ignore the Premier League dispensation recommending that visiting clubs' had to receive 3,000 seats, thus making the ground for home fans only, which made the atmosphere rather subdued with no one from the opposite end of the East Lancs Road to shout at. But as the season progressed and work continued ahead of schedule (and to budget), United sought to alter this and give visiting clubs a limited number of tickets. The lack of atmosphere even prompted the Independent Manchester United Supporters Club to draw up a twenty-plus point plan and forward it to Chairman Martin Edwards in the hope that Old Trafford could be restored to a noisy arena in the future. A couple of the suggestions made were that the entire Stretford End of the ground could be designated an area where fans could stand if they wished, with K stand and East Stand Lower (the old Scoreboard Paddock) also being allowed similar usage. Another point was that singing areas should also be created to help improve the atmosphere.

November 1995 saw part of

the stadium take on a sponsor for the first time, with Express Cargo Forwarding signing a three year deal with the Museum and Tour Centre. More than 500,000 people had visited the museum since it first opened in 1986.

The visit of Southampton on November 18th saw the crowd capacity break the 39,000 barrier for the first time that season, as an addition 7,000 seats had been installed and a safety inspection saw the site pass without any problems, six weeks ahead of schedule. With the North Stand Lower having been available since the end of September, things were returning to normal. Even away fans were re-admitted, with the Hampshire side receiving eight hundred tickets for J Stand, although segregation reduced the overall ground capacity by 1,000. The advanced stage of re-building was believed to have earned the club an extra £1m in gave revenue.

A month later came the 'Topping Out' ceremony on the triple-decker construction. This was a traditional ceremony which saw Chairman Martin Edwards hammer in a golden bolt and a piece of yew branch was tied to part of the roofing to ward off evil spirits.

The F. A. Cup-tie against Manchester City on February 18th 1996 allowed some supporters the privilege of watching the game from the brand new executive boxes at the back of the North Stand, with around 13,000 fellow Reds, in the crowd of 42,692, seated below, thanks once again to the rapid progress being made on the construction front. April was still looked upon as the likely date to see the project completed, with at least one game towards the end of the season having spectators in every section. It would certainly all be ready for the European

Championships, when United, who along with Liverpool, would host the north-west section - Group C - comprising Germany, Italy, Russia and the Czech Republic. The feast of football was enriched with the prospects of a quarter-final and a semi-final tie also taking place at Old Trafford.

Having sold three experienced, and popular, players during the summer in the shape of Ince, Hughes and Kanchelskis, and begun the League campaign with a 3-1 defeat at Aston Villa, many thought that season 1995-96 would be one of rebuilding both on and off the pitch at Old Trafford. However, as the months passed by United maintained steady progress and by early March they had clawed back Newcastle's twelve point advantage with some sterling performances. They were also in the quarter-finals of the F. A. Cup and the home draw against Southampton would see spectators admitted to the second tier of the new stand for the first time. Despite the

previous weeks of rather severe weather, work had continued well and it was hoped that the last two home fixtures would see the attendance move close to the 55,000 capacity.

Supporters arriving at the ground for the Southampton tie on a very wet Manchester evening could reach the stadium by a new route, as a pedestrian footbridge had been constructed across the Bridgwater Canal, allowing access from Trafford Park Road. This provided easy entry into the new North Stand for spectators using that side of the ground for parking. The Cup-tie also saw the new floodlights along the stand roof used for the first time, with the three temporary pylons which provided a partly obscured view for some spectators due to their situation in the lower section of the North Stand, being removed following the previous home fixture. The attendance for that Southampton Cup-tie, which saw United move to within one game of their third consecutive Wembley Cup Final appearance, was 45,446, almost 3,000 more than the season's previous best.

On the night of Thursday March 12th, Old Trafford had a rare and unwelcome visit by cat-burglars, who caused £10,000 worth of damage in an attempt to break into Chairman Martin

Edwards' office. Having scaled a fifty foot wall, they smashed a hole in the stadium roof before crawling through a heating duct to gain entry into the office block. Surprisingly the alarm system did not go off and they managed to obtain entry into the Chairman's second floor office, where they located a safe and proceeded to throw it out from a window onto the concourse below. Having exited the ground, they failed to remove the safe and disappeared into the night. One would have thought that it was impossible for such an incident to occur and even more surprisingly, nothing more was heard of the incident!

The 1-0 victory over Arsenal on March 20th saw the first 50,000 plus crowd for seven years, as the Championship challenge was maintained. The 50,028 attendance was then bettered by 129 four days later, when the other North London club, Tottenham, were the visitors.

Sunday March 31st was F. A. Cup Semi-Final day and as United travelled south to Villa Park, the followers of the Birmingham side took the opposite route to Old Trafford to face Liverpool in the other tie. Ticket pricing by the Football Association was criticised, and as a result many seats at both Semi-Final venues were left

empty, with the 39,072 at Old Trafford being perhaps the most disappointing. United's 2-1 victory over Chelsea saw them move a step closer to a unique second 'double' in three years, something never before achieved.

Easter, the crunch time of any Championship or relegation battle, saw a Manchester 'derby' on April 6th at Maine Road. Such was the interest in the game, with City fighting against the drop into the First Division, that the match was televised live at Old Trafford. Eleven days later, on Wednesday April 17th brought Yorkshire rivals Leeds United across the Pennines to Old Trafford and some of the red army had the privilege of obtaining tickets for a bird's eye view of the game from the very top tier of the North Stand for the first time. Some ten levels and fifty-five meters up, a climb of one hundred and seventy steps would leave even the fittest breathless, and it was certainly not advised to arrive at the ground five minutes prior to the kick-off and hope to be in your seat on time!

People suffering from vertigo or climbing difficulties were advised not to buy seats in this section for the Leeds match, as the lifts were not yet working, but what were the opinions of some of those who ventured into the unknown? "An excellent view where you can see all the action" one said, while another thought it was "too far from the action and would not like to sit there again". The majority of opinions, however, gave it the thumbs up.

On Friday April 26th, a giant crane moved onto the Old Trafford forecourt, but this time it was not for any major construction work, instead it was to manoeuvre an 11ft high bronze statue of Sir Matt Busby onto a podium below the Munich Memorial, on the roof of the entrance into the executive boxes facing Sir Matt Busby Way. The specially commissioned statue, weighing more than one ton, was the work of sculptor Philip Jackson, and inside the hollow figure were some of the scarves and shirts which had been placed on the forecourt following the great man's death. The following day, a special ceremony was held when members of Sir Matt's family, civic dignitaries and club officials were present at the unveiling.

A ceremony of a different kind took place at the ground a week later, when a Heaton Mersey couple became the first to be married at the stadium, following the club's successful application in February to be able to hold marriage ceremonies. Unfortunately the law did not allow the ceremony to be carried out on the actual pitch, so the Premier Suite was used.

April 28th brought Nottingham Forest to Old Trafford, and a victory would put United within touching distance of the Championship. A crowd of 53,926 were present that afternoon as three vital points were won with a memorable 5-0 victory. Cautious play and a couple of near misses looked like all the opening half would produce, but Paul Scholes lifted the pressure a little in the forty-first minute, stabbing home, before David Beckham

added a second three minutes later with an opportunist header. The same individual increased the lead ten minutes into the second half to put the outcome beyond any doubt, and further goals from Giggs and Cantona in the seventieth and ninetieth minutes sent the crowd home dreaming of another title triumph.

The smiles soon disappeared off some faces when it was announced a couple of days later that 2,300 seats in the central section of the new stand would be an executive area the following season, with higher quality catering and parking facilities. Previously priced at £340, the new area would cost a staggering £1,169, preventing most (if not all) of the supporters who sat there - many from its opening in 1965 - from returning to their old places. A further executive area

was earmarked for another 1,300 seats in the first twelve rows of the second tier. The front row in the centre of this area provided what was arguably the best view in the house.

A week after the victory over Forest, a 3-0 win at Middlesbrough secured the Championship, while the following Saturday, a late Eric Cantona goal clinched a remarkable 'double-double' with a 1-0 win over Liverpool in the F. A. Cup Final at Wembley, bringing to an end a remarkable season in the club's history.

An almost empty Old Trafford was the venue for an England .v. Holland under-fifteen international on May 4th, but attendances would be much different for the forthcoming Euro '96 matches which were beginning to capture the imagination of the public. Groundsman   Keith Kent and the other backroom staff had the stadium looking in superb nick, and the introduction of the latest technology from Canada in the form of a germinating blanket for use in the goalmouths, which increased temperatures by eight degrees to encourage growth, helped towards a perfect playing surface.

Old Trafford had never looked better as the club prepared to entertain thousands of supporters, players, officials and media representatives from all over Europe. A special media centre had been constructed within the ground for the use of the three hundred plus journalists covering the games in Manchester. It was boasted that the facilities were so good that a journalist could report on the whole of the tournament from this room, without having to watch a game live.

There was also a new facility for the fans, a Midland Bank Cash dispenser. So, if you ran out of cash for your Mega Store purchases or the ticket tout prices were more than you had in your wallet, your immediate problems were now over.

It had been some three decades since a newly refurbished Old Trafford had played host to Portugal, Hungary and Bulgaria, as the summer of 1966 simmered towards a bubbling cauldron of national frenzy. Thirty years on, with England staging Euro '96, Old Trafford once again welcomed overseas visitors for a major football competition. But it was to be a more colourful and vocal generation of supporters who flocked to the Salford Quays area.

The Championships got under way at Old Trafford on June 9th, with the opening Group C match between Germany and the Czech

Republic, watched by 37,300. The beaten finalists in 1966 were the eventual winners this time around and got off to the perfect start, defeating their opponents (who they would meet again in the Final) 2-0. Seven days later they went one better with a 3-0 defeat of Russia in front off 50,760. At one point this match looked like being postponed due to a bomb explosion in central Manchester the previous day, but it went ahead as planned. Sadly the Germans third game in the group (against Italy) failed to produce any goals to satisfy the appetite of the 53,740 present.

Old Trafford, and Manchester, remained the German's 'home' for the Quarter-Finals, with Croatia narrowly losing 2-1 in front of a somewhat disappointing 43,412. The Semi-Final tie between the Czechs and France, which attracted just over four hundred more than the previously mentioned game, remained goalless after ninety minutes. Extra time also failed to produce a goal, so it was down to penalties with the Czech's eventually winning 6-5 to proceed to the Final.

As the players made their way off the pitch, Keith Kent and his staff moved into their normal after match routine, but waiting outside the ground

was a much larger squad of workers, who were ready to move onto the United groundsman's precious patch. Scheduled for Old Trafford on the eve of the Wembley Euro '96 Final was 'The Crowd Are on the Pitch - Euro '96 Extravaganza'. This was a special concert, featuring Manchester band Simply Red, along with M People, Madness, and Dodgy, with clowns, stilt walkers and a troupe of acrobats. Normally preparations for such an event took a week, but the 320 workers had only 60 hours to transform the ground. The riggers and roadies worked in twenty-four hour shifts to complete the job, with thirty trucks bringing the equipment to the stadium.

Around 60,000 flocked to the ground on a fine Manchester night, and on a huge elevated stage in the centre of the pitch, complete with large video screens, United manager Alex Ferguson appeared to open the concert with the words - "Welcome to the Theatre of Dreams", before introducing Simply Red fronted by United fanatic Mick Hucknall. The special Old Trafford atmosphere was soon in evidence and the evening turned into something special. The

The Gibson Guarantee: *A plaque commemorating the contribution of former chairman James Gibson.*

pitch was covered with fans, security and technicians and the support group M People soon had everybody in the stadium dancing as they blasted out their hits, with the mood continuing as Simply Red brought a unique evening to a close. Old Trafford had not experienced so much singing and dancing since the Blackburn Rovers match of season 1992-93, following that first title triumph for twenty-six years.

Prior to the United .v. Chelsea fixture on November 2nd 1996 (a 2-1 defeat), a plaque was unveiled in the players tunnel area, in memory of Mr James Gibson, who had came to United's rescue in December 1931, ploughing some £3,000 into the club funds. The sum, a modest amount by today's standards was enough to keep the club afloat, providing some secure footing on which to build, with Manchester United quite

possibly not being in need of a stadium like today's, or perhaps not even being in existence at all, if it had not been for his investment, one of the reasons behind the club's decision to erect this permanent memorial. A member of the Gibson family had maintained a place on the United board from 1931 until 1996 upon the death of James Gibson's son Alan. Present at the unveiling was James Gibson's nephew, Alan Embling, along with his wife, manager Alex Ferguson, Chairman Martin Edwards and director Les Olive.

A similar plaque was unveiled opposite the one to Mr James Gibson a couple of months later, this time in memory of Mr John Henry Davies, who had performed a rescue act of his own, saving the club from

GREEN FLAG

PATRON
HER MAJESTY THE QUEEN
PRESIDENT
H.R.H. THE DUKE OF KENT
CHAIRMAN   CHIEF EXECUTIVE
K.ST.J. WISEMAN   R.H.G. KELLY, FCIS

GREEN FLAG
INTERNATIONAL MATCH

ENGLAND
v
SOUTH AFRICA

TO BE PLAYED AT
MANCHESTER UNITED FOOTBALL CLUB
OLD TRAFFORD, MANCHESTER
ON
SATURDAY, 24th MAY, 1997
KICK-OFF 18.00 hrs.

Programme of Arrangements

bankruptcy during the bleak season of 1901-02, whilst also playing a major part in the change of name from Newton Heath to Manchester United. Present at this unveiling were Bobby Charlton, Martin Edwards, Jo Russell, Cynthia Thomas and Toby Russell, grand daughter, great grand daughter and great great grandson of Mr

Davies respectively.

A few weeks after the first of those tunnel plaques were unveiled, there was yet another unveiling ceremony at the ground, when UEFA President Lennart Johansson officially opened the North Stand, prior to the Champions League fixture against Juventus, a match the Italians won 1-0 thanks to a Del

Piero penalty following a clumsy Nicky Butt challenge on the same player.

International fixtures were nothing new at Old Trafford, but there was something of a first on Saturday May 24th 1997, when England played host to South Africa for the first time in what was a 'Green Flag International'. A colourful crowd of 52,676

packed the ground, enjoying a 2-1 'home' win, with United favourites Phil Neville, Nicky Butt, David Beckham and Paul Scholes all taking up positions in the England line up. This was the second 'big occasion' at Manchester M16 in a matter of weeks, with the F. A. Cup semi-final between Chesterfield and Middlesbrough having been played at the ground on Sunday April 13th.

Thirteen days prior to the above England international fixture, on Sunday May 11th, no-one present in the 55,249 crowd could have sensed that they were actually witnessing an abdication, rather than a crowning. It had been an afternoon of continuous silverware, as first the United 'A' team, 'B' team and reserve sides had collected their respective League Championship trophies, Ken Doherty, the United supporting World Snooker Champion, had shown off his recently won trophy and had there been any connection with the winners of the Grand National or the Boat Race, then it was odds on that they too would have shared the Old Trafford stage.

As it was, after a rather non-descript ninety minutes against West Ham United, which United won 2-0 (goals from Solskjaer and Cruyff), recording their first home win since March 15th, Eric Cantona stepped forward to lift the Premiership trophy, United's fourth in five seasons. The enigmatic Frenchman had already received the Player of the Year trophy and as he saluted his adoring public for the second time that afternoon, he gave away nothing as to what was really passing through his mind. Seven days later he announced that he was leaving United and

retiring from the game.

Few players who have graced the Old Trafford turf had made such an overall impact on the club as Eric Cantona. Perhaps his final forty-five minutes in the red shirt of United had been little to write home about, but over his one hundred and eighty odd appearances he created numerous Old Trafford memories. His return from suspension and scoring a penalty against Liverpool on October 1st 1995 and more recently, a sublime piece of individual footballing skill against Sunderland on December 21st 1996, (a 5-0 win), when he coolly chipped the stranded Sunderland goalkeeper for one of the stadium's most memorable goals. If gone in body, he would certainly remain in spirit.

Prior to the above mentioned West Ham United fixture, a large number of supporters had gathered at the Streford End of the ground, outside the large red gate that serves as the player's entrance, but on this particular occasion, they were not there in the hope of catching a glimpse of one of their favourites, with the opportunity of obtaining an odd autograph, they were there to see yet another plaque unveiling. This time, it was on the outside of the ground, high on the wall above the player's entrance and was the United supporters tribute

to Sir Matt Busby. The life size engraving, in black stone, cost around £9,000 and was so heavy that it had to be shipped from the United States where it had been carved.

Despite the shock and dismay at Eric Cantona's retirement, interest in Manchester United never wavered, with the world-wide support reaching towards an all-time high. So much so, the directors announced in early August 1997, that they had applied to the Premier League for permission to screen home fixtures live from Old Trafford to Bury's Gigg Lane, where they expected to attract around 7,000 supporters to each showing. It was, however, a plan that was never to get off the ground, as a week later, the board pulled the plug on the idea, due to 'licensing reasons'.

Supporters were well to the fore in the early days of the 1997-98 campaign, with

Red Star Sports: *The shops at the corner of Sir Matt Busby Way and Chester Road have become an assembly point for United fans.*

the *Manchester Evening News* carrying an article on October 6th, entitled 'United They Stand', debating the issue of standing at football matches. It was something that United were reported to be leading a campaign for, with chief executive Martin Edwards posing the "shall we stand?" question. Dipping his toe into the water to test the temperature of public opinion, the man the fans loved to hate, was surprised to find that it was surprisingly warm.

Former United favourite Lou Macari came out as a strong supporter of the standing issue, saying "I'm mindful of the Hillsborough disaster, but we are a long way down the road and much progress in ground safety has been made. You often find people standing on seats during exciting moments and that in itself can be dangerous – and then of course they block the view of a whole section of fans behind them." Speaking of Martin Edwards, Macari continued, "He is a clever man. He realises it would benefit the club because more fans would get in and it would also appeal to supporters because they would get cheaper tickets and everyone wins."

For the second time in a matter of months, United failed to see their plans develop further, as the Football Association opposed Martin Edwards's suggestion regarding the standing issue, saying, "We would consider such a move a backward step by clubs in the top division". This, however, would not be the end to the standing debate, not by a long shot.

Such was the atmosphere at the ground on Saturday November 22nd 1997, that standing was more or less an obligation amongst the 55,243 crowd in attendance for the first appearance of Rugby Union at Old Trafford for the first time in over one hundred years, to watch England play the New Zealand 'All Blacks', with the latter recording a 25-8 victory. At the end of the game, England were given a standing ovation despite their defeat, with manager Clive Woodward saying "I've never experienced anything like this in my life. I honestly believe this atmosphere affected the

opposition. They walked into a lions den. Our dressing room was unbelievable and I wish Twickenham was more like this."

1998 did not get off to the best of starts, as the standing debate continued to roll, gathering so much momentum, that the club had to issue a warning to supporters regarding the continual persistent standing at games. This was mainly due to the widespread trouble during the Boxing Day fixture against Everton, as offending fans were thrown out of the ground, as others stayed on their feet despite the threats of ejection, whilst chanting "stand up for the Champions", whilst also screaming obscenities at chairman Martin Edwards.

Despite warning notices and public address announcements that those who continued to stand were flouting the ground safety rules, many continued to do so, leading to scuffles with security staff, offenders being ejected from the ground and their season tickets being confiscated. Letters were also sent to all club members, warning of sections of the ground being closed, while the local Trafford Council were reportedly ready to send out those closure notices.

It was certainly an edgy situation and a worry for club officials, but by mid January something of a truce had occurred, with the withdrawal of security staff from the East Stand Lower for the match against Tottenham Hotspur on the 10th of the month, following

talks with the Independent Manchester United Supporters Association.

*

Old Trafford and the surrounding area was forever changing and anyone who had moved away from the area a couple of decades

previously would certainly not recognise the place upon their return, and in the final few paragraphs of the first edition of 'Old Trafford – The Theatre of Dreams' published in 1996, I wrote "will adjoining areas to the ground see something along the lines of a 'Fred the Red' theme park, with a hotel to generate further income….". It was simply a tongue in the cheek suggestion, but in March 1998, it was announced that the club were to build a £5million hotel. Nobody, however, had picked up on the suggestion of a 'Fred the Red' theme park!

As it turned out, it wasn't entirely a "United" hotel, as they were simply to become major shareholders in the one hundred and ten bedroom, three star hotel, sited a mere goal kick from the ground opposite the popular Red Army haunt of Sam Platt's pub. The new hotel would feature

United memorabilia in the reception area, but nothing along the scale of the new look club museum, which was officially opened on Saturday April 11th 1998, by none other than the legendary Pele, who had also kindly loaned many of his own items of memorabilia for the first of many special displays.

The new look museum, which had cost £4million and taken around seven months to complete, was built on three floors and would be the new starting point for the stadium tours. Incorporating its own café, shop and audio visual theatre, the museum contained a mixture of traditional showcase displays, along with graphic, historical and contemporary film footage, as well as modern techniques to involve and entertain visitors of all ages.

The displays also revealed much material collected by the club and previously hidden away in storage, finally see the light of day. Those items would be incorporated into a number of themes, including 'The Trophy Room', 'Legends', 'Munich', 'Playing Kits' and so forth. There would also be an archive for researchers and a dedicated classroom to reflect the demand of schools and groups.

One item that did not find its way into any of the museums showcases, but became instantly in demand by many supporters, was a square of the hallowed Old Trafford turf. With the 1997-98 season at a close, United decided to replace the playing area, which had been used for some seven hundred odd fixtures over the past eleven years and was now showing signs of wear. Replacing the turf would also give the club the opportunity to also improve the under soil heating and drainage systems.

"The main problem was the drainage," explained United groundsman Keith Kent. "It was becoming antiquated, with areas of the pitch becoming flooded during heavy rain. We decided that it was imperative that both the pitch and drainage was replaced during the summer."

Following the decision to re-turf the pitch, it was also decided that it would be cut into 10,000 strips and given away to supporters who filled in a special card in the museum. The names of those who would be able to claim their own piece of United history would be drawn at random and would have to come to Old Trafford in person to collect it. How many reading this can boast of a piece of Old Trafford turf in their back garden?

The new turf that adorned Old Trafford for the opening fixture of season 1998-99 had seen the club go to the other side of the world to ensure that the playing surface would be one of the best around. Finding the ideal turf had taken head groundsman Keith Kent to Australia and the Melbourne Cricket Ground on a fact finding mission and upon his return, the new turf was grown in Yorkshire and laid by a Scottish company, making it quite an international affair.

With the earlier setback of showing fixtures from Old Trafford live to a big screen at Bury's Gigg Lane, United lowered their sights to a slightly smaller screen, while at the same time looking towards a much wider audience, with the announcement that they were going to launch MUTV, broadcasting from a purpose built studio in the heart of Old Trafford. This joint venture with BSkyB and the Granada Media Group made United the first club in the world to have its own daily television channel.

Although there were early teething problems, the channel continued to grow, producing a variety of excellent documentaries, and today is still a big part of the Manchester United brand.

On Monday December 15th, after a request from former United player John Doherty, on behalf of the Manchester United Former Players Association to chairman Martin Edwards, it was announced that the club were going to honour those who had been involved in the 1958 Munich air disaster, by playing a special match to commemorate the 40th anniversary of the tragedy, with all proceeds going to the survivors and families of those who had lost their lives. Bayern Munich or Red Star Belgrade were touted as possible opponents.

Director, Maurice Watkins

said, "It is hoped that there will be a game at the beginning of the year to commemorate the 40th anniversary. It's just a question of sorting out the best date. We also hope that it will be against appropriate opposition."

At first, Martin Edwards was hesitant, but once Eric Cantona hinted that he would like the opportunity to say farewell to the United supporters, the event took on more momentum, with the United chairman deciding to combine the two – the Munich Memorial match and Cantona's farewell. From that moment on, the game seemed to take on a comletely new agenda that did not sit well with many people. More so, when it was announced that due to the Frenchman's unavailability for the planned February date, the match would not take place until August, with the opposition now a Cantona selected European X1.

Edwards, not for the first time since becoming chairman, was severely criticised from various sources for turning the match into something of a publicity stunt, while Elizabeth Wood, the divorced wife of Munich survivor Ray Wood compared the treatment of the Munich victims to that of "dancing bears at the circus".

So, on Tuesday August 18th 1998, some four hundred and fifty-seven days after

surprisingly announcing his retirement, Cantona returned to Old Trafford for one last *adieu* and despite the fixture being given the title of the Munich Memorial match, the whole evening soon revolved around one man only – Eric Cantona and the Frenchman received a tumultuous reception from the 55,210 crowd as he ran out onto the pitch accompanied by his son Rafael, wearing the black and white shirt of the European XI for the first forty-five minutes, a team which included the likes of Blanc, Robson, Gascoigne and Hughes, changing into the more familiar red of United for the second forty-five.

A one minute silence preceded the kick-off, but it was obvious from the outset that the evening was going to be treated as little more than an exhibition game. Entertainment was certainly high on the agenda and the crowd were treated to everything that they could have wished for as the game unfolded. The only thing that was missing as the game moved into its final stages was a goal from the enigmatic Frenchman.

With ten minutes remaining, the supporters eagerly watched in anticipation, as the number seven beneath the trademark upturned collar beat his brother Joel (one of the numerous substitutes on the night), avoided another half-hearted challenge, side stepped goalkeeper Olmeta (who had earlier threatened to steal the evening from Cantona with some eccentric play), before audaciously placing the ball into the back of the Stretford End goal as another defender lay sprawled on the line. For the record, United won 8-4, with goals from Ryan Giggs, Paul Scholes, Jordi Cruyff, Phil Neville, Nicky Butt, Alex Notman (2) and the man himself. Jean-Pierre Papin, Laurent Blanc, Martin Dahlin and United's Mark Wilson, guesting for the visitors, scored for the European XI.

There had been much debate in the weeks and days leading up to the memorial match, as to how the money raised would be distributed and it was finally agreed that so much would go to any passenger still living, next would be the widows of those who died. If there was no living widow, then that share would then go to any children. If there should be no children, then it would go to parents, or brothers and sisters. If none of the above applied, then that particular share of the money would be given to charity.

Various questions were raised as to why this person should receive that amount, or why that was paid out, with each dependant receiving just over £47,000, with that figure broken down accordingly, but the biggest gripe of all, and what soured the whole occasion, came when it was later announced that Eric Cantona had recouped over £90,000 in expenses directly from the testimonial fund, rather than from the club. Included in these expences was the cost of flying himself and his family from Paris to Manchester in a private jet and the hotel bill from the exclusive Mottram Hall Hotel, where Cantona stayed for three nights and his family for four or five.

On Monday September 7th 1998, the news broke that Manchester United Football Club was near to being sold to media mogul Rupert Murdoch, the owner of BskyB, much to the fury of many supporters. But amid the flurry of takeover rumours and news came the announcement that the club were preparing to turn Old Trafford into a 67,000 capacity stadium by the year 2001.

Plans had been submitted to Trafford Council for the redevelopment of both the East and West Stands at a cost of around £30million. This 12,000 rise in capacity was to be achieved by adding two tiers to the existing structures. The club were also quick to state that the planned expansion had nothing at all to do with the recent takeover moves.

The goalless draw with Newcastle United on November 8th did not cause manager Alex Ferguson too much concern, but what did worry the United manager that Sunday afternoon, was the state of the Old Trafford pitch. Large divots were being kicked up, with a mass of holes clearly visible after the match. This was certainly not something that you would expect from a newly laid surface and by a strange coincidence, the pitch consultant, John Souter, was actually at the match and the following morning inspected the pitch closely with groundsman Keith Kent. The rumours that blue nosed worms were behind the poor condition of the pitch were firmly scotched...

Following the game against Blackburn Rovers on November 14th, the pitch was once again dug up and re-laid with a heavier turf, much to the club's embarrassment. The grass, once again grown in Yorkshire, was grown to a depth of two inches and cut into ten metre strips, each weighing half a ton. Nearly one thousand strips were required to cover the pitch and were delivered six at a time by a fleet of lorries. This was only a temporary measure, as it would be dug up again at the end of the season and replaced by younger shoots which would hopefully bed into the drainage.

On Sunday January 10th 1999 West Ham United travelled north to Manchester, hoping to pull level on points with United, who sat in fourth place in the Premier League with thirty-five points from their twenty games, with the game scheduled for the usual Sunday afternoon television slot of 4pm.

United's title aspirations, however, were surprisingly plunged into darkness when workmen severed a mains electricity cable outside the ground, putting the game itself into some considerable doubt. With the majority of the crowd already in the ground and the usual late arrivals making their way towards the turnstiles, there was now a frantic race against time to repair the damage. Discussions between the club, the workmen and the police led to the decision to delay the kick off for forty-five minutes.

The power outtage also created a major safety concern at the end of the match. When the game eventually started, power had been restored in some form to all parts of the ground, although in the North Stand, where the fault had originated, lighting was reduced to practically nil.

As the game moved towards full time, supporters in the North Stand, who decided to leave early, as many were apt to do for a variety of reasons, were initially turned back from their planned decent by stewards, until torches could be found to enable them to be escorted safely down the countless steps. But by then the scenes had became somewhat chaotic, with many supporters concerned that there might be a major safety issue. Fire stairs with emergency lighting were eventually used as the final

DO YOU CARE ABOUT YOUR FOOTBALL CLUB?

DOES ITS HISTORY MATTER TO YOU?
DO YOU WANT TO GET BEHIND YOUR TEAM?
IF THE ANSWER TO THESE QUESTIONS IS YES,

JOIN US

Murdoch's papers were quick enough to stick the boot in when Eric was banned. Fergie has been noticably quiet about supporting the bid. If you, like us, want to fight this takeover:

▶ Display this card.

▶ Sing Calypso at 8.30pm, 15 mins before half time against Liverpool.

▶ Boycott all Murdoch products.

▶ Cancel your Sky subscriptions by phoning 0990 102030 the day before your October payment.

If you wish to do more to preserve your football club, contact IMUSA PO Box 69 Stretford Manchester M32 0EL, our website (www.imusa.org.uk) or phone us on 0161 829 9941.

whistle blew.

"Neither the police nor the stewards knew what was going on. They were in complete disarray," said one supporter who had been sitting in that area of the ground. "The police had blocked off the normal exits and people were only allowed to get out via two passages, one at either end, and they were only three feet wide. I then decided to turn back, because I had my son with me and I didn't get out of the ground until an hour afterwards."

Another supporter asked – "Where was the organisation? By the time we tried to leave the ground, they had known about the problems of emptying the stand for three hours. They should have made an announcement before the end of the game for those people who wanted to leave early. It took me nearly fifteen minutes to walk down two flights of stairs in pitch blackness. People were screaming and getting squashed and crushed. Someone grabbed hold of my hand when the lights went out on the stair because of the pushing."

Some supporters were led out of the ground through a restaurant area, lit only by candles. United assistant secretary Ken Ramsden, however, denied that there had been any problems. He said – "I personally started making announcements to the fans in the North Stand well before the final whistle, asking them to remain in their seats. Only certain areas of the concourse were illuminated

and we considered it of paramount importance to guard against any crush developing. It was all very carefully supervised and everyone was very patient. The whole exercise went off without a hitch and the last few fans were out of the ground and on their way home by 7.30pm."

Urgent enquiries took place in the aftermath of the afternoon's drama, which saw United win 4-1 in front of 55,180 spectators, with electricity suppliers Norweb and Trafford Council both very much involved. The reduction in power had been originally caused by a fault in United's own power system, which was why no neighbouring homes had been affected. Rather surprisingly, Norweb had a private box at the ground, but it took three tannoy announcements for their engineer to attend the fault, while United's own electrician tried to solve the problem.

One steward later contacted the *Manchester Evening News*, saying, "I would like to know just whose decision it was to let the game go ahead, knowing that the North Stand was only running on back up power. They should realise that they cannot put people's lives in potential danger."

Following the blackout problem, United only had a week to sort out things out and convince Trafford Council, the stadium licensing authority, that everything was working to order, allowing them to hold their F. A. Cup clash with Liverpool. Norweb laid extra cables at the ground, while the emergency

UNITED 2 TOTTENHAM H 1

As early as the fifth minute Dwight Yorke had the majority of those who were not already standing, on their feet, but to everyone's disappointment his block on Walker's attempted clearance hit the post. United continued to dominate the early exchanges, but slowly, Tottenham came into the game and in the twenty-fourth minute, they stunned the United supporters in the 55,189 crowd into silence. A long ball over the top of the United mid-field, was flicked on by Iverson and Les Ferdinand reacted quickly to lob the ball over Schmeichel and into the roof of the net.

Beckham and Giggs failed to conjure up anything on the flanks. Sheringham was booked, as well as being continuously barracked by the Spurs contingent in the away section of the ground who had at one time sung his praises, as a frustrated United looked to be going in at the interval a goal behind.

With a mere three minutes remaining before the break, an audible sight of relief echoed around the ground. Paul Scholes dispossessed Sherwood, exchanging passes with Giggs, before picking out Beckham as the winger moved into the Tottenham penalty area. Keeping his cool, he sent a rising drive past Walker, just between the angle of the post and the crossbar, and into the back of the net for the equaliser.

Manager Alex Ferguson had made the half time substitution of replacing Teddy Sheringham with Andy Cole and one minute forty-seven seconds after coming on, with United attacking their favoured second half Stretford End goal, he looped the ball over the head of Walker in the Tottenham goal, following an excellent through ball from Gary Neville. Many were still scrambling back to their seats, having enjoyed a welcome nerve quenching half time drink, when the ground erupted.

A most welcome goal without a doubt, but its timing meant hat there were still approximately forty three minutes still to play!

Radio earpieces were fiddled now employed with the regularity than those at a bodyguards convention, as the afternoon slowly progressed. From the touchline, Alex Ferguson shouted, pointed and kept his players focused, but as the minutes and the finger nails wore away and the final whistle eventually came, United were once again Premier League champions and one step closer to that treble.

▲ **East Stand:** *An artist's impression of what was to become the East Stand, housing club offices and the new megastore.*

▲▶ **The Statue of Sir Matt Busby before it was moved.**

▲ **Two views of the work in progress**

power supply was boosted just in case. The only problem which materialised during the Liverpool cup-tie was the length of time that it took for United to win the game, their two goals, from Dwight Yorke and Ole Gunnar Solskjaer coming in the final two minutes.

*

Second in command's rarely receive the accolades that they deserve, although more than a few former United players would be quick to point out the contribution Jimmy Murphy made to their professional

careers and indeed to the club itself in those darkest of days following the Munich disaster. So it was perhaps fitting that on the evening of Tuesday February 3rd 1999, in a week that saw Steve McClaren appointed as Alex Ferguson's assistant, that a bronze bust of Matt Busby's right hand man was unveiled in the Old Trafford museum, commanding a special place in the 'Munich' section.

The Stretford End has witnessed countless memorable moments, with the red bedecked, singing and swaying occupants acclaiming the achievements of their heroes. But on Friday March 26th, the area considered to be the heartbeat of the vast stadium was silent and empty, with the red and white seats the only witnesses to the movement down in the goalmouth.

There, a group of individuals, who would have been totally unfamiliar to the Stretford Enders, gathered with the stars from previous decades – the likes of Noel Cantwell, David Herd, Nobby Stiles, Albert Scanlon and Denis Law, as they paid their last respects to United legend Dennis Viollet. Viollet, a Mancunian by birth, from the blue heartland around Maine Road, had joined United in 1950, scoring 179 goals in 293 appearances before joining Stoke City in 1962 and later moving to America where he shone as a coach and where he had died earlier in the month. Dennis had fought as bravely against his illness as he had played for the club and it was fitting that his ashes should be scattered at the ground by his wife Helen as other members of his family and friends looked on.

Tottenham Hotspur travelled north to Old Trafford on Sunday May 16th 1999, carrying the hopes of the country's non-United supporters, as they attempted to prevent United

from lifting their fifth Premier League title. It was, however, with mixed emotions, as a draw could hand the championship to their north London rivals Arsenal, who sat in second place one point behind United.

This ninety minutes of football kicked off an unprecedented eleven days which would the club attempt the unprecedented treble of Premier League, FA Cup and European Cup. On that particular Sunday afternoon, Old Trafford was a sea of red and white, except for the usual corner containing the three thousand or so away supporters adjacent to the main stand. Prior to kick-off, Russell Watson worked the crowd into a frenzy, with 'Nessun Dorma', whilst reminding them of what was to come just over a week later, as if that was required, with a rendition of 'Barcelona'. The stage was set. (see report)

Step two of the treble was achieved at Wembley six days later, when Newcastle United were defeated 2-0 in the F. A. Cup Final, which could be best described as totally one-sided. Four days to go. Four days that could see United crowned kings of Europe and the first English side to claim the treble of the two domestic crowns and the European Cup.

As the history books show, United reached the Promised Land with a dramatic 2-1 victory over Bayern Munich in Barcelona. A goal behind at the interval and as the second half wore on, it slowly began to look as though time had finally

caught up with Alex Ferguson's side. With the fourth official signalling three minutes of injury time to play, United won a corner and from Beckham's kick, a scrambled effort from Giggs, was forced over the line by Sheringham. Thirty seconds later, United won another corner, on the same side of the ground and this time Sheringham rose to nod Beckham's kick down towards Solskjaer, who instinctively stuck out a foot and the ball rose into the roof of the Bayern Munich net. United were European Champions and the Norwegian had written his name into United folklore.

On the morning of May 27th, Old Trafford was buzzing as the regular workforce, who had not made the trip to Spain, turned up for work. There was a spring in their step, despite the soreness in some of the heads and the tiredness in some eyes. In the museum, there was work to be done, with space having to be cleared to make way for yet another trophy.

Fortunately, I got a view of Old Trafford as never before. The pilot on my flight back from Barcelona took us back over the stadium and thankfully I had a window seat. I had been fortunate to have seen the ground (and most of Manchester) from the roof of the

North Stand, during the building of that particular structure, but from a couple of miles, or whatever, up in the sky, it was something else. Particularly that morning!

The building work on the East and West Stands progressed on schedule, taking shape above the existing structures, with no affect on the ground capacity. New entrances and exits had to be put into place, with a thoroughfare under the building work, but a central barrier came down at the East Stand an hour and a half prior to kick off, with only those holding tickets for that section being allowed through. The construction work, however, did not all go according to plan, as a high-rise crane worker suffered an asthma attack one hundred and twenty feet above the ground and had to be rescued by fire brigade officers who were winched up to the worker, who was lowered to the ground and taken to hospital.

October 11th 1999 saw a crowd of 54,842 inside Old Trafford to salute the man who above all others was responsible for the modern day stadium – Sir Alex Ferguson. If the Old Trafford of the 1960's was Sir Matt Busby's, then there was no doubt that the present day stadium was the Glaswegian's legacy. Forget

DENNIS VIOLLET R.I.P. Died 6th March 1999

The family would like to invite you to a Memorial Tribute to be held in the Trafford Suite (South Stand) at Manchester United Football Club on Friday, 26th March at 5.00 pm.

At Dennis' request, this is to be a happy occasion and not one for mourning.

Please present this invitation at Door D3

the architects, draftsmen and their like, forget the United board who countersigned each development, if it had not been for the success of the man from Govan's teams then there would have been little need for a stadium capable of holding over 67,000 supporters.

The Sir Alex Ferguson testimonial match was played between United and a Rest of the World side, managed by Ottmar Hitzfeld the Bayern Munich manager in Barcelona on that memorable May evening, and was a night which conjured up everything that a football match should. Flair, fun and memorable individualistic goals.

Against the evening's script, the Rest of the World, whose ranks included Schmeichel, Cafu, Gascoigne, Weah, Larsson, Vialli, Rio Ferdinand and of course Eric Cantona, took the lead through Vialli. Peter Schmeichel meandered up field at every possible opportunity, while his second half replacement, Pascal Olmeta, the crowd pleasing entertainer from the recent Munich Memorial fixture, once again stole the show as he had done fifteen months previously.

After the interval, the current United side made way for the stars of Fergusson's early tenure at Old Trafford, with Paul Parker, Clayton Blackmore, Steve Bruce, Gary Pallister, Mark Hughes, Bryan Robson, David Beckham, Lee Sharpe and Darren Ferguson taking the field, with Cantona and Schmechel changing sides. Beckham, Robson and Cantona all wore number seven shirts.

By mid-October 1999 the Old Trafford pitch was replaced for the fourth time in eighteen months, with the ground staff and other workers moving in following the match against Watford on the 15th of the month. They had four days in which to complete the job. The main cause of its problems being given as the size of the stadium, a complaint apparently common across Europe, with the towering stands, blanking out the sunlight.

George Johnson, the group property manager at Old Trafford said, "Grass grows better in an open space and a bigger stadium means worse growing conditions. In addition, much higher standard pitches are now expected at top clubs. The pitch at United is something that we take sensibly, a key factor in the whole organisation. We are always looking to improve the turf and it will be under constant review."

While the United team, and the usual "where the Reds will play…." members of the Red Army, were sunning themselves on the highly controversial trip to Brazil for the World Club Championship, the bulldozers moved into Old Trafford. Not to assist in any new stadium development, but to once again dig up the pitch for the sixth time in two years and the third time since the previous summer. With over £1millon already

spent trying to find a solution to the ongoing problem, the bill for the sought after 'perfect surface' could easily double.

The Boxing Day fixture against Bradford City left the pitch little more than a bog, following a downpour, with Sir Alex Ferguson commenting that it was "taking the zip out of our attacking play. You have to be a Trojan to get through it." When captain Roy Keane had been asked about the state of the playing surface, he replied – "Don't ask me about the pitch, just ask my hamstrings." Just as frustrated as the previous two, head groundsman Keith Kent said that the latest work was little more than "a repair job to get us through until May. After that we will get it right, you mark my words."

Even the so called "repair job" came in for criticism, with a member of the Institute of Groundsmanship saying that the work should not have been carried out, as he would not advise anyone to re-turf their back garden at this time of year, never mind a Premier football pitch. As it turned out, the repair job, carried out by a team of Dutch specialists, took less than a week and proved to be such a success that it was not lifted as planned during the following summer, but kept in place.

Compared to the pitch, increasing the stadium capacity with the extension of the East and West Stands created little

in the way of problems, with the Arsenal fixture on January 24th 2000 seeing the release of the first batch of 3,000 seats in the East Stand, creating a new Premiership record attendance of 58,293. It was a record that was to last only five days, as a further 3,000 seats were released for the match against Middlesborough, when the attendance rose to 61,267. This also beat the British record attendance, 60,506, which was held by Celtic. Not surprisingly, United's own record was broken again as the season progressed, with the highest attendance of the season coming against Derby County, on March 11th, when 61,619 were present.

The second tier of the East Stand had been completed seven months ahead of schedule, while work on the West Stand was also well ahead of time, thanks mainly to a brainwave by Birse Construction who were responsible for the £30million ground expansion. The company suggested that United should close their Megastore, situated behind the old Stretford End, and move it to temporary accommodation, so that work could be speeded up and the contract time drastically reduced. A spokesman for Birse said, "Originally we had to complete the East Stand and the Megastore by February 2000, which would allow the West Stand work to begin in May, without affecting trade in the store. The key to the stadium being completed twelve months ahead was the suggestion to

move the store." The store moved to portacabins in the main car park.

The completion of the East Stand saw the moving of a familiar Old Trafford landmark back to more or less its original site. Sited above the entrance to the executive boxes at the old Scoreboard End, Sir Matt Busby's statute had been moved to inside the entrance to the United Museum in North Stand, but it was restored to a position above the entrance to the new Megastore.

The defence of the European Cup was a not altogether smooth road, but hopes were high that the trophy would remain at Old Trafford for at least a further twelve months. The two group stages were navigated safely, and a 0-0 draw in Spain, against Real Madrid in the quarter-finals, was thought by some to give the team the advantage in the Old Trafford second leg. As it was, the lack of the 'away goal' proved fatal, with the Spaniards snatching three in Manchester, with United only managing a couple in reply.

But it was the second group phase fixture against Italian side Fiorentina that captured the headlines and not for the emphatic 3-1 victory. Much to the annoyance and embarrassment of the club, there was once again a power failure prior to a match. This time, it was the floodlights above the South Stand going off, just before 7.30pm, with the match due to kick off at 7.45pm. There was, however, no repeat of the West Ham fiasco, as technicians fixed the problem in twenty minutes

▲ **The completed stadium:**
After a decade of construction work on and off the pitch Manchester United and Old Trafford had been transformed

and the game kicked off only a mere fifteen minutes late.

8 - 100 YEARS ON

THE STANDING ISSUE was still a major headache for the club on match days and on the eve of the season 2000-2001, the *Manchester Evening News* revealed that United fans would be issued with a "three strikes and you're out" warning if they persistently stood at Old Trafford, as safety difficulties threatened to close parts of the ground. It was believed that any prohibition order by the licensing authorities would cover two home games.

Despite these problems, the club were rumoured at have put plans to Trafford Council to re-develop the South Stand. However, a statement issued by chief executive Peter Kenyon seemed to knock the idea on the head. "We have just extended to 67,500 which was where we wanted to go," the Chief Executive said. "we feel it satisfies our requirements. We think that 67,500 is right in the changing media environment. Our objective is to fill Old Trafford every game." This was also due to the fact that the board were concerned about the proposed pay-per-view screening of games and that the lack of Saturday afternoon fixtures would affect attendances.

United certainly had no fears in reaching their objective as regards to filling Old Trafford for every home fixture, as the new upper section of the West Stand was completed during the close season and for the opening fixture of season 2000-2001, against Newcastle United, the attendance was recorded at 67,477 and it only dropped below the 67,000 mark for the Champions League fixtures. The highest attendance was recorded against Coventry City, on April 14th, with 67,637 present for the 4-2 victory, a win which left the players and spectators waiting three hours to find out if they were to be Champions again due to the kick-off timing of other games. The chase for the championship obviously created a wealth of exciting moments, whilst at the same time causing considerable problems, as a majority of supporters continued to stand during matches and not simply when their red heroes were on the attack.

As in the previous campaign, United marched through both group phases in the Champions League into the quarter-finals, where Bayern Munich were waiting with thoughts of revenge. But as United sought to gain advantage in the first leg home fixture, the horizon was darkened with thoughts of a

much different kind, as Trafford Council threatened to close part of the ground if the team reached the semi-final stage. Town Hall chiefs insisted that supporters left them with no choice after continuously breaking safety regulations by standing and if the semi-finals were reached, then the upper section of the West Stand would be closed. At the time of the announcement, it had not been decided if the whole of the stand, or only a certain number of seats would be affected, but the *Manchester Evening News* believed that it would only be around one thousand seats at the front of that particular stand that would be effected. As it was, the Council did not have to worry about a supporter backlash, as Bayern Munich followed up their 1-0 victory in Manchester with a 2-1 win back in Germany, knocking United out of the competition.

Old Trafford began to rival town and city centres due to the number of statues and memorial plaques sited around the ground, with the latest addition being unveiled prior to the home match with Aston Villa. Situated within the West Stand, Denis Law paid a rare visit to the ground to unveil a ten foot tall statue of himself, by sculptor Ben Panting and situated on the concourse of the upper tier of the stand.

"I'm very glad to be here doing this" said the former 'King' of the Stretford End. "And I hope my family are happy I'm here too, because usually when you unveil a statue it's when

▲ **King of the Stretford End:** *Denis Law mid-goal celebration.*

the person is no longer around. This would truly be a great honour for any footballer, but it is especially so for me to be back in the Stretford End where the fans will always hold a special place in my heart." The statue showed a typical Law pose. Shirt cuffs tightly gripped and finger pointing skywards, saluting yet another goal.

Despite United having countless problems with their playing surface, the stadium itself was perfect and UEFA soon announced that Old Trafford was to host the Champions League Final of 2003. If ever a team needed inspiration to reach a Final, this was it. Sir Alex Ferguson was determined to taste European glory again and having missed out on the opportunity of claiming the coveted trophy in his native Glasgow, when Hampden Park staged the 2002 Final, where better to be crowned Champions

of Europe than at Old Trafford?

Negotiating the two group stages once again caused few headaches, but to progress further down the path to the dream Final they had to overcome old adversaries Real Madrid in the quarter-finals. The first leg in the Spanish capital did not exactly produce the ideal result for progressing further, with a 3-1 defeat, but there was that all important away goal to consider. A 2-0 win was all that was required for United to go through.

Wednesday April 23rd saw Real Madrid visit Manchester and it turned out to be a typical night at the theatre, a magical memorable night for the 66,708 present and one which kept them on the edge of their seats, or for many nervously shuffling their

23RD APRIL 2003
EUROPEAN CUP
QUARTER-FINAL, SECOND LEG

UNITED 4 REAL MADRID 3
REAL WON 6-5 ON AGGREGATE

The game was only four minutes old when Ruud van Nistelrooy squirmed past Helguera and Roberto Carlos, before unleashing a drive that Casillas did well to turn over the bar. Ten minutes later, with play moving from end to end, came the opening goal of the night. Former Liverpool player Steve McMannaman, amid a crescendo of boos, pushed the ball down the line for Zidane, who moved inside from the left before passing the ball on to Guti. A quick glance, a touch of the ball and Ronaldo was past Ferdinand. Seconds later, the ball was in the back of Barthez's net.

Figo came close to adding a second in the twenty-first minute, Veron was booked for a lunge at Makelele. Giggs watched in agony as his shot beat Casillas and also the outside of the post, while Solskjaer also kept the Madrid 'keeper on his toes.

Two minutes prior to the interval, United finally got back into the game. Giggs, again the thorn in the Madrid defence fed Solskjaer, who in turn squeezed the ball beyond Casillas to van Nistelrooy, who had the simple job of prodding the ball home from a couple of yards out. Old Trafford was now alive, there was still a chance. There would have been more to contemplate during the half time interval, if Casillas had not been able to kick away a van Nistelrooy shot amid a goalmouth scramble.

Forty-five minutes to go. 4 -2 to Madrid, but within five minutes of the restart, it was 5-2, Ronaldo again doing the damage. Figo, running on to a Zidane pass could only watch his chip rebound off the far post, but the United defence failed to clear the ball properly and the portly Brazilian accepted Roberto Carlos's pass to net his second of the evening.

Scoring four was a tall order for any team over ninety-minutes, but with less than forty to go, it looked all over for United. To their credit though, they did not let up and pulled a goal back almost straight from the restart, when Helguera surprisingly turned a Veron shot past his own goalkeeper.

It was suddenly all United, with Casillas flinging himself at a Solskjaer effort, before stopping a Veron volley. However, play suddenly swung to the opposite end with Ronaldo taking a Figo pass in his stride, beating Brown, before unleashing a stunning drive past Barthez from twenty yards. This goal brought polite applause from the United supporters, but soon afterwards the Old Trafford crowd stood to a man and applauded the Brazilian off the pitch as he was substituted by Solari.

A reshuffle by Sir Alex Ferguson saw David Beckham, somewhat surprisingly left on the bench, thrown into the fray and the out of favour United man soon made his mark on the evening with a trade mark free kick from outside the Madrid area, before scrambling home a fourth for United. Two goals were still required, as they had been at the start of the extraordinary evening, but with only minutes remaining, it was to prove an impossible dream.

feet as they stood, from start to finish, with drama, excitement and a standing ovation for the star performer. As the night unfolded, there was to be no dramatic fight back. United did indeed pull back the two goals they knew that they had to score, scoring four in fact, but for the Old Trafford faithful, they still tasted disappointment amid the enjoyment, due mainly to the performance of one man (see report).

*

European nights have always been special and this was yet another to stand alongside the likes of Barcelona in 1984, Porto in 1977 and the rest of those magical nights at the Theatre of Dreams. Real Madrid, were not to make a return to Manchester in May to contest the Champions League Final, that honour fell to two other old adversaries of United, AC Milan and Juventus. That quarter-final tie would have provided a much better climax to the season and given the worldwide television audience a more entertaining ninety minutes than the boring goalless affair produced by the Italian giants.

Old Trafford was awash with supporters long before kick-off, with horns, hooters and claxons echoing around the streets and the perimeter of the stadium in the early evening. Down behind the Stretford End, in one of the car parks, was the hospitality village, where a huge marquee was erected for the main sponsors of the competition, with a red carpet laid out for the guests between there and the North Stand.

Twenty large inflatable footballs were suspended above the pitch, while Atomic Kitten did their best to generate some pre-match entertainment and they might have been better performing a complete set, as the game itself failed to live up to its expectations, despite Old Trafford providing a fitting backdrop for Europe's top club match. It was not until the penalty kicks that the crowd were given anything to get excited about, with AC Milan converting three, while the Juventus players could only manage two.

Whilst Old Trafford was adorned with the Champions League logo, the ordinary run of the mill fixtures were not played out in front of the rather bland backdrop of the stands, as there had been a dash of colour at the Stretford End of the ground since the new millennium, with various banners hanging from the second tier of this stand.

The idea of such adornments had come from supporter Charlie Watson, whilst trawling through an unofficial supporter's website. "I came up with the idea of a banner fund, after reading that someone suggested making banners like the European 'Ultra's', to try and create some of the old atmosphere." Charlie's idea was soon picked up on and before long, there was a selection, including "The Flowers Of Manchester", "The Real Treble"

– especially for the visits of Liverpool, hinting at their minor treble of three recent cup wins, "Republic Of Mancunia" and one showing the number of years since neighbours City had last won a trophy, which could be changed every year, among the seventeen banners which were rotated every now and again.

It was not only the banners hanging from the front of the stand which added to the colour and passion of the Stretford End, as the second tier concourse also saw a makeover, thanks to the 'Vocal Fans Committee'. A large banner – "Manchester United – Streford End" appeared on the wall behind the statue of Denis Law, while boards detailing the Munich Air Disaster and the players of that period, were placed around the walls. Those boards, having first been used in the United Museum as part of their display for the 40th Anniversary of the crash in 1998.

With Old Trafford more or less full for every fixture and countless supporters being constantly unlucky in the ballot for match tickets, there was from time to time a cry to expand the ground further. Following the 3-1 'derby' victory over Manchester City, in December 2003, an "exclusive" appeared in the *Daily Star on Sunday* by Paul Hetherington, "Manchester

United are exploring the possibility of increasing the Old Trafford capacity by 8,000 to 75,000. United originally vetoed the plans, but are now having second thoughts due to the huge demand for tickets at Old Trafford. Every United match is a sell out and the club know they could easily maintain that situation with a greater capacity. To increase the size of the ground, United would have to redevelop South Stand. It would mean building up and over the railway station on that side of the ground."

Numerous "exclusive" articles that appear in the press are neither exclusive, often appearing in other newspapers on the same day, or simply not true. Paul Hetherington's article, however, whilst not entirely correct did reveal that United were indeed looking into the possibility of increasing the ground capacity yet again. To redevelop the South Stand, which Paul hinted at, would have been an expensive

and exhausting exercise. Not only would the club have been forced to build up and over the railway, they would also have had to purchase a considerable number of the houses on Railway Road, in order to create suitable entrances and exits in line with crowd safety regulations. As it was, the planned redevelopment, which would be announced at a later date, centred round the areas between the East and West Stands and the North Stand.

In March 2004 United's Communications Director, Phil Townsend, officially revealed the club's proposed plans, proving that while Paul Hetherington had grasped the initial idea, he had been a bit off the mark about the precise developments.

"Manchester United is considering plans to improve further and develop facilities at Old Trafford, including an additional 7,500 seats, increasing the capacity of Old Trafford to around 75,000," said the club statement. "A feasibility study is underway to evaluate the technical, financial and planning issues on completing the North East and North West Quadrants of the stadium and consultation on these issues will now commence. Any decision to proceed will be taken by the board in due course and announced thereafter."

"For several years, virtually every United home game has been sold out. Successive developments, representing over £170m of investment in the stadium, have been swallowed up by a seemingly insatiable demand for tickets. These new improvements, should they go ahead, may not cater for all that demand, but they would provide more than 7,000 extra seats. They will also maintain Old Trafford as one of the finest and best equipped stadiums in the world." The cost of this planned development would be around £45 million.

This in reality meant that the club planned to extend the second tier of the North Stand at either end, so it would join up with the East Stand, the old Scoreboard End and the West Stand, the old Stretford End. It was, however, not a forgone conclusion that the plans would progress from the drawing board and into concrete and metal.

Plans for such a project would obviously have to go before Trafford Council before getting the green light, but the United board must have considered it worthwhile submitting them, as the relationship with the local council was not exactly lovey-dovey.

Having commissioned a report on Old Trafford, the results revealed by the Council were not what the club would have liked, or indeed wanted to have heard. It claimed that 75% of the fans at the front of

the upper tier of the Stretford End – West Stand, faced a 75% risk of a catastrophic accident when celebrating a goal. As a result of the report, United made changes to the seating layout and standing. They did not, however, accept the "75% risk". Trafford Council, on the other hand, decided to keep the matter under review.

*

Fixtures against Liverpool are always eagerly looked forward to, many creating memorable moments of drama and excitement, but the meeting between the two clubs on April 24th 2004 took on an entirely different profile. In the week leading up to the fixture, there had been ten arrests in Manchester with reported links to terrorism and when tickets for the Old Trafford fixture were found at the house where the arrests had been made, there was immediate speculation that the ground could possibly be a target for suicide bombers.

The fixture against the team from the opposite end of the East Lancs Road is normally a high profile match, but the events in the run up to this one saw police and the club re-structure its security to an unprecedented level. Sniffer dogs were in

evidence as was additional security, with supporters searched as they approached the stadium and prior to entering the ground. A journalist from a tabloid newspaper managed to breach security, dressed as a steward, but once inside the ground, he was arrested before the game, and to his own disappointment, failed to get much of a story. The threat of a terrorist attack did little to put the Old Trafford faithful off and 67,647 were inside to witness the 1-0 defeat at the hands of their Merseyside rivals.

With planning permission for the new quadrant extensions still to be approved by Trafford Borough Council and the PLC, United took a bold step in beginning work on the proposed £40m project. If they had waited on the scheme being rubber stamped by both the board and the council, then the early ground work would not have been able to get underway until the following summer, with the new sections not in use until 2007. The North-West quadrant (at the Stretford End) was expected to be completed by May 2006, with the one at the opposite end due to be completed in August 2006.

Work was also being carried out at Wembley, creating a brand new stadium to replace the

rather antiquated, but well-loved north London ground, with the familiar twin-towers becoming nothing but a mere memory. Whilst this construction was underway, a new home had to be found to host England international fixtures, if not the show-piece F. A. Cup Final which went to the neutral Millennium Stadium in Cardiff. It was obvious that there was only ever going to be one outright choice... With five home 2006 World Cup qualifying games to be played, the Football Association recognised the quality of Old Trafford and announced that four of the five fixtures would be played in Manchester.

Pre-season games, certainly for United, are usually spent venturing to some outpost or other where there is a large red shirted following and sometimes involve a small tournament along with two or three other clubs in preparation for the season ahead. So, it was something of a surprise when it was announced that the pre-season of 2004-2005 would feature a four club tournament at Old Trafford, yet another first for the ground. Contesting the 'Vodafone Cup', along with the host club, were Urawa Red Diamonds, PSV Eindhoven and Boca Juniors, with the games being played over two nights, Tuesday August 3rd and Thursday August 5th. On the first night, United defeated PSV 1-0, while Boca Juniors had an emphatic 5-2 victory over the Red Diamonds, the former game kicking off at 6.45pm, while the home support had to wait until

9pm for the start of the United match.

Two nights later, Boca Juniors and PSV were to enjoy the early start, with United again bringing up the rear, however, the unsuspecting United and Red Diamond supporters were destined to be heading home slightly earlier than they expected. With Boca leading the Dutch side 1-0 and around fifteen minutes still to play, the 15,000 crowd were rather surprised to see referee Mark Halsey stop the game and take the two teams off the pitch, as rain pelted down and cracks of thunder and flashes of lightning giving the ground a strange and unfamiliar backdrop. The referee soon announced that he had abandoned the game, as the storm continued. Lights in the stand fizzled, creating something of a safety issue.

After consulting United officials, and the Met office for a local weather report, Mike D'Urso, the referee for the United match, which was due to start at 9pm, decided that it was unsafe to continue, much to the disappointment of the 15,000 or so spectators in the ground, many of whom greeted the news with derision. Whether the disappointment was due to missing out on ninety minutes football, or because they had to go out in the pouring rain is not recorded. As it was, United refunded ticket money, which amounted to around £300,000. Despite the ferocity of the storm, there was no damage to any sections of the ground, as

each stand has its own lightning conductor.

It was not only Old Trafford and the aforementioned Wembley that was enjoying something of a make-over, or indeed a complete re-construction, as Arsenal, one of United's biggest on-field rivals in recent years, had decided that Highbury, with its listed main stand, was no longer big enough for the club's needs. So, it was decided to move a short distance to Ashburton Grove and a brand new stadium, which would see the club (that had run up debts of £60m last season) having to borrow £260m from a flotilla of banks in order to finance the project. United, on the other hand, were expanding their ground as they had done in the past, without borrowing a penny, paying the £45m for the latest developments in cash. Gold Trafford indeed!

One area of the ground rarely seen by the rank and file supporters, unless on a stadium tour, is the press area under South Stand. For a number of years, it resembled little more than a small hotel lounge bar, with toilet facilities at a minimum. (I know, as on one European Cup night, I had to queue behind a couple of the main United correspondents from the national press, with former United player, Mick Martin, behind me). Now, however, the members of the national and world press had state of art facilities.

Approaching the area via a stair with images of events in

28TH SEPTEMBER 2004
CHAMPIONS LEAGUE PHASE 1 MATCH 2

UNITED 6 FENERBAHCE 2

A crowd of 67,128, some six thousand odd more than had filed into the ground for the previous European fixture against Dinamo Bucharest, certainly received value for money, coming away after the final whistle enthusiastically praising the first appearance in a red shirt of a player destined to join the long line of Old Trafford favourites.

Seven minutes gone and a precise Kleberson cross allowed Ryan Giggs to open the scoring with a glancing header. But all eyes were on Wayne Rooney, and within the opening fifteen minutes, he had shown that not only was he fully fit, as it had been rumoured otherwise, but that he clearly meant business. Chasing a ball to the by-line, that looked to many in the ground to be going out of play, he not only caught it, but beat the Turkish goalkeeper and went narrowly close with a shot that swerved just over. Two minutes later, however, moving on to a van Nistelrooy through ball, he took it calmly in his stride before blasting it past the helpless goalkeeper.

In the twenty-eighth minute, he made it 3-0. Taking a pass from Ryan Giggs, a dip of the shoulder was enough to take him past Ozat, the Fenerbache captain and before any other defender could react, a thirty yard drive was screaming towards the back of the net. The Turks pulled a goal back two minutes after the interval, but United reclaimed their two goal advantage in the fifty-fourth minute, when Rooney grabbed his hat trick, firing a free kick past the helpless Recber, who only minutes earlier had done well to grab a twenty-five yard effort at the second attempt.

The Turkish side again punished some slack defending, when Sanli followed up a shot from Nobre, which Roy Carroll had failed to hold. A long ball from substitute Diego Forlan set up Ruud van Nistelrooy for United's fifth and David Bellion, enjoying a rare run out, added a sixth in the eighty-first minute. It was certainly a debut, and yet another memorable European night to remember.

United's history and of players past and present, the lounge itself is very modern and spacious, with a 'working area' off this, which contains facilities for laptops etc. Alongside this, is the conference room and also the United Radio studio. This particular area was buzzing, as was the whole stadium, on the evening of September 28th 2004.

Debuts at any age, for any footballer, are usually an occasion to remember. Some are also fortunate enough to score on this noteworthy occasion, making the day even more memorable. Harold Halse found the back of the net after a mere thirty seconds of his debut in March 1908. Joe Spence, as we noted a number of pages back, scored four goals on his debut, while a burly, Scottish born, English schoolboy internationalist called Alex Dawson scored on his United debut in the League, FA Cup and Football League Cup. Neil Webb went one better, scoring on his first outing in each of the domestic competitions as well as in the European Cup Winners Cup. Tommy Reid managed to score twice on his United League debut, following that with a hat trick on his FA Cup debut. Prolific goalscorer David Herd found the net on his FA Cup debut, League Cup debut and on his debut in the three major European competitions – European Cup, European Cup Winners Cup and the old Inter Cities Fairs Cup, but failed to do so on his League debut. In 1905, Charlie Sagar helped himself to a

hat trick in his first appearance. Ole Gunnar Solskjaer became the first United substitute to score on his debut. The likes of Bobby Charlton, Tommy Taylor and Paul Scholes all netted twice on their initial appearances. There have been others who managed a solitary strike to mark their first appearance for Manchester United, but few can claim to have as a rewarding, high profile Old Trafford debut than Wayne Rooney.

Signed by Sir Alex Ferguson on August 31st 2004, in a deal said to be worth around £23million to Everton, the stocky built Liverpudlian was brought into the United side for his debut against Turkish side Fenerbahce on September 28th, a fixture that was a 'must win' game, as in the previous Group D Champions League fixture, against Olympique Lyonnais, United had struggled to come from behind to earn a 2-2 draw.

Rooney's goals, and United's overall performance (see match no. 19), had the Old Trafford crowd on its feet, but the standing issue during games remained a thorn in the club's side and one that certainly did not kook like going away. So much so, that Trafford councillors once again met to discuss the on-going problem, but it proved to be a waste of time, as there was nothing they, or the club could do to stop those who persisted in standing during games.

October 9th saw Old Trafford host England's international with Wales and

with the protests relating to the proposed takeover of the club by American businessman Malcolm Glazer increasing, as well as the possibility of crowd trouble between rival sets of supporters, policing at the game would be much tighter than for an ordinary Old Trafford fixture. United's reserve fixture at Altrincham two nights previously had been disrupted with a pitch invasion of masked protesters, who set fire to an American flag on the pitch and neither the club, nor the police, wanted anything similar to occur at Old Trafford. The game, won 2-0 by England, went off without any major incidents.

The proposed takeover of the club began to take up more column inches than matters on the playing front, with every day throwing something different into the melting pot. Many supporters, although concerned, felt that there was little that they could do as it was something completely out of their control, while others felt so strongly, that they simply could not sit back and allow events to take their course. Both sides, however, suddenly became united on Sunday October 24th, when a 'World Exclusive' in the *Sunday Express* proclaimed that within "top secret and highly sensitive documents" seen by the newspaper, Malcolm Glazer, should he succeed in taking over the club, had been advised to sell Old Trafford.

Details within the dossier explained that one of the ways of raising funds to buy the club

was to sell the ground and then lease it back to United. This would apparently generate capital of around £250 million in the short term, but leave the club having to pay rent to the owners before having an option to repurchase. It read: "There is the potential to perform a sale and lease-back of the stadium to provide additional finance which can be rolled into the financing package."

Shareholders United chairman, Nick Thorne commented, "This is frightening and nightmarish. He could find somebody else to borrow money from, but who would lend him money. The other option would be the sale and lease back of the ground, which could bring in around £200 million. Selling Old Trafford would mean losing the club's most valuable asset and having to pay the new owners money to use the stadium to play games".

By a strange co-incidence, with United at home to Arsenal that same Sunday, protests had been arranged to coincide with the fixture and the breaking news in the morning papers only added fuel to the already well-ignited fire. Hundreds of supporters marched in protest down Sir Matt Busby Way before flooding into the Megastore, blocking the aisles and check-outs, and disrupting sales.

Inside the ground, the protests continued, with a large banner unveiled from the Stretford End proclaiming – "Warning, using MUFC may result in serious damage to your health" with an effigy of Malcolm Glazer dangled over the edge of the stand on a noose. Even the ninety minutes of football was not without its drama. It was after all Arsenal in opposition and over the years, this particular fixture seems to always conjure up something unusual.

The Gunners had arrived in town unbeaten in their forty-nine previous fixtures, while United needed to win in order to keep themselves within striking distance of the top of the table. As it was, United secured a notable 2-0 victory, with goals from a Ruud van Nistelrooy penalty and Wayne Roooney, but it was the after match events that ultimately captured the headlines.

In the player's tunnel at the end of the game, with feelings already running high following confrontations between numerous players, Sir Alex Ferguson had soup and pizza thrown at him by an unidentified Arsenal player, following a flare-up involving the United boss and Arsene Wenger. Strangely, none of the match officials or the police actually saw what happened, but it was certainly not missed by the media as it filled considerable column inches for a few days after the match.

The visit of Lyon to Manchester on Champions League business on Wednesday November 24th 2004, was not simply a game that United had to win in order to take over top spot in Group D from the French champions, but it also marked a significant landmark in the career of Sir Alex Ferguson – his 1,000th game in charge of Manchester United. Having recently celebrated eighteen years at the helm, itself a notable achievement in the modern game, having managed a club for 1,000 games is equally significant. Especially when you consider that the likes of Wayne Rooney and Cristiano Ronaldo were mere toddlers when their manager first stepped into the United dug-out.

As he emerged from the tunnel prior to kick off, the crowd rose to give him a much deserved standing ovation, as well as a chorus of "stand up if you love Fergie" while UEFA abandoned protocol insisting that he took his place alongside his team for the obligatory pre-match photograph. Before leaving the pitch to take up his customary position in the dug-out, United chief-executive David Gill presented him with an engraved case of wine to mark the achievement.

Thankfully, the result fitted the occasion, although a dreadful mistake by United 'keeper Roy Carroll, five minutes before the break, gifted Lyon the equaliser, after Gary Neville had opened the scoring in the nineteenth minute. A van Nistelrooy goal, eight minutes after half time, was enough to give United a 2-1 victory and top place in the group.

Towards the end of January 2005, the first images of the 'new' Old Trafford were exclusively revealed in the *Manchester Evening News* in an artist's impression and a computer generated photograph. A special public meeting had been pencilled in to take place at the ground, but this was scheduled for a mere two days before the actual planning meeting was due to be held by the local council and as such, would be too late to change anything despite the fears of local residents that there had been inadequate consultation.

Councillor Steve Adshead said: "For people living right next door to the ground, there is the height and massing of the extended stands to consider, but there are also horrendous traffic implications. Even if people come two-to-a-car, you are talking about an extra 4,000 cars trying to get into the area. Then there's the noise, litter and other problems. We will be wanting to discuss all these things with the club."

One local resident told the paper, "United are not good neighbours. We have had years of problems with over- parking, rubbish and noise from concerts. I will be going to the meeting to oppose the plans, but they are like an American company – nothing can stop them."

Early February 2005, saw the Trafford Metropolitan Borough council agree to United's proposed plans for re-developing the ground with the filling in of the North-East and North-West Quadrants. To gain such permission, United had to satisfy the council of certain aspects of the new developments, as the local residents, as they had been in the past, were not altogether too happy to have a further 7,500 football supporters on their doorsteps every other week.

Stretford and Urmston MP Beverley Hughes criticised the club, saying "I think local people are just exasperated, because they want to meet the club half way, but they've got a history of broken promises and because of that, local people are just very cynical about this." Another Councillor felt that the increased number of cars in the area would cause a problem, as would the amount of litter.

United's group property manager, George Johnstone revealed that "It was a long process, involving detailed negotiations with the local authority. We agreed on a package of measures to reduce the impact on the transport system and the local community. We have made a commitment to contribute £1 million over a ten year period, with the first payment to be made when the new seating is fully licensed."

Having secured the permission, it was now all systems go, with contractors sending in tenders for the work. As George explained, "Until we have appointed a main contractor, we can't be clear about specific details. But it is our intention that building work will not affect the current stadium capacity, although we can't rule out losing some seats at certain stages of the project. The scoreboards will have to be re-located, but our aim will be to ensure that everybody inside the ground can still see a scoreboard. We are grateful to supporters for their patience and understanding during the preparatory work, and we'll be asking fans to please bear with us during the construction work."

The towers of the new structure were to become a major feature of the new quadrants and in the terms of architecture, George Johnstone added: "We have asked our architects to look at the Imperial War Museum North and the Lowry and reflect that kind of style. We think they have done a superb job. The appearance of the stadium, both inside and out, will be amazing. Once the re-development is complete and the gables removed, the new configuration will make for an improved atmosphere. The new bowl effect will allow noise to roll around the stadium rather than being trapped in specific stands as at present".

The re-development was of course about much more than adding a few more red seats to the stadium interior. The outside of the ground would also take on a 'new look', with towers at either end, which would be the structural element of the quadrants, designed in such a way that they would give it a modern look. It would also make it the third largest stadium in Britain, behind the New Wembley (90,000) and Twickenham which was due to increase to 82,000.

Underneath the seating areas, there would be a variety of bars and lounges, a club

brochure read, "Welcome to the Quadrants: Evolution of the Ultimate Venue". "The Quadrants will increase overall capacity to over 75,000 seats and along with a series of new hospitality, hosting and private box facilities, will raise the curtain on a new era of this magnificent sporting stage. Welcome to the unrivalled sporting experience that is Manchester United at OLD TRAFFORD… the Theatre of Dreams."

There would be a 'Sports Bar' on level five, providing elevated pitch views, with pre and post match refreshments "in an environment that will provide all the passion and excitement of the match day experience", while the 'Lounge Bar' would offer the "perfect location to enjoy match day in style".

On levels two and three were the Executive Lounges, "for the fans who want it all", where you could enjoy a three course meal before proceeding to your seat in the stand, returning for a pre-ordered drink at half time. Level three would also offer a 'Fine Dining' experience, called 'The Gallery', costing each person £7,500 per season. The 'Evolution Suite' on the other hand, "with fabulous views overlooking the Quays" was £1,000 per person less. There would also of course be new executive boxes in both areas.

In an effort to stave off the threat of a takeover by Malcolm Glazer, the club decided to increase the cost of watching games by 24% for the best seats

in the house, making the top season tickets £684, with those in the centre of the North Stand and upper sections of the South Stand seeing the cost per match increasing from £29 to £36.

A statement from the club read: "The club realises that no price rise will ever be welcomed and that many fans would like to see ticket prices cut. However, there continues to be excess demand with, on average, more than 7,500 ticket requests being turned down for each Premiership League game. It remains the Club's firm intention to remain as one of the most affordable grounds in the Premier League, while still competing with the biggest clubs in the game to fund a top-quality team in a world-class stadium and with the finest training facilities and staff.

"This commitment is demonstrated by the fact that the lowest-priced adult season-ticket has been frozen at £20.50 per game, with only six Premiership clubs offering a lower adult price this year – before any rises for next year have been taken into account. Over the last few years the standard rise of £1 has narrowed the relative gap between the lowest priced seats (which have been frozen for next season) and the highest priced seats in the ground. As a result of the review, and taking on board the opinions expressed by fans as well as the recommendation of the Football Task Force, the Club has rectified this to create what we believe is a fairer relationship between the location of the seat

and the price of the seat, and therefore have increased the top price level."

This announcement raised the threat of empty seats appearing around the ground in the years ahead, when the stadium capacity was increased to 76,000, with the Independent Supporters Association believing that although the demand for tickets was indeed high, the Club was now reaching saturation point.

Work on the £39m project was set to begin in late April/ early May 2005, with the planned date of completion of August 2006. Prior to the Champions League fixture against AC Milan on Wednesday February 23rd 2005, Sir Matt Busby Way vibrated to the noise of around 2,000 United supporters, who were protesting at the proposed takeover by the Glazer family. Led by thirteen police officers on horseback, the fans had marched from the cricket ground at the opposite end of the old Warwick Road to the forecourt area, carrying numerous banners of displeasure, whilst at the same time causing rather chaotic scenes outside the turnstiles as kick off approached.

For the ordinary supporter, whose income would perhaps not stretch to such lavish match day fare of the proposed new lounges, they could always make there way past the early exploration work at the corners of the North Stand and head for the N1 car park where the 'Fanzone' was sited. This was a large marquee, capable of

The development of the quadrants in 2005-6 further raised capacity beyond the 70,000 barrier.

Anti-Glazer Protests:
2005 saw the prospect of a hostile takeover by Malcolm Glazer grow.

holding around 1,000 and was first open for business against Blackburn Rovers on April 2nd 2005. For the sum of £5, supporters could obtain meal and drinks in relative comfort, whilst listening to the exploits of former players, with Jimmy Greenhoff and Lee Martin at the inaugural session. Initially, it was for a trial period only, but proved to be yet another money spinner for the club and became a regular match day feature.

If you had little more loose change in your pocket, then the news of the club building a casino adjacent to the ground would have been of much interest. Eight mega-casino licences were due to come up for grabs under the new Gambling Bill, with others venues such as the City of Manchester Stadium, Salford Reds and Blackpool also wanting to create a Las Vegas style complex on their doorstep.

United had already become involved in talks with the local Trafford Council and Las Vegas Sands, a major casino operator in America who were interested in taking advantage of the new more liberated gambling laws once they were up and running and a spokesman said, "We are looking at all possibilities to take the business forward. It's way too early to start talking about applying for licenses which don't exist yet. No decisions have been made. We are looking at any possibilities there may be in the proposed changes to the legislations." The development was planned for the area on the Trafford Park side of the ground, presently occupied by two car parks.

By May, the government might have had a change of heart regarding the ideas of the eight super-casino's being scattered across the country, but United, having got their teeth into the idea, revealed plans that they were very much involved in creating something of a "cultural village" at nearby Salford Quays, with the plans including a five-star hotel, restaurants, a health club, sports bar, a new Metrolink station, improved bus routes and car parking and of course a casino. Trafford Council, having viewed the plans, had agreed in principle to support them. The plans, however, were abandoned by October, with the club announcing that it had had a change of heart and had decided not to tie up their resources, allowing them to use the land for alternative future ventures.

On 12th May 2005 the Glazer family finally took over the club in a deal that valued the club at £800 million. Further protests against the Glazer takeover were held prior to the Champions League qualifier against the relatively unknown Hungarian side Debrecen, on August 9th, with hundreds involved in angry clashes with police prior to the kick-off. Demonstrators, many carrying banners, whilst yelling personal insults about the Glazer family, marched from the Trafford pub on Chester Road down to the ground and as mounted police fought to gain some sort of control, bottles and cans were thrown. Inside the stadium, with the Glazer brothers, Joel, Avi and Bryan in attendance, there were rows of empty seats, as fans boycotted the fixture, giving the tie an official attendance of 51,701, one of the smallest for a European tie at the ground.

With the Glazer takeover still very much a thorn in the side of the United supporters, some of the banners which adorned the Stretford End were removed as a form of protest, but the club's stance against the protesting fans reached a new low at the game Aston Villa on the opening day of the 2005-06 season, when a supporter, sitting with his wife and daughter in the lower section of the stadiums East Stand, was asked by a steward to cover up his "Glazer Out" t-shirt, as it might be picked up on television. The supporter had already received a warning from a steward outside the ground that if he did not cover it up, he would not be allowed in. Having pulled a replica top over it, he had removed the top once inside the ground, before being approached by the second steward. As he did not want to his wife and daughter to miss the match, he decided to once again cover up the t-shirt.

More fan fury erupted at the end of the month, when it was revealed that a seventy-eight year old supporter and his disabled son, who had enjoyed watching games from their South Stand seats for more than forty years, were being evicted for Champions League fixtures, along with two hundred other supporters, as their seats were required by the club for Category A tickets for UEFA sponsors.

A club spokesman said: "Fans who follow the club for a long time and grow up supporting the club are exceptionally important to us and it's unfortunate we have had to inconvenience them. We are bound by our contract with UEFA to give them a certain number of the best seats for their sponsors. If people want to be relocated in the South Stand that should be possible, but we can't guarantee the seats will be as good as before. However, we will do our very best to take into account personal circumstances."

Such is the modern game, where sponsorship and television play a major part due to the financial clout that they carry, often pushing to one side the origins of the game and the thoughts of the people who mattered and without whom there would be no game at all – the supporters.

For many of those supporters, Manchester United Football Club plays a major part in the lives, for others, Manchester United is their life. So much so, that the club wasted little time in making the ground available

as a venue for weddings and christenings, a move that was soon to prove extremely popular. But for those whose life evolved around everything United, what could be more apt than the ultimate send-off with a funeral service at Old Trafford?

Although the scattering of supporter's ashes on the pitch is not allowed by the club, the approach by a Sale-Moor based funeral service – Natural Endings, to hold wakes at the ground, in a function room overlooking the pitch was something that would be considered, adding yet another aspect to the never ending usage for Old Trafford. At the end of September, there was the announcement of yet another attraction at the ground, with news of a £400,000 skating rink being built in the shadow of the East Stand. The reinforced plastic dome, which would house the rink, would be available for skaters for six weeks from the end of November. Whatever would be next?

Despite the club often, or perhaps many would say frequently, coming under-fire for their pricing of match-day tickets, they acknowledged that supporters attending Carling (League) Cup ties, when an under-strength side was often fielded, should be charged less than for normal League and F. A. Cup fixtures. So much so, that they reduced ticket prices by a third, with juniors paying only £5 for last seasons fixtures against Crystal Palace, Arsenal and Chelsea.

They had planned to continue with such a scheme for season 2005-06, but their plans became unstuck when Third Round opponents Barnet complained about United pricing of the tickets, which they were entitled to do, due to the fact that they would receive 45% of the gate receipts, with a potential £500,000 cheque coming their way. With the reduction in costs, this windfall would be quite a bit less.

United had proposed prices of £5 for juniors and between £15 and £25 for adults, but Barnet, who had asked United for 6,000 tickets, although allowing something of reduction, forced United into pricing the tickets at £8 for juniors and a third off normal prices only for those in the automatic cup-tie scheme. All other supporters, around 20,000, would have to pay the normal match day price. That was the only victory that the League Two side managed, however, as United ran out easy 4-1 winners.

Chelsea's forty game unbeaten Premiership record was brought to an end on November 6th 2006, by Darren Fletcher's thirty-first minute goal, as the 1-0 victory took United to third place in the table. There was, therefore, little need for Sir Alex Ferguson to switch on the renowned "hairdryer" at either half or full time in order to inspire his troops to a more involved performance. This perhaps was just as well, as unbeknown to those within the sacred confines of the United

dressing room, everything that was said that afternoon was being recorded by a hidden transmitter.

"Bugged – Traffordgate" proclaimed the headline of the *Manchester Evening News* on the morning of November 12th, six days after the Chelsea fixture, with *The Sun* splashing – "Exclusive – Man Utd dressing room is bugged" across its front page. So, what was the big story? Apparently, a transmitter had been smuggled into the dressing room prior to the fixture and two hours of conversation was recorded on to cassettes, which were then offered by a middle man, to a national newspaper (*The Sun*), who in turn handed them over to the club.

When replayed, the voice of Sir Alex Ferguson could be clearly heard, encouraging his players before going out to face Chelsea and again at half time. At the interval, he could be heard telling Rooney and van Nistelrooy as to how they could improve their performances, while stressing that the team as a whole must stop giving away unnecessary free kicks, the need for tighter marking on Makelele and that they should stop sending high balls into the Chelsea area. At the end of the game, the United players could be heard celebrating their victory, with much laughter and mimicking after their manager is heard swearing during a Sky Sports interview.

How the transmitter was smuggled into the United dressing room was a huge cause

George Best Tributes:
The death of the legendary footballer in November 2005 led to tributes from supporters of all persuasions arriving at the ground.

for concern for the club and obviously treated as a major security matter, but it was believed that someone planted the device whilst on a stadium tour prior to the Chelsea fixture, removing it again the day after.

Crowd trouble occurred around the stadium on something of a regular basis a couple of decades ago, but one man, whose mere presence, never mind the punches that he was capable of throwing, would have all those would be trouble makers running for cover, strolled into the stadium on November 20th 2005, receiving a two minute standing ovation of the type normally reserved for those who wore, or had worn, the famous red shirt of Manchester United.

Mike Tyson, the youngest ever world heavyweight boxing champion, strolled into the Old Trafford Manchester Suite for a specially arranged, £130 per head dinner, which would earn him £40,000, taking in the applause of the nine hundred boxing fans present, as well as other boxing guests such as Frank Bruno, John H Stracey and John Conteh.

While one sporting legend was wallowing in the acclaim being showered upon him at Old Trafford, another legend, one more associated with Manchester United and its famous stadium, was fighting a battle of his own. He had done so on numerous previous occasions, and like Mike Tyson, had a history of coming out on top. This time, however, he was down on the canvas, so to speak, and was not going to beat the count. George Best was seriously ill in a London hospital and on the afternoon of Friday November 25th 2005, the final whistle blew.

As news of the United legend's death spread, fans began assembling outside the ground, opposite the megastore and the Sir Matt Busby statue, but compared to that last non-match day gathering of supporters, there was silence, the cold afternoon air carrying no cries of discontent, with only a muffled sob being heard from time to time. A small bunch of flowers, a scarf and a photograph were placed along the wall in front of the car park, soon to be joined by countless others, as the Red Army began to pay its respects to one of its favourite sons.

Best, forgiven for all his failings, was now remembered for his football, especially that in the red shirt of Manchester United. His debut, as a seventeen year old, a somewhat nondescript ninety minutes against West Bromwich Albion in September 1963 does not find its way into the 'Old Trafford Memorable Moments' top ten or whatever, but there were other occasions when the tousle haired Irishman memorised his audience, giving them never to be forgotten memories.

There were goals against Real Madrid and against Tottenham, which easily spring to mind, but perhaps two George Best Old Trafford goals in particular stand out amongst all others. The first is from a Football League Cup tie against Chelsea on October 28th 1970. Standing just inside the Chelsea half and almost in line with their last defenders, George took a pass from John Aston, turned and sprinted away, with the three blue shirts in hot pursuit. As he neared the penalty area, Ron Harris, not the gentlest of defenders, attempted a lunging tackle in the hope of bringing George down. Bonetti moved out from his goal to narrow the angle, as Harris's attempted challenge momentarily unsteadied the red shirt in full flow, as three other Chelsea defenders moved closer. As the crowd held its breath, George steadied himself, took the ball round the Chelsea 'keeper, before slipping it into the empty net as the 47,322 crowd went wild. Even the Chelsea support had to acknowledge the goal. The second memorable strike came on a sunny afternoon almost a year later, on October 2nd 1971, against Sheffield United as detailed in an earlier chapter.

Since his untimely death, the area facing the main entrance to the ground and the statue of his old manager on Sir Matt Busby Way, had been turned into a shrine to the wayward Irishman, with flowers, scarves, shirts, photographs and candles covering the pavement and railings and stretching some hundred yards. By a strange quirk of fate, United's first home fixture following George's death was a fourth round Carling Cup tie against West Bromwich Albion, on November 30th, the team that he had made his League debut against all those years ago. It was a truly

emotional evening, with the club paying its former legendary forward a unique and fitting tribute.

The electronic advertising boards around the ground flashed up a continuous message –"George Best – Manchester United 1963 – 1974, 470 appearances, 179 goals, 1 genius", as his 1968 European Cup winning team mates filed onto the pitch, along with members of the current squad, the United directors, Graham Williams, the West Bromwich defender who had marked George on his League debut, along with some of his team mates from that afternoon and Calum Best, George's son.

As the strains of Don Farden's "Belfast Boy" echoed around the stadium, Sir Alex Ferguson and West Bromwich Albion manager, and former Red legend Bryan Robson walked from the tunnel, ahead of the United and West Bromwich teams, carrying two large wreaths as the players of today faced the players of yesterday on either side of the centre line.

Master of Ceremonies for the evening, David Meek, a man who had, as the United correspondent for the *Manchester Evening News*, written thousands upon thousands of words on George, introduced Sir Bobby Charlton. It was often suggested that the United director and his former team-mate did not get on, but there was no hint of such differences in Bobby's message.

"George Best was a giant of the game of football." said

Charlton, "On the behalf of the Manchester United family here in this stadium, and all the fans around the world, I would just like to say a big thank you to George Best. You'll never be forgotten".

Following this, Sir Alex and Bryan Robson laid their wreaths alongside a banner made by the supporters stating – "George – Simply The Best" and seconds later, the stadium fell silent amid the rustle of paper, as the supporters held aloft the colour poster of George that they had been given upon entry into the ground as part of the club's tribute to the genius. For one individual, the silence and the emotion of the evening became too much as Calum Best, wiped away the tears before being comforted by Pat Crerand. As a matter of interest, United won the football match that followed 3-1.

For many, or perhaps most, the financial side of the club was of little interest, but since the takeover by the Glazer family, such matters have become more meaningful. In terms of match-day income, no other club in the world could touch United, who, in the season 2005-06 took in a total of £70.0m. Twelve months previously, it had been £68.8m, compared to Chelsea's £56.1m and Real Madrid's £42.7m. Next season, that figure was expected to increase to £90 million, due mainly to increased ticket prices, while season 2010-11 was expected to increase again, to £109.8 million due to stadium expansion and further price

increases.

Looking at those 2005-06 figures, it is worth noting, that catering brought in 10% of the takings, while the domestic cup competitions and the Champions League brought in 8% and 7% respectively.

By the turn of the year, work on the new Quadrants was progressing well, with contractors Laing O'Rourke confident that parts of the new stands could be in use prior to the end of the season. Work had been taking place on the two sections simultaneously, although the North West quadrant was slightly further advanced than its opposite number.

United project manager Gary Hepplewhite said that the club was more than happy with the progress made. "With a development like this, spectator and visitor safety is paramount. But with our experience of expanding the stadium over the past decade we believe that there has been very little disruption on match days. They've been times when we've had a lot of home fixtures in a short space of time, but we've got a procedure in place that we feel has been a real success and we've managed to maintain stadium capacity."

The whole project was expected to take sixty-two weeks and by week forty-one, some 270,000 man-hours had been spent on it, with around one hundred and sixty workers on site at any one time. 1,642 tonnes of steel had been erected, with 4,000 cubic meters of concrete poured and a total of 1,000 pre-cast units put together to form the terracing sections. Following the construction of the roof above the present structure, work could begin inside the ground as piece by piece, the old roof would be dismantled and seating fitted, with the stadium taking on a more complete look.

It had been hoped that by April some of the seats in the North West quadrant could be in use, with the ground record attendance of 70,504, in place since Aston Villa's visit on December 27th 1920 clearly in sight.

January 2006 saw the biggest away support converge on the ground since Old Trafford became an all-seater stadium. Taking over the East End of the stadium on Wednesday January 18th, the supporters of Burton Albion, a Conference side, one hundred and four places below United, arrived at Old Trafford for an FA Cup third round replay, having held their illustrious opponents to a 0-0 draw some eleven days previously.

Their 11,000 supporters, who had commandeered some one hundred and twenty-two coaches for the ninety mile trip, had to endure a 5-0 United victory, but despite the Burton players giving their followers little to sing about, they enjoyed the occasion, whilst also being present for an unusual Old Trafford debut. Or at least it was the first time that it had been spotted. With the action elsewhere, a small mouse appeared running along the goal-line, with the away fans begging it to "shoot" Another apparently appeared after the final whistle. Fred the Red had a new rival!

With the seemingly bottomless purse of Chelsea's Roman Abramovich taking the Londoners to previously unknown heights, United were looking to the income due to be generated from the 'new-look' Old Trafford, as providing the cash which would enable Sir Alex Ferguson to give the Stamford Bridge club a run for their money. By March 2006, work on the new quadrant sections was progressing to schedule and with approximately one-third of the 8,000 seats earmarked for 'executive' use, it was estimated that somewhere in the region of £3 million a game would be generated in gate receipts alone.

"The stadium expansion is one of the ways we can grow our business and remain competitive" said David Gill, United's chief executive. "The expansion will significantly improve our turnover and we are confident we will continue to sell out all our Premier League home games. Coming to Old Trafford is still a special experience. I don't wish to compare us to any other club but our stadium has history and heritage.

"We have the biggest following in the UK and the biggest commercial income of any Premier League club. This is a continuation of the re-investment in the club. We have re-invested the success we had in the 90's back into the club whether it be the training ground or the stadium expansion, players, transfer fees and contracts. The money we make on the pitch we re-invest in the club and from that we go from strength to strength."

When quizzed on further expansion of the ground, the chief executive said: "To expand the South Stand is not on the agenda. It would cost an arm and a leg. You have to build over the railway and you have the terraced houses in Railway Road. We looked at it years ago when we did the West Stand but dismissed it on the grounds of cost and return. It is not something we would look at now."

The visit of Birmingham City to Old Trafford on March 25th saw the release of 1,500 seats in the new West quadrant, with an attendance of 69,070 recorded creating a Premier League record. The previous best being the 67,989 who had watched United's game against Portsmouth the previous season. The record was then broken again three days later, when 69,522 clicked through the turnstiles to see West Ham United beaten 1-0, with a solitary goal from Ruud van Nistelrooy, his 150th for the club.

Old Trafford is always under consideration as a big match venue for both football and rugby and was chosen by the Football Association to host the 2005-06 FA Cup semi-final between Liverpool and Chelsea. Greater Manchester Police had voiced their concerns about the club hosting the fixture, due to the traditional animosity between United and the Merseysiders, suggesting that Villa Park should be used instead. They were also concerned about the tea-time kick-off, which allowed the supporters of both teams more time to drink before the game. However, with its overall capacity and the income that it would generate, there was little chance of the Football Association considering switching the game to an alternative venue.

As it turned out, following a massive security operation, which included contacting all known troublemakers to warn them to stay away from the city and also visit pubs to ensure that alcohol was not sold to drunken fans, it would prove a costly move for the Football Association, as following the match, the police sent them a bill for £120,000. A further bill was sent to the Football Association by United, who were seeking compensation for damage caused to Old Trafford by visiting Liverpool supporters who went on a wrecking spree at full time when toilets were smashed and graffiti was daubed on the walls, including references to the Munich air disaster. To pay for this, the FA would withhold some of the £3m gate money due to go to Anfield.

Billing costs for normal United fixtures is generally around £45,000 - £50,000 depending on the opposition, while England international fixtures held at the ground would cost between £97,000 and £135,000, again depending on the opposition. There was little need for police at the Old Trafford on May 28th, despite there being a crowd of some 72,000 in the stadium, as there would certainly be no need for segregation, crowd control measures, or any potential trouble to deal with.

The crowd were just as appreciative as those of a normal match-day, some possibly even more enthusiastic than if it had been United playing, as they paid in excess of £500,000 to watch an "England XI" take on the "Rest of the World" in a charity match in aid of the United Nations International Children's Emergency Fund (UNICEF), with a further £2m raised by the vast television audience watching the game live.

So instead of Ronaldo, Giggs and van Nistelrooy, the crowd got Robbie Williams, Maradona, Gazza and Zola, but it mattered little to those in attendance, the majority of whom would certainly not have been able to pick out some of the lesser

known United players if they had turned out. The celebrities on the other hand, were more to their liking.

On the evening of Thursday May 13th a crowd, small by normal match day proportions, gathered around the stadium, despite there being no match on and the gates firmly locked. There were also no chants or songs of praise for their red heroes, instead there was shouts of hatred and protest, with banners proclaiming "Not For Sale", "£800 million Won't Buy Old Trafford" and "No Customers – No Profit" fluttered in the night air, as once again the supporters voiced their complaints about the takeover which had become a reality and had cost Malcolm Glazer seven hundred odd million. Some fans, after marching around the ground, staged a sit down protest on the corner of Chester Road and Sir Matt Busby Way.

The anti-Glazer support was again out in force on June 30th, another non-match day, when it became known, that the three Glazer sons, Joel, Avram and Bryan, were visiting Old Trafford. News of the 'secret' visit was soon out in the open via the internet and mobile telephone calls and around five hundred supporters were soon assembled outside the stadium.

The fans were soon busy building makeshift barricades of metal gates, traffic cones and anything else which came to hand, across the access routes from the stadium. The portable player's tunnel, which had been

outside the ground was also used. Effectively, the three Glazer sons and United officials were trapped inside Old Trafford.

Police were called and following a five hour stand off, officers managed to pull down some of the barriers, allowing two police vans, with blacked out windows, to leave the ground amid ugly scenes of confrontation between the two factions, as fans threw missiles and sat in the road in an attempt to prevent the brothers leaving. Such sights were new to Old Trafford, adding to the history, heritage and mystique of the stadium.

Much of that mystique comes to life during the ever popular stadium tours, but there are areas of the stadium that the public do not see. Doors that are closed but to a select few. One of those doors, is that of Sir Alex Ferguson's personal lounge area, which prior to the start of season

Battle of Old Trafford:
The visit in June 2006 of United's owners to the stadium provoked a furious reaction.

2006-07 received a complete makeover. Apparently, this inner sanctum had changed little in forty years and had resembled the carriage of a 1940's train, but with 'Jam Design' given a free hand, they adapted a RS4 car from Audi, the official car supplier to the club, and came up with a superb hi-tec room.

Engine valves were used as door handles and a head gasket for a wine rack. Two RS4 seats were also included, with Nike boot studs supporting the glass on the mini-bar.

With a trio of mouth watering home fixtures lined up for September 2006, against Tottenham Hotspur on Saturday 9th in the Premiership, Glasgow Celtic on Wednesday 13th in the Champions League and another

Stretford End Quadrant:
A view of the work in progress from inside the ground

Premiership fixture against Arsenal on Sunday 17th, it was not simply the turnstiles that would be clicking away merrily, but the cash tills would also be pushed into overdrive. All three were obviously, like every other home fixture, sold out weeks in advance, but the above three Old Trafford fixtures were set to generate somewhere in the region of £3 plus million per game, with the tea-time visit of Tottenham Hotspur set to be the first English League fixture to pull in such a figure. Gate money alone would come to almost £3m, and with the club shop and catering added on to this, it was a sum that many a small club would be delighted with over a season, never mind one fixture.

It had also been expected that the visit of Tottenham would set a new ground record of more than 76,000, with the two new quadrants filled for the first time,

but expectations were slightly high, as the attendance was a mere 75,453, a figure beaten at the Arsenal match by 142. The previous best had been on the opening day of the season against Fulham, with 75,115, but as the season progressed, it was obvious that the record was going to change on a weekly basis, although, it was not until the visit of Portsmouth on November 4th, that the 76,000 barrier was broken – by four! By the end of the campaign, the record stood at 76,098, set with the visit of Blackburn Rovers on March 31st.

The previously mentioned fixture against Tottenham did see a few more luxury seats filled, but they were not in either of the new quadrants. They were in the dug-out area, with Sir Alex Ferguson, members of his background team and the substitutes for the day, as well as the staff of the opposition club, enjoying the comfort of the newly installed seating. None of the plastic tip-up seating for

those in that particular section, as they now had, courtesy of sponsors Audi, padded red seats, with the dug out also heated for additional comfort during the winter months.

Despite the vast numbers congregated at Old Trafford, the overall atmosphere at times could leave a lot to be desired and following the atmospheric evening against Celtic in the Champions League, helped by the presence of some 6,000 visiting supporters, Sir Alex Ferguson launched a scathing attack on the United support. "Sometimes on a Saturday, some of them come here and they're half asleep" said the United manager. "They come wanting to be entertained, entranced and to see magic. A lot of them want to be bewitched. They say 'Oh, this is a magical place. It all happens here'. But we need their spirit to ignite the team at times. It shouldn't be the other way round all the time. A fan can stir his team - be behind the players in good times as well as bad.

I wish every club could bring 6,000 here. It creates a really competitive element between fans. Our fans are better when it happens. Wednesday night was a great atmosphere and we need to get that big-European tie atmosphere more often."

Mark Longden of the Independent Manchester United Supporters Association was quick to reply to the manager's broadside saying: "The atmosphere is bad at the weekend but that is because most of the games are played at stupid times. They agreed to midday kick-offs, 5pm kick-offs and Sunday kick-offs. There are also too many corporate fans at the moment and not enough stalwarts. If the club want a better atmosphere they should encourage local fans to come."

Since the death of George Best, almost a year previously, the club had been under pressure to commemorate the player with a statue, as a lasting memorial to his place in the history of Manchester United. Behind the scenes, however, there had been on-going talks regarding not just George Best, but the other two members of the 'holy trinity', Bobby Charlton and Denis Law and the announcement in late November that the club had commissioned world famous sculptor Philip Jackson to create a life size, bronze statue of the trio. This news was well received by the supporters, who were even more pleased to learn the following day that there were also plans afoot to create a special memorial at the ground to those who had died at Munich.

*

It cost the Glazer family £831 million when they purchased Manchester United in May 2005, with £540 million of that borrowed. Of that amount, there were the interest rates of 14.25% per cent on a further £275 million. This was payable at £20 million a year, but in the background the debt that the family had taken on steadily increased. Figures that the ordinary man at the match finds mind boggling to say the least. But what sort of money did Old Trafford generate and how did it compare with other club's?

Looking back at the figures released for the 2005-06 season, the total revenue was £163.5m, broken down as follows – Match day revenue - £70.0m, Television revenue - £46.4m and Commercial revenue - £47.1m.

Despite the opposition of the Football League regarding the invitation to take part in the 1956-7 European Cup competition, Matt Busby felt that this was the way ahead and, with the backing of the Football Association, took those tentative footsteps into the unknown world of European football, never to look back, except to wrongly question himself for doing so in the wake of the Munich disaster.

2006 saw the club launch the Manchester United Foundation, to mark the 50th anniversary of the Busby Babes first championship, in season 1955-56, with the aims of this organisation to "provide a legacy to communities in Manchester, the North West and around the World." One of the fund raising events organised by the Foundation was a special match, which would also celebrate the 50th anniversary of the Treaty of Rome, between United and a European X1.

Since hosting its inaugural European tie against Real Madrid back in 1957, Old Trafford, over the years, has provided the stage for the cream of continental (and world) football to display their wide array of talents. From Di Stefano to Platini, Maradona to Zidane and Ronaldo (the Brazilian version) to Eusbebio. As well, of course, as the individuals who have pulled on the red shirt of United.

On the evening of March 13th, it was little different, despite a few call-offs from the original selection of guest players such as Ronaldhino and his Brazilian team mate Ronaldo, with the likes of Ayalla, Materazzi, Gerrard, Ibrahimovic, Gattuso and Larsson, who received a hero's welcome following his loan stint at the club, lining up to face the Reds.

Giant screens flashed up images of past glories, while Alex Stepney and Brian Kidd from the 1968 European Cup triumph, Brian McClair and Denis Irwin from the 1991 European Cup Winners Cup success in rainy Rotterdam and who else but Ole Gunnar Solskjaer from Barcelona in 1999, took their bow in front of an appreciative crowd.

David Beckham, who had initially hope to have played, made a half-time appearance, receiving a rapturous welcome, in a somewhat emotional farewell, telling the crowd: "It is amazing to be back. I have waited four years for this and it is nice to be back on such an occasion. I was devastated to be injured two weeks ago and unable to play. It's the first time that I have been back when the stadium has been full of United fans and I just want to say the times I spent at the club were the best in my entire football career."

As for the game itself, watched by a crowd of 74,343, an Old Trafford record for a non-competitive fixture, raising the sum of £1.2m for the Foundation, they were treated to a highly enjoyable evening of football, which saw United eventually run out 4-3 winners. Wayne Rooney took five minutes to open the scoring, tapping a Paul Scholes pass into an empty net. Wes Brown, with a rare goal, made it 2-0 three minutes later, after Giggs had ghosted past Gattuso. Malouda reduced the leeway for Marcello Lippi's side with a scorching left-foot drive, but Ronaldo restored the two goal advantage with a stunning, trade mark free-kick. Ibrahimovic failed to reduce United's advantage, when he hit the crossbar from the penalty spot six minutes before the interval. The second half, as could have been expected, saw the pace drop a little, while second half substitute Hadji Diouf, making it 4-2 with a header seven minutes after the re-start, before rounding off the

10TH APRIL 2007
CHAMPIONS LEAGUE
QUARTER-FINAL, SECOND LEG

UNITED 7 AS ROMA 1
UNITED WON 8-3 ON AGGREGATE

2-1 down from the first leg, it took United twelve minutes to draw level on aggregate. Ronaldo moved forward, before jinking inside and feeding Carrick with a ball that he bent past Doni at the near post from outside the

Roma penalty area. Five minutes later, it was 2-0. Heinze, on the left picked out Ryan Giggs and with Chivu failing to cut out the Welshman's through pass to Alan Smith, the former Leeds man was in the clear to pick his spot. Ronaldo once again teased the Roma defence, before passing to Smith, who in turn found Giggs. Looking up and spotting Rooney, his inch perfect pass was quickly placed beyond the helpless Doni to put United 3-0 ahead.

Having been involved in the previous goals, it was deserving that Ronaldo scored the fourth, cutting inside from the right and beating Doni, again at the near post, one minute before the interval.

If many suspected the second half would see the pace slow, then they were wrong, as United kept up the tempo and increased their lead within four minutes of the re-start. The Roma defence lost the ball as it attempted to clear and it was immediately despatched to Giggs out on the left. His cross somehow eluded Smith, but Ronaldo was on hand to force the ball home to make it 5-0 on the night.

"Are you City in disguise" taunted the Old Trafford crowd as the atmosphere continued to bubble away and on the hour mark Carrick hammered a pass from Heinze high past Doni from twenty yards for United's sixth.

Roma, to their credit, kept plugging away and were rewarded with something of a consolation goal through Rossi in the sixty-ninth minute, but they were soon to find themselves once again six goals behind on the night, when, with United reduced to ten men, Ferdinand going off injured, Evra joined in the attack to round off the scoring with United's seventh, nine minutes from time.

scoring with a cheeky penalty, which bounced into the net.

The Champions League fixture in Rome's Stadio Olimpico on Wednesday April 4th 2007, was completely overshadowed by the treatment dished out to some of the 4,500 United support in the away section of the ground by the rather heavy handed Italian police. Following Roma's first goal in their 2-1 victory, missiles were thrown between the two sets of supporters, with the baton weilding police wading unceremoniously into the United support, with many fans being struck, but thankfully not too seriously injured. Incidents had also occurred outside the ground prior to kick-off, thus causing feelings to be run high for the return leg in Manchester six days later.

Despite Sir Alex Ferguson not anticipating any problems due to the fantastic security at Old Trafford, there were violent clashes between both sets of supporters prior to kick-off, with many innocent supporters being caught up in the ugly scenes between the rival factions and the riot police and dog handlers. Italian and English yobs hurled bricks and bottles in the direction of each other as the police tried to keep them apart, with several people being led away with blood pouring from head wounds. According to the police, one small group of black clad United supporters, with their faces covered, had been intent in causing trouble, running down Sir Matt Busby

Way towards the ground and charging towards the Italian fans, but they had been dispersed by riot police.

Although many of the travelling 3,800 Italian support cowered for safety near their entrances at the East Stand and it was later suggested that United should have opened the turnstiles earlier to avoid the congestion outside, whilst also allowing the visitors to find safety within the ground, others were happy to exchange insults and missiles with their United counterparts, some surprisingly enough brandishing knives, as the police, at times, struggled to keep the rival groups separate as helicopters swirled overhead. A total of twenty one supporters were arrested, fourteen English and seven Italians.

Inside the ground, the problems outside, coupled with the events of the previous week, added to an electric atmosphere, as the teams entered the arena to a wall of noise and colour. A scene that would have done Rome's Coloseum proud in days gone by (see report).

"In European terms that has to be my greatest moment at Old Trafford" said a jubilant Sir Alex Ferguson after the game." The quality of our game was so high that once we scored the second and third goals I was in the dugout thinking 'this could be something really big here'. But even so, I wasn't expecting that."

Marching through to the semi-final stages in style had many within the rank and file support believing that nothing would stop United from going all the way to the actual Final itself. Sadly they were to be disappointed, as despite a 3-2 victory in the home first-leg against AC Milan, the dreams were to disappear in the away leg when the Italians won 3-0. A sixth minute Ronaldo header was cancelled out by a Kaka double in the twenty-second and thirty-seventh minutes to dampen proceedings. Rooney equalised on the hour, following a sublime Scholes chip and then mustered a dramatic last minute winner, but the second leg in Milan, was to end the dreams of an appearance in the Athens Final against arch-rivals Liverpool, although thankfully the Italians went on to win the final 2-1.

Down and out after losing in Milan, Sir Alex Ferguson had to pick up his troops for the visit to neighbours City on the morning of Saturday May 5th, knowing that a victory could go a long way towards securing United's sixteenth Championship. A penalty kick from Ronaldo and another saved by Edwin van der Sar gave United their three points, while just over twenty-four hours later a 1-1 draw between Arsenal and United's nearest rivals Chelsea, kicked-started a party for some 2,000 supporters gathered outside Old Trafford. A party that would stagger along for another seven days, until the trophy presentation following the final fixture of the season against West Ham United. An afternoon only dampened by the rain and West Ham's 1-0 victory.

Pre-season friendlies are fixtures that many show little interest in, unless they are at some foreign location or a previously unvisited stadium. On those occasions the real die-hard supporters can be found, no matter where the red shirts are playing. So, when United announced that as part of their pre-2007-08 season warm-up, they were to play Inter Milan, it didn't exactly grab the imagination, despite the English Champions versus the Italian Champions banner.

But games such as this, before the real bread and butter league and cup fixtures get under way, offer the supporters who normally don't get the opportunity to visit Old Trafford, for one reason or another, the chance to watch the United stars in the flesh, as the tickets are readily available on open sale to anyone who wants them. Few, however, could have expected this particular fixture to conjure up a crowd of 73,738, a record for a pre-season friendly at the ground.

There is little in the way of significance to be extracted from such games, which is perhaps just as well, as the Italians hit United with three first half goals after Rooney had given the home side the lead in the seventeenth minute. An own goal twelve minutes after the break gave the score line a bit of respectability, but despite the occasion, the score would give the United manager some food for thought.

Honours and Old Trafford go hand in hand, certainly in recent times, with the never ending array of trophies heading to the club museum, but in December 2007, it was a different kind of honour that found its way to the ground. In a local residents "Pride of Place" poll, the stadium, with forty percent of the votes captured the award.

Invited to select from between ten places within the area, including the Trafford Centre, which could claim some 30 million visitors during 2006, and the Imperial War Museum North, there was only ever going to be one winner. Although, even Old Trafford could not match the attendance figures of its near neighbour, plans were well to the fore for a permanent exhibition at the ground, which would certainly be a big attraction on both match and non-match days.

*

With February approaching, thoughts turned to that fateful day in 1958 when disaster struck British European Flight 609 ZU at Munich's Rheim airport - February 6th 2008 marked the 50th anniversary of the crash, with the club holding a special service at the ground, and unveiling a special, permanent memorial to the team affectionately known as "the Busby Babes" on the walls of the South Stand that would chart the story of that legendary side, through to the winning of the European Cup in 1968.

Atmosphere is something that Old Trafford has never lacked, but when the stadium became an all seated arena, it, like countless others up and down the country lost something unique to the game of football. Yes, long gone are the swaying, pushing and shoving crowds, when you would begin watching the match on one spot, only to find yourself several yards away as the half time whistle blew. Also gone was the need to be outside the ground for the turnstiles opening at one o'clock (for those bygone days of the regular three o'clock kick-offs), as you could now stroll down to the necessary gate and walk in a mere five minutes before the referee's whistle.

New Year's Day 2008 saw United struggle to overcome a dour Birmingham City side, with the only goal of the game coming after twenty-five minutes from Carlos Tevez. It was not the ideal performance to begin another year with, but it did maintain United's pressure on league leaders Arsenal. Rather surprisingly though, Sir Alex Ferguson diverted the rather disappointing performance from his players to the supporters, with his after-match comments stirring up a hornet's nest.

"The atmosphere in the

ground wasn't very good – the crowd were dead. That is the quietest I have heard the crowd. You need the crowd to create a good atmosphere here. Players will respond to that. It is all right saying the way the players play will make the crowd respond but in some situations like this you need them to get behind you. It was like a funeral. It was so quiet. It was dead. I don't think that helped us. There have been days like this in the past. It has happened before. Some years ago when we were dominant the crowd were coming to be entertained but you need them to get behind you so we can produce the right performance and get the tempo of the game up. There are times when you need a lift but we didn't get that today."

The managers comments, coupled with condemnation of criticism towards the Glazer family, despite his standing amongst the supporters, was like a red rag to a bull to some, while others agreed with him, at least as regards to the atmosphere within the ground.

"You reap what you sow and SAF (Sir Alex Ferguson) siding with the Glazers is a large reason for the lack of atmosphere." Said 'philnevlegend' on United fanzine Red Issue's online message board, who continued: "He helped them in, to sting the working class fans and put tickets up 75 per cent and price out most of the lads who went for the singing. Now it is half-full of corporates and day-trippers."

"Too many new faces where

I sit, most of whom don't speak with a local accent. Yesterday was a joke, with people sitting down in the Stretford End" said another fan on BBC 606, while another on the same 'phone-in said: "I'm a season ticket holder at Old Trafford and I agree with Fergie that it was quiet but he has no right to disrespect the fans who pay him and his players' wages. It is a poor excuse to cover up a poor performance."

Another contributor to one of the numerous websites added: "The new regime prefers the day-tripping, glory hunter supporter over the die-hard Red, because the latter is going to turn up for the match, sing his heart out, then go home, whereas the day-tripper will peruse the club shop, pick up some memorabilia, maybe a replica kit or two for friends, maybe take in the stadium tour the day before, and generally part with far more cash. So while we lose out in terms of atmosphere, 'we' gain financially."

Perhaps Colin Hendrie, of the Independent Manchester United Supporters Association, hit the nail on the head when he said; "A lot of people are pretty upset because it shows a lack of understanding about what it's like to be a football fan in 2008. Fergie's going back to the days ten years ago when it was

absolutely fantastic, you could stand. But you can't do that now and the football authorities need to make up their minds whether they want to have fans sitting neatly in a row not being able to do anything, or if they want an atmosphere in the football grounds again. I think Fergie could benefit from sitting in the ground. You can't stand up and make a noise. If you try to stand up, you've got stewards who are ejecting you and then taking your season ticket away from you. It's almost like a police state in a football ground now and, if you do stand up, people will take your arm, put it behind the back of your neck and throw you out of the ground. Under those circumstances, what atmosphere does he want?"

So, was the United manager right in his observations regarding the Old Trafford match day atmosphere? A survey from October 2007, which compared the noise levels from the different Premier League club's saw Sunderland supporters crank out an average of 129.2 decibels, making them the noisiest, while United found themselves in seventeenth on a level of 117.5, with only Wigan, Reading and Fulham below them.

In mid-January, work began on what was to be a temporary 50th anniversary tribute to the

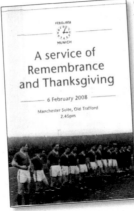

'Babes', with the familiar last line-up prior to their final game against Red Star in Belgrade, being erected across the glass frontage of Old Trafford, behind the statue of Sir Matt Busby. Alongside the image of the players was some of the words from the terrace anthem – 'The United Calypso', but unfortunately, these had not been properly checked before the tribute was erected, as the line – "Manchester, Manchester United, a bunch of bouncing Busby Babes, they deserve to be knighted" had seen the word "Busby" omitted. Following numerous complaints, this was quickly corrected. Equally annoying to many supporters was the fact that the logo of club sponsors AIG also appeared on the tribute and red paint was later thrown at the logo, although it was removed equally as quickly as the panel with the missing word.

Plans for the memorial service at the ground had been on-going for some time, with special invites going out to the families and friends of those who died, to the survivors, players from that period, team-mates

▶ **50th Anniversary of Munich:** *The club produced a number of worthy tributes to commemorate the disaster. The Munich Tunnel (under The South Stand) features a moving display of all the passengers on the ill-fated aircraft. The players of both United and City donned special sponsor-free kits for the day, an idea prompted by supporters.*

United Review v Manchester City 10.02.08

FEB 6th 1958

MUNICH

"MANCHESTER ❖ MANCHESTER UNITED A BUNCH OF BOUNCING BUSBY BABES, THEY DESERVE TO BE KNIGHTED ❖ IF EVER THEY'RE PLAYING IN YOUR TOWN ❖ YOU MUST GET TO THAT FOOTBALL GROUND ❖ TAKE A LESSON COME TO SEE FOOTBALL TAUGHT BY MATT BUSBY"

THEY PLAY ON IN OUR MEMORIES AIG

BEFORE THE TRAGEDY AT MUNICH THE CITY BELONGED TO MANCHESTER BUT AFTERWARDS MANCHESTER UNITED CAPTURED THE IMAGINATION OF THE ENTIRE WORLD

FEB 6th 1958

MUNICH

SOUTH STAND

Geoff Bent   Tom Cable   Eric Thompson   Liam Whelan   Frank

and representatives of Red Star Belgrade, with a number of supporters also being able to attend the memorial service which was to be held in the Manchester Suite within the North Stand. But as well as those with invitations, the Old Trafford forecourt was packed, as never before, with a crowd that many club's would have relished on a Saturday afternoon, reported to be more than 1,500 gathered to pay their respects.

The service was relayed from within the stadium to those outside in the winter sunshine, with the same emotions being felt wherever you were. Inside the Manchester Suite, screens showed the 'Babes' in action, whilst a children's choir enlightened the occasion, as did the likes of Nobby Stiles and Harry Gregg. Club captain Gary Neville lit twenty-three small candles, each in a specially engraved holder, for those who had died, while the area beneath the memorial plaque on the wall of the East Stand was awash with floral tributes.

Although the hands on the Munich Memorial clock on the wall close to the memorial plaque were fixed at 3.04, the exact time of the crash, silence enveloped both those inside and out as that fateful time approached, with tears being shed by many who found the occasion too much.

As the service drew to a close, Harry Gregg, Bill Foulkes, Bobby Charlton, Albert Scanlon and Kenny Morgans, along with David Gill and Roger Byrne jnr

made their way outside, where waiting cars took them round to the South Stand tunnel, now to be re-named the Munich Tunnel, where the latter two unveiled a special plaque at the start of a new permanent exhibition stretching the length of the stand, which re-told the story of the 'Busby Babes' and the rebirth of the club following the tragedy.

By a strange quirk of fate, the fixtures for the league programme two days later paired United with neighbours City, something that caused sleepless nights for so many, as the threat of the match-day tribute and a further minutes silence would be disrupted by visiting supporters who knew no better. It had even been suggested that the minute silence be changed to a similar period of applause, but United, correctly, stood firm to their original plans. Both teams were to wear special one-off shirts carrying no sponsors logos, with the United kit similar to that worn in 1958.

As it turned out, there need not have been any cause for concern, as the visiting City support were impeccable in their respect, making the pre-match occasion one to be remembered. Red and white and blue and white scarves had been placed on every seat within the ground, which were held high as the minutes silence was celebrated following the laying of wreaths in the centre circle by Sven Goran Eriksson and Sir Alex Ferguson. Everything didn't quite go to plan, however, as City swung the title advantage towards Arsenal

by upsetting the form books with a 2-1 victory.

As another season moved towards its climax, with United jousting with Chelsea and Arsenal for the Premiership title, the Gunners came to Old Trafford with the hopes of upsetting their red shirted rivals, but by the end of an eventful afternoon, in front of a 75,985 crowd, goals from Ronaldo, with a twice taken penalty, in the fifty-fourth minute and a free-kick from Hargreaves in the seventy-second minute, wiped out Adebayor's goal three minutes after the interval, which had given Arsenal the lead. The result saw United go nine points clear of Arsenal and six in front of second placed Chelsea, requiring two wins to secure the championship for a second successive season.

Not only was the Premier League title within their grasp, it was also possible to secure a notable double as Alex Ferguson's team were also in the semi-final of the Champions League, with Barcelona standing between them and a place in the Final. It was exciting times around Old Trafford, but for some, who were looking forward to the forthcoming Champions League semi-final tie against Barcelona, there was to be disappointment.

Season tickets are usually, in many cases, for life, but in order to generate additional income, the club decided to issue "one-year" season tickets, which were eagerly snatched up by supporters fed-up with being

unlucky in the ballot for match day tickets. Payment for such tickets was no different to that for a normal season ticket. Pay up-front, in some cases £700, and join the dreaded and highly controversial 'automatic cup scheme', which meant that you had to pay for any home cup-tie tickets whether you wanted to go to the game or not.

With the Barcelona fixture less than two weeks away, more than 1,000 supporters received letters from the club that they would not automatically receive tickets for the forthcoming tie. The reason given for this was that the club had to provide UEFA with more tickets than it had done for the quarter-final tie against Roma. Larger advertising boards and increased press facilities were also given as reasons behind this move. For those unlucky supporters, they had little option but to watch the game unfold on television.

Having drawn the first leg in Spain 0-0, hopes were high that victory could be achieved and the Final in Moscow reached, where either Liverpool or Chelsea would provide the opposition. As it was, it took only one goal to secure that victory, scored by Paul Scholes, who had ironically missed the 1999 Final in Barcelona due to suspension, in the fourteenth minute.

The evening started almost chaotically for the ginger-haired mid-fielder, as within twenty-five seconds of the start, he brought down Messi within inches of the United penalty area. Thankfully, the resulting free-kick came to nothing, but van der Sar did little to quell the United supporters in the 75,061 crowd, as he mis-kicked a clearance straight to the dangerous Eto'o. Again the opportunity was missed.

With fourteen minutes played, Ronaldo moved past Toure and Zambrotta, but failed to keep control of the ball, with Zambrotta gaining possession. The defender, however, carelessly sent the ball straight to the feet of Scholes, who did little more than look up before sending a stunning right-footed drive into the top corner of the Barcelona net from all of twenty-five yards. It was a goal worthy of winning any game, never mind a Champions League semi-final, but with seventy-six minutes still to play, anything could happen. As it was, United bravely held on to that solitary goal lead and the rest, as they say, is history.

Thousands had flocked to Old Trafford over the weekend of April 19th and 20th, hoping to catch the eye with their own particular talent and go on to fame and fortune. But they were certainly not out to impress Sir Alex Ferguson or any of his numerous talent spotters, as this was the television reality show – the X Factor and Simon Cowell was the man who the talented and the definitely not-so talented had to win over.

Up to 3,000 people queued in the car park outside the main entrance to the ground, some even camping out overnight and by 4am there were already two long lines of wannabe stars. Most, however, had as much

chance of doing so as the some of the Red Army had of making Moscow for the Champions League final without any problems. With the penalty-kick drama of the Champions League Final and United's ultimate success still monopolising most meaningful conversations, there was a brief diversion at Old Trafford on the afternoon of Thursday May 29th, when a small ceremony took place opposite the imposing structure of the East Stand.

Beneath the blue Manchester sky, around five hundred supporters and one hundred invited guests gathered for the unveiling of the 'Holy Trinity' statue, a lasting tribute to the legendary trio of Denis Law, George Best and Sir Bobby Charlton, forty years to the day since United won the European Cup for the first time, with that 4-1 defeat of Benfica at Wembley.

Unveiled by David Gill and Sir Alex Ferguson (a statue of the latter will surely follow somewhere in the vicinity) those present were treated to vintage highlights of the player's careers and goals and the trio were then joined on the small platform by former team mates from 1968 – Pat Crerand, John Aston, Brian Kidd, Francis Burns, John Fitzpatrick, Nobby Stiles, Jimmy Ryan, Bill Foulkes, David Sadler, Jimmy Rimmer, along with Jack Crompton, Sandy Busby and Barbara Best.

Across Manchester, City's Eastlands stadium had been chosen by UEFA as the venue for the Final of the UEFA Cup, but

THE UNITED TRINITY
BEST   LAW   CHARLTON

with Glasgow Rangers as one of the finalists, the other being Zenith St Petersburg, there was more than a possible chance of thousands of Scottish supporters travelling south without tickets.

In order to avoid any problems outside Eastlands on the evening of the match, it was suggested that large screens could be installed at Old Trafford to accommodate those without match-tickets and who wanted to see the game in surroundings where an atmosphere could be created. Greater Manchester

▶ **Best, Law and Charlton**
Three of the finest talents to ever grace a football field got a worthy tribute when a statue was unveiled in 2008.

Police, however, had very different ideas and certainly did not want the travelling hoard's anywhere near Old Trafford. Not that they were all United supporters, wishing to keep their hallowed ground in one piece, it was simply because it would be easier to try and control the supporters if they were generally in the same area. As events unfolded, and with the problems caused in Manchester city centre, it was certainly the correct decision, as who knows what damage might have been done to Old Trafford and the surrounding area.

The visit of Villarreal on Champions League business does not exactly stir the emotions, but on the evening of September 17th 2008 and the Spaniards visit to Manchester, it was much more than the emotions of some of the United support that was stirred, as around three hundred found themselves locked out of the ground when their season ticket cards failed to register when swiped at the turnstiles. That season, along with the 14% rise in season ticket prices, the club had introduced the much despised, automatic cup scheme, where supporters had their credit cards debited for all cup tie tickets (except the Carling Cup if they chose to opt out), whether they wanted to go or not.

The problem at the turnstiles was caused due to the expiry of the holders credit card details after they had paid for their season tickets and because of this, the club had sold those seats for Villarreal again. Those refused admission made their way to the Ticket Office where they were told the reason for their non-admittance and that letters had been sent out previously explaining this. Surprisingly, one supporter who had spoken to a number of

others in the queue said that no-one had received such a letter.

Most were offered alternative seats at £55, while the club were quick to

point out that it was up to the individual to ensure that their credit cards were valid. With the continued interest in all things United and their media arm of MUTV now an established part of the club, it was planned to build a three storey, sixty foot high building alongside the existing Membership and Ticket Offices. This would house office space and also a new studio, but one of the obligations was that it would be screened by some ninety-three trees.

This, however, was not something that could be done, as there was no room, or anywhere that the trees could be planted, so the club had to agree to pay £21,823 for off-site planting for the community forest project, which covered, Manchester, Salford, Bolton, Bury and Wigan. A further £22,000 was to go towards roads and public transport improvements. These plans were, however, put on hold for the time being.

Having broken Chelsea's slender grip on the Premiership trophy two seasons ago, United were once again in a challenging

position to make it three in a row, as the 2008-09 campaign moved into a critical period. Although the Stamford Bridge side were once again in the race for the title, it was arch-rivals Liverpool who looked to be the team who would run United the closest and with consecutive defeats, 2-0 at Fulham and 4-1 against Liverpool, in one of Old Trafford's more forgettable matches, the next fixture was indeed crucial.

On April 5th, a solitary Liverpool goal had earned the Merseysiders three points at Fulham, taking them two points clear of United at the top, although they had played one game more, while a visit to Old Trafford by a re-juvenated Aston Villa under Martin O'Neill was no guaranteed three points for the home side. A poor Milner back pass in the fourteenth minute, forced Friedel to handle outside his area and from the resulting free-kick, Giggs calmly rolled the ball into the path of Ronaldo, who made no mistake with a drive into the top corner of the Villa goal.

Although jolted by the early set back, Villa clawed their way back into the game and before the clock hit the hour mark, they were 2-1 in front through goals from Carew (30th minute) and Agbonlahor (58th), both with headers which outlined a flaw in the makeshift United defence.

With ten minutes remaining and United looking down and out, Ronaldo hit a low drive through a crowded penalty area to level the scores and with the

home crowd more than happy with the possible point when none at all looked more than likely. But the afternoon was far from over. Having little to lose, Sir Alex Ferguson decided to give the unfamiliar Federico Macheda his senior debut as a sixty-first minute substitute. It was thought the muscular seventeen year-old Italian could perhaps unsettle the Villa defence if little else. Slowly, the minutes ticked away, with the Old Trafford scoreboards soon showing that the ninety were up. On the touchline, the fourth official's board indicated that there would be an additional five minutes to play. United had a lifeline. The noise level rose in encouragement, urging the red shirts towards the Stretford End goal.

With two of the additional five minutes played, Neville pushed the ball through to Macheda, but his effort was blocked by a defender. Possession, however, was quickly regained and Giggs found the young Italian just inside the Villa area. Despite having his back to goal, 'Kiko' turned Davies before wrapping his foot round the ball and sending it past Friedel's desperate dive and into the far corner of the net. Old Trafford erupted and Macheda took off towards where his family were seated down beside the tunnel and was booked for excessive celebrations by referee Riley, but who cared. A new hero was born and the title dream was back on track with one of those special Old Trafford moments.

With television ruling the roost as regards to kick-off times, United once again found themselves playing catch up on Saturday April 25th, with the visit of Tottenham Hotspur to Old Trafford. Liverpool had defeated Hull City 3-1 earlier in the day, so United knew that they needed a point, at least, in order to regain top spot. By half time, it looked as if not only was the point not going to materialise, but the title hopes were once again slipping away.

The warning signals were there as early as the eighth minute, when Bent should have put Tottenham in front from Lennon's cross, but Van der Sar managed to push the ball away for a corner. Bent, however, did get the better of the Dutchman twenty-one minutes later, when he gave the Londoners the lead. Three minutes later, United were two goals behind. Lennon, again tormenting the United defence, crossed into the area. The ball evaded Bent, but fell to the unmarked Modric who beat Van der Sar. Gomez in the Tottenham goal thwarted Ronaldo minutes before the break and as the second half got underway, the gangly 'keeper was once again in the thick of the action, saving from substitute Tevez, before being involved in the incident which put United back in the game.

Twelve minutes into the second half, Carrick moved into the Tottenham penalty area and as he pushed the ball forward, Gomez dived at his feet and although getting his fingertips

to the ball, brought down the United mid-fielder. Referee Howard Webb immediately pointed to the spot and Ronaldo fired the ball home. Ten minutes later, a Berbatov – Tevez – Rooney move ended with the latter beating Gomez at the near post to put United level and with the celebrations still on-going, Ronaldo's diving header, from a Rooney cross, put United in 3-2 in front. With the scent of victory in the air, United continued to press forward and made it 4-2 in the seventy-first minute through Rooney and rounded things off with a fifth, eight minutes later through Berbatov. Whilst not as dramatic a victory as that against Aston Villa, it was still one to remember, as the title inched closer.

The games were now coming thick and fast and it wasn't simply Premier League fixtures that pulled the masses into Old Trafford, as four days after Tottenham's visit, their north London neighbours Arsenal were in town on Champions League business, hoping for a favourable semi-final first leg result. As it turned out, there wasn't the drama, or indeed the goals of the Aston Villa or Tottenham encounters, with a solitary John O'Shea effort all that separated the sides on the night.

More notable perhaps, was the fact that the visit of Arsenal saw Ryan Giggs chalk up his 800th United appearance, when he came on as a sixty-seventh minute substitute for Anderson. As Kevin McCarra wrote in his

report for *The Guardian*, "…he can take pride in the fact that there was nothing in the least ceremonial about this outing. He was simply needed."

Strangely, when asked to name the Old Trafford "greats", it is names such as Billy Meredith, Johnny Carey, Duncan Edwards, Bobby Charlton, Eric Cantona and of course George Best, (with whom he was compared in his early days) which readily come to the fore, but none of those previously mentioned legendary Red Devils can come anywhere close to matching the achievements within the game of Ryan Giggs OBE, who in the years to come, will rightly take his place alongside the other United legends, with a trophy haul which will never be beaten. It was perhaps fitting that it was the Gunners who marked

such a momentous occasion, as Giggs's finest moment in the red shirt came against the north London side, in the 1999 FA Cup semi-final at Villa Park, scoring that solo goal that took United to Wembley and kept them on course for the treble.

Heady times indeed for the Old Trafford faithful, but the match day experience and indeed a visit to Old Trafford at

any time, could prove different from person to person. Certainly for supporters with a disability the experience was different in the sense of access to the stadium and the actual viewing of the game. For disabled supporters, the facilities within the stadium were as impressive as those for the more active fan, with Old Trafford being ranked as one of the country's top tourist attractions for the disabled. This was mainly due to the work done between the club and its Disabled Supporters Association, creating excellent facilities for both home and away supporters.

Situated in a corner of the ground, underneath the away section, the disabled area is on three levels, with spaces alongside the wheelchair for carers. The sightlines from level one were considered not as good as those of two and three, so the club installed television screens, ensuring that their disabled supporters enjoyed the same view as everyone else in the stadium as Ryan Giggs lifted the Premier League trophy high above his head for a record breaking eighteen time, following the 0-0 draw with Arsenal, who they had crushed 3-1 (4-1 on aggregate) at the Emirates in the second leg of the Champions League semi-final.

In the opposite corner from the disabled section, in the north-west quadrant, there was little problem with the sightlines or indeed missing any of the action, as the first phase of a multi million pound investment in the stadium's hospitality facilities saw outdoor balconies added to eight suites, which formed the Centennial Club. Each of the "private terraces" had sixteen luxury seats, with those able to afford them able to gain entry three hours prior to kick-off and remain there for two hours after the final whistle, enjoying a complimentary bar, champagne and canapés on arrival to a five course meal from a table overlooking the pitch. A far cry from the pie and Bovril days!

Also a far cry from the days of the flat caps, travelling to the match on your bicycle and leaving it for two old pence in someone's garden, while on a wet afternoon or evening, having simply to stand there and endure it as there was only limited cover at the ground, is the money involved in the game today, as has been mentioned often within these pages.

With season 2009-10 not too far off, United announced a world record profit of £71.8m according to the latest figures, which covered the 2007-08 season, on the same day that the club also announced the signing of a new shirt sponsorship deal with American financial giant Aon Corp. Premier League revenue pulled in £257.1m, outperforming all their rivals. Yet the huge debt incurred by the Glazers remain and now totalled some £500m.

With such sums of money being bandied about, anyone wishing to buy Manchester United and its Old Trafford

ground, the sum required does not bear thinking about, but if you did fancy purchasing the latter, you could obtain it, for a figure significantly less than purchasing the whole club would cost you if you were prepared to accept a scale model of the famous stadium, rather than the real thing.

Hand crafted by artist Peter Oldfield-Edwards, the model, scaled at approximately 1:220 and measuring approximately four feet square, was offered for sale by Graham Budd Auctions, with a price of between £20,000 and £30,000 put against it.

So what would the buyer get for his outlay? Certainly not some cornflake packet and toilet roll job, held together with sellotape, but a superbly constructed model, which was everything that the real thing was. But why did the artist want to construct a model of Old Trafford in the first place and what was the inspiration behind it all?

"I wanted to build a model of a stadium that would grace any home, museum or institution; a model that would draw you in and captivate you, a model that would wow the kids and fascinate the parents. When I first visited Old Trafford in 2004 to look into the possibility of building a model of this stadium, I immediately felt inspired to the challenge of creating a work of art that was instantly recognisable as one of the great sporting arenas of the world, and a piece that would be correct to the eye in all its intricate detail.

At the same time I wanted put my own interpretation into this piece. I felt excited at the thought and it was something I had an innate desire to do, but where would I start?

"I began researching and studying as many aerial images as I could find, along with my own photographs I had taken during the 2004 visit. I needed to familiarise myself as much as possible with the stadium and also read as much as I could about its history. Then I thought about sizing the piece. I decided to work in 1:220 scale and finalising how much of the surrounding area around the stadium I would need to incorporate. The finished size would be about 4 ft. square, which would be a good workable and practical size by the time it was presented in a display case.

"The first thing I do with all my models is to put a rough pitch guide in called a prop. This will be replaced later with a finished pitch and surround track. The model is built in sections and is easily dismantled. This allows me to work easily on any part of the model at any time, and on completion also allows the model to be disassembled for transportation. The upper decks and both quadrants come out as does each roof. Every part of the stadium comes apart in sections so that all is left is the base with its pinewood surround. I started with the inside of the stadium first building the South Stand terrace up to executive box level, and continued this all the way

around the stadium finishing in the south west corner, incorporating the players tunnel area in the south-west corner, disabled area in the south-east corner and dugouts on halfway.

"This is the base for the whole stadium and has to be absolutely correct to guarantee success and is a highly involved process. I calculated the degree of angle for each section of terrace. The South Stand in fact has three different degrees of angle which all conjoin on one level. Being Old Trafford`s main stand it houses all the privileged seating and hospitality areas. The other three sides of the stadium and the four corners only have two degrees of angle. The seats were carved in blocks.

"With the bowl of the stadium now in place I could then build the North, East and West upper decks and their supports, and furnished them with seating before adding both quadrant terraces with their respective seating. The next task was to cut all the vomitory passages, these are all the entry and exit points for spectator seating throughout the stadium. I then painted all the seats in a high gloss enamel paint. Work could now begin on forming the stadium`s perimeter and surroundings. Because Old Trafford was redeveloped in stages, each side of the ground is remarkably different from

▶ **A perfect facsimilie:**
Peter Oldfield-Edwards' model of the stadium took over 3,000 man hours to complete.

the outside and has very little uniformity.

"Gradually I created the outside walls and columns from balsa wood, leaving the first level of detail till later. Once proportioned, I started thinking about the land surrounding the stadium. This is built in one piece using a wooden frame, carved to the camber of the land, with a separate section behind the South Stand to incorporate the railway and platform area. Both these sections are screwed down to the base, and mounting card is then used to cover the entire frame. Next I started putting in the first layer of detail to the back of the stands starting with the North Stand. Plastic sheets are corrugated and etched by a scalpel, cut to size and fitted, then painted. This is repeated all around the stadium. I then installed the finished pitch which is fabric-based and mounted on a balsa wood platform. The goalposts are removable and the nets are made from a very fine nylon mesh.

"It was now time for the roof structures, which required lots of experimentation to get right. I wanted to stay clear of the simpler method of photo-etching so as to maintain the complete hand-built integrity of the work. The model has five separate roofs and all use a cantilever design, which means they all have to support themselves individually. I started with the North Stand and used a clear Perspex for the general surface area while achieving the corrugated effect with a scalpel

and then painted the non-clear sections. A plastic coated wire was used for the basic cantilever structure, using cotton threads as guide lines. I then strengthened this structure with diagonal rods made of nylon and cut precisely to size and glued into place. The East, West and Quadrant roofs were made in a similar way but using different diameter rods. The South roof proved the hardest to make because the cantilever structure was a lot smaller in diameter. I had to use brass rods supported with plastic diagonals again cut precisely to size and glued. Using tweezers, over 700 individual pieces were installed on this one roof! In fact the stadium`s entire roof structure would take in excess of 350 man hours to complete.

"Next I cut and installed Old Trafford`s vomitories, all 111 of them. These are made from 1mm. plastic and all cut using a scalpel. Fascia boards were then printed and positioned. I then sculpted the railway lines using modelling clay and formed the station platform and grass bank behind the South Stand. The canal behind the North Stand is made from 6 mm. glasses with clay used again to shape the banks. Then the turnstiles were printed and cut in. In fact it required another visit to Old Trafford to take some photographs of all the turnstiles and outbuilding detail. All the turnstiles in this model have the correct signage printed, although the scaling is minute and takes a keen eye to read them.

"There are also turnstiles

housed under the North, West and Quadrant areas employing the same high level of detail. Then all the glass panelling is made for the East Stand and Quadrant areas. These panels are removable. With all the main features now made and fitted, it would take me several months to add all the fine, finishing details such as outbuilding, roads, bridge, tarmac areas, trees and foliage, car parks, signage and other miscellaneous detailing. Even the vehicles are hand made and painted. With the sole exceptions of the human and canine figures, the model has been constructed entirely by my own hands.

"A wide range of materials has been used to build this piece. Hardwoods like balsa, which is lightweight, versatile and easy to work, have been used for the main structure. Plastics were used in many forms, including 2mm. clear thick sheets for the roof, and 0.5mm. to 1mm. used in a lot of finishing surfaces. A range of nylon and brass rods of varying diameters have been used for the cantilever structures. Decoration has been achieved with both water and oil base paints. Although started in 2004, the project had to be mothballed temporarily while Old Trafford was being redeveloped further with additions of the East and West Quadrants. Most of this model was built between June 2008 and September 2009. Around 3,000 man hours have been spent on this piece.

"The Old Trafford model is a hugely complex piece of

art and has challenged me in so many different ways I can't begin to communicate it fully. It's the best model I have built in my career to date. It is the only fully detailed scale model of Old Trafford in the world and I will never repeat it. I have found this project to be a massive learning curve. I am enormously proud of the finished piece and of the degree of workmanship which is true to the standards I had set myself from the outset of the project. Although naturally a part of me doesn't want to let it go, I of course look forward with great anticipation to personally installing the model in its new home." Unfortunately, the model stadium did not reach the required reserve and so, on this occasion, did not sell.

Living in the vicinity of Old Trafford, certainly for myself, would be something of luxury, saving me countless early morning rises and also getting to bed in the early hours, but for the residents of Manchester 16, life, at times, is far from a bed of roses, with match days (and nights) bringing much disruption and annoyance. The close-season must be looked forward to like a child does for Christmas, but the summer of 2010 looks as though it will bring added distractions, with United hoping to hold seven concerts at Old Trafford over a six week period. If that wasn't bad enough, there were plans for some running for four nights in a row.

Residents living near to the ground were up in arms at

the news, but with such events bringing in considerable sums of money, it was an avenue that the club found worth considering, even at the cost of damaging the pitch and preventing necessary growth during the close season.

There were even pre-season fixtures for the locals to contend with, unless, having consulted the fixture lists, they decided to disappear for a few days, something, if they did not enjoy

the endless stream of supporters passing their doors, would have been advisable prior to the start of the 2009-10 season. Few, however, would have expected a mere friendly to spoil a summer evening, as such fixtures were often low key affairs, with attendances often restricted to those unable to make the regular pilgrimage to Old Trafford, with the 'regulars' giving them a wide berth.

On this particular occasion, even with opponents Valencia not really a major draw, they were wrong if they thought a smaller attendance than normal would be present on August 5th, as some 74,311 clicked through the turnstiles, surpassing the previous record of 73,738 set two years previously when Milan came to town. The atmosphere of a Premiership fixture was obviously missing, substituted

by numerous Mexican waves, but the debuts of new signings Michael Owen and Antonio Valencia did attract much attention, but in the end, it was goals from Wayne Rooney and youngster Tom Cleverley, that sent the crowd home happy.

Since you first turned the pages of this book, we have travelled through one hundred years, a century of not only football, but rugby, cricket, tennis, music concerts, boxing, weddings and whatever else has taken part within the bowels of the vast arena that is Old Trafford, but what of the future?

Expansion is not impossible, constructing two quadrants on the South Stand side, similar to those already in place is not beyond the imagination, although building over the railway looks less a possibility, due to the houses in Railway Road (rumour had it that the club already own the area lying vacant due to two of the houses having already been demolished, but this is untrue) and the overall cost involved. Perhaps taking the current South Stand upwards, as suggested to me by United secretary Ken Ramsden, is the most viable option.

I wrote at the end of first publication of this book – "Will the adjoining areas to the ground see something along the lines of a Fred the Red theme park, along with a hotel to generate further income, or other United associated ventures?" Well, the hotel did appear, but the theme park remains a figment of the imagination, although something akin to one does appear in the main car park, when the club hosts its open training days on the eve of every season.

Old Trafford on a match day is an experience to be savoured and enjoyed, with the area around Chester Road and Sir Matt Busby Way resembling a Middle Eastern Market, with countless traders doing brisk business from early morning. Fast food outlets, an off-licence and nearby pubs satisfy the hunger and thirst that United cannot satisfy, while stalls set up by independent traders sell everything from badges to flags and t-shirts, to old match programmes of past seasons. Slightly less audible than the stallholders declaring their wares are the mumbled voices of the ticket touts offering to buy or sell those precious pieces of paper that are required to gain admission to the ground.

Many, however, who cross the railway bridge on Sir Matt Busby Way (still affectionately known to many as Warwick Road), will remember completely different scenes, with the 'United Café' a notable landmark, situated where the United Foundation offices are today. There was also 'Holy Joe' Pennington who, along with his wife and brother would stand at the forecourt end of the bridge, proclaiming the sins of man, with a large banner which warned the crowds flocking towards the ground that 'The End Is Nigh'.

The trio, who first appeared around 1962-63, were to become prominent match-day figures, dressed at first in long white, market style coats, with the two men wearing bowler hats. They later stood out even more in their yellow fluorescent jackets as they proclaimed "Only God Can Save" and "Repent Your Sins", exchanging good humoured banter with the passing supporters. With exchanges such as Joe shouting: "It's Hell in there" to which a passing supporter replied "we know".

There was also the yellow *Manchester Evening News* van, which sat on the roadside opposite the forecourt and would print stop press news and the full time scores, as you filled out of the ground at the end of the match.

Back in the present, as kick-off approaches, Sir Matt Busby Way and the surrounding streets become busier, as the supporters from far and near make their way towards the turnstiles in anticipation of the forthcoming ninety minutes. From the city centre, the local buses drop their fares along Chester Road, while from the opposite direction come the majority of the members of the vast Red Army who have journeyed from all corners of the country in their various supporter's club coaches. Many others have arrived in the city by train and make the short journey towards the ground by either Metrolink or to the small station a short pass from the main stand.

Each match day differs, but for want of the perfect example of what Old Trafford means to so many people, I will bring this amazing story to a close with the events of Sunday September 20th 2009 (see report).

For some, it was the ultimate match day experience. What football and a visit to Old Trafford is all about.

Drama, goals, excitement and controversy, welcome to Old Trafford, the Theatre of Dreams, home of Manchester United Football Club.

Take me home,
United Road,
To the place I belong,
To Old Trafford,
To see United,
Take me home,
United Road.

UNITED 4 CITY 3

It was 'derby' day in Manchester, but today, the fixture took on a completely new perspective due to neighbours City, suddenly finding themselves enriched with the seemingly bottomless purse of the Abu Dhabi United Group. The usual volatile atmosphere was also pumped up by the summer signing of former United terrace favourite Carlos Tevez, whose every touch was greeted by a backdrop of boos. Now just as despised as anyone else in a light blue shirt.

Many were still making their way to their seats, when the majority of the crowd erupted as the ball bulged the back of the City net, following Wayne Rooney's second minute strike, prodding the ball over the line from Evra's pass. The goal settled United and they enjoyed most of the ball, but the visitors drew level rather unexpectedly in the sixteenth minute, when a long, aimless ball forward by Lescott should have been cleared by Foster in the United goal. Dwelling too long on the ball, he suddenly found himself under pressure from Tevez and the former red prized the ball away from the 'keeper before setting up Barry to slip the ball into the unguarded net from the edge of the area.

Some who missed that first goal may well have also missed United's second. Four minutes after the restart, Evra lays the ball off to Giggs, who beats Richards on left before sending over a high looping cross into the City penalty area. Fletcher, unexpectedly, rises high above everyone at the Stretford End goal to head past Given into the bottom corner. City were only monetarily knocked off their stride and took only three minutes to once again draw level. Tevez, again a thorn in United's side, sets the ball up for Bellamy and the Welshman cuts inside O'Shea before beating Foster with a rasping drive from twenty yards.

Play swung from end to end. Given in the City goal made two impressive stops from Berbatov headers whilst also tipping a Giggs effort over the bar. At the opposite end, Wright-Phillips saw Foster redeem his earlier mistake with a fine save and Petrov flashed another effort across the face of the United goal. But with ten minutes remaining, United scored what in reality should have been the winner, when a Giggs free-kick, ten yards in on the left, was floated towards Fletcher who headed powerfully past a helpless Given. That should have been that as the minutes ticked away, with the crowd preparing to celebrate three points against their old enemy and the four scoreboards around the ground ticking towards the ninetieth minute. Down on the touchline, in front of the two dug-outs, fourth official Alan Wiley, held up his board showing that there were still four minutes of stoppage time to play.

However, there was still drama to unfold. Ferdinand, inexcusably and lazily, attempted to flick the ball over the head of Petrov, but could only watch in anguish as the ball was cut out, with the City player quickly releasing Bellamy, who scampered down the left and away from the stranded United central defender before sending an angled drive past Foster.

That for many United supporters was that, leaving their seats and dejectedly, making their way towards the exits and away from the ground, contemplating the two points that had been needlessly thrown away, as the City support unmercifully taunted their red rivals.

The additional four minutes, signalled as the fourth official held up his board, left City manager Mark Hughes showing his displeasure, whilst also cranking up the atmosphere from the United support, for one final joust at the opposition goal. Not for the first time in this magnificent arena, the crowd paid as much attention to the time as to the match action.

With seconds remaining, Giggs, once again at the heart of everything United, picked out Carrick, who in turn found substitute Michael Owen. Taking one touch, the former Liverpool favourite quickly despatched the ball past a helpless Given to clinch the three points for United, leaving the City players dejected, as the stadium erupted into a wall of noise, whilst at the same time becoming a cult hero with the home support.

There was certainly no time for a fourth City comeback, with the final action of the afternoon coming from a United supporter invading the pitch before being scrambled to the ground by a handful of stewards. Before he could be led from the pitch, a frustrated Bellamy appeared to strike the trespasser, much to the displeasure of the red following. City manager Mark Hughes was obviously furious with the referee for allowing the game to continue for so long, whilst Sir Alex Ferguson, disappointed with his team's mistakes was more than happy with the victory, describing the game as the "greatest derby match ever"

THE LOVE OF MONEY IS A ROOT OF ALL EVIL

POSTSCRIPT

WITH 2010 STILL in its infancy and this book in its final stages before publication, news began to filter through regarding a proposed £500 million Bond issue by the Glazer family, as they attempted to juggle the books in order to try and reduce the staggering £700 million debt hanging over the club. It also produced, with the 100th anniversary of Old Trafford on the near horizon, further drama in the history of the home of Manchester United Football Club.

In a three hundred and twenty-two page prospectus document, produced to promote the proposed bond issue, the possibility of the stadium being sold was raised. The club's owners stated that the legal contract governing the bond "….will not prohibit us from selling certain key properties", which included, "our training ground facilities and our stadium".

This certainly did not mean that eviction notices were going to suddenly appear on the gates of both sites, but it created the possibility of United, or to be more precise, the Glazer family, selling both, or at least one of the two properties and then agreeing a lease back arrangement (although at a special "road show" in Edinburgh, promoting the bond, the sale of Old Trafford was ruled out).

Analysts estimated that the sale of Old Trafford could bring in around £300million, with any prospective freeholder looking towards a five per cent rental yield. This would create an annual bill for the club of around £15million.

The prospectus continued that anyone who acquired either the stadium, or the training ground, "will be required to enter into a long term lease with us, to enable us to continue to have substantially the same access to such property as we currently do."

There was also the warning that "If we sell or transfer either or both of these properties, we will no longer control them", whilst also conceding that "the failure by the freeholder in respect of either or both of these properties to maintain the properties or to make capital expenditures to improve the facilities at such properties could have a material adverse effect on our business and results of operations."

Included within the pages of the prospectus was a fifteen page section which, as required by law, notified prospective buyers of the bonds of the degrees of risks in making such an investment, listing the threat of terrorist activity at Old Trafford.

"We are one of the highest profile sports clubs in the world, with a global fan base", mentioning the possibility of threats towards the players, adding, "in addition, Old Trafford is an iconic stadium and a potential target for terrorism. We insure against certain acts of terrorism and other disasters and use security screening to protect fans and visitors."

Much more worrying to the supporters than the threat of terrorism at Old Trafford, were the implications raised by the bond issue and the actual financial state of their beloved United. Internet message boards were soon overflowing with the thoughts and opinions of supporters and meetings of protest were soon arranged prior to the first home fixture following the breaking of the bond news, against Burnley on January 16th.

On the pitch, the lacklustre performances of recent weeks continued, forcing the supporters to spend the majority of the game giving the red shirts as much vocal encouragement as possible, but with victory more or less assured following United's second goal scored by Rooney in the sixty-ninth minute, there was a sudden change in the atmosphere in the heartland of United's vocal support – the Stretford End second tier.

As defiant chants of "We Want Glazer Out" echoed around the stadium, a large "Love United – Hate Glazer" banner was unfurled from over a scoreboard amid cheers from those who could see it. Suddenly, orange jacketed security staff rushed to the front of the stand to apprehend the owner of the flag and his attempted escape into the neighbouring quadrant was thwarted by even more members of the security staff. The actions of both the flags appearance and the owner's immediate rejection, brought an increase in the anti-Glazer vocal protest and soon after another smaller banner appeared, again causing activity from the orange jackets. Again, the two people responsible were bundled away by security staff, but a minor scuffle resulted amid further abuse aimed at both staff and the Glazer's.

Seven days later Hull City visited Old Trafford for what was a re-arranged fixture due to United's surprise home defeat to Leeds United in the 3rd round of the FA Cup and once again the voices of discontent echoed around the ground. Prior to Hull's visit, it was suggested that supporters adopted the old green and gold colours of Newton Heath instead of the familiar red and white and many could be seen sporting the "new" colours. Banners against the Glazer regime were also in evidence, but this time, no-one was removed from their seats and between the encouragement for the team, and Wayne Rooney in particular as he claimed all the goals in United's 4-0 victory, and anti-Glazer chants, it was again a far cry from the often subdued atmosphere against teams from the lower end of the Premiership.

The new look fan's attire was even more in evidence four days later, when City crossed Manchester for the second leg of the Carling Cup semi-final hoping to erase the thirty-four wait for a piece of silverware. Old Trafford, as expected, was a cauldron of noise, but as the opening forty-five minutes came to a close, there was still anxiety in the air, with the finger nails coming in for some close attention as City still held that one goal advantage.

Although United enjoyed the majority of the play in both the first half and the opening exchanges of the second, It wasn't until the fifty-second minute that they managed to make that all important breakthrough. City, attacking the scoreboard end, won a corner on the far side and as Bellamy prepared to take the kick, he was hit on the head by an object thrown from the crowd.

After a short delay, the corner was eventually taken, but was cleared out of the United penalty area by Paul Scholes to the feet of Wayne Rooney.

The United front man in turn sent Ryan Giggs racing through on goal, but it looked at first as if the Welshman had overrun the ball, but he turned and pushed it to Nani. The winger was unable to get in a shot and as the ball bobbled about the penalty area, it broke to Paul Scholes, who drilled it past Given and into the corner of the net from the edge of the area.

This cranked up the atmosphere a further couple of notches and gave United the impetus to go for the kill. The baying Old Trafford crowd had to wait a further nineteen minutes, however, before that vital second goal came. Nani, enjoying a new lease of life, almost produced a second as his tantalising cross was diverted by Boyata over his own crossbar. The smile was soon back on the face of the Portuguese winger, as he brilliantly found Fletcher on the right, with the Scottish

▲ "Green and Gold until the club is sold"

Protests re-emerged in January following the publication of a bond prospectus. It remains to be seen how successful they will be.

midfielder cutting the ball back to Carrick, whose shot flashed across the face of the City goal and into the net off the post.

A third United goal would have finished the tie and as the ball flashed across the City area towards Rooney in the seventy-second minute, around six yards out, it looked as though the end result was going to be put beyond question. However, United's top scorer failed to add to his total with an uncharacteristic miss.

Play suddenly swung to the opposite end and any thoughts of a United victory soon evaporated and the cheers of United supporters in the 74,576 crowd caught in their throats as old boy Tevez flicked beyond Van der Sar to level the tie on aggregate.

With the game on a knife-edge, Carrick shot narrowly wide, while a Fletcher header was blocked by Given as the reds continued to attck the Stretford End goal. As the Old Trafford scoreboard ticked down and extra time loomed United won a second successive corner. Giggs played a one-two with Valencia, and the evergreen Welshman curled a cross into the packed City penalty area. As if by some magnetic force, the ball found the head of an un-marked Wayne Rooney, who made up for his earlier miss by heading firmly past a helpless Given to put United 3-1 in front.

There was no way back for the visitors this time. United were on their way to Wembley and the banner hanging from the Stretford End stand mocking City's years without success would continue to turn.

As for the owners, there will doubtless be further protests and who knows what will have happened within the Old Trafford environs between now and the next edition of this book…

SPECIAL OFFER: £8
PAPERBACK

BACK FROM THE BRINK
by Justin Blundell
The Untold story of Manchester United in the Depression Years 1919-32

If Manchester United revelled in innocent childhood during the Edwardian era, winning two league titles and an FA Cup within 9 years of the club's establishment, it endured a painful adolescence as the inter-war years saw it absent from the honours lists. In this amusing, irreverent and fascinating account, Justin Blundell traces the events of the club's lost youth between the end of the Great War and the worldwide economic crisis that almost scuppered the club yet ushered in a new era under James Gibson.
Blundell's punchy account deserves to stand alongside the many volumes written about the post-war glory years - it tells the story of how United survived the Depression Years and came back from the brink.

Morrissey's Manchester
by Phill Gatenby
Second Edition

SPECIAL OFFER: £6
PAPERBACK

Lyrically unique, Morrissey saw 1980s Manchester differently. Where most recognised the derelict remains of a Victorian warehouse, he saw humour, where others saw post-industrial squalor, he felt the frisson of romance.
As a result the city became as much a part of The Smiths output as the guitars, drums and vocals. Unusually, these places still exist and provide the devotee with a place of pilgramage. Now updated, Morrissey's Manchester has added new places to visit, more lyrical references and more background information on one of the world's most influential bands.

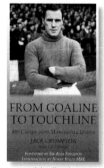

Hardback
Special offer £12

From Goal line to Touch-line
My Career with Manchester United
by Jack Crompton

Jack Crompton is one of the surviving members of Manchester United's swashbuckling 1948 FA Cup winning side and the first to pen his autobiography. Jack served the club as goalkeeper, trainer and caretaker manager for over 40 years playing a major part in the triumphs of the immediate post-war years and witnessed the rise of the Busby Babes first hand before leaving for a coaching role with Luton Town in 1956.
Now a sprightly octagenarian, Jack is in a unique position to discuss the considerable changes in the game during his lifetime and look back on a seven decade long association with Manchester United.

THE COMPLETE ERIC CANTONA
BY DARREN PHILLIPS
ISBN: 1901746585 - £10.95 - PAPERBACK

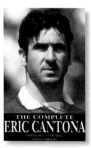

SPECIAL OFFER: £8
PAPERBACK

ERIC CANTONA'S CAREER at Old Trafford lasted only 5 years but its lasting impact is still being felt today. During that comparatively small span, Cantona's dedication and self-confidence enabled a club to emerge from over a quarter of a century of failure and self-doubt. THE COMPLETE ERIC CANTONA details every game Eric played for Manchester United, Leeds United and the French national team as well as potted summaries of his career in France. Darren Phillips has painstakingly researched his remarkable career in France, England and in the French national team. The Complete Eric Cantona sheds new light on a football career that altered the dynamics of English football.

SPECIAL OFFER: £8
PAPERBACK

18 TIMES AND THAT'S A FACT!
BY JUSTIN BLUNDELL
400PP - PAPERBACK - £10.95

This was the season when Sir Alex Ferguson's long-held wish to 'knock Liverpool off their f**king perch' was made flesh. A season so successful that even European Cup Final defeat to Barcelona couldn't fully diminish the club's achievements. Justin Blundell tells the story of United's triumphs in a punchy, rabidly red-eyed review of every single match and goal.

Written with an eye for the humour and pomoposity surrounding the modern game, Justin Blundell brings the matches, goals and managerial spats back to life in an entertaining, minute-by-minute guide to the matches that really mattered. "18 times" is a book for everyone who lives and breathes United, not just on match day but every single day.

Memories... Of a Failed Footballer
AND A CRAP JOURNALIST
BY PAUL HINCE

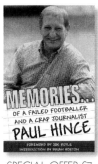

SPECIAL OFFER £7

PAUL HINCE BEGAN his football career with boyhood heroes Manchester City under the legendary Mercer-Allison partnership of the late 1960s before continuing his first class football career at Charlton, Bury and Crewe Alexandra. After retiring from the game he worked his way up to the heights of Manchester Evening News Manchester City correspondent and, later, that paper's first, and only, 'Chief Sports Writer'. Famed in later years for getting up the noses of both United and City fans in equal measure courtesy of his weekly columns, Paul retired from the Manchester Evening News in 2006.

sPECIAL OFFER £9

BEFORE THEY WERE FAMOUS
the story of NEWTON HEATH 1878-1902
Charbel Boujaoude
Published: 12th January 2010

THIS IS THE rivetting story of Newton Heath's formation. Told as a prequel to Justin Blundell's acclaimed Back from the Brink published in 2007, it seeks to answer the age old question: what was exceptional about the bunch of Victorian railway workers that formed the football club that would go on to be Manchester United? Relying on extensive research and written in a snappy style, Charbel Boujaoude brings to life a late Victorian era where football mushroomed to become the national pastime.

Reminiscences of Manchester
And its surrounding areas from 1840
by Louis M Hayes - Originally published 1905

WRITTEN OVER THE course of his lifetime, Louis Hayes' memoirs of Manchester life 'Reminiscenes of Manchester' is an evocative look back at the city's formative years. As well as outlining the social changes in the city, Hayes profiles the key characters, many he knew personally, to make a mark in Manchester life.

An invaluable guide to those keen to know more about the formative years of the city and those who wonder what life was like for Mancunians over a century ago, Reminiscences of Manchester is a remarkable work re-printed here in full with additional footnotes and the illustrations published in the original edition.

special offer £9

COMPLETIST'S DELIGHT - THE FULL EMPIRE BACK LIST

ISBN	TITLE	AUTHOR	PRICE	STATUS†
1901746003	SF Barnes: His Life and Times	A Searle	£14.95	IP
1901746011	Chasing Glory	R Grillo	£7.95	IP
190174602X	Three Curries and a Shish Kebab	R Bott	£7.99	IP
1901746038	Seasons to Remember	D Kirkley`	£6.95	IP
1901746046	Cups For Cock-Ups+	A Shaw	£8.99	OOP
1901746054	Glory Denied	R Grillo	£8.95	IP
1901746062	Standing the Test of Time	B Alley	£16.95	IP
1901746070	The Encyclopaedia of Scottish Cricket	D Potter	£9.99	IP
1901746089	The Silent Cry	J MacPhee	£7.99	OOP
1901746097	The Amazing Sports Quiz Book	F Brockett	£6.99	IP
1901746100	I'm Not God, I'm Just a Referee	R Entwistle	£7.99	OOP
1901746119	The League Cricket Annual Review 2000	ed. S. Fish	£6.99	IP
1901746143	Roger Byrne - Captain of the Busby Babes	I McCartney	£16.95	OOP
1901746151	The IT Manager's Handbook	D Miller	£24.99	IP
190174616X	Blue Tomorrow	M Meehan	£9.99	IP
1901746178	Atkinson for England	G James	£5.99	IP
1901746186	Think Cricket	C Bazalgette	£6.00	IP
1901746194	The League Cricket Annual Review 2001	ed. S. Fish	£7.99	IP
1901746208	Jock McAvoy - Fighting Legend *	B Hughes	£9.95	IP
1901746216	The Tommy Taylor Story*	B Hughes	£8.99	OOP
1901746224	Willie Pep'+	B Hughes	£9.95	OOP
1901746232	For King & Country*+	B Hughes	£8.95	OOP
1901746240	Three In A Row	P Windridge	£7.99	IP
1901746259	Viollet - Life of a legendary goalscorer+PB	R Cavanagh	£16.95	OOP
1901746267	Starmaker	B Hughes	£16.95	IP
1901746283	Morrissey's Manchester	P Gatenby	£5.99	IP
1901746313	Sir Alex, United & Me	A Pacino	£8.99	IP
1901746321	Bobby Murdoch, Different Class	D Potter	£10.99	OOP
190174633X	Goodison Maestros	D Hayes	£5.99	OOP
1901746348	Anfield Maestros	D Hayes	£5.99	OOP
1901746364	Out of the Void	B Yates	£9.99	IP
1901746356	The King - Denis Law, hero of the...	B Hughes	£17.95	OOP
1901746372	The Two Faces of Lee Harvey Oswald	G B Fleming	£8.99	IP
1901746380	My Blue Heaven	D Friend	£10.99	IP
1901746399	Viollet - life of a legendary goalscorer	B Hughes	£11.99	IP
1901746402	Quiz Setting Made Easy	J Dawson	£7.99	IP
1901746410	The Insider's Guide to Manchester United	J Doherty	£20	IP
1901746437	Catch a Falling Star	N Young	£17.95	IP
1901746453	Birth of the Babes	T Whelan	£12.95	OOP
190174647X	Back from the Brink	J Blundell	£10.95	IP
1901746488	The Real Jason Robinson	D Swanton	£17.95	IP
1901746496	This Simple Game	K Barnes	£14.95	IP
1901746518	The Complete George Best	D Phillips	£10.95	IP
1901746526	From Goalline to Touch line	J Crompton	£16.95	IP
1901746534	Sully	A Sullivan	£8.95	IP
1901746542	Memories...	P Hince	£10.95	IP
1901746550	Reminiscences of Manchester	L Hayes	£12.95	IP
1901746569	Morrissey's Manchester - 2nd Ed.	P Gatenby	£8.95	IP
1901746577	Before They Were Famous	C Boujaoude	£10.95	TBP (12/1/10)
1901746585	The Complete Eric Cantona	D Phillips	£10.95	IP
1901746593	18 Times	J Blundell	£9.95	IP

* Originally published by Collyhurst & Moston Lads Club + Out of print PB Superceded by Paperback edition

† In Print/Out Of Print/To Be Published (date)

EMPIRE PUBLICATIONS

Dear Reader,

If you have read this far it's probably safe to say you've enjoyed the book. As the list opposite indicates we are an independent Mancunian publisher specialising in books on the sport, music and history of our great city.

If you would like to receive regular updates on our titles you can join our mailing list by email: **enquiries@ empire-uk.com**, by sending your details to: **Empire Publications, 1 Newton St., Manchester M1 1HW** or by calling **0161 872 4721**.

We also update our website regularly: **www.empire-uk.com** with our latest title information.

Cheers

Ashley Shaw
Editor